THE WEB PAGE DESIGN COOKBOOK

All the ingredients you need to create 5-star Web pages

William Horton

Lee Taylor

Arthur Ignacio

Nancy L. Hoft

John Wiley & Sons, Inc.
New York • Chichester • Brisbane • Toronto • Singapore

Publisher: Katherine Schowalter
Editor: Theresa Hudson
Managing Editor: Mark Hayden
Book Design and Composition: William Horton Consulting

Library of Congress Cataloging-in-Publication Data:

The Web page design cookbook: all the ingredients you need to create 5-star Web pages/ William Horton ... [et al.].

    p. cm.

Includes index.
ISBN 0-471-13039-7(paper:alk. paper)
1. Hypertext systems.   2. HTML (Document markup language)

  I. Horton, William K. (William Kendall)
QA76.76.H94W43   1996
025.04—dc20   95-41350

                                              CIP

Printed in the United States of America
10 9 8 7 6 5

PREFACE

Why are you reading this preface instead of creating Web pages? Isn't making Web pages more fun and more productive than reading prefaces? Well, as long as you are still here, we'll be brief.

If you are thinking about buying this book

You've considered how the colorful spine will look on your bookshelf, evaluated the book's heft as a potential doorstop, and considered whether the CD-ROM in the back will make a good coaster. Still not convinced? How do you know if this book is for you?

This book is for people who want to create Web pages without making a career of it. If you want to set up a Home page or an entire Web site for your department, small business, or community group, this book will get you up and online with Web pages you can take pride in, and that your users can find information in.

If you know how to use a word processor and you're already hooked to the Internet, you have more than enough technical savvy to produce effective Web pages. Not on the Internet yet? Don't worry, we'll talk you through the process of getting hooked up and finding a home for your Web pages. Actually, we'll tell you who to call and how to speak their language.

On the other hand, if you'd rather spend your time memorizing arcane computer codes, have at it. This is probably not the book for you. Rather show off your programming skills? Not here. We show you how to create effective pages without a lot of programming.

To help you decide whether this book is for you, here are the principles on which it is based.

Even the best cooks use recipes

Good cooks learn by using the recipes of more experienced cooks. That's why we've organized this book like a cooking school, starting you off with simple, easy recipes and gradually taking you to the level of master chef where you can dazzle us with your original dishes.

Never draw or type something you can cut and paste

The quickest, most reliable way to get effective Web pages up and running is to copy something that already works and make it work for you. That's why throughout the book and CD-ROM we've included literally hundreds of templates and examples.

Instead of staring at a blank screen and what looks like a foreign-language dictionary, you just pick and choose from dozens of pages of templates and many more page ingredients.

Start with a complete working page, like the one you want to create. Delete a button here and a paragraph there. Add a list or table, again by copying a working model from the CD-ROM. Voila! You've got a Web page that works for you.

Show, don't tell

This book shows you how to create effective Web pages by presenting examples, examples, and more examples. Park a thumb here and quickly flip through the book. See what we mean? And the examples are on the CD-ROM.

Your Web pages also need to show things. That's why we tell you how to include music, voice, sound effects, animation, video, and other media on your Web pages. We'll help you decide where each is appropriate and show you how to include them.

The Web is a global medium

Through the World Wide Web you can reach the whole world. Literally. We'll tell you how to take advantage of the international reach of the Web and how to design your Web pages for people who don't speak your language, who don't understand your culture, and who consider your icons obscene.

A Web page is not a paper page

Merely replicating pages designed for paper is a sure way to produce Web pages that fail. Differences of display characteristics and users' expectations require new design techniques that account for the differences between the printed page and the computer screen—and take advantage of them. If you know a few HTML commands, you can create Web pages. But it takes a lot more knowledge to create Web pages that attract, inform, and delight people. We'll show you how.

If you have already bought this book

If you already own this book—first, thanks. Now you probably want to know how to get the maximum amount of information with the minimum amount of reading. Hey, you're not lazy. You're a good time manager.

We've tried to leave out all the stuff that really does not matter. We've included the information we have found essential in our own efforts at creating Web pages, most of them done under impossible deadlines with minimal budgets. Sound familiar?

Let us briefly describe how the book is organized so you know where you can jump in. The book is structured like a double funnel. It starts with a broad view, focuses in tightly, them pulls back for the big view again.

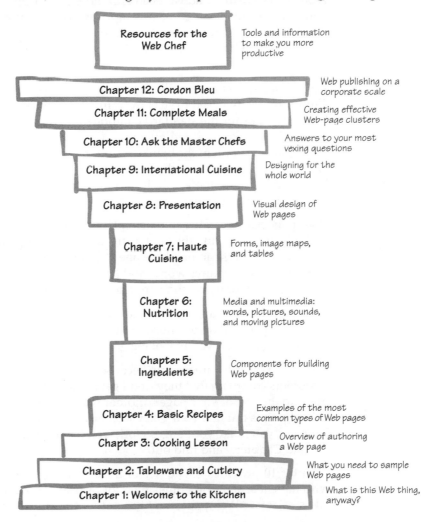

Resources for the Web Chef	Tools and information to make you more productive
Chapter 12: Cordon Bleu	Web publishing on a corporate scale
Chapter 11: Complete Meals	Creating effective Web-page clusters
Chapter 10: Ask the Master Chefs	Answers to your most vexing questions
Chapter 9: International Cuisine	Designing for the whole world
Chapter 8: Presentation	Visual design of Web pages
Chapter 7: Haute Cuisine	Forms, image maps, and tables
Chapter 6: Nutrition	Media and multimedia: words, pictures, sounds, and moving pictures
Chapter 5: Ingredients	Components for building Web pages
Chapter 4: Basic Recipes	Examples of the most common types of Web pages
Chapter 3: Cooking Lesson	Overview of authoring a Web page
Chapter 2: Tableware and Cutlery	What you need to sample Web pages
Chapter 1: Welcome to the Kitchen	What is this Web thing, anyway?

Kind of Dante-esque, eh? If you're new to the Internet and the Web, Chapter 1 will get you up and netspeaking with the best of 'em. If you've not yet developed the Web-surfing addiction, Chapter 2 will show you what you need to get hooked (in both senses of that word). On the other hand, if you're already whiling away your evenings (we know you wouldn't do it on company time) wandering the Web, then you can skip the first two chapters.

If you've never created a Web page before, you may feel daunted by the task. Chapter 3 will let you watch as an intrepid, but real, person creates a Web page, installs it on a server, and announces it to the world. Then it won't look so scary anymore.

If your boss just said "We need a Web page announcing our new Glub-o-tronic 2000 Water Purifier and we need it by noon," go right to Chapter 4 where you will find ready-to-go page templates. Just flip through till you find one that looks like what you want, replace our example content and placeholders with your words and pictures, and you've got time for an early lunch.

A week later, you get e-mail suggesting you add a list of the benefits of the Glub-o-tronic. No need to start over. Just turn to Chapter 5 where you will find templates for the standard components you are likely to find in Web pages, things like lists, and menus and pointers to other pages. Just pick, copy, paste, and fill in the blanks. If someone requests you add a sound bite of the cute gurgling noise the Glub-o-tronic makes, Chapter 6 can tell you how. While you're there, you'll find hints for making your text and pictures look better and display more quickly.

Your page has generated so much interest from customers that you decide to add a table comparing the Glub-o-tronic to the competition, and an order form so customers can purchase one at 2 am. Chapter 7 will show you how these advanced features work. And again, you can do most of the work by copying and modifying the templates from the CD-ROM.

Your pages look okay, but you know they could look better. Chapter 8 shows you what you can do to improve the balance, legibility, and attractiveness of your pages. Now you're looking good.

Your overseas sales are way up because of your Web pages. But some foreign customers complain that they don't get some of the clever puns you carefully put into the text of your page. Another wants dimensions in metric units, and a third points out that your Okay icon is an obscene gesture in his country. How can you make your pages work well for users throughout the globe? Turn to Chapter 9 and find out.

Chapter 10 provides the advice of master chefs, those Web-page creators who have learned, sometimes by a lot of trials and a few errors, what it takes to create Web pages that are not just pretty faces but that actually communicate information. They'll tell you how to avoid the most common blunders and how to make your pages more efficient.

A page here, a page there. Your Web publishing effort is getting out of hand! Chapter 11 to the rescue. With sage advice and copy-and-use models, Chapter 11 tells you how to organize sprawling collections of separate pages into effective Web sites.

Your Web publishing efforts have been so successful, that you've been asked to set standards and plot a strategy for use of Web technology throughout your organization—now and in the future. How do you use Web pages for marketing literature and customer support? What other technologies should you be considering? What's the next big thing? Chapter 12 will help you focus on the big picture and look into the future.

At the end of the book is a special section titled "Resources for the Web Chef ." It lists the sources of software, icons, and information to make your efforts more productive.

Credits

Any project this large requires a lot of work. Roll credits!

Authors	**William Horton**, William Horton Consulting
	Lee Taylor, Telluride Wordcraft
	Art Ignacio, Arthur Ignacio Consulting
	Nancy Hoft, International Technical Communication Services
Most of the graphics in Chapter 4	**Larry McGowan**, LM Publications/Graphics
Graphics elsewhere	**Katherine Horton**, William Horton Consulting
Some of the examples in Chapter 4	**John T. Devlin**, International Technical Communication Services
Book layout and design	**Katherine Horton**, William Horton Consulting
Time management & whip cracking	**Terri Hudson**, John Wiley & Sons, Inc.
CD-ROM disk art	**Katherine Horton**, William Horton Consulting
Downloading and link testing	**The good folks at ZoneWorks and the Telluride InfoZone**

CONTENTS

CHAPTER 6: NUTRITION   307

CHAPTER 12: CORDON BLEU   539

WELCOME TO THE KITCHEN

What's this Web thing, anyway?

On the cover, in large, friendly letters,
the book said "Don't Panic!"

—*Hitchhiker's Guide to the Galaxy*

Congratulations.

You survived the hype. You withstood the media onslaught. Wisely (or with luck), you waited out the gee-whiz phase of the World Wide Web (WWW), letting it grow and take root, watching it become a place where real work can get done.

Web-speak 101

Web pages are the online hyperlinked documents that you create and make available on a *Web server*. A Web page is more like a window on the WWW than an actual page in a book.

Your users *browse* (or view) your Web pages, following your links to other pages and resources.

The total collection of your Web pages (and other media and resources) is known as your Web *content*.

Finally, your content is stored at your *Web site*. When it is made available to the WWW through the Internet, you have *published on the Web!*

You probably already know what has happened: the Web's benefits—point-and-click ease of use, its ability to hyperlink to any other Web resource or document on the Internet, and the (relative) simplicity of creating those documents and links—have attracted a tidal wave of users to the Internet. Thanks in large part to the Web, you've seen the popularity of the Internet explode, going from a nerdy academic hangout to an international marketplace, classroom, and playground faster than you can say "MTV."

In short, the WWW is now a place where you (or your company, group, or organization) are becoming conspicuous by your absence.

Web users come from all levels of experience and technical sophistication, use all kinds of systems, and have a wide range of agendas and interests. It's a wild and free-form information feast, and everyone wants to dig in. Everyone, including you—the budding Web author.

You're here at the beginning because you've got something you want to (or have to) offer the world:

- Information about your business, products, or services.

- Topical knowledge related to your research, your skills, your experience, or your beliefs.

- Interactive (or even 3-D) samples of your artistic, creative, or professional output.

- Technical, professional, or legal reference works.

- Other great stuff that we've never seen before!

Now you're ready to get down to the nuts and bolts of creating your own homestead on the electronic frontier.

Well, we've written page 1—and the 600-plus pages that follow—to help you get there. Using this book and its companion CD-ROM, you'll be able to create effective and attractive Web pages in minutes, and build well-designed and functional clusters of Web resources in a few hours. With the assistance of our samples, examples, and guidelines, you'll be able to craft your own presence on the World Wide Web. With a little effort and commitment, you can establish a captivating Web presence that ensnares users with the quality of your content, the effectiveness of your design, and the usefulness of your links—rather than a Web warehouse growing cobwebs from lack of use!

WHY WOULD I WANT TO DO THIS WEB THING?

There are a variety of compelling reasons to represent yourself or your organization on the World Wide Web. (Of course, you probably already have a few reasons of your own, or you wouldn't be reading this book.)

Since you may need ammunition when you ask The Powers That Be in your organization for more time, money, or resources to support your Web page development, we'll briefly describe some of those reasons here.

To attract business or offer a service

There are whole books on this subject (more on that in a minute), so we'll just point out that your Web page can be many things:

- An electronic customer service desk that never closes. Once online, your customers have "24 x 7" access to your goods, your services, and your support (24 hours, 7 days a week, not counting down time for backups).

- A virtual storefront where customers can buy (and even take delivery of) your products, without talking to sales staff.

- An interactive billboard for passersby, describing you and your offerings in detail no print or television spots can match—with sound, video, virtual reality, or animation, to boot.

- A digital forum for your pro bono contributions to your profession, your industry, and the world at large—a very cost-effective karma bank.

- A tireless market researcher that tracks real prospects from actual (and self-initiated) contacts, in real time.

- The cheapest way to reach 35 million prospective customers, and counting: You can go from paying ten dollars a lead to ten cents a lead, and improve the quality of those leads in the bargain.

Well, you get the picture; obviously, there are sufficient reasons for your business or organization to have a Web presence.

To share a special skill, knowledge, or perspective

The founding ethos of the Internet was a spirit of cooperation and coexistence, where share and share alike was (and still is) expected behavior. If you have a particular skill, a special knowledge, or an area of interest that others may share, you may want to provide this knowledge in a Web page or related resource.

That ethos takes a pragmatic turn if you have specialized content that's of particular interest to specific users. Don't worry if your subject matter is a little arcane—that's another founding principle of the Internet: No information is too obscure, no knowledge too unusual, no image too unorthodox to have its own place in cyberspace. (Trust us, there are some, shall we say, unique Web sites out there.)

To give specific answers whenever users need them

A 24 x 7 access to your Web resources puts all kinds of information at your users' disposal, and makes it available when and where they need it. You can combine a library, newsstand, shopping mall, and help desk into one Web site that's always open for business, all for about three square feet of space on a user's desk (or one airline seat tray, for those compulsive laptop users).

For example, your technical specifications, data sheets, or monthly report instructions can be available to online customers or field staff, when they need them, for pennies apiece. Your personnel policies and job postings are instantly available (and always current) for in-house network users—even the graveyard shift.

In short, the Web is an excellent mechanism for distributing information and resources on demand—freeing up your human resources for more important and rewarding work.

To shrink distances and reduce isolation of all kinds

The Web is an ever-expanding panoply of social, educational, and professional resources, all available through the phone (or network) jack on your computer. No matter where users live, their telephone or network connection gives them the same access to your Web site as the New Delhi consultant, or the Wall Street financier, or the London bureaucrat.

As a Web author, this means that the whole world is your oyster—or marketplace, audience, classroom, or playing field, as the case may be.

This sheds new light on your content, doesn't it? Suddenly, there are no regions, no boundaries, no limits. Of course, that also means that there are new exposures and protections, too.

To support learning and intellectual stimulation

One of the most difficult things about using the Web is trying to browse around without learning anything. As a Web user, you can wander around, search for particular topics, or zoom to specific locations on a daily or hourly basis—it doesn't matter, the odds are you'll learn something new every time. At the very least, you'll spot new places to go or links to try in order to learn something next time. There are even "Web roulette" sites that will link you to purely random Web pages on the fly. Try:

```
http://www.yahoo.com/Reference/Indices_to_Web_Documents/
Random_Links/
```

when you have your browser up and running.

Your users are seeking this learning and stimulation, too. This gives you, as a Web author, an opportunity to give back to the Web community—and attract even more users to your Web site. Consider the intellectual resource that your Web content represents, and design your Web pages accordingly. Your home page can be your soapbox to the world—the best part is, not only can you tell people what you think they ought to know, you can find out if anybody is paying attention.

To pursue personal interests

No matter what topic or issue you're personally interested in, it's a good bet that there are other Web users out there who would benefit from your effort or knowledge about your personal topic; like to agree (or disagree) with you; or be eager to give you more information or direct you to additional resources about your topic.

The possibilities are endless. You can share experiences with other left-handers, point to some helpful hints on filing tax claims, sample new magical realism literature from South America, or set up links to the home pages of your favorite places to eat in Rio de Janeiro. Seen in this light, Web pages become not only an effective tool for business or professional communication, but also a vivid and dynamic means of self-expression and self-exploration.

Many Web users are strollers who just want to sample various Web sites, or look up people or places of interest—helping themselves to the online sports news from ESPN, for example, making hotel reservations in San Francisco, or even sampling the latest musical release from the Bang On A Can All-Stars. As Dave Barry says, "I am NOT making this up!" Lest you think we're kidding, try these Uniform Resource Locators (URLs):

`http://espnet.sportszone.com/`

`http://www.hotelres.com/`

`http://www.music.sony.com/Music/FeaturedArtists.html`.

Consider whether your personal content is of interest to these strollers—and if so, how you can make your Web pages an attractive and welcome place for them to visit.

THE WEB AS SUPERNOVA

If you're a breathing, living consumer of popular media, you may have heard or read some numbers describing the Web's growth, numbers that are too large to comprehend, and that change too rapidly to publish in this book. But if you really want to know, check out these Web pages:

Remember, line breaks in URLs are shown by necessity. When you type in an URL, don't leave any spaces.

`http://www.yahoo.com/Computers/World_Wide_Web/`
`Statistics_and_Demographics/`

`http://www.openmarket.com/info/internet-index/current.html`

`http://sunsite.unc.edu/boutell/faq/www_faq.html`

Suffice to say that all measures—Web usage, number of Web sites, number of Web resources added daily, international distribution of commercial and noncommercial servers, everything—are increasing rapidly. We're talking geometric rates of growth, here: big, hairy numbers.

To get a handle on these boggling numbers, think of the Web as a 24-hour library that adds several dozen new shelves of materials (all types, of course: books, posters, videos, lobby exhibits, the works) on every conceivable topic, every time you walk through the door. Imagine that you live above this library, so you might pop through those doors five or six times a day, seven days a week—often to add something new to the shelves yourself.

Amazing, isn't it?

What has happened? The Web has put an easier and more usable face on the vast resources of the Internet, and a whole range of users has responded enthusiastically. The technical barriers have been swept aside; you no longer have to be a UNIX guru to be able to access the Internet's global riches.

The WWW bandwagon rolls along so relentlessly because it's valuable, it's rewarding, it's interesting, and it's fun. That's a pretty tough combination to beat; when it comes with an easy to use (and essentially free) interface, it's pretty near unstoppable. Of course, the newness of the Web (and general public access to the Internet itself, for that matter) means that there are a lot of newbies out there, going for Sunday drives, bumping into each other, getting stuck in the digital mud, and generally having a whale of a time. *Newbie* is Internet lingo for a new and inexperienced user. You knew that, of course, but we had to put it in for the less experienced.

Maybe it's the old hunter-gatherer instinct coming out in us again—only instead of saber-toothed tigers and wildebeests, it's illumination and communication that we seek. Not in bits and bytes—which we don't see and don't care about—but in images, information, and answers.

THE JOURNEY BEGINS . . .

So you're probably familiar with the Internet; let's assume you have used the Web to roam around a bit, or you've seen others do it. Perhaps you've visited a number of good and bad home pages, and have logged your fair share of hours watching that globe spin or meteors streak by the big "N," while your computer pumps in data from some site halfway across the planet. You've seen enough Web sites that are trying to do what you could do—but maybe you've got better information, better graphics, or just better ideas about how to present that information.

So now you're ready to tackle your first home page, or to finally put those company or department documents out there for the whole world. Perhaps you've already done your experimenting, and are ready to start more substantive work. (More likely, of course, your boss promised to have that catalog online for your customers by third quarter, and the days of September are waning.)

If you're in this group somewhere, then this book is for you.

However, just in case you haven't spent any time online, cruising the Web, we offer ...

(PROBABLY GRATUITOUS) INTRODUCTION TO THE NET

> Been there, done that? Then skip ahead to "Okay, So What's HTML?" on page 14, or if you're already an experienced Web surfer, head on into Chapter 2.

Even though this book is not intended to be an introduction to the Internet—we figure that you, Dear Reader, already know at least the basics—we'll offer the following condensed version for anyone who can benefit from it:

- The Internet is not a physical network of wires going from one individual computer to another, although it functions like a network to share information and connections between computer users.

- The Internet is not a specific place, company, or service, although places, companies, and services are accessible via the Internet.

- The Internet is not a government subsidy for university students and X-Generation slackers to hang out and play endless games of Dungeons and Dragons, although that certainly *does* happen on the Internet.

So much for what it's not—now, what *is* it?

The Internet is a sizable community of cooperation that circles the globe, spans the political spectrum, and scampers up and down the ladder of economics. It's a collective society, really, in the largest sense of the word—a wiry ball of agreements between the administrators and users of a bunch of independent computers hooked up to (or dialing in to) shared or linked computer resources.

Everyone who accesses the Internet uses hardware and software (or online services) that agree on certain things:

- **Technical details**—how their computers are going to exchange packets of information, how they'll check for errors, what kinds of transmission formats they will use.

- **Social behaviors**—agreeing to forward mail not addressed to them, providing free and anonymous access to file repositories in a certain manner, and so forth.

Needless to say, these agreements are international standards as well; an Internet node in Ireland is meeting the same technical and social requirements as a company connected to the Internet in South Africa.

There's no Internet, Inc., no stockholders, no layers of management. But there are several key components:

- **Groups of volunteers**—including the Internet Society, the Internet Architecture Board, the Internet Engineering Task Force, and the Internet Computer Emergency Response Team (CERT)—who maintain standards and help the Internet police itself.

- **Several physical "backbone" networks**—originally set up and maintained by the U.S. government to support Defense Department research at universities across the country and the world, but now a private consortium that provides high-volume connectivity between major distribution sites (whether commercial, research, or educational in nature) all over the world.

- **Various government agencies and quasi-agencies of countries connected to the Internet**—that participate in setting standards and data exchange practices, pay for development of the "backbone," directly or indirectly support Internet access and resources, and occasionally try to control its content.

- **Outside contractors**—who are hired to maintain certain collective assets of the Internet community, such as a central registration of domain names (the technical term for addresses on the Internet) or a default "What's New" home page that announces new sites, new resources, and other items of interest to World Wide Web (WWW) users.

- **Commercial entities, universities, and other organizations**—that maintain and provide pro bono (free!) resources, tools, and data repositories. (Given the universities' contribution to the development and maintenance of the Internet, it could almost be called the Ivy-net.)

Other than that, the Internet consists of its users (you, you humble authors, and another 30 million or so) and the providers who give or sell access to those users. Once you're connected, you can reach (and be reached by) anyone else, anywhere in the world, who is also connected.

That's the simple version, of course, but it's pretty much what you need to know at this point. We'll get into the technical details as we need to; there are also some excellent additional references starting on page 605, if you're interested.

OKAY, OKAY, SO WHAT IS "THE WEB," THEN?

Well, there are four or five answers to that question varying in complexity and comprehensibility, and those answers change nearly every day. We'll offer one we feel is most pertinent to you as a Web page author:

> The World Wide Web is the collective name for all the computer files in the world that are a) accessible through the Internet; b) electronically linked together, usually by "tags" expressed in HyperText Markup Language (HTML); and c) viewed, experienced, or retrieved through a "browser" program running on your computer.

This is not an all-inclusive definition, of course; at the rate of change and growth the Web is currently experiencing, there's no telling what the linking mechanism will be in four or five years, much less whether browsers will exist or what form they will take. In the here and now, however, we use Web pages, tagged in HTML, to access other Web resources.

Don't let the terms *hypertext*, *hyperlink*, or *hypermedia* intimidate you, either: They all simply refer to things on a computer screen (buttons, text, or graphics) that you can select to tell the computer to show you other things. (Don't worry about HTML yet; we'll get to it.)

Of course, that defines the Web, but it doesn't really describe it—any more than your neighborhood library is just a building on the corner that holds lots of books. So, now we can put it another way: The Web is a hyperlinked global information and interaction system, carried on the Internet, that's made up of three components. They are:

- Web browsers and servers.

- Web content.

- Links between Web resources.

You are considered "on the Web" when, as a user, you crank up your browser and access Web resources. You've "published on the Web" when you make information or other resources accessible to other WWW users. As the first two W's imply, these users can be anywhere in the world.

Web browsers and servers

Technically speaking, of course, you can simply distribute your Web pages as files that users would then store on their own computers and access locally through their browsers. There are even good reasons for doing so. Since this book is primarily about designing and publishing for the World Wide Web, however, we won't go into the details of this special application.

To look at Web pages and access Web resources, you need a *Web browser* application running on your computer to interpret the tagged files, navigate the links, and display or perform the results. (It actually does a lot more, but we'll discuss that later, too.)

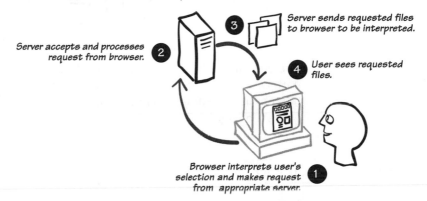

Server accepts and processes request from browser. **2**

3 Server sends requested files to browser to be interpreted.

4 User sees requested files.

Browser interprets user's selection and makes request from appropriate server. **1**

When other users link to your Web pages (using their own browsers, of course), your *Web server* responds to their requests and displays or delivers your corresponding content. To offer your great Web pages to the world (outside your home system or network), you need to store them on a computer that runs Web server software and that is accessible to the Internet. To publish your Web pages internally within your own networked organization, your pages should be on an internal Web server.

Web content

It is the worldwide body of text files that have been tagged with HTML, plus all the images, animations, sound files, videos, virtual reality, programs, and data that those files are stuffed with or linked to—in effect, any digitized resource that a user can access via the Web, regardless of its source or format.

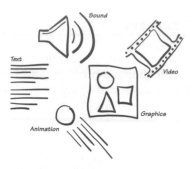

The content of the great Web pages that you'll create follows the same pattern: HTML-tagged text, and linked or integrated resources. When we talk about content in this book, we're generally speaking of the content of *your* Web pages.

Links between Web resources (also called hyperlinks)

Links are special HTML codes that instruct the browser to fetch a resource, run a program, or otherwise do something constructive. A hyperlink consists of HTML tagging that tells the browser what type of link it is, and a Uniform Resource Locator (URL) that tells the browser where to go or what to do. (We'll talk about URLs further on, too.) In effect, when a hyperlink is selected or clicked on by your users, it sends a request (whether for information, resources, or results) to the Web server defined in the tagging. In your browser, a link typically appears as highlighted, underlined, or colored text; it can also be shown as a button or graphic element.

Web servers and browsers use an Internet-standard protocol called HTTP (HyperText Transfer Protocol) to send, receive, and respond to the requests issued by Web hyperlinks. HTTP is simply a specific computer dialect that's used as a common language to handle text and resource transfers between different computers (such as a Macintosh-based browser and a Silicon Graphics server) via a network such as the Internet.

That's just the high-level version, of course; we'll discuss each of these components in turn. But first, here's what the whole picture looks like:

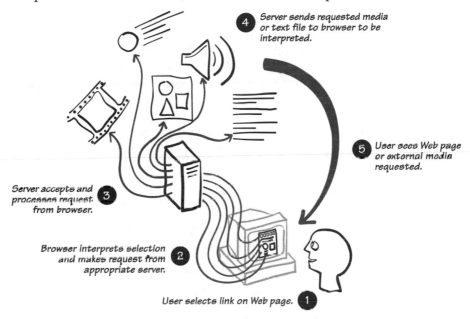

4 Server sends requested media or text file to browser to be interpreted.

5 User sees Web page or external media requested.

3 Server accepts and processes request from browser.

2 Browser interprets selection and makes request from appropriate server.

1 User selects link on Web page.

WHERE DID THE WEB COME FROM?

The Web was born in the bright and fertile mind of Tim Berners-Lee, a computer specialist at the European Particle Physics Laboratory (CERN). In 1989, he saw the need for "a collaborative knowledge-sharing tool" to support the work of CERN and international teams of scientists in high-energy physics, and envisioned the usefulness of such an environment for other disciplines and interests as well. He and colleague Robert Cailliau expanded a hypertext notebook that Berners-Lee had developed in the early 1980s for personal use, and devised an original version of the WWW as a way to keep track of CERN's own network systems. He then offered it to the Internet community for testing, use, and comments (via the newsgroup `alt.hypertext`, among other outlets), and the WWW was hatched.

So who's in charge?

The World Wide Web Consortium (known as W3C) is a volunteer industry organization that has taken on responsibility for developing and maintaining common standards for the continuing evolution of the WWW. W3C is run by the Laboratory for Computer Science at the Massachusets Institute of Technology (MIT), in collaboration with CERN and INRIA, the European W3C center.

The W3C serves as the standard-setting body for Web specifications, and provides a repository for those specifications (see `http://www.w3.org`). The consortium also develops prototype and sample applications to demonstrate new technologies, and makes software tools (such as the HTTPD Web server application) available for general public use.

OKAY, SO WHAT'S HTML?

HTML is a language of "tags" that you use to mark:

- The logical structure of a Web page: `<H1>` is a head, `<TR>` is a table row, and so forth.

- Links to other Web resources or other parts of the Web page. `<IMG SRC>` is an inline image, for example.

- Attributes for certain components of the document structure: `<... ALIGN=LEFT>`, `<...WIDTH=200>`, and so forth.

- A limited (but growing) number of visual formatting effects, from bold `<B>` and italics `<I>` to more esoteric things like colored or textured Web page backgrounds:

  `<BGCOLOR'"#666666" BACKGROUND'"gc_pattern2.gif">`

For example, visual formatting in your typical word processor might look like this ...

[Helv Bold 18 pt][TOC Level 1]
What Is This Web Thing, Anyway?

while HTML tagging looks like this:

`<H1> What Is This Web Thing, Anyway?</H1>`

When a user looks at your Web page with his or her browser program (which is, by definition, HTML-compliant to some degree), the browser retrieves a copy of the file containing the Web page, interprets the HTML tags you've put into that file, and displays the results onto the user's screen—assigning fonts, margins, and so forth more or less automatically. It can also interpret the tags into a hard-copy format, should the user choose to print it.

HTML was originally defined as a structured markup language that supported tagging based on the structure and relationship of the document components, and not primarily on their font, emphasis, or appearance. Of course, having offered that statement, we now have to qualify it (that didn't take long, did it?):

- There are some standard HTML tags that try to define a *structured contextual relationship* (PRE, EMPHASIS, and STRONG, for example), but in real life they are used for visual effect. EMPHASIS, for example, actually formats *italics* on screen, and STRONG usually displays as **bold**, and that's just how they are used in common tagging practices.

- Although HTML started out as a standardized, bedrock set of structure tags, it has rapidly developed a topsoil layer of formatting tags that are really more conventions than standards, more visual than structural, and more functional than hierarchical. (And yes, it's been noted that HTML might really stand for "HTML Tagging Mirrors Life.")

Does HTML mean "SGML Lite"?

This is one of those religious questions that can disrupt an otherwise civil discussion or newsgroup for days. Here are the basics:

- SGML stands for Standard Generalized Markup Language. It's an older and more powerful implementation of the same structure-based tagging *concept* that HTML is based on. Although SGML is especially effective for handling large, hierarchical content—say, the parts catalog of a Boeing 777 airliner—it can be (and is) used to format a wide range of information.

- SGML (technically, International Standard ISO8879-1986) allows you to create plain text files (with links to other file types, like graphics) that are *device-independent*, which means that they can be printed or viewed on any system running software that knows how to interpret the SGML markup.

- This interpretive software, typically called a *parser*, looks at a file containing a set of rules that define what the SGML tags mean, and then interprets the tags in the plain text file according to those rules. This rules file is known as a *document type definition* (DTD).

- HTML works essentially the same way SGML does, but it's simpler because there are fewer tags to use. The tag rules are defined in the browser, which interprets the tagged file and displays the results. There's even an HTML version of a DTD, so that an SGML parser can "understand" a file tagged in HTML.

So, the answer is ...

Yes, HTML *is* a structured formatting language that is both SGML-like and SGML-compliant. It does use standard tags to structure both the document as a whole and its component parts—including links to media, processes, and virtual realities.

And ...

No, HTML is *not exactly* a subset of SGML. Think of HTML as an SSSML—a Sort of Standardized Specific Markup Language, designed to support device-independent, electronic distribution of data, media, and (virtual) experience.

So what's the real difference?

- HTML does support some tags specifically for visual formatting; because it is designed to be used in a graphic, visual environment, there's increasing emphasis on pushing the HTML standard into design and layout territory.

- Web browsers are generally more forgiving than SGML parsers; if they don't understand a tag they'll show raw text, but they won't usually blow up.

- A few browsers are designed to interpret specific nonstandard HTML tags. Some browsers can support types of formatting or functions—like tables or graphic backgrounds—that other browsers can't, even though they're all reading HTML. As a result, certain browsers support, in effect, their own flavor of HTML.

So HTML is that functional oxymoron, a flexible standard?

Web-speak 101

A *Web author* is the person who prepares a particular page or set of pages for Web distribution (whether or not he or she writes the actual content of those pages).

A *Webmaster* is the person responsible for the successful operation of a whole Web site, which may contain the works of many Web authors.

In real life, of course, these are often the same person.

Bingo. The bedrock of underlying standards is definitely there, and the standards continue to evolve; HTML 2.0 is now *almost* official, and 3.0 is under discussion. Pretty much any browser out there will at least support the standards that have been blessed by the W3C. If you stick to standard HTML tags to create your Web pages, your audience won't have to deal with any blown pages, raw text, or other surprises (good or bad).

But the creative ferment of the Web—not to mention the energy of millions of Web-savvy high school and college students with time on their hands—continues to push the Web envelope with new visual effects, operating tricks, and gizmo scripts that go well beyond the HTML standard (and perhaps a few other conventions as well, like common sense or personal modesty). These mutations get developed:

- **Out of boredom**: "Hey, I wonder if we could write a tag that would display all text in reverse, so that you'd have to read it in a mirror?"

- **To support some advanced function or effect** that a Web author or Webmaster decides he or she needs on their Web site. Fill-in-the-blank forms, for example, evolved in part to allow users to place orders—a pretty critical function to many commercial Web sites.

- **To produce some visual effect** that is designed to improve legibility; impress friends and colleagues; express some creative or personal opinion; or add color, motion, or some other attractive and unique experience to your Web page(s).

Once developed, the mutations are distributed (online, of course), played with, fought over, and then either absorbed into common acceptance or left behind.

A few of the companies that develop browser and server software (Netscape Communications Corp. is best known for this) are deliberately adding support for nonstandard tags and functions to their products. Besides battling the competition for bragging rights ("Wow, the new BrowzerMan has a teleporting feature!") and market share, these companies argue that the visual reality and actual use of the Web demand design effects, formatting, and functions that the HTML standard can't keep up with.

And I care about all this because . . . ?

Well, when you create your Web pages and other resources, you have to decide:

- What—if any—nonstandard effects (and their tags) do you need to use?

- How important are these effects to your pages and your users?

- What browser(s) will support these effects (and are they available for all platforms)?

- Will all, most, or some of your users be using that browser—and if not, can they get a copy of it *and* will they think your pages are worth the effort of doing so?

Your decisions should be based primarily on what works best for the user, not what will land you on this week's "Top Ten Cool URLs" list—unless, of course, that was your goal all along.

Enough already—how do I use HTML?

Fair enough; let's get back to the HTML basics.

At the beginning of a print document you might have a primary or level 1 head, followed by several paragraphs, which are then followed by the first of several subheadings and text, like this:

Tableware and Cutlery: What You Need to Surf the Web

Now that you have a working knowledge of what the World Wide Web is, you naturally want to know how to gain access to its riches. In this chapter we'll review the tools and connections you need to access Web resources—and, not incidentally, view and test your own Web creations before you put them out on the Internet!

We'll try not to get too technical, but of course you can't make an omelet without breaking a few eggs. FWIW, this is *supposed* to be the technical chapter—after this, we get to the fun part!

The Big Picture

Since a picture is worth 1,000 words (and this is supposed to be a short chapter) here's an indelible image of the Complete Web Surfer:

In a word processing or desktop publishing program, you might define this level 1 head to appear in, say, centered 24-point Helvetica Bold Italic. Nowadays, you'll probably use the named styles feature of your word processor or DTP program (Head1, bullet, body, and so forth) to do this visual formatting.

In HTML, you physically tag this same head as:

```
<H1>Tableware and Cutlery: What You Need to Surf the Web</H1>
```

and let the user's browser program worry about its font, emphasis, and placement. That's what a browser does—interprets the HTML code into its own screen formatting.

Here's what this same sample page looks like as an HTML document:

```
<H1>Tableware and Cutlery: What You Need to Surf the
Web</H1>

<P>Now that you have a working knowledge of what the World
Wide Web is, you naturally want to know how to gain access
to its riches. In this chapter we'll review the tools and
connections you need to access Web resources - and, not
incidentally, view and test your own Web creations before
you put them out on the Internet!</P>

<P>We'll try not to get too technical, but of course you
can't make an omelet without breaking a few eggs. FWIW, this
is <EM>supposed</EM> to be the technical chapter - after
this, we get to the fun part!

<H2>The Big Picture</H2>

<P>Since a picture is worth 1,000 words (and this is
supposed to be a short chapter) here's an indelible image of
the Complete Web Surfer:</P>
```

The HTML code elements may look kind of arcane and alchemical, but they're really not that complicated. Many codes have a beginning tag, like <P>, and an ending tag, like </P>; ending tags usually put a slash "/" prefix in front of the beginning tag. Most tags are also fairly logical: the "P" in this case stands for "paragraph."

Some code elements also have attributes that modify how the tag works. A hypertext link tag, for example, includes an attribute that references the thing linked to, such as a heading in another file, a picture, or a short audio segment. For example, the code element:

```
<A HREF="http://satftp.soest.hawaii.edu/pub/video/manoa/
last.mpg"></A>
```

creates a link to a continually updated video clip of the Manoa Valley and Mount Konahuanui in Hawaii. When your user selects or clicks on the link in his or her browser, the target attribute tells the browser where to go (and what to do) next—in this case, to download the video clip to the user's system and then play it, if an MPEG viewer is available on that system.

If you like, you can refer to "Just enough HTML ..." (page 22) for additional specifics about the parts of an HTML tag.

To complete our picture, here's what the same HTML file looks like through a couple of different Web browsers.

Netscape for Windows

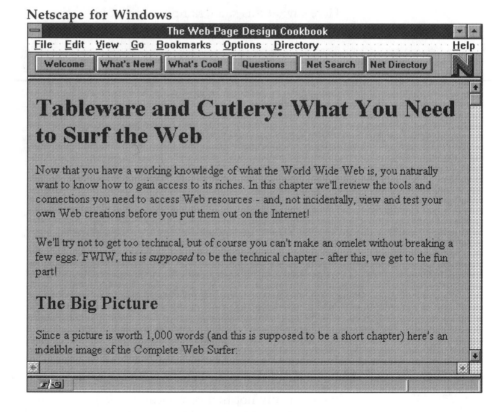

MacWeb

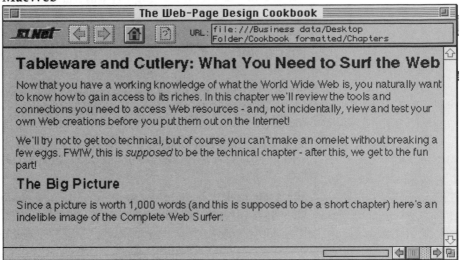

Mosaic

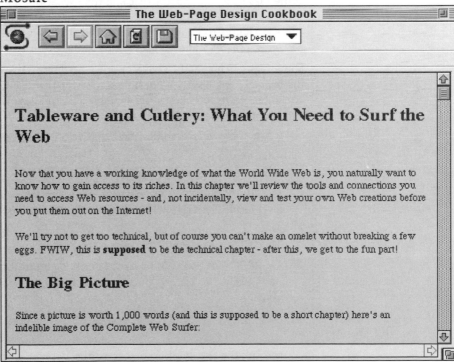

Remember, the file behind a Web page is a plain text file containing only letters, numbers, and (most) keyboard characters, with *no* formatting or special characters—nothing but words, punctuation, and HTML tags. That's why the formatting looks slightly different in each of these browsers. Each browser interprets the HTML file in light of its own formatting conventions.

Just enough HTML to keep reading ...

HTML files are made up of *tags* and *content*. Web pages are a browser's display of the HTML file's content, based on its interpretation of the HTML tagging in the file.

Tags are enclosed in <angled brackets>. The *content* of the HTML file is the stuff enclosed between tags: <EM>this text would be emphasized (usually in italics)</EM>

Some tags have to be used in pairs, with a beginning tag (such as <P>) and an ending tag (such as </P>) that format all the contents in between. (Sort of a tag team deal.) Ending tags usually start with a forward slash (/).

Browsers do not display the tags themselves, so users can't see them. Instead browsers display the tags' effects, such as font size and indentation.

Some tags include *attributes* that fine tune what the tag does. For example, the tag <HR> inserts a horizontal rule (that is, a solid line) on the Web page. Adding a few attributes to control the width and thickness of that line: <HR width'45 size'4> creates a line 45 pixels wide and 4 pixels thick.

Some tags (such as <HR>) have optional attributes; if you don't include them, the browser will display its default setting for that tag. Other tags *require* attributes—a hyperlink tag, for example, has to know what you want to link to, and you define the *target* in an attribute.

Here are some very common tags that you'll see frequently:

- <P>This would be a new paragraph.</P> This would format this sentence as a new paragraph.
- <H2>Okay—So What's HTML?</H2> This tags this phrase as a secondary-level head. The tags <H1>, <H3>, and so forth work the same way.
-
  This tag forces a line break within the text.
- <A HREF="http://www.myorg.com/myhome.htm">My home page</A> lists my hobbies. A browser would display this sentence as:

  My home page lists my hobbies.

  and link the text My home page to the Web page myhome.htm, which is located on the Web server www.myorg.com.

Since the whole point of our cookbook is to save you from looking up and figuring out how to use all these tags, we're not going to include a long, boring definition of all the tags and attributes. (Besides, you can get the most current ones online at `http://www.ncsa.uiuc.edu` and other locations.)

In Chapters 5 and 7, we provide lots of examples of the most common and standard tags, used in some sample context so that you have templates for tagging your own information. Of course, we also want you to care about how your Web documents look, so we'll be giving you some design advice along the way.

HOW ABOUT THOSE URALS?

Well, the Urals are some impressive mountains in the western part of the former Soviet Union (considered to be the dividing line between Europe and Asia, by the way). And there is a nice picture of them on the Web. Point your browser at the URL:

`http://www.glas.apc.org/ascbrant/test3.html`

when you want a change of scenery.

SORRY, I MEANT URLs

An URL (Uniform Resource Locator), on the other hand, is the how-and-where instructions for the Web resource that the browser is supposed to retrieve next. (You can pronounce it U-R-L ["you-are-el"], but we mostly hear it as "earl.") We've shown you several already, and here's another one:

`http://www.nando.net/pctravel.html`

It's not a pretty sight, we know, but don't panic: Everything is there for a reason. This URL, for example, simply displays the home page of the PC Travel Company, a place in North Carolina where you can book travel arrangements via the Web.

This URL displays a specific section of the *Second Survey of Web Usage*, which is published by Georgia Tech:

```
http://www.cc.gatech.edu/gvu/user_surveys/survey-09-1994/
html-paper/survey_2_paper.html#results
```

This kind of URL works just like a cross-reference in a paper document, but instead of telling a reader to "see page 7," you create an URL that tells the user's browser to go fetch the Web Survey and turn directly to the Results section. Pretty neat, huh?

A similar URL might simply display an inline graphic—in this case, a GIF file showing the national weather map, updated regularly:

```
http://rs560.cl.msu.edu/weather/Lsa.gif
```

Here's a different kind of URL, one that downloads a musical sample of Wynton Marsalis playing the "Hummel Trumpet Concerto":

```
http://www.music.sony.com/Music/SoundClips/
WyntonMarsalis_HummelTrumpetConcerto_8bit.wav
```

This one retrieves a sampler animation sequence (in this case, spaceships from a television show) from the "Animators Wanted" page run by pixelMotion Gallery:

```
http://www.supercomp.ns.ca/pix/mpg/star.mpg
```

Remembering that not all URLs start with `http:`, here's the URL to retrieve a full-sized picture of the Rana Dorada or Golden Frog (*Atelopus zeteki*), the most cherished frog in Panama, now facing extinction:

```
file://photo1.si.edu/images/gif89a/science-nature/GFROG.GIF
```

URLs are decoded and demystified in gaudy detail in Chapter 5, starting on page 286.

SEEMS REASONABLE, BUT WHAT DO I DO WITH URLS?

As a Web author, you do two things with them: You publicize the URLs of your own pages (to attract users, naturally), and you use URLs in your pages as links to view other pages or retrieve other resources.

Here's what we mean:

- **Publicize them**—Once you have your own Web pages up, running, and available on a Web server, you broadcast the URL of the front door that you want users to come through (hence, *home* page):
  - Announce it in the appropriate Internet newsgroups, or in a press release.
  - List it in your next catalog, annual report, or mass mailing.

- Include it in your newsletters, your letterhead, and business cards—in fact, all your printed material.

BTW (By the Way) ...

In this book, and in the gobs of goodies on the enclosed CD-ROM, we standardized on the extension .htm for files containing HTML tagging. As you may know, DOS can't handle more than three letters in its filename extension, and we wanted the goodies to be usable on as many systems as possible. You can rename any of the pages or links we provide to whatever convention you want to use—just be sure to change any URLs that refer to those pages!

- **Use them as links**—If you want to create a link within one of your Web pages to another Internet resource—so that anyone reading your home page can link out to the home page of your alma mater, for example, or to the home page of an association to which you belong—you enter the URL into the HTML document, enclosed within beginning and ending link tags. (More on this in Chapters 4 and 5.)

  Conversely, if you just want to access a Web page—or any other Internet resource—yourself, just type the URL into the appropriate place in your Web browser, and it will attempt to take you there. Almost all browsers have some kind of Go To: field, Open button, or URL prompt (and thank goodness for cut-and-paste!).

THE FLAVOR OF THINGS TO COME

Since the resources and riches available via the Web resemble, as much as anything, a smörgåsbord of exotic tastes and culinary delights, we've followed that analogy to present the information in this book. After a whirlwind tour of the kitchen in Chapter 2, we'll give you an overview of how to whip up a simple Web page, using some of the recipes and goodies on the CD-ROM—a quick cooking lesson, if you will.

Progressing from there, you'll find the basic dishes of Chapter 4 quite useful as recipes for your own pages, and you can use the ingredients of Chapter 5 to tastefully season your Web site. Subsequent chapters lead you through a full-course meal of resources and templates.

Consider yourself a Web chef-in-training, and keep this book propped up in the recipe holder. Flag it, tag it, and generally make use of its examples and samples as you concoct your own presence on the Web.

Now, on to Chapter 2, where you'll learn about browsers and servers. Bon appetit!

TABLEWARE AND CUTLERY

What you need to sample Web pages

Now that you have a working knowledge of what the World Wide Web is, naturally you want to know how to dive in and start grazing at the buffet table.

This chapter will get you to the table by describing how to get connected to the Web. We'll try not to get too technoid here, but of course, you can't make an omelet without breaking a few eggs.

FWIW (This is the netspeak equivalent of "for what it's worth." Initials and acronyms are a big thing in cyberspace!), this is supposed to be the technical chapter—after this, we get to the fun part!

So here's how this chapter is organized:

- After a quick pair of caveats, we'll start with an overview of the reasons why Web authors have to be Web users, too, and describe a few of the things to keep an eye out for as you surf the Web.

- "The Fast Track to Web Access" gives you a quick checklist of the stuff you need to access and view Web pages. (The gory technical details are offered at the end of the chapter.)

- Unless you're developing an internal-use-only Web site, you'll need to check out "Getting Internet Access" for some guidance in finding and selecting an Internet provider—it's a quick review of what to ask and what to watch out for.

- Then we'll dive into some specifics about the two main types of software programs you'll need: one or more browsers to view Web pages, and helper applications to handle multimedia and virtual reality. We'll also show you a few samples of Web pages and images available on the Web.

- And finally, for those who can't stand not knowing, "Through the Kitchen Doors" describes TCP/IP and SLIP/PPP software, other client applications, and the nuts and bolts of Web access.

Caveat Webspinner

For simplicity's sake, we've assumed that most of you will be connecting to the Internet via SLIP/PPP and using a graphical browser for your Web work. There are a couple of alternatives, however, that we'll mention in passing:

Using a text-only browser—If you have a dial-up (or shell) Internet account, you may already be using Lynx (or some other text-only browser) to explore the Web. However, many (if not most) of your users will be viewing your Web pages through their graphical browsers. As you can imagine, you need to know what your pages will look like to those users —even if you don't use any browser-specific tagging or functions.

So, even if you don't use graphical browsers yourself, you should equip yourself with several browsers to test your Web pages before you make them publicly available. You can certainly continue to use a text-based browser for your own Web traveling, of course.

Using imitation SLIP/PPP access—There are a growing number of SLIP/PPP work-arounds, software applications that effectively emulate a SLIP/PPP connection so that you can use a regular dial-up Internet account for your Web access. Some work-arounds, like Pipeline New York, come bundled with an Internet account; others, like SlipKnot, will work with any Internet provider.

There's certainly nothing wrong with emulating SLIP/PPP access; be aware that the installation and configuration of the software can be a bit tricky, though. If this is the route you've taken, just skim past any of the technical stuff that doesn't apply to you.

THE CHEF HAS TO EAT, TOO

There are four key reasons why you'll want to browse the Web and sample the information smörgåsbord yourself.

- **To "taste test" other Web pages**, searching for good (and bad) examples, tips and tricks that you want to emulate, and new ideas for structure, design, and content.

- **To locate other resources** that you want to link to from your own pages. These may be anything from Web pages on related topics, to pointers to sources for software, to downloads of other resources (such as multimedia players, if your pages include such content). You'll want to collect and test the URLs to such resources so that you can include them in your pages.

- **To test the formatting and links** of your own Web pages externally before you announce them to the world.

- **To tap into the riches of the Web** for your own benefit.

Since this book is about authoring Web pages, we're mostly concerned with browsers from the author's perspective. Of course, anything that we describe about your authorial use of browsers also applies to you as a user.

THE FAST TRACK TO WEB ACCESS

If you're pretty Net savvy (or have someone working with you who is), then perhaps all you need is a checklist of things to do to start surfing. Here it is:

- ☐ Set up an Internet SLIP/PPP account (or reasonable facsimile thereof) with the Internet service provider (ISP) of your choice.

- ☐ If your operating system doesn't have it built in, get TCP/IP stacks and a dialer program from your ISP or some other source.

- ☐ Test and troubleshoot your ability to connect to the Internet using the TCP/IP software.

- ☐ Obtain, install, test, and configure one or more graphical Web browsers.

☐ Obtain, install, test, and configure additional SLIP/PPP client applications—typically, you'll want e-mail, Telnet, FTP, and newsreader applications—as needed.

☐ Learn how to use the Hotlist feature of your browser(s), then start cruising.

GETTING INTERNET ACCESS

The first thing you need is access to the World Wide Web, whether you're going to publish your pages and other resources "out there" on the Web, or simply provide them in house on an internal system for internal users. You need either an account with an Internet service provider (ISP), or an account with Internet access on the computer network within your organization.

Here's how to get going:

- **See your system administrator** for help getting access if your computer is part of a computer network—such as a corporate LAN or WAN. (Buy 'em lunch while you're at it—they'll be valuable allies in making your Web pages dynamic and effective, and in keeping them running.)

- **Track down a good provider** if you'll be connecting to the Internet from your home or office. There is a wide range of community, regional, and national providers out there, and eventually the telephone and cable companies will probably get into the act, too.

Finding a ISP

This being the Internet, there are several lists of ISPs available online, but of course you have to have an e-mail account to get to them! If you do have access to e-mail (or know someone who does—like maybe the neighbor's nine-year-old), you can get a copy of the public ISPs by sending an e-mail message to:

info-deli-server@netcom.com

Your message should contain the text "Send PDIAL" in the body of the message. (The Info Deli and PDIAL are maintained by Peter Kaminski; thanks, Peter!)

Here's a few tips to help you shop around:

- Try to find a provider within your local telephone calling area (so you don't have to pay long-distance charges). If you can't find one, or if you travel a lot, look for an ISP that offers an 800 number that provides cost-effective access to their Internet POP. (This means literally *Point of Presence*, a geeky term for a rack of modems and hardware that lets you connect to their Internet service.)

- Make sure your ISP has some staying power—it's easier to set up a server and sell accounts than it is to stay in business over the long haul.

- Make sure that Internet services are a primary or important part of their business, and not just something they offer on the side to rake in monthly account charges. (We won't name names, but it's been known to happen.)

- Ask for customer references, and make the effort to talk to them. With Internet use increasing so rapidly, many providers are scrambling to keep up with the exploding volume of users—and the quality of customer and technical support seems to suffer first.

- If you find a provider you think you like, talk to their technical support staff. Find out what Web and TCP/IP software they have available for download (and how to get to it); in the process, see how professional and customer-oriented they are.

- Ask around (in online newsgroups, professional associations, or at your local community college, perhaps) for references to a responsive and reliable ISP. Your account won't do you any good if you can't log in because the system is down or clogged up all the time. You also won't want to use this ISP as your Web server if your users can't get expedient and reliable access to your Web pages.

- **Check into the cost and other details for storing and making your own Web pages available to the Internet** if you are setting up an account with an ISP.

JUST BROWSING, THANKS

As we defined earlier, a browser is an application that users run on their computers to access World Wide Web resources. (Technically it's a SLIP/PPP client application, but we're more interested in what it does than what it is.) When the user—we'll call her Julie—selects a link, clicks on a graphic button, or enters a URL to go to one of your pages, her browser can, for example:

- Retrieve the Web page Julie has selected, interpret your HTML markup, and display the results on her screen.

- Download that hot new sound file of your fledgling garage band, or that video clip of your dog's Frisbee tricks.

- Allow her to place an order for her upgrade of your construction project software.

- Let Julie query your membership database using a specific set of search criteria, and display a report of the results.

- Register her responses to your survey or product registration form.

- Send an e-mail message to your technical support department.

In theory, since all browsers interpret Web pages containing *standard* HTML markup, there shouldn't be much difference between the way pages are displayed in various browsers. Indeed, the explosive growth of the Web is largely due to a general agreement on technical standards—such as TCP/IP, HTTP, and (in the beginning, at least) HTML. One might even wonder why there are more than one or two browsers for any operating platform.

As computer users know well, however, the term standard has a rather fluid meaning in the digital arena. In the real world, although there is a baseline of standard HTML interpretation, browsers actually support a wide range of functions, and even implement the standard functions in a variety of ways. To put it more simply:

- Most browsers do most of the same baseline things.

- Some browsers do things others can't do.

- Some browsers do certain things better (or differently) than others.

What sort of things, you ask? Well, Netscape, for example, supports a text attribute that makes text blink on the screen (a bit tacky, perhaps, but certainly attention getting). Hot Java, the new interface from Sun Microsystems, sports a 3-D interface and 3-D objects. This is just a sampling, of course; the nonstandard functions are, shall we say, numerous.

The result: Your Web users get to select the browser that best suits the way they want to access and use the Web's resources. (Of course, as a Web user yourself, you get to make the same selection.) This can be a significant issue for you as a Web page author; the range of browser variations means that you usually can't entirely predict how (or how well) your Web pages will look to your users.

Caveat author

As the lawyers would say, "Mentioning specific products does not constitute an endorsement. The authors have no business relationship with any of the companies or products described herein."

So, we strongly recommend that you obtain and install several browsers from the shopping lists in Resources for the Web Chef, and use them to test your pages before you publish them on the Web. Your best bet is to have a high-end graphical browser (such as Netscape), one of the flavors of Mosaic, and one of the lower-end browsers, such as WinWeb or MacWeb. If you have the computer horsepower for it, you may want one of the 3-D browsers, also.

Remember, too, that while most of your Web page visitors will be using browsers that display inline graphics, an unknown number of them may be using Telnet sessions or some flavor of Lynx, a text-only Web browser. Text-based browsers may be limited and uncool, but they are a fact of life in academic and community-access circles—so be sure to tag your HTML files to support text-only users, no matter who your anticipated audience is. We'll show you some examples of well-mannered tagging in Chapters 5 and 7.

What are my browser choices?

There are a number of browser applications out there for each operating system platform; they may be available in limited versions as freeware or shareware, included with the operating system, or sold as independent commercial products. A fairly complete list of browsers for each platform (those available at deadline time, anyway) is offered in Resources for the Web Chef. You can also browse over to the World Wide Web FAQ (Frequently Asked Questions), located at the URL:

`http://sunsite.unc.edu/boutell/faq/www_faq.html`

or, cruise over to:

`http://www.yahoo.com/`

for information on browsers available for your operating platform.

Let's take a look at a few of them, just for comparison's sake. We'll use our Generic Web page template—copied straight from the CD-ROM—as our sample page.

InternetWorks

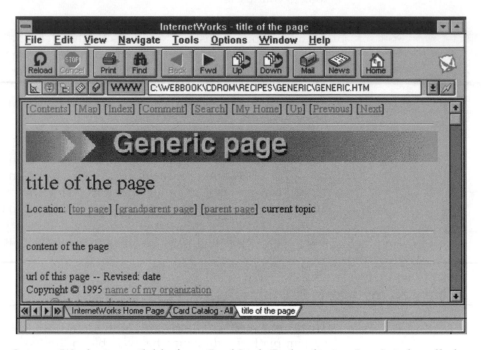

InternetWorks is available from BookLink Technologies, Inc. It is bundled with their Internet service subscription. A beta version is available to download.

MacWeb/WinWeb

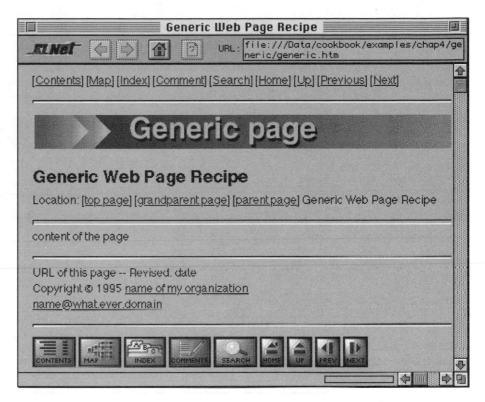

Developed by TradeWave Corporation, MacWeb and WinWeb are available as freeware.

NCSA Mosaic

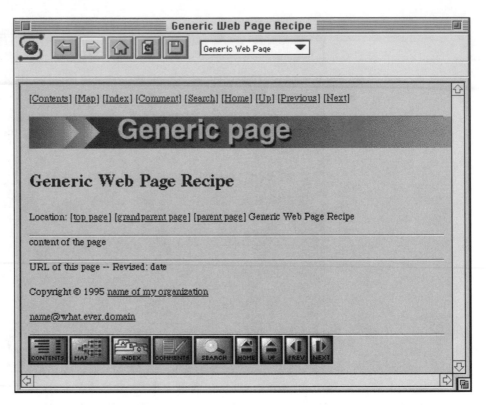

Mosaic is the original graphical Web browser, developed by the National Center for Supercomputing Applications at the University of Illinois for Macintosh, Windows, and X-Windows platforms. It can be argued that Mosaic played a large part in the blossoming of the Web as the place to be in cyberspace; indeed, in the early days of the WWW it was common to equate the Web and Mosaic (although by now you know they are not the same thing).

Since its original development, NCSA has licensed Mosaic development and support to a company named Spyglass, which in turn licenses it to other companies to serve as the basic engine for their own browser and related products. Thanks to that license transfer, NCSA can get out of the product development business, and Web users can get a variety of flavors of Mosaic to choose from.

Netscape Navigator

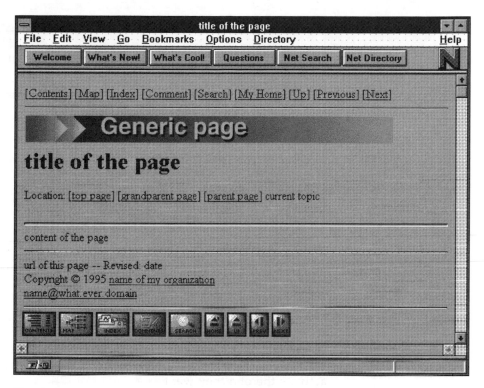

This browser is from Netscape Communications, a Web tools development company that includes several of the developers of the original NCSA Mosaic browser. Netscape has already made a name for itself by pushing the standards envelope aggressively, supporting a variety of functions and features that are not part of the HTML 2.0 standard. As a result, you can do some neat stuff with your Web pages that only a user with a Navigator browser can handle or appreciate. (When we say, "some browsers can do XYZ," we're usually referring to Navigator.)

Navigator is available as shareware (free to evaluate, $39 to license) for Macintosh, Windows, and X-Windows.

Lynx

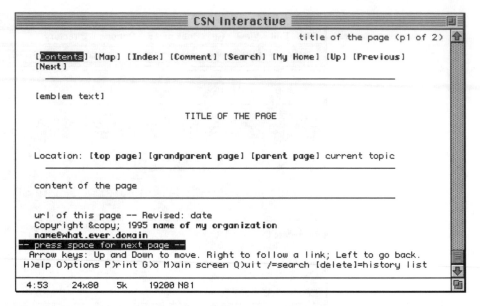

Lynx is the most popular text-only browser. It lets users with only VT-100 style alphanumeric monitors or terminal emulation programs sample the fare at the WWW banquet. Lynx displays the text and hypertext links of Web pages. Users can skip among the link triggers on a page and then activate the one they want.

Lynx is widely used in campuswide information systems (CWIS) and community-access systems where cost is the major concern and where users will not have graphical user interfaces. It is available for UNIX, DOS, and VMS operating systems.

How do I select a browser?

Well, that's partly a matter of personal taste, partly a matter of technical requirements, and partly a question of timing—that is, which browser has the newest version out when you're ready to make a decision. The operating platform you use will also play a part, although many browsers are now available on multiple platforms.

Our advice is to download and try out the freeware versions of several browsers before you make your decision. As we've suggested, you need to have several different browsers available for testing your Web pages. We've included a couple of browsers on the accompanying CD-ROM, but that's not a recommendation or anything; those are just the browsers for which it was practical for us to get permission to provide.

The periodicals that concern themselves with the Internet and the Web also monitor browser development and perform periodic reviews.

Browser basics

Regardless of which browser you use, there are some common or necessary functions that your browser should support. You can also assume that your users have the same functions available to them in their browsers.

The well-behaved browser will let you:

- Define a default home page for your starting point.

- Page forward and backward through the Web pages you've visited during the current Web session.

- Reload the Web page located at the current URL.

- Stop loading a Web page.

- Load images, so that you can see images from the current Web page, even if you've got the browser defaults set to suppress images.

- Create and maintain a hot list of URLs that you visit frequently; the browser should allow you to add the URL of the currently displayed Web page to your hot list with a simple click. You should also be allowed to edit the hot list fairly easily.

- Review a history list of URLs that you've visited in the current Web session—useful for backtracking to previous pages, without paging through all of them.

- View or save a source file of the HTML tagging used in the currently displayed Web page.

- Print the current Web page, with some semblance of appropriate formatting.

- Send Internet e-mail on the fly during a browsing session. Some browsers also allow you to include, in the body of the message, either a formatted text version or an HTML-tagged version of the current Web page.

The authorial perspective

Several of these browser functions have special significance to you as a Web author:

- For efficiency's sake, it's a good idea to set the browser's default home Page to a local file that's on your system. There are several reasons for this:

  - It loads the first page faster, so you can get up and running.

  - It cuts down on unnecessary network access time (and cost).

  - It makes it easier to test pages locally as you author them, before you put them out on the Web for general use.

- It's also a good idea to create an "author's bookshelf" page that contains only links to the various pages you have authored. Include this bookshelf page in your browser's hot list, and you'll have a means to quickly test or monitor your own pages. You might even prefer to start with this bookshelf page, rather than your own home page.

- The reload function is your best friend when you're creating Web pages. Here's how you can use it effectively:

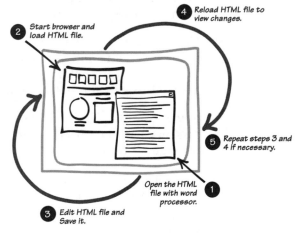

1. Open your HTML file in your preferred editor or word processor.

2. Open your browser and point it to the HTML file.

3. Make changes or additions to the HTML file as necessary, and save the changes.

4. Use the reload function in your browser to refresh the screen with the new HTML-tagged content.

5. Repeat steps 3 and 4 as necessary.

- The stop button tells the browser to interrupt the loading of the current Web page; you'll usually use it when a page is taking too long to load, or when a search is continuing without results. Keep in mind that users accessing your Web pages have the same button on their browsers, and they (like you) won't hesitate to use it. If your pages take too long to load, your users will stop the transfer and move on to other pages.

- Our own experience tells us that many users access the Web via dial-up SLIP/PPP accounts, using 14.4 kbps (or at best, 28.8 kbps) modems. At those speeds, graphics take a long time to load, and we suspect that many of these users have their browser defaults set to suppress images.

  So, you can't assume that your users are displaying those full-page illustrations you carefully scanned, or the detailed 32-bit button graphics that you labored so hard over. This suggests two precautions for your Web authoring effort:

BTW ...

Good ALT descriptions are particularly helpful to sight-impaired users, by the way; a speech synthesizer connected to a browser can pronounce "company logo" as easily as it can say "image here."

  1. Be sure to use meaningful ALT="Description of image" attributes for images, so that users with text-based browsers understand what they're missing, and users who have turned off display of images can determine whether they want to go to the trouble of loading your graphics. (See Chapter 5 for examples of the ALT attribute; it's just part of the HTML tagging for images that we describe later.)

  2. Unless graphic impact and illustrative content are the essence of your Web pages, be careful not to overdo graphic content. Use graphics effectively and sparingly. Be sure to test your page loading via a 14.4 modem, unless you know that you won't have any dial-up users.

- One of your goals (we assume) is to win a spot for your Web pages on your users' hot lists—to build a core of regular users. As you do your own browsing, keep in mind the reasons why you add URLs to your hot list. Look for the criteria or impressions that motivate you, and apply those to the design of your own pages.

- Notice how, when you add an item to your personal hot list, the browser (typically) adds the title of the page to your list. Make sure you use clear, concise, and logical titles on all your pages (even the ones linked at a subordinate level in a hierarchy), so that users can readily identify them in their hot lists. You never know which page(s) users will choose to link to—once they've found your archives in the basement, they may not come in through the front door again.

- Use the e-mail feature to distribute draft Web pages (which are not Internet- or network-accessible yet) to reviewers, editors, and co-authors. You can send them the HTML source files in (or attached to) an e-mail message, and they can look at the files locally with their own browsers, without accessing the Web site.

- If you expect users will frequently print your Web pages, be sure to test the print output from browsers running on all the operating platforms your users will be likely to use. Use the e-mail feature again, this time to send your pages and resources to friends or colleagues using various platforms. (Remember, a small bribe like cookies or a pound of special coffee works wonders for your response rate!)

These are just some of the main points to consider in selecting and using your browser. For more details about the finer points of authoring, see Chapter 3.

Go Web, go

The usual disclaimers apply: These URLs worked when we published them, but the Web changes every minute, so YMMV (Your Mileage May Vary).

Of course, no discussion of browsers would be complete without a few referrals of places on the Web to visit. Most browsers these days come equipped with a default hot list of common sites; here's a minuscule sampling of our own favorites that may be of interest to you as a Web author.

Description / Source	URL
Announcement services	`http://www.yahoo.com/Computers/World_Wide_Web/Announcement_Services/`
Ask Dr. Internet	`http://promo.net/gut/`
Home Page Construction Set	`http://nyx10.cs.du.edu:8001/~esasaki/hpcs/`
HTML/WWW Mentor Page	`http://www.mindspring.com/guild/index.html`
Multimedia Tutorials	`http://galen.med.virginia.edu/~smb4v/tutorial.html`
NetLinks! Newbie Help Link	`http://www.interlog.com/~csteele/newbie.html`
San Diego Supercomputer Center's VRML Repository	`http://www.sdsc.edu/vrml`

Description / Source	URL
Tim Berners-Lee's HTML Style Guide	`http://www.w3.org/hypertext/WWW/ Provider/Style/Overview.html`
Web (everything you wanted to know and then some)	`http://www.yahoo.com/Computers/ World_Wide_Web/`
Web Developers's Virtual Library	`http://WWW.Stars.com`
WWW FAQ	`http://sunsite.unc.edu/boutell/faq/ www_faq.html`
Yale C/AIM WWW Style Manual	`http://info.med.yale.edu/caim/ StyleManual_Top.HTML`

THE MEDIA WEB: HELPER APPLICATIONS

One of the killer advantages of the Web is its ability to allow your content to be expressed in a variety of media—including full-color graphics, sound, video, virtual reality, and animation—to any user who asks for it.

For more on particular media (pictures, sound, video, and so forth), see Chapter 6.

Adding such content to your Web page can be simple, hard, or impossible. It all depends on which media you are adding and whether your users are prepared to display the media. To ensure that Web users can play back the media you include, you must understand a little about how Web pages include various media and what each requires from the user.

Caveat Webspinner:

The most important factor in your users' enjoyment of your multimedia offerings is the one most completely out of your control: their computer and monitor hardware. To put it bluntly, the show is only as good as the equipment by which it is delivered.

This brings the dreaded lowest-common-denominator factor into play. Your best bet is to design with lower-end systems in mind, and test your stuff on a less impressive hardware configuration than the one on which it was developed.

There's more information on choosing and using media in Chapters 6 and 8.

Inline versus external media

The biggest distinction for authors and users is whether information is presented as inline media or external media. *Inline* media are words and pictures displayed by browsers in place within the browser's window. *External* media are ones displayed in a separate window by a *helper application (or helper app)*. Video, animation, sound, music, voice, and some pictures are displayed as external media.

For a list of popular helper apps, consult the "The Work Tools Shopping List" on page 565.

There are two basic kinds of helper apps (so far this week, anyway): *viewers* that display graphics files of various formats (or digital paper documents), and *players* that run video, animation, sound clips, and virtual reality. The main difference is that viewers let users view a static picture and players let users play sounds and dynamic pictures.

How do external media work?

Power has its price. The power of using multimedia in your Web pages comes with the price of complexity. Your users must master this complexity before they can play back your media.

What happens when the user summons external media?

Here's a diagram showing the complex series of events that occur:

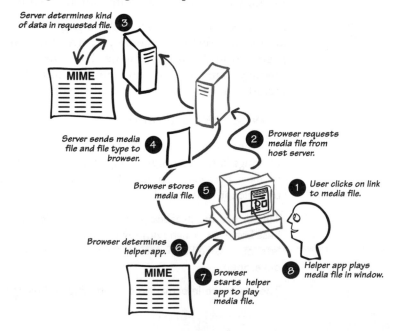

Server determines kind of data in requested file. ③

MIME

Server sends media file and file type to browser. ④

Browser requests media file from host server. ②

Browser stores media file. ⑤

User clicks on link to media file. ①

Browser determines helper app. ⑥

MIME ⑦ Browser starts helper app to play media file.

⑧ Helper app plays media file in window.

1. The user clicks on a link to play an external media file.

2. The browser asks the server to send the media file.

3. The server determines what kind of data the file contains.

4. The server notifies the browser of the type of data in the media file and sends it along.

5. The browser stashes the media file in memory or makes a temporary copy on the user's hard disk.

6. From the kind of data, the browser determines that it cannot display the file but that a particular helper app can.

7. The browser instructs the helper app to display the media file.

8. The helper app displays the media file in its own window. The user may interact with the helper application.

When the user quits the helper app, the browser will usually delete the temporary file that held the external media file.

MIME? Marcel Marceau in my computer?

How, you might ask, does the server *determine* the type of data in the file and how does the browser *determine* the helper app for a particular kind of data? The answer is MIME. MIME stands for "Multi-purpose Internet Mail Extension." It is a system developed originally so that Internet e-mail messages could include media other than text. The WWW uses it to help the browser figure out which helper application to fire up in order to play back a particular media file.

For WWW purposes, you can think of MIME as two tables, not the kind you eat from but the kind with rows and columns. The table on the server determines the type of data in a file. This table lists the various MIME types and the file extension (.gif, .txt, .mov, and so forth) that contain data of that type. Thus, the server can determine that the file vacation.mov is of MIME type video/quicktime. This table converts:

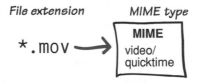

Each MIME type has two parts. The first part is the main type. It is a general category, such as video, image, audio, or application. The second part is called the subtype and it specifies the specific file format. For example, the MIME type video has subtypes of mpeg, quicktime, and x-msvideo.

The browser can assign a specific helper app to handle data of a particular MIME type. Thus, when the server says, "Here comes `vacation.mov` and it's MIME type video/quicktime," the browser can consult its table of helper apps assigned and determine to give the job of playing the file to the helper app MoviePlayer. This table converts:

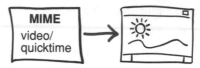

But how, you ask, does the browser determine the MIME type when it is reading a local file and not connected to a server? Most browsers also include a similar table to connect file extensions to the MIME types. The whole flow of information goes like this:

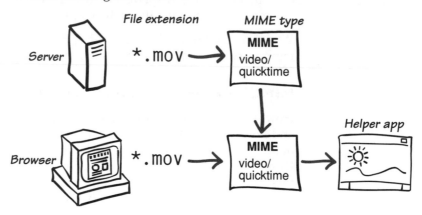

Okay, where do these magic tables come from? On the server the table is stored in a configuration file. On an NCSA-style server, if you look in the configuration subdirectory, you find a file named `mime.types`, which contains a line something like this:

```
video/quicktime mov qt
```

This indicates that the files whose names end in `.mov` or `.qt` have a MIME type of `video/quicktime`. Other servers may do it differently, but the principle is the same.

Where do the tables come from on the browser? Partly from the vendor of the browser and partly from the user's actions in setting up the browser. Here's were it gets complex. Most browsers include a default table listing common extensions, MIME types, and helper applications. However, the vendor of the browser can't guarantee whether the user actually has those helper apps installed. And no vendor can anticipate new MIME types that will be added. So, users must open the hood and configure their browser's MIME table to match their particular situation.

Doing so is not too hard—after surmounting two hurdles. The first is finding out how to do it in the particular browser. Each browser hides these options in a different place. Look under menus called Options or Preferences for something called Helper applications or MIME types. The second hurdle is filling in the blanks. Again the procedure varies from browser to browser. Here's the dialog box from Netscape.

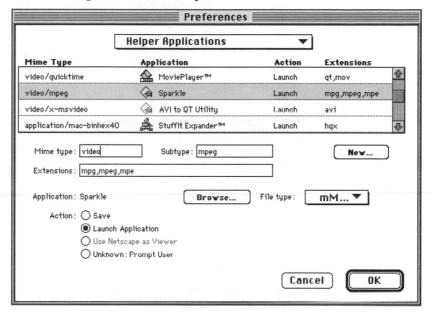

And here's the equivalent dialog box from Mosaic.

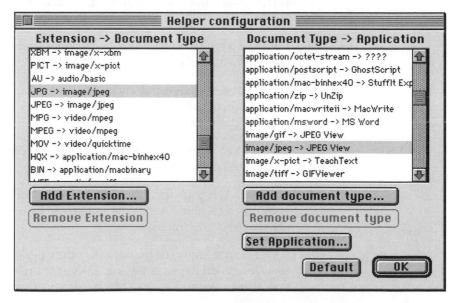

On UNIX systems, the helper apps may be specified in a `mailcap` file, which also specifies helper apps for e-mail tools. A simple `mailcap` file might look like this:

```
application/postscript; ghostview %s
image/*; xv %s
audio/*; showaudio %s
video/mpeg; mpeg_play %s
video/*; genericmovie %s
```

Compared to getting TCP/IP and SLIP running, specifying MIME types and helper apps is like floating downstream. But it is still a bit daunting to some users.

Bottom line on using external media

It all boils down to this. You cannot use external media in your Web pages unless your users:

1. Have helper apps to play the media.

2. Configure their browsers to trigger the right helper app for each medium.

Helping with helper apps

If you cannot count on your users to obtain helper apps or configure their browsers correctly, as an author you have two choices. You can limit your use of media to inline text and graphics and use external media only for secondary, noncritical information. Or, you can provide help to users unable to perform these tasks for themselves. What can you do? You can:

*   Link to a page recommending helper apps and showing how to configure the browser to trigger these helper apps.

*   If you have a captive audience—such as internal network users— provide them with the necessary helper apps and browser preconfigured to trigger those apps.

*   On the Web page, recommend a specific helper app for displaying the media elements.

*   On your Web page include a link to download the appropriate helper app from a reliable source. The source can be one you maintain or one elsewhere on the Internet.

*   If you do not know (or cannot infer) the operating system, provide a link to a Download page containing links to sources of helper apps for each operating system. You have to maintain this page and its software

libraries, but you gain better control over which helper apps are used with your pages. (We've included a Download menu recipe in our pantry; see page 185.)

Links to external media

You can place links to external media anywhere in your Web page content. The external media might be sitting on your Web server; others may be anywhere else on the Web; still others may be generated on the fly. For example, there are places on the Web where you can link to a video shot or segment that's generated in real time (usually by a robot or security camera), either at fixed time intervals, or on your request.

Now some good news. The links for external media are exactly the same as those for inline media. No special codes. No extra syntax.

URL is just the path to the file

The form of the URL for an external media element is the same as that for an inline graphic, or for a Web page, for that matter. It is just the location of the file containing the media element. Here's the URL for a Web page out on the Web:

`www.wherever.com/goodies/blowfish.htm`

Here's the URL for an inline gif file at the same location:

`www.wherever.com/goodies/blowfish.gif`

And here's one for a QuickTime movie at the same site:

`www.wherever.com/goodies/blowfish.mov`

What makes one inline and the other external? Just the file extension. The browser consults its MIME table to determine whether to display the file in its own window or whether to call on a helper application for the task.

Links can be buttons

You encode links to sounds the same as to any external media. These links can be separate buttons, like this:

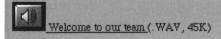

```
<A HREF="greeting.wav"><IMG SRC="sndicon.gif" ALT="[Sound
icon]"> Welcome to our team </A> (.WAV, 45K)<BR>
```

For the button, use a small icon that identifies the type of media. The recipe for a Multimedia page, page 213, includes these icons:

Icon	Medium	File
	Sound	sndicon.gif
	Speech	spkicon.gif
	Music	musicon.gif
	Picture	picticon.gif
	Animation	animicon.gif
	Video	vidicon.gif

For a visual medium, you can use a thumbnail—a miniature image of the visual. For animations or video, pick an especially revealing or intriguing still.

Links can be text

Links to external media can also occur within a paragraph of text:

> You can recognize this problem by listening for the grinding sound (.WAV, 45K) the disk drive makes as it starts up.

```
<P>You can recognize this problem by listening for the <A
HREF="diskstrt.wav">grinding sound</A> (.WAV, 45K) the disk
drive makes as it starts up.</P>
```

Make sure the context of the link makes clear what the user will receive by clicking on the link.

Whichever link you use, remember to indicate the size and format of the media file, so your users don't get any mega(byte)-surprises!

FutureMedia: virtual reality and the Web in 3-D

As this book was staggering to press, there were several exciting new developments brewing in browser and server technology, developments to present WWW worlds in three-dimensional, virtual, visual space. Although much of the initial thrust is on UNIX-based workstations (two of the first three products out of the gate were from Silicon Graphics and Sun Microsystems), it won't be long before most Web browsers support or incorporate 3-D environments.

Although we can't afford to display this in a hologram illustration (publication budgets being what they are), here's a two-dimensional example of the first Windows 3-D browser, WorldVision for Windows, from Intervista Software, Inc.

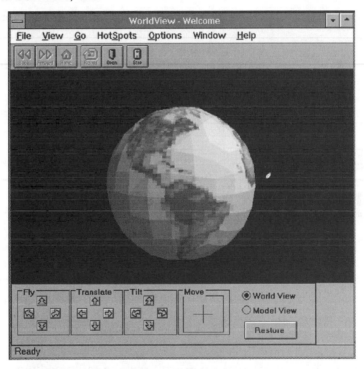

These browser companions (in effect, 3-D players) display three-dimensional versions of images and illustrations obtained from the Web. The next step is fully interactive 3-D worlds in which a 3-D browser lets the user navigate, make choices, select links, and so on through a 3-D representation of a particular Web site. Instead of reading a text or icon link that says "video clip of Sparky's stupid tricks," you'll walk over to the virtual TV, select the same video from a virtual kiosk, and play it. Instead of browsing Web pages and linking to other media, you'll be wandering Web worlds and experiencing Webness. (Hmmmm, does that make your Web self's virtual person a *virtson*?)

These 3-D worlds will likely be expressed in Virtual Reality Modeling Language (VRML), the growing standard for expressing VR attributes in basic text. VRML is based in large part on Silicon Graphic's Open Inventor toolkit, and is being developed to work much like HTML does: to provide a coded, plain-text description of a three-dimensional world that can then be interpreted and delivered by a 3-D browser on any operating platform. Once you've developed, say, a description of your products expressed in VRML (think of an animated version of your recent trade-show booth), you can deliver this living catalog to VRML-compliant browsers on any computer system.

Exactly. "Wow!" is right!

We've listed known 3-D browser applications and authoring tools in "The Work Tools Shopping List" in Resources for the Web Chef. But keep in mind that this is the Web's Next Big Thing (NBT, of course), so the names and companies involved will change significantly in a short period of time. If you have the content and the audience that makes 3-D VR a compelling delivery environment, go for it; if you see potential future possibilities, keep an eye on the periodicals and the appropriate newsgroups for the latest in authoring and browsing in 3-D.

DIGITAL PAPER AND THE WEB

One of the interesting recent Web developments is the growing use of digital paper as a content delivery medium. *Digital paper* (DP) is an electronic image of a formatted printout from any typical application, such as your word processing or spreadsheet program. A DP application functions like any other print driver on your system (for example, like a fax program that "prints" faxes directly to your modem). You just select it from your printer arsenal and let fly with your print job.

Digital paper isn't really a multimedium (yet), but it is another external media type that requires users to have a helper application. To create DP files, you print a job from your application software via a digital paper application—such as Adobe's Acrobat, No Hand's Common Ground, or Novell's Envoy—and instead of printing on the page, it "prints" an on-screen image of that page. Anyone with a compatible reader program can open the DP document (Adobe calls them *portable documents*) on their system, regardless of the platform they're on or the platform the document was created on.

DP reader programs are typically available as freeware, and in some cases you can embed them into the DP document files so that the whole thing runs like a program. Different DP programs have different capabilities, of course (isn't competition a wonderful thing?), but generally they do (or will) support:

- Hypertext linking among multiple documents.

- Annotations by readers.

- Word searching by readers.

- Printing (with a reasonable semblance to the formatting of the original).

- Integrated text and graphics.

Here's an example of a brochure page printed as digital paper via Novell's Envoy.

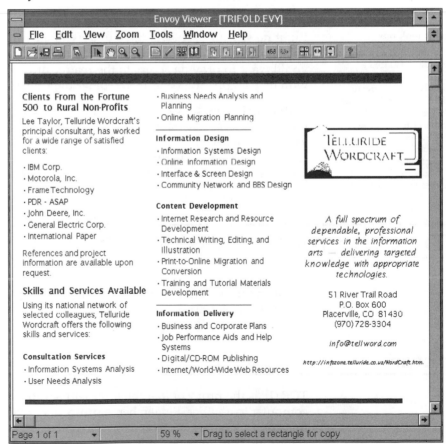

Why is digital paper important to you as a Web author? Well, for a couple of reasons.

- **DP is easy to do** (even easier than using our templates); you just select a digital printer and output your document to a file, then create a link to that file in your Web page. DP is a great way to distribute preexisting documents and information via the Web, without going through HTML conversion and cleanup. No codes, no muss, no fuss; just print 'em and link 'em.

- When you create a digital paper document, **it retains the formatting and design of the original**; you don't have to worry about the configuration and capabilities of your users' systems, and you know that what they see is what you wanted them to see, more or less. (We'll resist the temptation to do the acronym thing with this one; the results would be too horrible to contemplate.) So, you get more control over the format of your information than you have with HTML and the mayhem of nonstandard browsers. Don't you think predictable results are a good idea?

Don't look now …

True to form, Netscape recently announced a partnership with Adobe to teach Navigator how to read an Adobe PDF (Portable Document Format) file. In the future, your user's browser will probably be able to interpret and display a PDF or similar file, much as it handles HTML files now.

Right now, your users will have to download your digital paper files in order to view them. If you include links to DP files in your Web pages, you'll want to provide access to the reader programs, also. See "Helping with helper apps" on page 48 for some suggestions.

Web purists (yes, they do exist) might argue that using DP files doesn't really constitute publishing on the Web so much as distributing via the Web, but that seems a pretty thin distinction. The fact of the matter is, you can use the Web to distribute DP documents just as easily and effectively as you distribute external graphics or other resources.

THROUGH THE KITCHEN DOORS: TCP/IP & SLIP/PPP

So much for the fun media stuff. Last but not least, here's a look at the nuts and bolts of Web access.

TCP/IP

TCP/IP is the protocol that the Internet uses to transfer data from one computer to another. Remember, a protocol is a kind of computer dialect that computers use to understand each other. TCP/IP (which, by the way, stands for Transmission Control Protocol/Internet Protocol, a mouthful in any language) is the common dialect used by all the computers on the Internet, whether they are accessing the World Wide Web or not. Technically, TCP/IP controls the size, type, and transfer of the information packets that make up all Internet transmissions, from e-mail messages to Web page videos. Your computer has to speak TCP/IP in order for you to surf the Web with a snazzy and easy-to-use graphical interface. (And why would you want to do otherwise?)

You may already have TCP/IP software on your computer. It depends on which operating system runs your computer. UNIX, Macintosh System 7.5, Windows 95, and OS/2 Warp all include TCP/IP software. Consult your owner's manual to see what, if anything, you need to do to activate it. If your computer gets its marching orders from Macintosh System 7.0, Windows 3.1, Windows for Workgroups 3.11, or earlier versions of these operating systems, you'll need to obtain and install TCP/IP-fluent software to let your computer join in the conversation. Don't worry though: There are freeware and shareware versions for both platforms available.

SLIP/PPP

SLIP/PPP is the protocol that your TCP/IP computer uses to access the Internet via a modem. (SLIP stands for Serial Line Internet Protocol; PPP is the acronym for Point-to-Point Protocol. They serve the same function in slightly different ways.) It allows your computer to connect to the Internet in a client/server relationship. This sounds pretty technical, but it basically means that you are using the Internet as just a supplier (hence, server) of bits and bytes; the real work of interpreting and displaying that data is performed by programs (known as *clients*) that run on your computer.

If it helps, think of the Web as a galactic restaurant of information and entertainment: As the client, you order food from your server—and of course you then decide what to eat first, whether to mash together your peas and potatoes, and how to gracefully strip all the meat off that drumstick.

Why do you need two protocols? Well, SLIP/PPP is the pipeline or conduit for Internet information; TCP/IP is the format that this information takes in transit between you and the Internet. As long as both sides of the conversation are speaking the same dialect, everything's cool.

SLIP/PPP clients

Internet trivia time

Who was the popular product Eudora named after? (Answer: Eudora Welty, author of the classic short story, "Why I Live at the P.O."

SLIP/PPP clients are software applications running on your computer that know how to send and receive stuff over a SLIP/PPP connection, and are fluent in TCP/IP. You use these client applications to perform specific functions with different types of Internet data. For example, you use a Web browser client (such as NCSA's Mosaic) to wander the World Wide Web; an e-mail client (such as Qualcomm's Eudora) to read, send, and store e-mail; and a newsreader client (such as the freeware WINVN) to read and respond to Usenet newsgroups.

Web tools are evolving rapidly; even now, there are suites of tools available that have multiple clients included, and some client applications perform more than one function. Netscape, for example, is primarily a Web browser, but you can also use it to read newsgroups or send e-mail. This cross-functionality will continue to evolve as the market and the technology mature. In the not-too-distant future, you'll be able to do all your Internet activities from within one application, and operating systems will have TCP/IP and SLIP/PPP built in.

Since this book is specifically about the World Wide Web, we're primarily concerned with browser clients. If you want to know more about other SLIP/PPP clients, check with your ISP, look through some of the references in Resources for the Web Chef, or keep an eye on the various trade journals.

Are all clients created equal?

Nope. Just to make things interesting, your client software also has to know how to work with the flavor of TCP/IP software that you've installed. On the Macintosh side, this is pretty seamless stuff; the MacTCP software is supplied by Apple, so there aren't any consistency problems there. Windows users, on the other hand, have to make sure that their TCP/IP and client applications are compatible. This is rapidly becoming a nonissue, too, as the Windows Sockets Interface—the infamous Winsock of which you may have heard—is becoming the de facto standard. Most Windows-based TCP/IP and SLIP/PPP software that's now available in freeware, shareware, or commercial versions contains the necessary `winsock.dll` file to make the thing work.

This isn't a load-'n'-go thing, is it?

No, more like "plug and pray." Setting up your TCP/IP and SLIP/PPP connection is probably the trickiest thing you'll have to do—fraught with technobabble like domain server, netmask, IP addresses, and POPmail. Don't worry too much about this technical stuff, though: The ISPs that will be selling you accounts and storage are figuring out how to handle the support needs of less-technical new users. SLIP and PPP accounts are the ones most commonly opened these days, and a well-run ISP should be prepared to walk you through Winsock configurations and the like.

ISPs also typically offer downloads of TCP/IP and SLIP/PPP software that are already configured to work with their servers. You can, of course, also use the protocol software provided as a courtesy on the CD-ROM supplied with this book. "As a courtesy," means don't call us (or John Wiley & Sons, Inc.) for installation or technical support.

Now it's time to follow along while we show you how to create a Web page.

3

COOKING LESSON

Overview of authoring a Web page

With most chores (oops, we mean "challenges") in life, there's a hard way and an easy way to get 'em done. **The hard way to create Web pages** is to spend hours trying to figure out, type in, and debug arcane HTML codes. **The easy way** is to find a Web page that you like, copy it, and change it around as needed. (Just be sure not to violate any copyrights, or purloin any protected content!)

If you want to do it the hard way, starting from scratch for each Web page you create, this book is not for you. Instead, pick up a copy of *The HTML Sourcebook* by Ian S. Graham (John Wiley & Sons, Inc.), and have at it. We like cooking up Web pages, but we hate wasting time. So we do it the easy way—and you can too, especially since we've done a bunch of the work for you.

Consider this the just do it chapter: All the introductory stuff is behind us, the cybersoil has been prepared, the pregame warm-ups are done. Have a seat at your keyboard and let's get going, shall we?

We'll start by showing you the big picture (naturally): how to create a basic Web page using this book and the goodies on the accompanying CD-ROM to your best advantage. If you have a good idea of what content, design, and structure you want for your Web pages, you can dive right in at this point.

Next we'll launch into a detailed case study—a transcript, really—that shows exactly how one intrepid author created a well-organized and functional biography page and added it to her company's Web site. This is real blow-by-blow nitty-gritty stuff, right down to the modem commands for loading your pages; it comes complete with trenchant narration from your humble authors. (Don't worry, we edited it for a family audience!)

ON YOUR MARK, GET SET . . .

The procedure for creating Web pages with the CD-ROM resources is relatively simple and straightforward. It only takes nine key steps, as shown in this diagram.

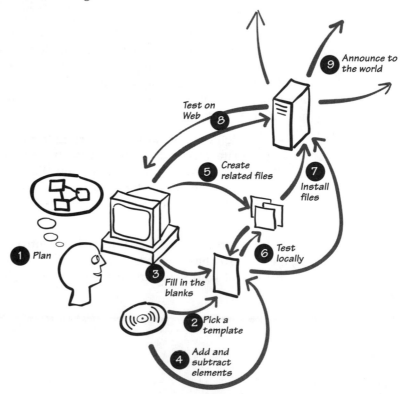

Overview, step 1: Get a plan.

Decide what you want to accomplish and gather the information and tools you will need. Make sure you:

- Have all your content source material—graphics, text, and media—close at hand.

- Have one or more browsers installed and working on your computer, and know how to view pages locally.

- Know who your target audience is, and what you want your Web pages to give them.

- Have an idea of the structure you want to use, and the scope of your Web site in general.

If you haven't thought of your Web pages in these terms, you may find Chapter 11 helpful; it talks about the different kinds of Web page structures (*clusters*, we call 'em) and what structure works well for which purposes.

Overview, step 2: Pick a template.

We stored the templates (we call them *recipes*) on the CD-ROM in a series of directories—entrées, if you will, since this *is* a cookbook.

Each recipe exists as both a template and an example. The template is a complete Web page with placeholders for each kind of information you might want to include. You can just replace the placeholders with real text, graphics, and other content. The example is just a filled-in template. Of course, you can use the example as if it were a template by just replacing the sample content with your own.

We carefully designed each recipe so that you can create your own Web page by just filling in the blanks without having to memorize or type in a lot of HTML codes.

Both forms of the recipes are on the CD-ROM. The templates are in separate folders within the `recipes` directory:

```
recipes
    biograph
    book
    catalog
    contents
(and more)
```

The examples are in the `chap4` subdirectory of the `examples` directory:

```
examples
    chap4
        biograph
        book
        catalog
        contents
```

(and more)

The template names are meant to be self-explanatory. For example:

- `biograph` is a biographical sketch that you might use to profile yourself or your staff members.

- `book` is for describing a book or presenting a book review.

- `catalog` is for describing a product in an electronic catalog.

If you want to see what recipes we provide or need more information about a particular recipe, see Chapter 4.

Otherwise, select one or more of the page templates and copy it to your hard disk from the CD-ROM. Be sure to:

- Create a directory (or folder) structure on your hard disk that matches the one that you'll use on your Web server. For example, if your Web site content is (or will be) stored in the directory

  `/marketing/catalog/`*`filenames`*

  then you should create this directory/folder structure on your hard disk (if you haven't already) and do all your work there. This will make it easier to move the finished Web pages (in technical terms, "mount" them) back to your Web server for release, since all the path names will be the same.

- Copy *all* the files in the selected directory—you'll need the graphics and other resources to reproduce the page you selected. You don't want to get halfway through and have to stop and figure out what's missing. (That's how an otherwise competent chef ends up burning the soup!)

Then, just to be safe, open the *`whatever`*`.htm` recipe file, using the View Local File function of your personal Web browser. Make sure you have all the contents. Check that all pictures and icons display correctly. Don't expect all the links to work, though. When you click on them you should get a response that the destination cannot be found. That's because these are templates and they do not know what you want to call the destination or where you have stored it. That's easy to fix, but that's part of the next step.

Overview, step 3: Fill in the blanks.

Now you're ready to edit the template source files and make them your own. Here's how:

- If you're using a word processor that can import or open files in Rich Text Format (`*.rtf`), then import/open the `*.rtf` file for your template. (Make sure that all the text is displayed in a fixed-width font, such as Courier, Letter Gothic, or Monaco.)

  If you have a color display, you will notice right away that the HTML code is in different colors. If your word processor knows about style sheets for paragraphs and characters, you may notice that different parts use styles. It may not look pretty, but the color-coding makes it easy to see what parts of the recipe you should change to create your own Web page, and what part you probably should leave alone. The styles and color codes are:

Type information	Paragraph style	Character style	Color
HTML code (stuff you should not change)	HTML	(none)	Black
HTML code you should change	HTML	variable	Red
Comments in HTML code	HTML	comment	Green

After you have made your changes, don't forget to save the RTF file first and then save it again as a plain-text HTML file.

Color blind? Don't like our choice of colors? Just redefine the corresponding style. It's your kitchen.

If you're using an editor program of some sort—line, text, or HTML—you can open the *whatever*.htm files that have been provided in ASCII; they're in the same directory. These text files have the same contents as the `*.rtf` versions, and you use them in the same way; unfortunately, you don't get the colored text, so you have to figure out which text to replace and which to leave alone. (Sorry about that.) You *can* use the printout of the HTML-tagged text for that template—reproduced in its section in Chapter 4—as a guideline, since the colored text shows up slightly grayed there.

- Replace our template content with your actual content. If you can run two programs at once, open your editor or word processor and start cutting and pasting to your heart's content. Obviously, be careful not to delete any HTML tags, or you'll create formatting or linking errors.

Sure beats thumbing through an HTML glossary, doesn't it?

Overview, step 4: Add, subtract, and modify elements.

Now you're ready to fine tune the page:

- Delete any parts of the template that you don't need or don't want.

- Add new elements to make your pages even better. We included snippets of HTML tagging for a whole catalog of helpful ingredients on the CD-ROM—we think of it as our spice rack.

If you want more information about what ingredients are available or how to use a particular ingredient, see Chapter 5.

You can get your ingredients from one big file that contains all the ingredients or from individual files for each ingredient. Why do we provide both?

The consolidated file is better if you are shopping for a particular ingredient to copy and paste into your file. You can window shop for ingredients to liven up your Web page. You can also compare similar ingredients. The consolidated file is definitely more convenient if you do not know the name of the ingredient you want (and this book is not at hand).

The consolidated file is available in two formats: RTF (`allinone.rtf`) and plain text (`allinone.txt`). The RTF has the color-coding and styles we bragged about on page 63. You will find these files down this path:

```
ingrdnts
    as_rtf
        allinone.rtf
    as_txt
        allinone.txt
```

The ingredients are also available in individual files. These individual files are for expert chefs who know exactly the ingredient they need, say a dash of bullet list or a pinch of horizontal rule, and want to plug it in directly. Many word processors provide an "insert" or "import" command to let you suck in a complete RTF or plain-text file. You just move to the point in your Web page where you want to add the ingredient and import the file you need. These files, like the consolidated ones, come in both RTF (`whatever.rtf`) and plain-text (`whatever.txt`) formats and are found down the same path:

```
ingrdnts
    as_rtf
        address.rtf
        allinone.rtf
        baseform.rtf
        bycolor.rtf
      (and many, many more)
    as_txt
        address.txt
        allinone.txt
        baseform.txt
        bycolor.txt
      (and many, many more)
```

The snippets are provided for your convenience; find what you need and cut and paste (or import) it into your pages with abandon! (If you have the room, you may want to simply copy the entire `ingrdnts` directory to your hard disk, for easier access.)

At this point, if you haven't done so already, you should save your work file. If you're working in RTF remember to save the file first as an RTF file then again in ASCII (or equivalent) format for the real HTML file. (An RTF file viewed through a Web browser is not a pretty sight!)

Overview, step 5: Create and link related files.

Now you're ready to add the fun stuff: custom graphics, icons, digital paper, sounds, video clips, animation, and virtual reality. We know you won't add any gratuitous decoration; we're sure you'll restrict yourself to essential media components that add impact and clarity to your message.

You can create these components using whatever program you want; just make sure that you save them in formats commonly used on the Web. Be sure to provide access to appropriate viewer and player software, unless you're pretty sure that your users already have everything they need to enjoy your efforts.

Overview, step 6: Test locally.

Okay, you've added all your content. Now it's time to open your new Web page in your browser(s) of choice, using the browser's local mode. Test the page thoroughly to make sure it displays correctly and that all internal links work the way you expect them to. (*Internal links* being those links that don't include URLs that point outside your server.)

It's also a good idea at this point to have other people look at the pages; run a simple usability test to make sure that your ideas on perfectly logical structure and sequence make sense to potential users. (You know what they say about assumptions, right?) If appropriate, you can use your browser's e-mail feature to distribute copies of the test pages within your internal network.

Overview, step 7: Install files on the server.

Once you've tested (and fixed) everything, you can transfer your HTML and other files to the Web server where they will reside. In technical terms, this is known as "mounting" the files. (Hey, it's not our fault—it's a UNIX thing.)

The mounting process varies from server to server:

- If you're using an outside vendor as your Web site, they should have fairly explicit instructions on how to mount files for public access. Check with the folks in technical support to see how they want you to proceed.

- If you're mounting your files on an internal Web server, or a proxy server outside your company firewall, check with your system administrator.

> ### Some unsolicited advice
>
> Regardless of your pride of authorship, your looming deadlines, or your urgency to get your Web pages out there, always approach the technical gods with empathy for their struggles. Put yourself in their position, and phrase your request for help accordingly. You'll be amazed at what friendly sympathy will do for your place in the mounting queue (but don't hesitate to buy them lunch again, if you think it will help).

When the files have been mounted, check to make sure that:

- Your files are placed in the correct directory, and that all the files are there.

- All the files have the correct permissions set.

- All your internal links reference the right locations and subdirectories.

Overview, step 8: Test on the Web.

Test your pages by accessing them the same way you expect your users to: If that means dialing in by 14.4 modem, then do so. Check to make sure that:

- Your pages display as expected.

- All your links (internal or external) work as expected.

- Your pages are integrated into your Web site appropriately: If your new pages are part of a larger cluster of pages, you may need to modify other pages to link them to the newcomer.

- Your external files will download in a reasonable amount of time.

> ### What's a reasonable download time?
>
> Well, that depends on the quality of the content, its importance to your users, and the bandwidth available. If you're offering software upgrades or fixes, then your users will probably hang in there as long as necessary, even at 14.4 or less. If you're sending them navigational graphics (like buttons or interactive maps) or other graphic elements (like table grids and swashes) that help them use your pages more effectively, they'll stick with you. When you send them decorative but nonessential "screen candy," they'll hit the Stop button in a heartbeat.

Overview, step 9: Announce to the world.

Announce your new Web page to any potential new users. Invite interested Web patrons to stop by and have a look.

A Case Study: Web Craft in Real Life

On the CD-ROM ...

The template for this case study can be found in:

recipes
    biograph
        biograph.rtf

The media files and intermediate HTML files can be found in:

examples
    chap3
        final
        firstcut
        rawmtls

And now, the case study we promised you. This section follows Kit Horton, partner of one of the authors, as she creates a Biography page for herself and adds it to her company's Web site. Join us as we track Kit through all nine steps.

Clarity through typography

We've introduced a few typographic conventions to keep things straight:

Kit generates the main narrative of the case study by thinking out loud as she works through the Web craft process; we show this narrative in a sans serif typeface, like this. Since Kit will be, in effect, interviewing herself, we'll show her questions in italics, *like this*.

> Occasionally we Master Chefs will butt in with a timely observation, or some pearl of our collective wisdom. Chef comments will be shown in serif typeface, like this.

Step 1: Get a plan.

Before I can get started on this nine-step path to Webness, I need some information and resources. I'm going to need a plan, some content, tools, hardware, and also an Internet service provider.

First, the plan: I'll use the trusty Socratic method and interview myself (since I talk to myself all the time, anyway!).

> Yes, it is always best to do your planning before you sit down at the computer.

Okay, why am I doing this?

> It is a good idea to begin by answering this question. If you cannot explain why you are creating your page, you are not ready. How would you explain what you're doing to your boss, your customers, or your spouse?

One day I received e-mail from a client telling me how much she liked our Web site, but was disappointed there was no information about me. She has talked to me on the phone and written me so many e-mail messages that she wanted to know what I looked like. She also wanted to include my bio info in the description for a conference session I was going to lead for her.

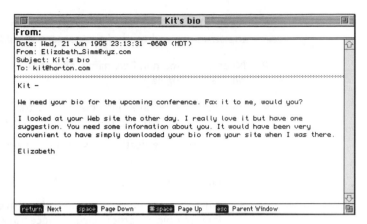

After getting the message, I wondered why I hadn't thought of it myself. It got me thinking, "Are there some additional reasons to put my biography 'out there' on the Web?"

I came up with:

- To explain my function within the company to our clients; it would probably help them to know whom to contact for particular kinds of information.

- Because a savvy client asked me why it wasn't already available.

- To prepare a standard biography that companies and organizations can download and use for publicity if I'm coming to their sites to speak or teach.

- Because I've been told to by The Powers That Be, who want to show off the staff as part of the corporate Web presence.

Knowing "why" I want to do this page will help me keep on track, both in tone and content.

How does it fit into the total Web structure?

Whenever your Web page must fit into a larger set of Web pages, you must plan ahead to make it harmonize and cooperate with those pages. Otherwise your Web page becomes an informational pariah: even worse, you might make Mirsky's Worst of the Web[tm] list (http://mirsky.turnpike.net/wow/Worst.html, if you have that kind of fascination with things morbid).

Consider how you will make your new page consistent with the other pages on your Web site; think about other pages that may need to change to take advantage of your new page.

Our company has a well-established Web site of over 40 pages. This imposes some design guidelines right from the beginning. For instance, my page will:

- Need a similar look and feel to the existing Biography page. What I mean is the structure and tone of the content should be similar.

- Need the same number, name, and configuration of navigation buttons as are on the existing pages.

- Need to be integrated into our Web site. This means that I must make changes to some of the existing pages. For instance, I'll have to:

  1. **Change** the destinations of the Previous and Next buttons of the topics coming before and after my bio.

  2. **Update** the Contents and Index pages.

  3. **Add** pointers *to* my bio from other pages as appropriate, and pointers *from* my bio to other pages if necessary.

> If you maintain more than a few Web pages, you will find it well worth the effort to keep careful records of your pages. Otherwise, adding pages becomes an exercise in frustration and Error 404s, and takes much more time than necessary.

Thank goodness we have a spreadsheet of our Web site showing its organization and file naming conventions. Here's a portion of it:

Name	Subtitle	File name.html	Template
What is William Horton Consulting?		index	Home page
What do you do?	Activities by William Horton Consulting	whc	Generic
Who is William Horton?	Bill's biography	bill	Biography
Who is Katherine Horton?	Kit's biography	kit	Biography
How do we hire you?	Terms, conditions, and policies	terms	Generic
How can you help us on a project?	Consulting activities	consult	Generic
Reviews and suggestions		review	Generic
Designs and prototypes		design	Generic
Guidelines and standards		guide	Generic
What courses do you teach?		courses	Generic
Visual literacy	Say it in pictures	vislit	Course description
Online documentation	Use computers to communicate	online	Course description
New-media literacy	Author effective, low-cost multimedia	nmlit	Course description
Icons and visual symbols	Design a visual language	icon	Course description
Can you come speak to us?	Presentations and speeches by WH	speeches	Generic
Visual literacy	A crash course	vlcrash	Generic
Online vs. paper documents	Dangerous differences	dang	Generic

Adding a new Web page to an existing cluster of pages means a lot of surgery:

- You must not only insert the new page, but you must graft it onto existing pages.

- You must link from the new page to existing pages and vice versa.

- You must suture the gaps.

- You must test everything.

If you have a clear view of how your existing Web pages are organized, you have greatly simplified the task of adding a new page. With a spreadsheet, a list, or some other tracking mechanism, you can instantly see what other pages will need tweaking.

After inserting my biography page into the spreadsheet (between `bill.html` and `terms.html`) and naming it `kit.html`, I see that I'll need to make changes to the following pages:

Page needing changes	Change needed
What is William Horton Consulting?	Add a pointer to my biography page.
Who is William Horton?	Change the Next button so it points to my biography rather than to "How can we hire you?"
How Can We Hire You?	Change the Previous button so it points to my biography page.
Contents	Add a pointer to my biography page.
Index	Add references to my biography page.

I'll make these changes *after* I get the new page working.

Okay, now to plan the content . . .

Good idea; plan what you're going to do, then plan what you are going to say. It is usually best to write out your text and sketch your graphics before you begin filling in Web pages.

I have a color photograph, a short informational piece about myself, and a biography I used recently in a conference paper. This will be enough to get started; however, I may need more stuff later, depending upon the template I choose. Sounds like a content plan to me!

Now, what kind of tools will I need?

To avoid interruptions while you are in the flow of creativity, take a few minutes to make sure you have all the resources you need to do the job.

Here's a list of tools I will use to create my page and upload it to our Web site.

Hardware

The computer system I am using to prepare my page is a souped-up Macintosh CI with a 68040 accelerator card and 20 megabytes of memory, running System 7.5, with a 14.4 bps modem. Connected to this are a Microtek scanner and an Apple 300i CD-ROM drive.

> This is the equivalent of a PC with a 486 processor running at about 50 MHz—or an 8-year-old Sun workstation.

Web software

This is the software that allows me to view Web pages and play media files. I have three types of applications:

- **TCP/IP software**—I'm using Mac TCP/IP (which lets the Mac "speak" TCP, the language of the Internet), and VersaTerm Admin SLIP, which sets up the connection to our Internet service provider.

- **Web browser**—I use Netscape, but I also have Mosaic and MacWeb, so that I can check my pages in multiple browsers.

- **Helper application**—Since I might include sound, I need an application that will allow me to play it back. I'm using SoundApp.

> Chapter 2 explains the software types and requirements in some detail. Kit has the basics well taken care of here.

Production software

These are general-purpose tools that I'll press into service to create my Web pages. I need to make sure these programs are on my system or at least easily accessible.

- **Word processor**—I'm using Microsoft Word 6.0 for Macintosh, which can read and write RTF files.

> Any word processor that can open or import RTF (Rich Text Formatting) files will do. You can also get by with a simple text editor, since HTML files are plain text, and we include ASCII versions of the templates. However, we recommend a word processor that can read and write the color-coded RTF files for recipes and ingredients.

- **Graphics tool**—I've got Deneba's Canvas and Adobe Photoshop, both of which can edit and export GIF files.

> If you plan to include graphics, you will need tools for creating and editing graphics. These tools must be able

to save their results in common formats for Web graphics; usually this means GIF or JPEG format.

- **Graphics file-conversion program**—I rely on Equalibrium's Debabelizer for converting from one format to another. I use it mainly to convert plain GIF to interlaced GIF, because I've learned that interlaced GIF files load better in some browsers.

    If your drawing or paint program cannot save in common Web formats, you will need a file-conversion program. You may also need a conversion program if you are using graphics from clip-art libraries.

- **Terminal emulation program**—I prefer Zterm (version 0.9, at the moment) for uploading the Web files to the service provider—oops, I mean "mounting the files."

    You will need a way to transfer your files to your service provider or to the file server where they will reside. A simple file-transfer utility will do for this task. You may also need to arrange your files into specific directories, change their names, and set permissions. To do these you will need to interact directly with the server's operating system. Usually this requires a terminal emulation package, running an interactive session. You can also use a Telnet session, which is essentially the same thing.

- **Sound editing and recording tools**—I've got Macromedia's SoundEdit 16 and built-in Macintosh sound, so I'm in good shape.

    If you are using sound, you may need hardware to capture the sound and software to edit it. The same goes for video.

Service provider

Because William Horton Consulting does not have its own Web server, we contract with Colorado SuperNet (CSN), our Internet access provider, for this service. They provide:

- **An Interactive account**—This is the account I use to install Web pages on the server. I'll need to know our User ID and password for this account, and program Zterm to know how to dial it up.

- **A SLIP account**—This is the account I use to view Web pages—both our own, to test the way others will see them, and other Web pages that I want to look at. I'll need to know the IP address, User ID, and password for this account. Then I have to configure MacTCP to access this account, and set up VersaTerm SLIP to work properly with the account.

These are not trivial tasks, even for an experienced Mac user. Be sure to read any help documents that your ISP sends you with your SLIP account, and keep the tech support number handy. Getting these things configured can be tougher than creating the Web pages themselves.

By the way, not all ISPs do it this way, either; some allow you to set up one account, and then give you both SLIP and interactive access to it. Check with your ISP for specific details.

- **Server space**—I'll need to know the name of the server and directory where my Web pages should be stored, so I can create the same structure on my local system. That'll make mounting my files a lot easier.

  Kit doesn't say so here, but getting everything set up with a service provider can take a l __o__n__g ____ t__i__m__e. Months, not days.

  Plan ahead. Start yesterday.

  If you have a current Internet service provider (ISP), get on the phone *now* to have them send you information on their Web server pricing, service, and procedures.

  If you don't have a provider yet, include those issues in your discussions with potential ISPs.

- **Domain name**—CSN also helped us in obtaining a domain name (this is our Internet "address") for e-mail (kit@horton.com) and our Web pages (www.horton.com). I gather that it's not unusual for a company or organization to create a domain name when they establish a SLIP account. We like it because it gives us a company presence on the Internet; horton.com is more, well, *cool*.

  Of course, if you are publishing your Web pages on a Web server your own organization maintains for such purposes, your task will be simpler. Well, it should be simpler.

  You will still need to know how to transfer the files from your computer to the server, how to arrange them there, what to do about user permissions, and any other peculiarities of your system. Oh, and don't forget to get the proper permissions for your own internal account, so that you're allowed to add files, change permissions, and the like.

  On a well-run system [are you listening, system administrators?] the system administrator will do much of this work for you. As a minimum, you should insist on clear instructions.

Okay, I've got The Plan, I've got The Tools—now it's time to get to The Work.

Step 2: Pick a template.

On the CD-ROM ...

recipes
  biograph
    biograph.rtf

Now I can start weaving—or is it spinning?—my new Web page. The first step is to select a template as a starting point.

> I think she's got it! The way to create Web pages is to start with a template that does most of the work for you. Check out Chapter 4 for page templates.

I've flipped through Basic Recipes, Chapter 4, and have found a Biography page template. It looks like just what I need. To be sure, though, I'll look at it with my browser.

To do that, I:

1. Mount the companion CD-ROM.

2. Start up the browser; in this case, I'll use Netscape.

> On a PC, you have to open TCPMan (Winsock) first. SLIP applications won't run, even locally, without it.

3. I select Open File... from the File menu...

4. ... and pick `biograph.htm` within the `recipes/biograph` directory on the CD-ROM.

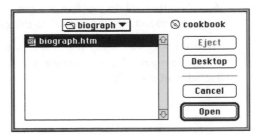

5.   I click "Open," and I check out this template page:

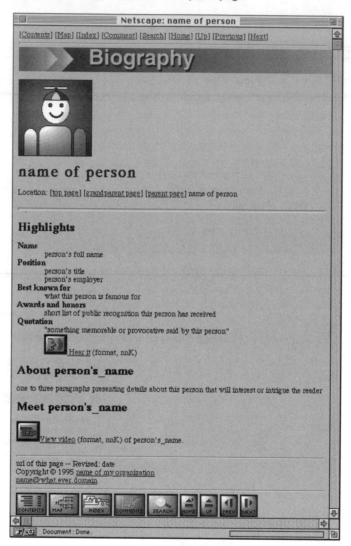

6.   Yep, this will do just fine. It's got a place for my picture, some details, even a little sound file to personalize things. I like it!

Before I start to modify the source file, though, I'll copy the entire `biograph` folder to my hard drive to make sure I have all the files I need. Let's see, that includes all these files:

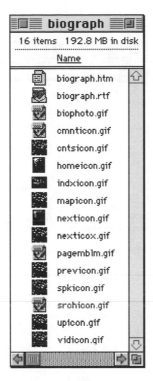

At this point, we Master Chefs recommend one extra step:

Open the Web page in the browser again, but this time use the file on your hard disk. We may be overly cautious, but we like to make absolutely sure everything copied over correctly and that all the pieces you need are in the folder you copied.

If you're in a hurry, we'll forgive you if you skip this step.

Using my word processor, I open the file, `biograph.rtf` from the folder I copied.

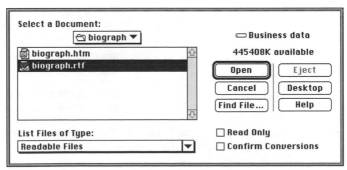

And this is what I see:

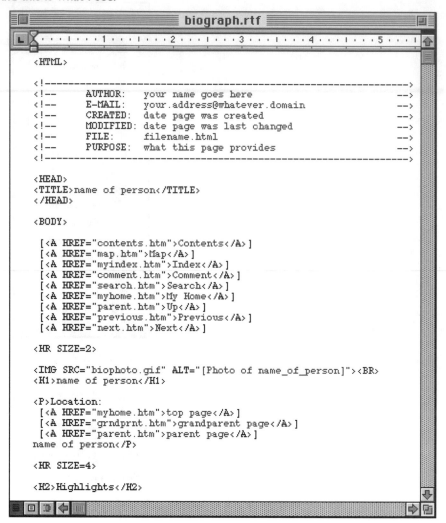

```
                                biograph.rtf
L    · · · I · · · 1 · · · I · · · 2 · · · I · · · 3 · · · I · · · 4 · · · I · · · 5 · · · I

  <HTML>

  <!-------------------------------------------------------------->
  <!--    AUTHOR:    your name goes here                      -->
  <!--    E-MAIL:    your.address@whatever.domain             -->
  <!--    CREATED:   date page was created                    -->
  <!--    MODIFIED:  date page was last changed               -->
  <!--    FILE:      filename.html                            -->
  <!--    PURPOSE:   what this page provides                  -->
  <!-------------------------------------------------------------->

  <HEAD>
  <TITLE>name of person</TITLE>
  </HEAD>

  <BODY>

   [<A HREF="contents.htm">Contents</A>]
   [<A HREF="map.htm">Map</A>]
   [<A HREF="myindex.htm">Index</A>]
   [<A HREF="comment.htm">Comment</A>]
   [<A HREF="search.htm">Search</A>]
   [<A HREF="myhome.htm">My Home</A>]
   [<A HREF="parent.htm">Up</A>]
   [<A HREF="previous.htm">Previous</A>]
   [<A HREF="next.htm">Next</A>]

  <HR SIZE=2>

  <IMG SRC="biophoto.gif" ALT="[Photo of name_of_person]"><BR>
  <H1>name of person</H1>

  <P>Location:
   [<A HREF="myhome.htm">top page</A>]
   [<A HREF="grndprnt.htm">grandparent page</A>]
   [<A HREF="parent.htm">parent page</A>]
  name of person</P>

  <HR SIZE=4>

  <H2>Highlights</H2>
```

If only the publisher had let us print this page in color, you would see that the stuff you change is one color and the stuff you leave alone is another. In testing these templates, we found that the color coding made them much easier to understand and quicker to change.

If you want to see what the whole file looks like, look at the example on page 164.

Hey, this is cool! All the HTML tags and code that don't need to be changed are in black, while all the sections I need to change are in red.

I guess now I get to take the authors up on their suggestion to modify these templates to suit my needs.

Step 3: Fill in the blanks.

First off, I'll make the obvious content changes, replacing the template's placeholders with my own content; my name here, my experience there. Oh, I guess I'll need to come up with a juicy quote, if I'm going to leave that sound byte in there.

To fill in the blanks you simply replace the example content and placeholders with your own content. To do this you select the text you want to replace and type (or paste in) a replacement.

Step 4: Add, subtract, and modify elements.

Okay, I've got my basic content in there. Now I need to modify the format a bit, to make it consistent with our other Web pages.

In our recipes, we tried to include most of the ingredients that most people need most of the time. We chose to err on the side of completeness, figuring it is easier to delete something you do not need than to type in something we left out.

In any case, you'll probably begin, like Kit, by removing parts of the template that you do not need. Go ahead— our feelings aren't hurt. That's the way we designed the templates.

Subtract

I need to remove several items from the template that I won't need. They are the Search and Comment navigation buttons, the video link button, and one of the location indicators.

Search and Comment buttons

The Search and Comment buttons need to be removed because they are not used on William Horton Consulting's other Web pages. It's easy to do, just select the appropriate code and delete it. (I need to be sure I delete those two icon buttons at the bottom of the page, too.)

Top of the page:

```
[<A HREF="contents.htm">Contents</A>]
[<A HREF="map.htm">Map</A>]
[<A HREF="myindex.htm">Index</A>]
[<A HREF="comment.htm">Comment</A>]
[<A HREF="search.htm">Search</A>]
[<A HREF="myhome.htm">My Home</A>]
[<A HREF="parent.htm">Up</A>]
[<A HREF="previous.htm">Previous</A>]
[<A HREF="next.htm">Next</A>]
```

Bottom of the page:

```
<A HREF="contents.htm"><IMG
SRC="cntsicon.gif" ALT="[Contents]"></A>
<A HREF="map.htm">    <IMG
SRC="mapicon.gif"  ALT="[Map]"></A>
<A HREF="myindex.htm"> <IMG
SRC="indxicon.gif" ALT="[Index]"></A>
<A HREF="comment.htm"> <IMG
SRC="cmnticon.gif" ALT="[Comment]"></A>
<A HREF="search.htm">  <IMG
SRC="srchicon.gif" ALT="[Search]"></A>
<A HREF="myhome.htm">  <IMG
SRC="homeicon.gif" ALT="[Home]"></A>
<A HREF="parent.htm">  <IMG
SRC="upicon.gif"   ALT="[Up]"></A>
<A HREF="previous.htm"><IMG
SRC="previcon.gif" ALT="[Previous]"></A>
<A HREF="next.htm">    <IMG
SRC="nexticon.gif" ALT="[Next]"></A>
```

Video link

To remove the video link button, I do the same thing: Select the appropriate code and delete it. Like this:

```
<H2>Meet person's_name </H2>

<P><A HREF="filename.mov"><IMG SRC="vidicon.gif"
ALT="[video]">View video</A> (format, nnK) of person's_name.
</P>
```

(Maybe I should rethink this. It could be my worldwide film debut.)

Location indicators

In the portion of the page after the heading "Location," I need to remove one of the location indicators because my hierarchy is not as deep. While I'm at it, I'm going to insert the correct URLs. I go from this:

```
<P>Location:
 [<A HREF="myhome.htm">top page</A>]
 [<A HREF="grndprnt.htm">grandparent page</A>]
 [<A HREF="parent.htm">parent page</A>]
current topic</P>
```

to this:

```
<P>Location:
[<A HREF="index.html">WHC home</A>]
[<A HREF="whc.html">What do you do?</A>]
Katherine Horton</P>
```

You will need to check, and possibly change, all the URLs in the template to make sure they refer to files that will exist at your Web site. Be careful with subdirectories and path statements; it's easy to make mistakes with all those slashes, backslashes, filenames, and abbreviations.

If your Web page is not part of a three- or four-level hierarchy of topics, subtopics, and sub-subtopics, you can delete the location buttons altogether.

Add

On the CD-ROM ...

ingrdnts
   as_rtf
      allinone.rtf

I know I'm going to need a text trigger in the body of my copy because I want to be able to refer readers to some Book description pages. Not to worry, I can copy the code for a text trigger from the `allinone.rtf` file on the companion CD-ROM.

The Web Chef Rule of Mouse: Never memorize what you can more quickly look up. Never type in what you can more easily cut and paste.

That's our philosophy on adding the things our recipes may have left out. Before you start typing, check out the goodies in Chapter 5. If you find what you want there, you can copy it from the corresponding directory or folder on the CD-ROM disk.

1. With Word, I open `ingrdnts.rtf`.

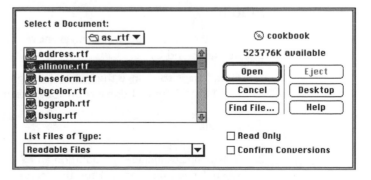

2. I scroll down the page until I come to:

Link with text trigger (linktxt)

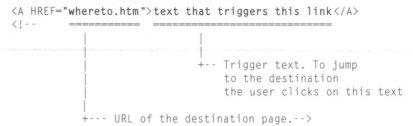

```
<A HREF="whereto.htm">text that triggers this link</A>
<!--      ===========   ============================
                |                     |
                |                     |
                |                     +-- Trigger text. To jump
                |                         to the destination
                |                         the user clicks on this text
                |
                +--- URL of the destination page.-->
```

3. I copy the "Link with text trigger" code snippet:

    ```
    <A HREF="whereto.htm">text that triggers this link</A>
    ```

4. With the code stashed on my clipboard, I'll find the spot in the template where I think I want it to appear and paste it there. I'll get back to it later.

    ```
    <P>Kit is the other half of William Horton Consulting, a
    Colorado-based firm specializing in applying human factors
    to the task of communicating technical information.</P>

    <A HREF="whereto.htm">text that triggers this link</A>

    <P>Aside from being the business manager for the firm, Kit
    (as she prefers to be called) is the lead animator, icon
    designer (using William Horton's <I>The Icon Book</I>),
    and all-around multimedia hacker. She has illustrated
    Bill's last three books, including <I>Illustrating
    Computer Documentation</I>, an STC International Award
    winner in 1992.</P>
    ```

Modify

I've made the basic structural changes, now I need to go through and modify all the file names and URLs.

1. First, I want to change the name of the photograph file from `biophoto.gif` to `kit.gif`, since I don't really look like the template person!

    ```
    <IMG SRC="kit.gif" ALT="[Photo of Katherine Horton]"
    ALIGN=right ><BR>
    ```

2. This template includes a quotation and a button the user can click to hear me say it. Since I decided to keep this feature, I need to rename the sound file and use that name when I create the sound. I'll call it `kit.wav`, I guess.

    ```
    <DD><A HREF="kit.wav"><IMG SRC="spkicon.gif" ALT="[Kit
    speaking her favorite quotation.]"> Hear it</A> (.wav,
    48k)
    ```

3. Remember that text trigger I copied into the template? It's time to integrate it into my text (I'm going to use it twice because I have two books I want to reference). I change it from:

> This is a tricky bit of brain surgery. Kit has to integrate the generic link structure into the flow of a paragraph of text.

```
<A HREF="whereto.htm">text that triggers this link</A>
```

```
<P>Aside from being the business manager for the firm, Kit
(as she prefers to be called) is the lead animator, icon
designer (using William Horton's <I>The Icon Book</I>, and
all-round multimedia hacker. She has illustrated Bill's
last three books, including <I>Illustrating Computer
Documentation</I>, an STC International Award winner in
1992.</P>
```

to:

```
<P>Aside from being the business manager for the firm, Kit
(as she prefers to be called) is the lead animator, icon
designer (using William Horton's
<A HREF="iconbook.html"><I>The Icon Book</I></A>),
and all-around multimedia hacker. She has illustrated
Bill's last three books, including
<A HREF="icd.html"><I>Illustrating Computer
Documentation</I></A>,
an STC International Award winner in 1992.</P>
```

> You may have noticed that Kit uses *.html* as the extension for her files. Because she is authoring on a Macintosh and her server is a UNIX system, she is not limited to a three-character extension as she would be on a DOS-based system.

I had better double check the Web site spreadsheet to verify the names of the two book files. They are indeed `iconbook.html` and `icd.html`.

4. After making sure all the necessary changes have been made to the navigation buttons and signature section, it's time to rename and save the file. Because I don't want to lose the color-coding in my file, I save it first as an RTF file.

> Kit could have saved her file as a regular Microsoft Word file at this point. By saving it in RTF, though, she does make it easier for someone with WordPerfect or Word for Windows to open the file later. This is particularly important if someone else within the organization might be responsible for maintaining and implementing changes to their Web pages.

```
┌─────────────────────────────────────────────────────────┐
│         ┌─ biograph ▼ ─┐          ▭ Business data         │
│      ┌────────────────────────┐   445536K available      │
│      │ 📄 biograph.htm      ▲ │  ┌──────────┐ ┌────────┐  │
│      │ 📄 biograph.rtf        │  │   Save   │ │  Eject │  │
│      │ 📄 biophoto.gif        │  └──────────┘ └────────┘  │
│      │ 📄 cmnticon.gif        │  ┌──────────┐ ┌────────┐  │
│      │ 📄 cntsicon.gif      ▼ │  │  Cancel  │ │Desktop │  │
│      └────────────────────────┘  └──────────┘ └────────┘  │
│                                  ┌──────────┐ ┌────────┐  │
│      Save Current Document as:   │ Options  │ │  Help  │  │
│      ┌────────────────────────┐  └──────────┘ └────────┘  │
│      │ kit.rtf                │     ┌──── New  ───┐       │
│      └────────────────────────┘                          │
│      Save File as Type:                                  │
│      ┌──────────────────────┬─┐                          │
│      │ Rich Text Format     │▼│                          │
│      └──────────────────────┴─┘                          │
└─────────────────────────────────────────────────────────┘
```

Here is what `kit.rtf` **looks like now:**

```
<HTML>
<!----------------------------------------------------------->
<!--      AUTHOR:    Katherine Horton                      -->
<!--      E-MAIL:    kit@horton.com                        -->
<!--      CREATED:   10 August 1995                        -->
<!--      MODIFIED:  10 August 1995                        -->
<!--      FILE:      kit.html                              -->
<!--      PURPOSE:   Meet Kit Horton                       -->
<!----------------------------------------------------------->
<HEAD>
<TITLE>Who is Katherine Horton?</TITLE>
</HEAD>

<BODY>
[<A HREF="contents.html">Contents</A>]
[<A HREF="map.html">Map</A>]
[<A HREF="whcindex.html">Index</A>]
[<A HREF="index.html ">WHC home</A>]
[<A HREF="index.html ">Up</A>]
[<A HREF="bill.html">Previous</A>]
[<A HREF="terms.html">Next</A>]

<HR SIZE=2>

<IMG SRC="kit.gif" ALT="[Photo of Katherine Horton]"
ALIGN=right ><BR>
<H1>Katherine Horton</H1>

<P>Location:
[<A HREF="index.html">WHC home</A>]
[<A HREF="whc.html">What do you do?</A>]
Katherine Horton</P>

<HR SIZE=4>

<H2>Highlights</H2>
<DL>

<DT><B>Name</B>
```

```
<DD>Katherine (Kit) Horton
<DD>William Horton Consulting

<DT><B>Position</B>
<DD>Partner

<DT><B>Best known for</B>
<DD>Being a slave driver with a sense of humor. Just ask
Bill.

<DT><B>Recent honors</B>
<DD>Invited to conduct a multimedia session for the
Technical Writer's Institute at Rensselaer Polytechnic
Institute (1995)

<DT><B>Quotation</B>
<DD>"I'm the boss around here" (raucous laughter is heard
in the background)!
<DD><A HREF="kit.wav"><IMG SRC="spkicon.gif" ALT="[Kit
speaking her favorite quotation.]"> Hear it</A> (format,
nnK)

</DL>

<H2>About Kit</H2>
<P>Kit is the other half of William Horton Consulting, a
Colorado-based firm specializing in applying human factors
to the task of communicating technical information.</P>

<P>Aside from being the business manager for the firm, Kit
(as she prefers to be called) is the lead animator, icon
designer (using William Horton's
<A HREF="iconbook.html"><I>The Icon Book</I></A>),
and all-around multimedia hacker. She has illustrated
Bill's last three books, including
<A HREF="icd.html"><I>Illustrating Computer
Documentation</I></A>,
an STC International Award winner in 1992.</P>

<P>Kit is the Web master for the William Horton Consulting
Web site.
<HR SIZE=2>

http://www.horton.com/brochure/kit.html -- Revised: 10
August 1995<BR>
Copyright &copy; 1995 <A HREF="index.html">William Horton
Consulting</A><BR>
<A HREF="MAILTO:kit@horton.com">kitm@horton.com </A><BR>
<HR SIZE=2>

<A HREF="contents.html"><IMG SRC="cntsicon.gif"
ALT="[Contents]"></A>
<A HREF="map.html"><IMG SRC="mapicon.gif"
ALT="[Map]"></A>
```

```
<A HREF="whcindex.html"><IMG SRC="indxicon.gif"
ALT="[Index]"></A>
<A HREF="index.html"><IMG SRC="homeicon.gif"
ALT="[Home]"></A>
<A HREF="whc.html"><IMG SRC="upicon.gif"   ALT="[Up]"></A>
<A HREF="bill.html"><IMG SRC="previcon.gif"
ALT="[Previous]"></A>
<A HREF="terms.html"><IMG SRC="nexticon.gif"
ALT="[Next]"></A>

</BODY>
</HTML>
```

5. To create an HTML file all I need to do is resave `kit.rtf` as `kit.html`
    (That is the filename I chose and entered in the Web site database), and be
    sure I change the file format to Text Only. Plain-text files (also known as
    ASCII) are the only kind the browser can open.

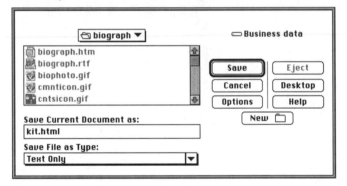

All that's left to do now (in the creation phase) is create those pictures and sounds
I referenced.

> At this point, Kit can delete `biograph.rtf` and
> `biograph.htm` from the `biograph` folder on her disk.

Step 5. Create related files.

Let's see, within my page I reference two files that do not yet exist: `kit.gif` (my
picture) and `kit.wav` (my quote)—so I've got a picture and a sound file to
create.

Some people like to create related files before they edit the HTML file. If you can't stand being told to do things in a particular order, here's your chance for some harmless rebellion. You can do this step any time after making your plan (step 1) but before testing the page (step 6).

Photograph

I'll do the photograph first, since it requires a few steps to go from my glossy photograph to the file I need for the Web page.

Chapter 6, "Nutrition," provides some suggestions for including graphics and other media in your pages. Check out Chapter 8, "Presentation," for some additional suggestions.

I scan in my photograph and open it with Photoshop. (Boy, the picture needs a lot of help. Most scanned photos do.) To make it presentable:

1. I crop it and adjust the color balance so that it's not so red.

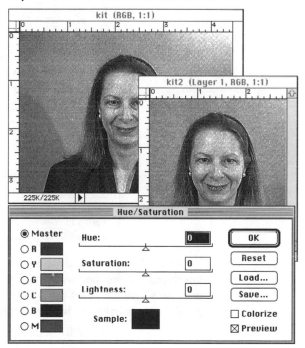

2. Then, I perform a little cosmetic surgery (removing the dark circles). I love this program!

3. When I've finished altering (enhancing) my picture, I save it as a CompuServe GIF file, one of the most common graphic formats on the Web.

4. I want to do one more thing to this photo. I want to convert it to an interlaced GIF file, because all the graphics at our Web site are interlaced, and because some browsers can use the interlaced format to display parts of the graphic as it is being loaded. Our users like that feature.

> Why bother with this step? The file was already in GIF format and would display okay.
>
> For an answer to this and other vexing questions about graphic file formats, see page 325.

So, to interlace the graphic, I open `kit.gif` with Debabelizer and save it as interlaced GIF.

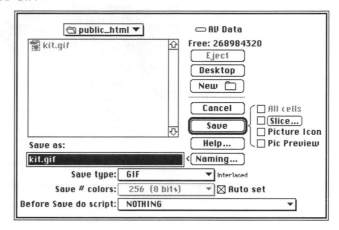

That's it for the photograph. (Hmmmm, I bet I could morph it with some movie star, and then ... well, maybe some other time.)

Quote

Now I'll prepare my sound file using SoundEdit 16:

1. First, I record and edit it.

   Chapter 6 also discusses ways to include voice and other sounds in your Web pages.

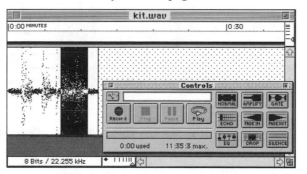

2. Then, I downsample it—this reduces the file size and lowers the sound quality. 8 bits at 11.127 kHz is good enough quality to play on most computer systems.

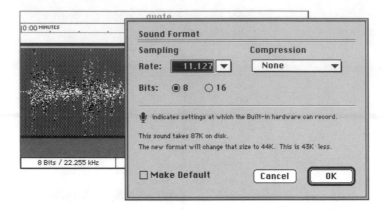

3. Finally, I save the sound as a WAVE file.

> Hey, wait a minute! Kit is working on a Macintosh—why did she choose a file format more common on PCs than Macintoshes?

> Good question. Kit knows her pages will be viewed and listened to by people on many different kinds of computers. So she picks a format for which many shareware or freeware helper applications are available.

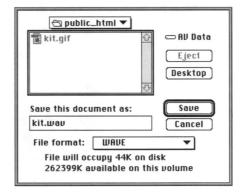

> That's it for the sound file! Now it's probably time to make sure the page still works.

Step 6: Test the page locally.

> I can upload now, right? Nope. The book says I should test it locally first. To do that I first copy my files `kit.html`, `kit.gif`, and `kit.wav` to the local directory where I keep all the other files of our Web site.

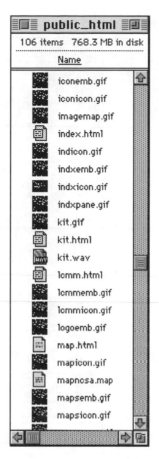

For testing, maintain on your local hard disk an exact duplicate of the files and directories on your server. That is, the files on your local disk should exactly mirror those of your Web server. That way you can test to make sure you have all the necessary files and that all the files are in the correct directories within your Web site.

To get ready to test, I open the file `kit.rtf` with Microsoft Word and the file `kit.html` with my Netscape browser. This way I can immediately fix any errors I find.

Remember that diagram on page 40, showing the Load/Reload cycle?

Here's what I've got:

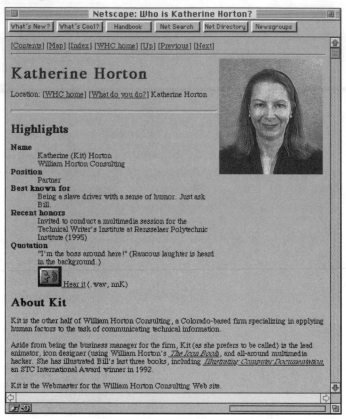

Oops! I see two problems. My picture is running through a rule. The other Biography page at our site doesn't have that rule; so, I'm going to remove it. Also, I forgot to fill in the file size next to my Hear it button. Both are easy since I have the RTF file open. I just:

1. Delete the line of HTML responsible for the rule:

```
<P>Location:
[<A HREF="index.html">WHC home</A>]
[<A HREF="whc.html">What do you do?</A>]
Katherine Horton</P>

<HR SIZE=4>

<H2>Highlights</H2>
```

2. Replace the nn in (format, nnK):

```
<DD><A HREF="kit.wav"><IMG SRC="spkicon.gif" ALT="[Kit
speaking her favorite quotation.]"> Hear it</A> (format,
50K)
```

3. Resave the RTF file (kit.rtf).

4. Save again as a Text Only file (kit.html). Yes, replace the existing kit.html file.

5. Switch back to Netscape and press the Reload button to see the fix.

> If you have the memory—RAM on your computer, that is—we suggest you do as Kit does and open the page with both your word processor and Web browser. That way, as soon as you spot a problem, you can fix it in your word processor, save it, and reload the page into your browser to verify the fix.

Continuing with the testing process, I make sure all the links to and from this page work. Then I'm ready to put my page up on the Web.

Step 7: Install pages on the server.

To install my page I need to:

1. Upload my page with its sound file and graphic file to the company's Web site directory, located on our service provider's disk.

2. Change the permissions of the files to allow users to access them.

Uploading the files

> If the server for your pages is on your local network, then you can probably copy the files directly. If your server is managed by a service provider, you will generally have to go through a procedure like the one shown here. Ask your service provider how they recommend you transfer files. Some let you use a separate file-transfer utility, such as FTP or FETCH. Others rely on standard file-transfer techniques, such as Xmodem and Zmodem, built into many terminal emulation packages.
>
> Make sure you know:
>
> 1. How to log in.
>
> 2. Where to load your files.
>
> 3. What program or protocol to use for the transfer.
>
> 4. What command to give to trigger the receiving end of the transfer.

I use my terminal-emulation program, Zterm, to log into my interactive account at my service provider. After entering my password and looking at welcoming messages I find myself at my service provider's main command prompt, `teal%`. (No, I don't know why it says `teal%` and not `Command:`.)

I move to the directory (`public_html`) that holds our Web pages by entering the UNIX change directory command:

```
cd public_html
```

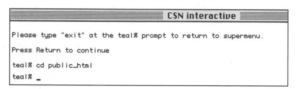

Now I'm ready to transfer my files.

Text file

1. I select the type of data I'll be transferring. In this case Text, because the first file I will transfer will be `kit.html`.

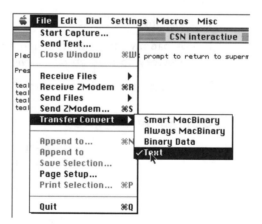

2. Then, I select Send ZModem . . . from the File menu. A dialog box appears.

3. I select the file I want to send (`kit.html`), press Add, then press Start.

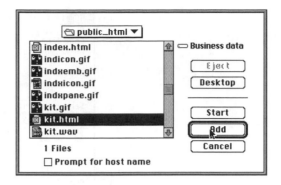

When my file finishes uploading, the dialog box disappears.

The procedure you follow will depend on the instructions from your service provider and the program you are using to transfer the files. Although the commands and menus will be different, in each case you must perform three steps for each transfer. You must:

1. Specify what files to transfer.

2. Specify how they are to be transferred.

3. Trigger the sending and receiving of the files.

Other files

Now it's time to upload the picture and the sound files.

1. I change the type of data I want to send to Binary Data, because I'll be sending a GIF file and a WAVE file.

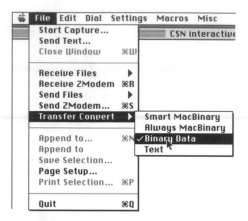

2.   I select Send ZModem . . . from the File menu and the dialog box appears.

3.   I add the files I need: `kit.gif` and `kit.wav` and press Start.

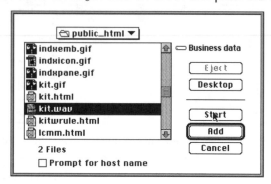

4.   Again, the status window appears while the files are uploading and then goes away.

Changing privileges

Now I need to change the access privileges of these new files. To do that:

1.   At the `teal%` prompt I type `chmod 644 kit.html` and press Return.

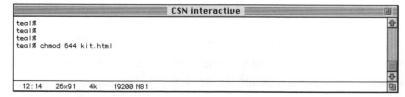

2.   I'll do the same thing for `kit.gif` and `kit.wav`.

I used to know what `chmod` stood for, but I forgot. Anyway it's the command I use to change permissions. The number `644` is the one my service provider told me to use. In any case, this command changes the HTML file so that other people on the Web can access it but only I can change it.

> Could Kit be taking a verbal jab at the obviousness of some UNIX commands? Doesn't everyone know that chmod stands for "change mode" and that access permissions are modes? Wouldn't you guess that the setting that allows others to view your files but not to change or delete them is "644"? For a traveler's phrase book of UNIX commands, see the UNIX survival kit that follows.

3.   I log off my interactive connection and quit Zterm.

I'm done! It's up there! All that's left to do is test and make sure all the files transferred correctly and everything works.

UNIX survival kit		
Most Web servers run the UNIX operating system. To install your Web pages on such a server you may have to know a few UNIX commands, but not many. Here's enough UNIX for 98 percent of the work you'll need to do on the server.		
If you want to	**Use this command**	**Notes**
See the files in the current directory	ls	ls stands for "list"
Move to another directory	cd *new_directory*	For example, to move to the directory /user/lee/web enter: cd /user/lee/web
Move to the parent directory	cd ..	cd .. is the abbreviation for the directory that holds the current directory
See what directory you are in	pwd	pwd stands for "print working directory"
Delete a file	rm *filename*	rm stands for remove
Rename a file	mv *oldname newname*	To rename myfile as yourfile: mv myfile yourfile
Create a directory	mkdir *itsname*	For example, to create the directory mypages: mkdir mypages

If you want to	Use this command	Notes
Move a file to another directory	`mv filename new_directory`	For example, to move the file myfile from the current directory to the directory /user/juan enter: `mv myfile /user/juan`
Copy a file to another directory	`cp filename new_directory`	For example, to copy the file myfile from the current directory to the directory /user/juan enter: `cp myfile /user/juan`
Change the protection of a file	`chmod nnn filename`	To make home.html so others can view it but not change or delete it: `chmod 644 home.html`
Refer to all the files in current directory with the same extension	`*.extension`	For example, to delete all .gif files: `rm *.gif`
Refer to all files in the current directory	`*.*`	For example, to move all the files in the current directory to the directory /user/sean, enter: `mv *.* /user/sean`
Get help on a particular command	`man command`	For example, to learn the format of chmod commands, enter: `man chmod`

Step 8: Test the page online.

This is the moment of truth. It's time to get onto the Web and test my new page. To start, I fire up my TCP/IP software.

It logs me into the service provider and establishes a SLIP connection.

```
╔═══════ UersaTerm RdminSLIP • Script ═══════╗
  Script waiting for:

                    Status:
   ┌ Abort  ⌘. ┐    ┌──────────────────────────┐
   └───────────┘    │ Login successful.        │
                    └──────────────────────────┘
```

Next, I start up my Web browser, Netscape, and tell it to display my new page.

```
╔════════════════ Open Location ════════════════╗

  Open Location: ┌────────────────────────────────┐
                 │ http://www.horton.com/brochure/kit.h │
                 │ tml                            │
                 └────────────────────────────────┘
                              ┌ Cancel ┐  ┌ Open ┐
                              └────────┘  └──────┘
```

> Notice that Kit has to specify the exact location of this page on the World Wide Web—its full URL.

Here's what the new page looks like:

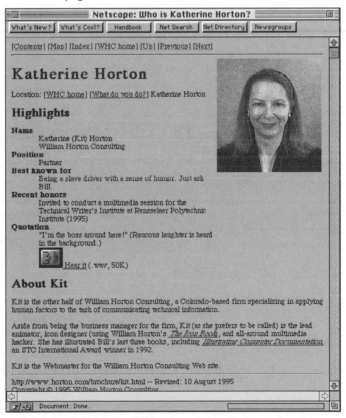

Now, I test all the links to and from the new page, and fix any problems.

Yippee! No problems to fix!

Remember those other pages I needed to change (`contents.html`, `whcindex.html`, etc.)? I'll make those changes now, following the nine-step path to Webness from step 3 to step 8.

Step 9: Announce the new Web page.

My page is up there and I want our customers to know it. So, I'm going to announce it in as many places as I can, beginning with a note to the client who started me on this odyessy.

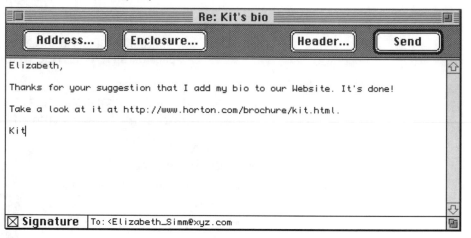

Also, I'm going to put a short news release up on our Web site linking to the new page.

If this is your first Web page, some of the places to announce your page are:

- On your business card

- In your brochure

- In any print ads you may have

- With your service provider—many have a listing of the Home pages of their clients

It's done. If you're saying, "I bet she didn't really do that stuff," check it for yourselves at:
`http://www.horton.com/brochure/kit.html`

Now it's your turn.

4

BASIC RECIPES

*Examples and templates for the
most common types of Web pages*

Ready to start cooking up Web pages? Here are our recipes for
eighteen of our favorite kinds of Web pages. Choose the one closest
to what you need, replace the example content with your own, and
voilà! Ready to serve.

If you've cooked up Web pages before, you can probably jump right into this chapter. If you're new to the whole process of authoring Web pages, we gently urge you to take the quick cooking lesson in Chapter 3. You wouldn't want to cut yourself on one of the sharp knives.

Where can I find the recipes?

Each recipe is in two forms: a *template* and an *example*. A template contains generic placeholders for the ingredients of the page. An example replaces the placeholders with specific content. The illustrations for this chapter show the examples.

Recipe	Page number	On the CD-ROM in examples/chap4/ and recipes/
Generic Web page	105	generic
Home page	113	homepage
Contents	119	contents
Index	123	index
Glossary	131	glossary
How-to procedure	139	howto
Troubleshooting procedure	145	trouble
Course description	151	course
Biography	161	biograph
Book description	167	book
News release	173	news
Organization page	179	organiz
Download menu	185	download
Registration form	191	register
Survey form	199	survey
Catalog entry	207	catalog
Multimedia sampler	213	mmedia
Research report	217	research

Everything you need for each recipe is in a separate directory on the CD-ROM. The path to each recipe is:

Examples
```
examples
    chap4
        biograph
            biograph.htm
            biograph.rtf
            biophoto.gif
                .
                .
                .
            upicon.gif
        book
        catalog
        and 15 more
```

Templates
```
recipes
    biograph
        biograph.htm
        biograph.rtf
        biophoto.gif
            .
            .
            .
        upicon.gif
    book
    catalog
    and 15 more
```

Within each recipe directory you will find two versions of the HTML code for the page. One is in a plain-text format and has a name ending in .htm. The other is in rich text format (RTF) and has a name ending in .rtf.

Put on your apron

Before you start editing one of the specific recipes, take a few moments to at least look over the recipe for the Generic Web page. Since all of the other pages are based on this one, your time will be rewarded by a clearer understanding of elements you can take for granted later. It's like learning to boil water.

Needs a little less salt?

As you begin working with our recipes, you will probably find more than you need. See a button that you cannot use? Delete it. An icon offends you? Zap it! We figure it's easier to delete something you don't want than to type in something we left out. We call it "design by decimation" and encourage you to exercise that Delete key. Anyway, you're the cook.

Find our recipes a bit bland? Think you can improve them? Go ahead. You won't hurt our feelings. Add some ingredients from Chapter 5.

If the resulting page is almost, but not quite, what you want, you can fine tune it. Each recipe lists the ingredients it uses. To make a slight adjustment in an ingredient, look it up in Chapter 5 to see how you can control its effect more precisely.

GENERIC WEB PAGE

The Generic Web page is the starting point for the design of all our Web pages. Even though the specific content, style, and design of each Web page will be different, each conforms to the structure established in this generic recipe. The Generic Web page not only contains the mandatory sections of a Web page, but also contains some additional sections we master chefs find useful.

Use it when none of the more specialized recipes works better.

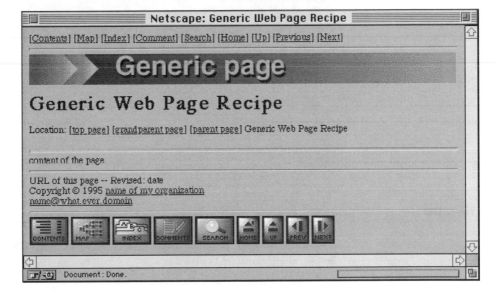

Here are the sections that well-designed (what other kind would you do?) Web pages include:

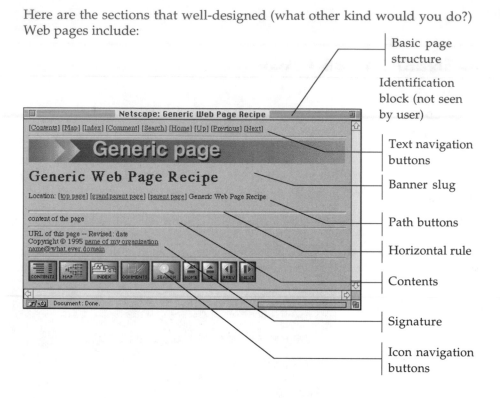

Basic page structure

Identification block (not seen by user)

Text navigation buttons

Banner slug

Path buttons

Horizontal rule

Contents

Signature

Icon navigation buttons

Recipe

The Generic Web page combines several basic ingredients to provide a basis for a wide range of Web pages.

Basic page structure

Ingredients

Page, p. 234

Behind every Web page, unseen by the reader, is a simple structure. It identifies the code as HTML and provides a space for <HEAD> and <BODY> tags.

```
<HTML>

<HEAD>
<TITLE>Generic Web Page Recipe</TITLE>
</HEAD>

<BODY>
content of the page

</BODY>
</HTML>
```

Identification block

At the beginning of the HTML code, just after the <HTML> tag, we recommend an identification block.

```
<!------------------------------------------------------------->
<!--     AUTHOR:   your name goes here                      -->
<!--     E-MAIL:   your.address@whatever.domain             -->
<!--     CREATED:  date page was created                    -->
<!--     MODIFIED: date page was last changed               -->
<!--     FILE:     filename.htm                             -->
<!--     PURPOSE:  what this page provides                  -->
<!------------------------------------------------------------->
```

Formatted as comments, this block is not displayed to the user. But it provides valuable information to anyone who needs to look at the HTML code behind the page—yourself, for example, six months from now. Or your boss on a large project trying to figure out who wrote which page. Or a user who wants to send you fan mail (most browsers let users view the HTML code behind a page).

Text navigation buttons

The first elements visible to the user are a row of text navigation buttons for jumping to other pages.

[Contents] [Map] [Index] [Comment] [Search] [My Home] [Up] [Previous] [Next]

```
[<A HREF="contents.htm">Contents</A>]
[<A HREF="map.htm">Map</A>]
[<A HREF="index.htm">Index</A>]
[<A HREF="comment.htm">Comment</A>]
[<A HREF="search.htm">Search</A>]
[<A HREF="myhome.htm">My Home</A>]
[<A HREF="parent.htm">Up</A>]
[<A HREF="previous.htm">Previous</A>]
[<A HREF="next.htm">Next</A>]
```

We put these navigation buttons at the top so they display immediately. That way users who realize that they are not on the right page can move on to another of your pages. We made them text buttons so they would not distract unduly from the page emblems and title and so they would load quickly. (We put the same controls at the end of the page as icons.) You will probably not need all of the buttons of either set. You may also decide not to use both sets of controls. Just delete what you don't need. You're the cook. What each button does is up to you. Here's how we recommend you use them:

- **Contents**—goes to a hierarchical view of the entire Web cluster just like the table of contents of a traditional paper book. The Contents recipe (page 119) shows what a contents page should look like.

- **Map**—goes to a graphical view of the entire Web cluster. The user sees the relationship of one Web page to another. More importantly, the user can jump directly to any other page shown on the map. You can create a map with an ingredient called an image-map (page 383).

- **Index**—goes to an alphabetical list of subjects covered in your cluster of pages, just like the index of a traditional book. Each entry lets the user jump directly to the page, or portion of the page, where that subject is discussed. You can use the Index recipe (page 123) to prepare an index for your cluster.

- **Comment**—triggers a form on which the user can give feedback or ask a question of the Webmaster or Web page designer. When completed, the form is sent electronically to the Webmaster or the designer. Use the Survey Form recipe (page 199) as a starting point to design such a form.

- **Search**—triggers a process that lets the user look for a particular Web page, typically by specifying a word or phrase that occurs on the page. There is no standard way to include such a search facility, but page 545 does provide some suggestions.

- **My Home**—goes to the home page of the current Web cluster. The Home Page recipe (page 113) will help you create a home page.

- **Up**—jumps up a level in the hierarchy to the parent page of the current page, that is, the one for which the current page is the subtopic.

- **Previous and Next**—lets the user move sequentially in the Web cluster just as if flipping the pages of a book. Previous and next links let you set up a browse sequence or guided tour through your Web site.

Banner slug

Ingredients

Banner slug, p. 237

The Banner slug introduces the page to the user. It usually consists of a page banner and the name of the page.

```
<IMG SRC="genbanr.gif" ALT="[emblem text]"><BR>
<H1>Generic Web Page Recipe</H1>
```

See page 414 for some suggestions on page banners.

You will need to create an image to use as a page banner. The name of the page appears as a first-order heading <H1>. If you incorporate the name of the page into the page banner, you may not need to repeat it as a heading.

Path buttons

Ingredients

Path buttons, p. 283

The second set of navigation controls provides a context for the current Web page with respect to related Web pages. These buttons show the path from the top of the hierarchy of pages to the current page.

> Location: [top page] [grandparent page] [parent page] Generic Web Page Recipe

```
<P>Location:
[<A HREF="myhome.htm">top page</A>]
[<A HREF="grndprnt.htm">grandparent page</A>]
[<A HREF="parent.htm">parent page</A>]
Generic Web Page Recipe</P>
```

These buttons not only show where the page occurs, they make it easy for users to jump to any page on that path, just by clicking on the corresponding button.

This recipe is for a page at the fourth level. If your page is deeper, add more buttons. If shallower, delete some.

Path buttons make sense only if the pages of your cluster are arranged in a hierarchy of topics and subtopics and subsubtopics. If your pages are arranged in some other pattern, you should omit the path buttons as they may confuse many users.

Horizontal rules

Ingredients

Horizontal rule, p. 238

Horizontal rules separate major sections of the page. Here is the rule between the title block and the content area:

```
<HR SIZE=4>
```

This rule is four pixels wide because it is the most important division in the page. Other rules are two pixels wide.

Content

See Chapters 5 and 6 to see what you can include in your Web pages.

Content is ... well, it's the reason people read and view your Web page. What goes in this section is entirely up to you. The other recipes provide examples of practical content for specific purposes.

Signature

Ingredients

Signature, p. 240

In our Web pages, we include a signature at the end of every page. Like the signature in a letter, the signature of a Web page tells where the page came from. Users who print a Web page with a signature, have all the information they need to find the Web site again and to contact the Web page designers for more information.

> URL of this page -- Revised: date
> Copyright © 1995 name of my organization
> name@what.ever.domain

```
URL of this page -- Revised: date<BR>
Copyright &copy; 1995 <A HREF="myorg.htm">name of my
organization</A><BR>
<A HREF="MAILTO:name@what.ever.domain">name@what.ever.domain</A><BR>
```

Every Web page needs a signature! A good signature answers these questions:

- **Where am I**? Provide the URL to the page so users who print out the page can find it again.

- **How current is the information on this page**? Provide the date that the page was last revised.

- **Who owns the information**? Provide any copyright information and indicate if use of the information is in any way restricted. For example, "For use by customers of Gizmobionics, Inc. only."

- **How do I get more information**? Provide the name of the Web page designer, or the Webmaster, or just an electronic mail address to one or more of these people. Our recipe includes a MAILTO link that users can click on to send you a message.

Icon navigation buttons

Ingredients

Icon navigation buttons, p. 282

The second set of navigation controls is graphical and consists of a set of icons. These sit at the bottom of the page and are for the user who scrolls through the whole page and is ready to move on.

```
<A HREF="contents.htm"><IMG SRC="cntsicon.gif" ALT="[Contents]"></A>
<A HREF="map.htm">     <IMG SRC="mapicon.gif"  ALT="[Map]"></A>
<A HREF="index.htm">   <IMG SRC="indxicon.gif" ALT="[Index]"></A>
<A HREF="comment.htm"> <IMG SRC="cmnticon.gif" ALT="[Comment]"></A>
<A HREF="search.htm">  <IMG SRC="srchicon.gif" ALT="[Search]"></A>
<A HREF="myhome.htm">  <IMG SRC="homeicon.gif" ALT="[Home]"></A>
<A HREF="parent.htm">  <IMG SRC="upicon.gif"   ALT="[Up]"></A>
<A HREF="previous.htm"><IMG SRC="previcon.gif" ALT="[Previous]"></A>
<A HREF="next.htm">    <IMG SRC="nexticon.gif" ALT="[Next]"></A>
```

These buttons work the same as the text navigation buttons at the top of the Web page.

HTML code

```
<HTML>

<!------------------------------------------------------------->
<!--     AUTHOR:   your name goes here                     -->
<!--     E-MAIL:   your.address@whatever.domain            -->
<!--     CREATED:  date page was created                   -->
<!--     MODIFIED: date page was last changed              -->
<!--     FILE:     filename.htm                            -->
<!--     PURPOSE:  what this page provides                 -->
<!------------------------------------------------------------->

<HEAD>
<TITLE>Generic Web Page Recipe</TITLE>
</HEAD>

<BODY>

[<A HREF="contents.htm">Contents</A>]
[<A HREF="map.htm">Map</A>]
[<A HREF="index.htm">Index</A>]
[<A HREF="comment.htm">Comment</A>]
[<A HREF="search.htm">Search</A>]
[<A HREF="myhome.htm">Home</A>]
[<A HREF="parent.htm">Up</A>]
[<A HREF="previous.htm">Previous</A>]
[<A HREF="next.htm">Next</A>]

<HR SIZE=2>

<IMG SRC="genbanr.gif" ALT="[emblem text]"><BR>
<H1>Generic Web Page Recipe</H1>

<P>Location:

[<A HREF="myhome.htm">top page</A>]
[<A HREF="grndprnt.htm">grandparent page</A>]
[<A HREF="parent.htm">parent page</A>]
Generic Web Page Recipe</P>

<HR SIZE=4>

content of the page

<HR SIZE=2>

URL of this page -- Revised: date<BR>
Copyright &copy; 1995 <A HREF="myorg.htm">name of my
organization</A><BR>
<A HREF="MAILTO:name@what.ever.domain">name@what.ever.domain</A><BR>

<HR SIZE=2>
```

```
<A HREF="contents.htm"><IMG SRC="cntsicon.gif" ALT="[Contents]"></A>
<A HREF="map.htm">     <IMG SRC="mapicon.gif"  ALT="[Map]"></A>
<A HREF="index.htm">   <IMG SRC="indxicon.gif" ALT="[Index]"></A>
<A HREF="comment.htm"> <IMG SRC="cmnticon.gif" ALT="[Comment]"></A>
<A HREF="search.htm">  <IMG SRC="srchicon.gif" ALT="[Search]"></A>
<A HREF="myhome.htm">  <IMG SRC="homeicon.gif" ALT="[Home]"></A>
<A HREF="parent.htm">  <IMG SRC="upicon.gif"   ALT="[Up]"></A>
<A HREF="previous.htm"><IMG SRC="previcon.gif" ALT="[Previous]"></A>
<A HREF="next.htm">    <IMG SRC="nexticon.gif" ALT="[Next]"></A>

</BODY>
</HTML>
```

HOME PAGE

A home page is usually the starting point from which Web users interact with your Web site. When you tell a client or a friend to look you up on the WWW, you give out the address, or URL, to your home page.

Screen shot is reprinted with permission from International Technical Communication Services.

A home page is both an introduction and a gateway to goodies. It's like the cover of a magazine, the headlines in a newspaper, a billboard, and an advertisement, all in one. The more inviting it is, the more likely the Web user will start clicking on links to linger, explore, and learn about you.

Recipe

This recipe builds upon the Generic Web page, p. 105

This example is the home page of International Technical Communication Services (ITCS), a company owned by one of this book's authors, Nancy Hoft. This home page sits atop a cluster of Web pages. Thus, it serves as both a jumping-off point and a table of contents to other pages in the cluster.

Banner

Ingredients

Inline image, aligned relative to text, p. 277

Text headings, p. 252

The banner contains the logo of the company and the name of the company within the banner. The banner here is prominent, since this is the home page. A smaller version of this banner is used on other pages in this Web cluster.

```
<IMG SRC="itcshead.gif" ALT="[itcs logo]"<BR>
<H1> International Technical Communication Services </H1>
<H2>Words that Travel. Internationally.(TM)</H2>
```

See p. 409 for more about different ways to position graphics on a Web page.

Popular home pages open with a splash and typically contain at least the logo of the company—and often much more. Many of the home pages for large companies, for example, open with an image-map (see page 383) that users click on to navigate through the Web cluster. The banner is often part of the image-map.

See p. 414 for more ideas about using banners.

Well-planned Web clusters repeat the banner, or some portion of it, on every major page within the cluster.

Introduction

The next part of our Home Page recipe introduces you or your organization.

Ingredients

Paragraph, p. 246

> International Technical Communications Services (ITCS) is an independent consulting firm specializing in the strategies required to develop information products that are world-ready. Information products include high-tech marketing material, Web pages, training materials, user interfaces, online and printed software documentation, and proposals. Information products that are world-ready minimize the costs associated with addressing a multilinguistic and multicultural audience.

```
<P>International Technical Communications Services (ITCS) is an
independent consulting firm specializing in the strategies required
to develop information products that are world-ready.  Information
products include high-tech marketing material, Web pages, training
materials, user interfaces, online and printed software
documentation, and proposals.  Information products that are world-
ready minimize the costs associated with addressing a
multilinguistic and multicultural audience.</P>
```

Keep your introduction short, say one to three paragraphs. Just tell users who you are, what you do, and why they should care. Consider including a picture of your primary product or some other object with which you are closely associated.

Details

Ingredients

Definition list, p. 261

Simple inline image, p. 276

Link with text trigger, p. 263

The remainder of this Home Page recipe offers a list to the wonders of this Web site. In this example the list is simple and uses a small portion of the logo as the bullet for each list item. Only the text, however, is *hot*, or linked to other parts of the Web cluster.

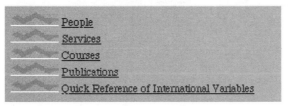

```
<DL>
<DT><IMG SRC="wave.gif" ALT="[button]">
<A HREF="people.htm">People</A>
<DT><IMG SRC="wave.gif" ALT="[button]">
<A HREF="services.htm">Services</A>
<DT><IMG SRC="wave.gif" ALT="[button]">
<A HREF="courses.htm">Courses</A>
<DT><IMG SRC="wave.gif" ALT="[button]">
<A HREF="pubs.htm">Publications</A>
```

```
<DT><IMG SRC="wave.gif" ALT="[button]">
<A HREF="quikref.htm">Quick Reference of International Variables</A>
</DL>
```

For other types of menus, see p. 269.

To create this menu, we use three ingredients: the definition list (without the <DD> tags), the simple inline image, and the link with text trigger.

Tips for great home pages

Popular home pages reflect the personalities of their creators and organizations. Some home pages use a colorful graphic or collection of graphics to draw a user's attention. Other home pages use simplicity and orderliness as their charm by identifying the information that's available at the Web site in a clear and easy-to-understand fashion.

Good home pages convey most of the information they need to convey within the initial scrolling zone. Users do not want to scroll down more than three or four times—if at all. So, keep your home page short and to the point.

Perhaps the most important aspect of popular home pages is that they contain or point to valuable content. Users frequent Web pages that offer information—not just a sales pitch.

HTML code

```
<HTML>
<!------------------------------------------------------------>
<!--      AUTHOR:   Nancy Hoft                          -->
<!--      E-MAIL:   itech@mv.mv.com                      -->
<!--      CREATED:  12 MAY 1995                          -->
<!--      MODIFIED: 12 MAY 1995                          -->
<!--      FILE:     homepage.htm                         -->
<!--      PURPOSE:  Home page for International           -->
<!--                Technical Communication Services     -->
<!------------------------------------------------------------>

<HEAD>
<TITLE>International Technical Communication Services</TITLE>
</HEAD>

<BODY>
[<A HREF="contents.htm">Contents</A>]
[<A HREF="map.htm">Map</A>]
[<A HREF="index.htm">Index</A>]
[<A HREF="comment.htm">Comment</A>]
[<A HREF="search.htm">Search</A>]
```

```
[Home]
[Up]
[Previous]
[<A HREF="next.htm">Next</A>]

<HR SIZE=2>

<IMG SRC="itcshead.gif" ALT="[itcs logo]"<BR>
<H1> International Technical Communication Services </H1>
<H2>Words that Travel. Internationally.(TM)</H2>
<HR SIZE=4>

<P>International Technical Communications Services (ITCS) is an
independent consulting firm specializing in the strategies required to
develop information products that are world-ready.  Information
products include high-tech marketing material, Web pages, training
materials, user interfaces, online and printed software documentation,
and proposals.  Information products that are world ready minimize the
costs associated with addressing a multilinguistic and multicultural
audience.</P>

<DL>
<DT><IMG SRC="wave.gif" ALT="[button]"> <A HRFF="people.htm">People</A>
<DT><IMG SRC="wave.gif" ALT="[button]"> <A
HREF-"services.htm">Services</A>
<DT><IMG SRC="wave.gif" ALT="[button]"> <A
HREF="courses.htm">Courses</A>
<DT><IMG SRC="wave.gif" ALT="[button]"> <A
HREF="pubs.htm">Publications</A>
<DT><IMG SRC="wave.gif" ALT-"[button]"> <A IIRCF-"quikref.htm">Quick
Reference of International Variables</A>
</DL>

<HR WIDTH=100% SIZE=2 ALIGN=left>

http://www.iquest.com/~itcs/itcs.htm-- Revised: 14 MAY 1995<BR>
Copyright &copy; 1995 <A HREF="services.htm">International Technical
Communication Services</A><BR>
<A HREF="MAILTO:itech@mv.mv.com">itech@mv.mv.com</A><BR>

<HR SIZE=2>
<A HREF="contents.htm"><IMG SRC="cntsicon.gif" ALT="[Contents]"></A>
<A HREF="map.htm">     <IMG SRC="mapicon.gif"  ALI="[Map]"></A>
<A HREF="index.htm">   <IMG SRC="indxicon.gif" ALT="[Index]"></A>
<A HREF="comment.htm"> <IMG SRC="cmnticon.gif" ALT="[Comment]"></A>
<A HREF="search.htm">  <IMG SRC="srchicon.gif" ALT="[Search]"></A>
                       <IMG SRC="homeicox.gif" ALT="[Home]">
                       <IMG SRC="upicox.gif"   ALT="[Up]">
                       <IMG SRC="previcox.gif" ALT="[Previous]">
<A HREF="next.htm">    <IMG SRC="nexticon.gif" ALT="[Next]"></A>

</BODY>
</HTML>
```

CONTENTS

This Contents recipe lets you include a traditional table of contents to your Web pages. It shows what kinds of information you provide and how you have organized it.

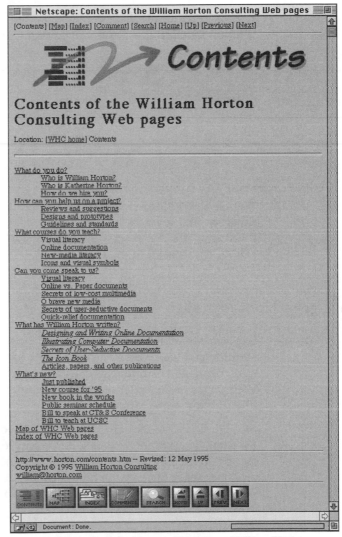

Screen shot is reprinted with permission from William Horton Consulting.

A contents page lets users get the big picture without getting lost in details. And it lets impatient users jump directly to a particular low-level page without having to traverse a long chain of links. It serves as both a navigation aid and a simple map.

All Web page clusters over a few pages long should have a contents page.

Recipe

This recipe builds upon the Generic Web Page, p. 105.

Ingredients

Definition list, p. 261

Link with text trigger, p. 263

This example is a table of contents for the Web site of one of our authors, William Horton. It is simple in design.

> **What do you do?**
> > Who is William Horton?
> > Who is Katherine Horton?
> > How do we hire you?

```
<!------------------------------------------------------------>
<DL>
    <DT><A HREF="whc.htm">What do you do?</A>
        <DD><A HREF="bill.htm">Who is William Horton?</A>
        <DD><A HREF="kit.htm">Who is Katherine Horton?</A>
        <DD><A HREF="terms.htm">How do we hire you?</A>
```

We use the definition list tag because it offers regular indentations for showing first-level topics, second-level topics, and so on. Note that we use the comments tag to separate top-level entries. These separators make the HTML code easier to read.

Tips for a great contents page

Exposure to tables of contents of traditional books will ensure that users should need little instruction as to how to use a contents page. Such exposure may also lead them to expect that the Next button takes them through your Web pages in the order listed in the contents page. Think twice before you violate this expectation.

Now that you've thought twice, consider creating a separate contents page for each group of target users. For example, if your cluster is a catalog of unrelated items, consider creating a contents page for one typical user group and another contents page for another typical user group. In each contents page, list only those entries that would appeal to that group of users.

HTML code

```
<HTML>

<!------------------------------------------------------------>
<!--     AUTHOR:     Kit Horton                          -->
<!--     E-MAIL:     kit@horton.com                      -->
<!--     CREATED:    14 April 1995                        -->
<!--     MODIFIED:   13 May 1995                          -->
<!--     FILE:       contents.htm                         -->
<!--     PURPOSE:    Contents of WHC Website              -->
<!------------------------------------------------------------>

<HEAD>
<TITLE>Contents of the William Horton Consulting Web pages</TITLE>
</HEAD>

<BODY>

[Contents]
[<A HREF="map.htm">Map</A>]
[<A HREF="index.htm">Index</A>]
[<A HREF="comment.htm">Comment</A>]
[<A HREF="search.htm">Search</A>]
[<A HREF="myhome.htm">Home</A>]
[<A HREF="parent.htm">Up</A>]
[<A HREF="previous.htm">Previous</A>]
[<A HREF="next.htm">Next</A>]

<HR SIZE=2>

<IMG SRC="contpane.gif" ALT="[emblem text]"><BR>
<H1>Contents of the William Horton Consulting Web pages</H1>

<P>Location:
[<A HREF="index.htm">WHC home</A>] Contents</P>

<HR SIZE=4>

<!------------------------------------------------------------>
<DL>
    <DT><A HREF="whc.htm">What do you do?</A>
        <DD><A HREF="bill.htm">Who is William Horton?</A>
        <DD><A HREF="kit.htm">Who is Katherine Horton?</A>
        <DD><A HREF="terms.htm">How do we hire you?</A>

<!------------------------------------------------------------>
    <DT><A HREF="consult.htm">How can you help us on a project?</A>
        <DD><A HREF="review.htm">Reviews and suggestions</A>
        <DD><A HREF="design.htm">Designs and prototypes</A>
        <DD><A HREF="guide.htm">Guidelines and standards</A>

<!------------------------------------------------------------>
    <DT><A HREF="courses.htm">What courses do you teach?</A>
        <DD><A HREF="vislit.htm">Visual literacy</A>
        <DD><A HREF="online.htm">Online documentation</A>
        <DD><A HREF="nmlit.htm">New-media literacy</A>
        <DD><A HREF="icon.htm">Icons and visual symbols</A>
```

```
<!------------------------------------------------------------>
    <DT><A HREF="speeches.htm">Can you come speak to us?</A>
        <DD><A HREF="vlcrash.htm">Visual literacy</A>
        <DD><A HREF="dang.htm">Online vs. Paper documents</A>
        <DD><A HREF="lcmm.htm">Secrets of low-cost multimedia</A>
        <DD><A HREF="obnm.htm">O brave new media</A>
        <DD><A HREF="secrets.htm">Secrets of user-seductive
documents</A>
        <DD><A HREF="quick.htm">Quick-relief documentation</A>

<!------------------------------------------------------------>
    <DT><A HREF="books.htm">What has William Horton written?</A>
        <DD><A HREF="dwold.htm"><CITE>Designing and Writing Online
Documentation</CITE></A>
        <DD><A HREF="icd.htm"><CITE>Illustrating Computer
Documentation</CITE></A>
        <DD><A HREF="seduce.htm"><CITE>Secrets of User-Seductive
Doocuments</CITE></A>
        <DD><A HREF="iconbook.htm"><CITE>The Icon Book</CITE></A>
        <DD><A HREF="pubs.htm">Articles, papers, and other
publications</A>

<!------------------------------------------------------------>
    <DT><A HREF="news.htm">What's new?</A>
        <DD><A HREF="dwoldtwo.htm">Just published</A>
        <DD><A HREF="newcours.htm">New course for '95</A>
        <DD><A HREF="cookbook.htm">New book in the works</A>
        <DD><A HREF="schedule.htm">Public seminar schedule</A>
        <DD><A HREF="softbank.htm">Bill to speak at CT&S Conference</A>
        <DD><A HREF="ucsc.htm">Bill to teach at UCSC</A>

<!------------------------------------------------------------>
    <DT><A HREF="map.htm">Map of WHC Web pages</A>

<!------------------------------------------------------------>
    <DT><A HREF="whcindex.htm">Index of WHC Web pages</A>

</DL>
<!------------------------------------------------------------>

<HR SIZE=2>
http://www.horton.com/contents.htm -- Revised: 12 May 1995<BR>
Copyright &copy; 1995 <A HREF="whcindex.htm">William Horton
Consulting</A><BR>
<A HREF="MAILTO:william@horton.com">william@horton.com</A><BR>

<HR SIZE=2>

                        <IMG SRC="cntsicox.gif" ALT="[Contents]">
<A HREF="map.htm">     <IMG SRC="mapicon.gif"  ALT="[Map]"></A>
<A HREF="index.htm">    <IMG SRC="indxicon.gif" ALT="[Index]"></A>
<A HREF="comment.htm"> <IMG SRC="cmnticon.gif" ALT="[Comment]"></A>
<A HREF="search.htm">   <IMG SRC="srchicon.gif" ALT="[Search]"></A>
<A HREF="myhome.htm">   <IMG SRC="homeicon.gif" ALT="[Home]"></A>
<A HREF="parent.htm">   <IMG SRC="upicon.gif"   ALT="[Up]"></A>
<A HREF="previous.htm"><IMG SRC="previcon.gif" ALT="[Previous]"></A>
<A HREF="next.htm">     <IMG SRC="nexticon.gif" ALT="[Next]"></A>
</BODY>
</HTML>
```

INDEX

On the CD-ROM ...

The example:
examples
  chap4
    index
      index.htm

The template:
recipes
  index
    index.htm

Main Ingredients

Generic Web page, p. 105

Link with text trigger, p. 263

Text headings, p. 252

Definition list, p. 261

Destination marker, p. 268

The traditional alphabetical index, found at the back of any good work of nonfiction, provides access and reassurance to readers searching for one particular piece of information or to those who are just curious about what the document contains.

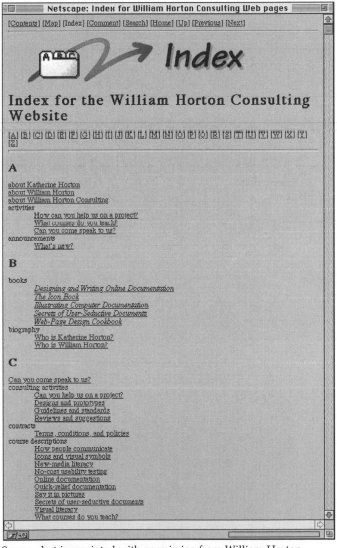

Screen shot is reprinted with permission from William Horton Consulting.

Create an index if you have a cluster of more than a few Web pages. An index is especially useful for those who may not know the terminology used in titles and, hence, cannot effectively look up things in a table of contents. In an index you can include synonyms that users will recognize, making it that much easier for users to find the information they need.

Recipe

This recipe builds upon the Generic Web page, p. 105.

This example is an index to the Web site of one of our authors, William Horton. Although the index is long, you can jump from the top directly to the entries for any letter of the alphabet.

Menu

Ingredients

Link with text trigger, p. 263

Destination marker, p. 268

Our example looks like a traditional index, but with links. The top row of letters serves as a quick navigation aid—much like the thumb tabs in a dictionary. Clicking on one of the letters scrolls the index to the first entry beginning with that letter.

[A] [B] [C] [D] [E] [F] [G] [H] [I] [J] [K] [L] [M] [N] [O] [P] [Q] [R] [S] [T] [U] [V] [W] [X] [Y] [Z]

If this looks cryptic, don't worry. You do not have to change it.

```
[<A HREF="#A">A</A>]
[<A HREF="#B">B</A>]
[<A HREF="#C">C</A>]
[<A HREF="#D">D</A>]
[<A HREF="#E">E</A>]
[<A HREF="#F">F</A>]
[<A HREF="#G">G</A>]
[<A HREF="#H">H</A>]
[<A HREF="#I">I</A>]
[<A HREF="#J">J</A>]
[<A HREF="#K">K</A>]
[<A HREF="#L">L</A>]
[<A HREF="#M">M</A>]
[<A HREF="#N">N</A>]
[<A HREF="#O">O</A>]
[<A HREF="#P">P</A>]
[<A HREF="#Q">Q</A>]
[<A HREF="#R">R</A>]
[<A HREF="#S">S</A>]
[<A HREF="#T">T</A>]
[<A HREF="#U">U</A>]
[<A HREF="#V">V</A>]
[<A HREF="#W">W</A>]
[<A HREF="#X">X</A>]
[<A HREF="#Y">Y</A>]
[<A HREF="#Z">Z</A>]
```

Even if you do not have entries for every letter, leave all the navigation letters in place. Imagine how disorienting it would be to open a Web page with an incomplete alphabetical list of letters at the top of the page.

Each letter in the menu is linked to the same letter later in the index using the destination marker `<A HREF>` and `<A NAME>`. For example, the HTML code for the menu entry for the letter D looks like this:

```
[<A HREF="#D">D</A>]
```

The HTML code for the letter D later in the Web page looks like this:

```
<H2><A NAME="D">D</A></H2>
```

Letter dividers

Ingredients

Destination marker, p. 268

Text heading, p. 252

Letter dividers mark the beginning of entries for each letter of the alphabet, for example the letter C:

```
<!  ------------------------------------------------------->
<H2><A NAME="C">C</A></H2>
```

You do not need to change these tags.

The comment tags `<!--` and `-->` frame a horizontal line. As you can see, this line is not visible to the user but does make the HTML code easier to read.

Index Entries

Ingredients

Definition list, p. 261

Destination marker, p. 268

Pointer to page in same directory, p. 290

Can you come speak to us?
consulting activities
        Can you help us on a project?
        Designs and prototypes
        Guidelines and standards
        Reviews and suggestions
contracts
        Terms, conditions, and policies
course descriptions
        How people communicate
        Icons and visual symbols
        New-media literacy
        No-cost usability testing
        Online documentation
        Quick-relief documentation
        Say it in pictures
        Secrets of user-seductive documents
        Visual literacy
        What courses do you teach?

To learn more about how to link to a specific page or place on a page, jump to page 290.

We use the definition list tag to organize the entries in the index. For example, here are the entries for the letter "C":

```
<DL>
<DT><A HREF="speeches.htm">Can you come speak to us?</A>
<DT>consulting activities
    <DD><A HREF="consult.htm">Can you help us on a project?</A>
```

```
          <DD><A HREF="design.htm">Designs and prototypes</A>
          <DD><A HREF="guide.htm">Guidelines and standards</A>
          <DD><A HREF="review.htm">Reviews and suggestions</A>
<DT>contracts
          <DD><A HREF="terms.htm">Terms, conditions, and policies</A>
<DT>course descriptions
          <DD><A HREF="ucsc.htm#ucsc5">How people communicate</A>
          <DD><A HREF="icon.htm">Icons and visual symbols</A>
          <DD><A HREF="nmlit.htm">New-media literacy</A>
          <DD><A HREF="ucsc.htm#ucsc4">No-cost usability testing</A>
          <DD><A HREF="online.htm">Online documentation</A>
          <DD><A HREF="ucsc.htm#ucsc2">Quick-relief documentation</A>
          <DD><A HREF="ucsc.htm#ucsc3">Say it in pictures</A>
          <DD><A HREF="ucsc.htm#ucsc1">Secrets of user-seductive
documents</A>
          <DD><A HREF="vislit.htm">Visual literacy</A>
          <DD><A HREF="courses.htm">What courses do you teach?</A>
</DL>
```

To learn how to create URLs to point to just about any place, see p. 286.

Many of the entries contain a pointer to related information located within a page, rather than a pointer to a whole page. For instance:

```
          <DD><A HREF="ucsc.htm#ucsc5">How people communicate</A>
```

This entry says to go to the destination marker #ucsc5 within the page ucsc.htm to find information about the course, "How people communicate."

Tips for a great index

Remember the golden rule of indexing: *Include entries the reader will recognize.* For each concept, include several entries. Ask yourself, "How would my different users express this idea?"

Consider hiring a professional indexer to do the index to your Web pages. Indexers are trained to know what kind of terms users are most likely to want to see in an index, and can create usable indexes.

If the index is very long, consider putting the entries for each letter or a group of letters on separate Web pages and link to these from the menu at the main index page.

If you have users whose native language is not English, consider providing an index in the native language of those users.

If your Web site uses a lot of icons or other graphics, consider adding these to the index to make a visual index. Here's an example of some visual index entries:

Ingredients

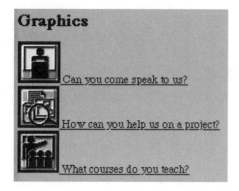

```
<!------------------------------------------------------------->
<H2>Graphics</H2>

</DL>
<DT><A HREF="speeches.htm">
<IMG SRC="spkicon.gif" ALT="[speaking button]">  Can you come speak to
us?</A>

<DT><A HREF="consult.htm">
<IMG SRC="consicon.gif" ALT="[consulting button]">  How can you help us
on a project?</A>

<DT><A HREF="courses.htm"><IMG SRC="couricon.gif" ALT="[teaching
button]">  What courses do you teach?</A>

</DL>
```

HTML code

```
<HTML>

<!------------------------------------------------------------->
<!--    AUTHOR:   Katherine Horton                           -->
<!--    E-MAIL:   kit@horton.com                             -->
<!--    CREATED:  16 Feb 1995                                -->
<!--    MODIFIED: 7 August 1995                              -->
<!--    FILE:     whcindex.htm                               -->
<!--    PURPOSE:  Index                                      -->
<!------------------------------------------------------------->

<HEAD>
<TITLE>Index for William Horton Consulting Web pages</TITLE>
</HEAD>

<BODY>

[<A HREF="contents.htm">Contents</A>]
[<A HREF="map.htm">Map</A>]
[Index]
```

```
[<A HREF="comment.htm">Comment</A>]
[<A HREF="search.htm">Search</A>]
[<A HREF="myhome.htm">Home</A>]
[<A HREF="parent.htm">Up</A>]
[<A HREF="previous.htm">Previous</A>]
[<A HREF="next.htm">Next</A>]

<HR SIZE=2>

<IMG SRC="indxpane.gif" ALT="[emblem text]"><BR>
<H1>Index for the William Horton Consulting Website</H1>

[<A HREF="#A">A</A>]
[<A HREF="#B">B</A>]
[<A HREF="#C">C</A>]
[<A HREF="#D">D</A>]
[<A HREF="#E">E</A>]
[<A HREF="#F">F</A>]
[<A HREF="#G">G</A>]
[<A HREF="#H">H</A>]
[<A HREF="#I">I</A>]
[<A HREF="#J">J</A>]
[<A HREF="#K">K</A>]
[<A HREF="#L">L</A>]
[<A HREF="#M">M</A>]
[<A HREF="#N">N</A>]
[<A HREF="#O">O</A>]
[<A HREF="#P">P</A>]
[<A HREF="#Q">Q</A>]
[<A HREF="#R">R</A>]
[<A HREF="#S">S</A>]
[<A HREF="#T">T</A>]
[<A HREF="#U">U</A>]
[<A HREF="#V">V</A>]
[<A HREF="#W">W</A>]
[<A HREF="#X">X</A>]
[<A HREF="#Y">Y</A>]
[<A HREF="#Z">Z</A>]

<HR SIZE=4>

<!------------------------------------------------------------>
<H2><A NAME="A">A</A></H2>

<DL>
<DT><A HREF="kit.htm">about Katherine Horton</A>
<DT><A HREF="bill.htm">about William Horton</A>
<DT><A HREF="whc.htm">about William Horton Consulting</A>
<DT>activities
    <DD><A HREF="consult.htm">How can you help us on a project?</A>
    <DD><A HREF="courses.htm">What courses do you teach?</A>
    <DD><A HREF="speeches.htm#">Can you come speak to us?</A>
<DT>announcements
    <DD><A HREF="news.htm">What's new?</A>
```

```
</DL>


<!------------------------------------------------------------------->
<H2><A NAME="B">B</A></H2>

<DL>
<DT>books
     <DD><A HREF="dwold.htm"><I>Designing and Writing Online
Documentation</I></A>
     <DD><A HREF="iconbook.htm"><I>The Icon Book</I></A>
     <DD><A HREF="icd.htm"><I>Illustrating Computer
Documentation</I></A>
     <DD><A HREF="seduce.htm"><I>Secrets of User-Seductive
Documents</I></A>

     <DD><A HREF="cookbook.htm"><I>Web-Page Design Cookbook</I></A>
<DT>biography
     <DD><A HREF="kit.htm">Who is Katherine Horton?</A>
     <DD><A HREF="bill.htm">Who is William Horton?</A>
</DL>


<!------------------------------------------------------------------->
<H2><A NAME="C">C</A></H2>

<DL>
<DT><A HREF="speeches.htm">Can you come speak to us?</A>
<DT>consulting activities
     <DD><A HREF="consult.htm">Can you help us on a project?</A>
     <DD><A HREF="design.htm">Designs and prototypes</A>
     <DD><A HREF="guide.htm">Guidelines and standards</A>
     <DD><A HREF="review.htm">Reviews and suggestions</A>
<DT>contracts
     <DD><A HREF="terms.htm">Terms, conditions, and policies</A>
<DT>course descriptions
     <DD><A HREF="ucsc.htm#ucsc5">How people communicate</A>
     <DD><A HREF="icon.htm">Icons and visual symbols</A>
     <DD><A HREF="nmlit.htm">New-media literacy</A>
     <DD><A HREF="ucsc.htm#ucsc4">No-cost usability testing</A>
     <DD><A HREF="online.htm">Online documentation</A>
     <DD><A HREF="ucsc.htm#ucsc2">Quick-relief documentation</A>
     <DD><A HREF="ucsc.htm#ucsc3">Say it in pictures</A>
     <DD><A HREF="ucsc.htm#ucsc1">Secrets of user-seductive
documents</A>
     <DD><A HREF="vislit.htm">Visual literacy</A>
     <DD><A HREF="courses.htm">What courses do you teach?</A>
</DL>
```

●
●
●

and more of the same

●
●
●

```
<!------------------------------------------------------------>
<H2><A NAME="W">W</A></H2>

<DL>
<DT><A HREF="courses.htm">What courses to you teach?</A>
<DT><A HREF="whc.htm">What do you do?</A>
<DT><A HREF="books.htm">What has William Horton written?</A>
<DT><A HREF="whc.htm">What is William Horton Consulting?</A>
<DT><A HREF="news.htm">What's new?</A>
<DT><A HREF="schedule.htm">Where can I hear you?</A>
<DT><A HREF="kit.htm">Who is Katherine Horton?</A>
<DT><A HREF="bill.htm">Who is William Horton?</A>
</DL>

<!------------------------------------------------------------>
<H2><A NAME="X">X</A></H2>

<!------------------------------------------------------------>
<H2><A NAME="Y">Y</A></H2>

<!------------------------------------------------------------>
<H2><A NAME="Z">Z</A></H2>

<!------------------------------------------------------------>

<HR SIZE=2>

http://www.horton.com/whcindex.htm-- Revised: 7 August 1995<BR>
Copyright &copy; 1995 <A HREF="index.htm">William Horton
Consulting</A><BR>
<A HREF="MAILTO:kit@horton.com">kit@horton.com</A><BR>

<HR SIZE=2>

<A HREF="contents.htm"><IMG SRC="cntsicon.gif" ALT="[Contents]"></A>
<A HREF="map.htm">     <IMG SRC="mapicon.gif"  ALT="[Map]"></A>
                       <IMG SRC="indxicox.gif" ALT="[Index]">
<A HREF="comment.htm"> <IMG SRC="cmnticon.gif" ALT="[Comment]"></A>
<A HREF="search.htm">  <IMG SRC="srchicon.gif" ALT="[Search]"></A>
<A HREF="myhome.htm">  <IMG SRC="homeicon.gif" ALT="[Home]"></A>
<A HREF="parent.htm">  <IMG SRC="upicon.gif"   ALT="[Up]"></A>
<A HREF="previous.htm"><IMG SRC="previcon.gif" ALT="[Previous]"></A>
<A HREF="next.htm">    <IMG SRC="nexticon.gif" ALT="[Next]"></A>

</BODY>
</HTML>
```

GLOSSARY

On the CD-ROM ...

The example:
examples
  chap4
    glossary
      glossary.htm

The template:
recipes
  glossary
    glossary.htm

Main Ingredients

Generic Web page, p. 105

Link with text trigger, p. 263

Text headings, p. 252

Destination marker, p. 268

Definition list, p. 261

A glossary lets users look up the meaning of unfamiliar technical terms, jargon, nomenclature, and even images. But wait, there's more! You can let users jump from other Web pages into the glossary, directly to the definition of any term you have linked to the glossary.

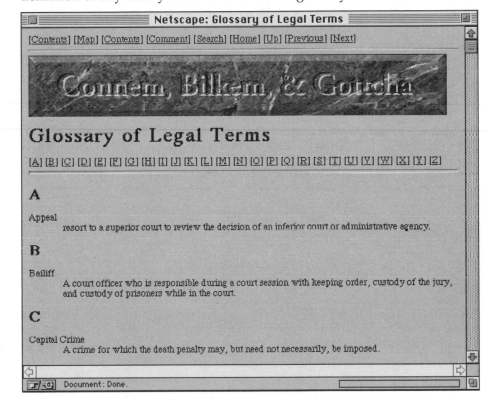

Recipe

This recipe builds upon the Generic Web page, p. 105.

Our example is a glossary of legal terms for the law firm of Connem, Bilkem, & Gotcha, PC.

Alphabetic lookup buttons

Ingredients

Link with text trigger, p. 263

Our example is a traditional glossary with links from the letters of the alphabet to the matching content in the body of the glossary. The top row of letters serves as a quick navigation aid. Clicking on a letter propels the user to terms beginning with that letter.

[A] [B] [C] [D] [E] [F] [G] [H] [I] [J] [K] [L] [M] [N] [O] [P] [Q] [R] [S] [T] [U] [V] [W] [X] [Y] [Z]

Sure it's complex, but relax. You never have to change it.

```
[<A HREF="#A">A</A>]
[<A HREF="#B">B</A>]
[<A HREF="#C">C</A>]
[<A HREF="#D">D</A>]
[<A HREF="#E">E</A>]
[<A HREF="#F">F</A>]
[<A HREF="#G">G</A>]
[<A HREF="#H">H</A>]
[<A HREF="#I">I</A>]
[<A HREF="#J">J</A>]
[<A HREF="#K">K</A>]
[<A HREF="#L">L</A>]
[<A HREF="#M">M</A>]
[<A HREF="#N">N</A>]
[<A HREF="#O">O</A>]
[<A HREF="#P">P</A>]
[<A HREF="#Q">Q</A>]
[<A HREF="#R">R</A>]
[<A HREF="#S">S</A>]
[<A HREF="#T">T</A>]
[<A HREF="#U">U</A>]
[<A HREF="#V">V</A>]
[<A HREF="#W">W</A>]
[<A HREF="#X">X</A>]
[<A HREF="#Y">Y</A>]
[<A HREF="#Z">Z</A>]
```

Here is the HTML code for the first few letter buttons and the HTML code for their destinations.

HTML code for letter buttons	HTML code for glossary entry "A"

`[<A HREF="#A">A</A>]`
`[<A HREF="#B">B</A>]`
`[<A HREF="#C">C</A>]`
	`<H2><A NAME="A">A</A></H2>`
	`<H2><A NAME="B">B</A></H2>`
	`<H2><A NAME="C">C</A></H2>`

Even though we do not have entries for each letter, we leave all the navigation letters in place. Imagine how disorienting it would be to open a Web page with an incomplete list of letters at the top of the page.

Letter dividers

Ingredients

Destination marker, p. 268

Letter dividers mark the beginning of entries for each letter of the alphabet, for example the letter P:

You do not need to change these tags.

```
<!-------------------------------------------------------------->
<H2><A NAME="P">P</A></H2>
```

The comment tags `<!--` and `-->` frame a horizontal line. This line is not visible to the user but does make the HTML code easier to scan.

Glossary entries

Ingredients

Definition list, p. 261

Destination marker, p. 268

We use the definition list for the glossary entries themselves. Here's the entry for the letter P, which has two glossary terms.

```
<DL>
<DT><A NAME="Probation">Probation</A>
<DD>a sentence releasing a defendant, or prisoner, into the community
under the supervision of a probation officer. Once on probation, the
individuals must conduct themselves in a suitable manner over a
specified period of time. While on probation, the individuals must meet
periodically with their probation officer.
<DT><A NAME="Pro bono">Pro bono
<DD>Legal services offered free of charge by attorneys.
</DL>
```

Each entry consists of a term, its definition, and a marker for jumping to that term. In general, entries have this format:

```
<DT><A NAME="marker-for-term">the term</A>
<DD>the definition of the term
```

If you do not want to let users jump directly to an individual term and its definition, you can leave off the target marker and its tags. In this case, the glossary entry is simply:

```
<DT> the term
<DD> the definition of the term
```

Tips for a great glossary

See Chapter 9 for more information on international considerations.

Index globally

For non-native readers of English, consider adding glossaries in additional languages. Because HTML supports the ISO-Latin-1 character set, you can create a glossary of terms in most European languages and list the terms according to the language's rules for alphabetical order.

Use phonetic pronunciations

You can add the phonetic pronunciation of the term, as is done in many dictionaries. Link the phonetic entry to the actual entry for the word, like this:

```
<DT>Zee-non. See <A HREF="Xenon">Xenon</A>
```

Include graphics

Consider including icons or other graphics in the glossary entries and provide a brief description of what each represents. For example, here are glossary entries for three of the navigation icons used for these recipe pages.

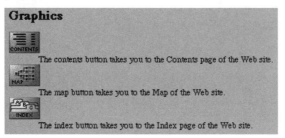

```
<!------------------------------------------------------------>
<H2><A NAME="graphics">Graphics</A></H2>

<DL>

<DT><IMG SRC="cntsicon.gif" ALT="[contents]">
<DD>The contents button takes you to the Contents page of the Web
site.

<DT><IMG SRC="mapicon.gif" ALT="[map]">
<DD>The map button takes you to the Map of the Web site.

<DT><IMG SRC="indxicon.gif" ALT="[index]">
<DD>The index button takes you to the Index page of the Web site.
</DL>
```

Let other documents use your glossary

Once you have created a glossary, you can use it to define terms found in any of your Web pages. Each time you use a term defined in the glossary, just link it to its definition. For example, suppose you use the term *pro bono*, which is defined in the glossary (`glossary.htm`) thus:

```
<DT>A NAME="Pro bono">Pro bono</A>
<DD>Legal services offered free of charge by attorneys
```

To let the user jump to this definition from another Web page, include a link something like this:

```
Our firm does considerable <A HREF="glossary.htm#Pro bono">Pro
bono</A> work in the communities served by our clients.
```

HTML code

```
<HTML>

<!------------------------------------------------------------->
<!--        AUTHOR:    Nancy Hoft                          -->
<!--        E-MAIL:    itech@mv.mv.com                      -->
<!--        CREATED:   05 APRIL 1995                        -->
<!--        MODIFIED:  08 MAY 1995                          -->
<!--        FILE:      glossary.htm                         -->
<!--        PURPOSE:   Glossary of Legal Terms for our Clients   -->
<!------------------------------------------------------------->

<HEAD>
<TITLE>Glossary of Legal Terms</TITLE>
</HEAD>

<BODY>

[<A HREF="contents.htm">Contents</A>]
[<A HREF="map.htm">Map</A>]
[<A HREF="index.htm">Contents</A>]
[<A HREF="comment.htm">Comment</A>]
[<A HREF="search.htm">Search</A>]
[<A HREF="myhome.htm">Home</A>]
[<A HREF="parent.htm">Up</A>]
[<A HREF="previous.htm">Previous</A>]
[<A HREF="next.htm">Next</A>]

<HR SIZE=2>

<IMG SRC="lawembl.gif" ALT="[emblem text]"><BR>
<H1> Glossary of Legal Terms </H1>

[<A HREF="#A">A</A>]
[<A HREF="#B">B</A>]
[<A HREF="#C">C</A>]
[<A HREF="#D">D</A>]
[<A HREF="#E">E</A>]
[<A HREF="#F">F</A>]
```

```
[<A HREF="#G">G</A>]
[<A HREF="#H">H</A>]
[<A HREF="#I">I</A>]
[<A HREF="#J">J</A>]
[<A HREF="#K">K</A>]
[<A HREF="#L">L</A>]
[<A HREF="#M">M</A>]
[<A HREF="#N">N</A>]
[<A HREF="#O">O</A>]
[<A HREF="#P">P</A>]
[<A HREF="#Q">Q</A>]
[<A HREF="#R">R</A>]
[<A HREF="#S">S</A>]
[<A HREF="#T">T</A>]
[<A HREF="#U">U</A>]
[<A HREF="#V">V</A>]
[<A HREF="#W">W</A>]
[<A HREF="#X">X</A>]
[<A HREF="#Y">Y</A>]
[<A HREF="#Z">Z</A>]
<HR SIZE=4>


<!------------------------------------------------------------->
<H2><A NAME="A">A</A></H2>

<DL>
<DT><A NAME="Appeal">Appeal</A>
<DD>resort to a superior court to review the decision of an inferior
court or administrative agency.
</DL>


<!------------------------------------------------------------->
<H2><A NAME="B">B</A></H2>

<DL>
<DT><A NAME="Bailiff">Bailiff</A>
<DD>A court officer who is responsible during a court session with
keeping order, custody of the jury, and custody of prisoners while in
the court.
</DL>


<!------------------------------------------------------------->
<H2><A NAME="C">C</A></H2>

<DL>
<DT><A NAME="Capital Crime">Capital Crime</A>
<DD>A crime for which the death penalty may, but need not necessarily,
be imposed.
</DL>
```

•
•
•

and more of the same

•
•
•

```
<!------------------------------------------------------------->
<H2><A NAME="W">W</A></H2>
```

```
<DL>
<DT><A NAME="Witness">Witness</A>
<DD>An individual who testifies at a trial on what he has seen, heard,
or otherwise observed.
</DL>

<!------------------------------------------------------------------->
<H2><A NAME="X">X</A></H2>

<!------------------------------------------------------------------->
<H2><A NAME="Y">Y</A></H2>

<!------------------------------------------------------------------->
<H2><A NAME="Z">Z</A></H2>

<!------------------------------------------------------------------->

<HR SIZE=2>

http://www.cbgpc.com/glossary.htm -- Revised: 08 MAY 1995<BR>
Copyright &copy; 1995 <A HREF="page.htm">Connem, Bilkem, & Gottcha,
PC</A><BR>
<A HREF="MAILTO:cbgpc@legal.com">cbgpc@legal.com</A><BR>

<HR SIZE=2>

<A HREF="contents.htm"><IMG SRC="cntsicon.gif" ALT="[Contents]"></A>
<A HREF="map.htm">     <IMG SRC="mapicon.gif"  ALT="[Map]"></A>
<A HREF="index.htm">   <IMG SRC="indxicon.gif" ALT="[Index]"></A>
<A HREF="comment.htm"> <IMG SRC="cmnticon.gif" ALT="[Comment]"></A>
<A HREF="search.htm">  <IMG SRC="srchicon.gif" ALT="[Search]"></A>
<A HREF="myhome.htm">  <IMG SRC="homeicon.gif" ALT="[Home]"></A>
<A HREF="parent.htm">  <IMG SRC="upicon.gif"   ALT="[Up]"></A>
<A HREF="previous.htm"><IMG SRC="previcon.gif" ALT="[Previous]"></A>
<A HREF="next.htm">    <IMG SRC="nexticon.gif" ALT="[Next]"></A>

</BODY>
</HTML>
```

How-To Procedure

On the CD-ROM ...

The example:
examples
    chap4
        howto
            howto.htm

The template:
recipes
    howto
        howto.htm

Main ingredients

Generic Web page, p. 105

Simple inline image, p. 276

Numbered list, p. 259

A how-to procedure shows how to do something. It's a set of simple, clear instructions.

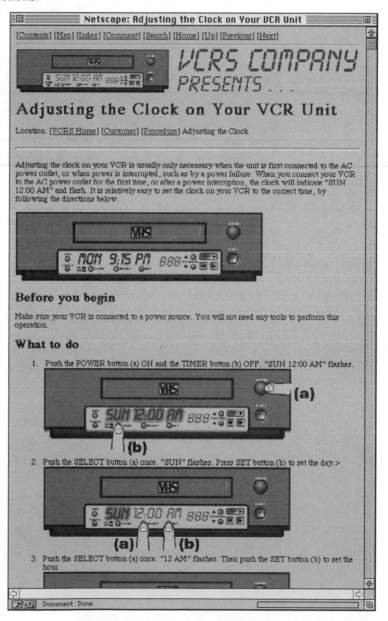

Recipe

This recipe builds upon the Generic Web page, p. 105.

Our example is a procedure for adjusting the clock on your VCR. It contains an illustrated step-by-step procedure.

Introduction

Ingredients

Paragraph, p. 246

Simple inline image, p. 276

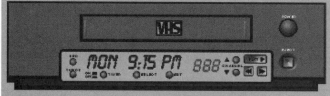

Adjusting the clock on your VCR is usually only necessary when the unit is first connected to the AC power outlet, or when power is interrupted, such as by a power failure. When you connect your VCR to the AC power outlet for the first time, or after a power interruption, the clock will indicate "SUN 12:00 AM" and flash. It is relatively easy to set the clock on your VCR to the correct time, by following the directions below.

```
<P> Adjusting the clock on your VCR is usually only necessary when the
unit is first connected to the AC power outlet, or when power is
interrupted, such as by a power failure. When you connect your VCR to
the AC power outlet for the first time, or after a power interruption,
the clock will indicate "SUN 12:00 AM" and flash.  It is relatively
easy to set the clock on your VCR to the correct time, by following the
directions below.</P>

<IMG SRG="results.gif" ALT="[Picture of VCR set to correct time]">
```

We open by describing the procedure and its results in a brief paragraph. We next include an image of the results. In this case, the results are that the VCR clock is not blinking and it's set to a time other than SUN 12:00 AM. Showing the results motivates the user to attempt the procedure. Think about the luscious photographs of finished dishes used in food magazines and cookbooks.

Prerequisites

Ingredients

Text headings, p. 252

Paragraph, p. 246

Before leading users into the details, we tell them what resources they will need to perform the procedure.

Before you begin

Make sure your VCR is connected to a power source. You will not need any tools to perform this operation.

```
<H2>Before you begin</H2>
<P> Make sure your VCR is connected to a power source. You will not
need any tools to perform this operation.</P>
```

Chapter 5 has recipes for lists, pictures, and links.

If your procedure requires tools, list or show them. If other procedures must be done first, list them and link to the Web pages that tell how to perform those other procedures.

Steps of the procedure

Ingredients

Inline image, p. 276

Numbered list, p. 259

The details are, of course, the steps of the procedure. Here, we establish a rhythm for users: We state the action they must perform, tell what the step accomplishes, and show a picture of what they do. Here are steps one and two.

```
<H2>What to do</H2>
<OL>
<LI> Push the POWER button (a) ON and the TIMER button (b) OFF.  "SUN
12:00 AM"  flashes. <BR>
    <IMG SRC="step1.gif" ALT="[picture of Step 1]">
<LI>Push the SELECT button (a) once.  "SUN" flashes.  Press SET button
(b) to set the day. <BR>
    <IMG SRC="step2.gif" ALT="[picture of Step 2]">
      .
      .
      .
</OL>
```

Results

Ingredients

Text heading, p. 252

Paragraph, p. 246

Tell users that they are finished with the procedure.

> ### Results
>
> Your VCR clock now shows the correct time. If your clock does not show the correct time, you probably need to look at our troubleshooting section.

```
<H2>Results</H2>
<P> Your VCR clock now shows the correct time. If your clock does not
show the correct time, you probably need to look at our<A
HREF="trouble.htm#wrong_time"> troubleshooting section</A>.</P>
```

Provide enough detail so that the user can tell whether the procedure succeeded. Also, tell the user what to do if the procedure fails.

Tips for great how-to procedures

- How-to procedures focus on actions. Begin each step with an action verb.

- Always tell or show users what the result of the actions are. They need information in your procedure that helps them evaluate whether they're successfully following the instructions or not.

- The Web is a multimedia environment. You can include audio clips of a narrator reading the steps. You can include an animation or a video of the procedure, too. Before you do, though, make sure these media are needed and that they really help the user to perform the procedure.

- If a procedure contains a caution or a warning, put the caution or warning *before* the step it refers to.

- Break up long procedures into subtopics, each covering a distinct phase of the overall procedure. How long is long? A procedure is long if it contains 10 or more steps or requires the user to scroll down more than four times to get to the end.

HTML Code

```
<HTML>

<!------------------------------------------------------------------->
<!--      AUTHOR:   Nancy Hoft                                    -->
<!--      E-MAIL:   itech@mv.mv.com                               -->
<!--      CREATED:  03 APRIL 1995                                 -->
<!--      MODIFIED: 08 MAY 1995                                   -->
<!--      FILE:     howto.htm                                     -->
<!--      PURPOSE:  Adjusting the Clock on                        -->
<!--                Your VCR Unit                                 -->
<!------------------------------------------------------------------->

<HEAD>
<TITLE> Adjusting the Clock on Your VCR Unit </TITLE>
</HEAD>

<BODY>

[<A HREF="contents.htm">Contents</A>]
[<A HREF="map.htm">Map</A>]
[<A HREF="1ndex.htm">Index</A>]
[<A HREF="comment.htm">Comment</A>]
[<A HREF="search.htm">Search</A>]
[<A HREF="myhome.htm">Home</A>]
[<A HREF="parent.htm">Up</A>]
[<A HREF="previous.htm">Previous</A>]
[<A HREF="next.htm">Next</A>]

<HR SIZE=2>

<IMG SRC="vcrshead.gif" ALT="[emblem text]"><BR>
<H1>Adjusting the Clock on Your VCR Unit</H1>

<P>Location:
[<A HREF="vcrshome.htm">VCRS Home</A>]
[<A HREF="customer.htm">Customer</A>]
[<A HREF="steps.htm">Procedure</A>]
Adjusting the Clock </P>

<HR SIZE=4>

<P> Adjusting the clock on your VCR is usually only necessary when the
unit is first connected to the AC power outlet, or when power is
interrupted, such as by a power failure.  When you connect your VCR to
the AC power outlet for the first time, or after a power interruption,
the clock will indicate "SUN 12:00 AM" and flash.   It is relatively
easy to set the clock on your VCR to the correct time, by following the
directions below.</P>

<IMG SRC="results.gif" ALT="[picture of results]">

<H2>Before you begin</H2>

<P> Make sure your VCR is connected to a power source.  You will not
need any tools to perform this operation.</P>
```

```
<H2>What to do</H2>

<OL>
<LI> Push the POWER button (a) ON and the TIMER button (b) OFF.   "SUN
12:00 AM" flashes.<BR>
    <IMG SRC="step1.gif" ALT="[picture of Step 1]">

<LI>Push the SELECT button (a) once.  "SUN" flashes.  Press SET button
(b) to set the day.><BR>
    <IMG SRC="step2.gif" ALT="[picture of Step 2]">

<LI>Push the SELECT button (a) once.   "12 AM" flashes.   Then push the
SET button (b) to set the hour.<BR>
    <IMG SRC="step3.gif" ALT="[picture of Step 3]">

<LI>Push the SELECT button (a) once.  "00" flashes.  Press SET button
(b) to set the day.<BR>
    <IMG SRC="step4.gif" ALT="[picture of Step 4]">

<LI>Push SELECT button and be sure the present time is displayed. <BR>
    <IMG SRC="step5.gif" ALT="[picture of Step 5]">

<LI>Repeat steps 2 through 5 if you enter the time incorrectly.
</OL>

<H2>Results</H2>

<P> Your VCR clock now shows the correct time. If your clock does not
show the correct time, you probably need to look at our <A
HREF="trouble.htm#wrong_time">troubleshooting section</A>.</P>

<HR SIZE=2>

http://www.vcrs.com/howto.com -- Revised: 08 MAY 1995<BR>
Copyright &copy; 1995 <A HREF="page.htm">The VCRS Company</A><BR>
<A HREF="MAILTO:fixin@vcrs.com">fixin@vcrs.com</A><BR>

<HR SIZE=2>

<A HREF="contents.htm"><IMG SRC="cntsicon.gif" ALT="[Contents]"></A>
<A HREF="map.htm">     <IMG SRC="mapicon.gif"  ALT="[Map]"></A>
<A HREF="index.htm">   <IMG SRC="indxicon.gif" ALT="[Index]"></A>
<A HREF="comment.htm"> <IMG SRC="cmnticon.gif" ALT="[Comment]"></A>
<A HREF="search.htm">  <IMG SRC="srchicon.gif" ALT="[Search]"></A>
<A HREF="myhome.htm">  <IMG SRC="homeicon.gif" ALT="[Home]"></A>
<A HREF="parent.htm">  <IMG SRC="upicon.gif"   ALT="[Up]"></A>
<A HREF="previous.htm"><IMG SRC="previcon.gif" ALT="[Previous]"></A>
<A HREF="next.htm">    <IMG SRC="nexticon.gif" ALT="[Next]"></A>

</BODY>
</HTML>
```

TROUBLESHOOTING PROCEDURE

Troubleshooting procedures help your customers solve specific problems on their own.

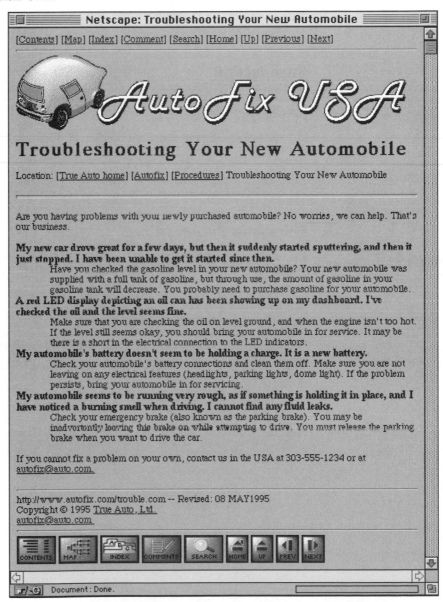

Given its purpose, you need to make troubleshooting procedures intuitive, easy to use, and easy to follow by an impatient and unhappy user. Your customers come here with a problem. If your Web page design is hard to follow, you give them another problem, not a solution.

Recipe

This recipe builds upon the Generic Web page, p. 105.

This example is a troubleshooting procedure for a new automobile. It lists common problems and provides solutions for them.

Introduction

Ingredients

Paragraph, p. 246

Open the procedure with reassurance. Set the tone and explain the page's purpose right away.

> Are you having problems with your newly purchased automobile? No worries, we can help. That's our business.

```
<P> Are you having problems with your newly purchased automobile? No
worries, we can help. That's our business. </P>
```

Problem-solution pairs

Ingredients

Definition list, p. 261

> **My new car drove great for a few days, but then it suddenly started sputtering, and then it just stopped. I have been unable to get it started since then.**
> Have you checked the gasoline level in your new automobile? Your new automobile was supplied with a full tank of gasoline, but through use, the amount of gasoline in your gasoline tank will decrease. You probably need to purchase gasoline for your automobile.
> **A red LED display depicting an oil can has been showing up on my dashboard. I've checked the oil and the level seems fine.**
> Make sure that you are checking the oil on level ground, and when the engine isn't too hot. If the level still seems okay, you should bring your automobile in for service. It may be there is a short in the electrical connection to the LED indicators.
> **My automobile's battery doesn't seem to be holding a charge. It is a new battery.**
> Check your automobile's battery connections and clean them off. Make sure you are not leaving on any electrical features (headlights, parking lights, dome light). If the problem persists, bring your automobile in for servicing.
> **My automobile seems to be running very rough, as if something is holding it in place, and I have noticed a burning smell when driving. I cannot find any fluid leaks.**
> Check your emergency brake (also known as the parking brake). You may be inadvertently leaving this brake on while attempting to drive. You must release the parking brake when you want to drive the car.

```
<DL>
<DT><B> My new car drove great for a few days, but then it suddenly
started sputtering, and then it just stopped. I have been unable to get
it started since then. </B>
<DD> Have you checked the gasoline level in your new automobile?
Your new automobile was supplied with a full tank of gasoline, but
through use, the amount of gasoline in your gasoline tank will
decrease. You probably need to purchase gasoline for your
automobile.
<BR>
```

```
<DT><B> A red LED display depicting an oil can has been showing up
on my dashboard. I've checked the oil and the level seems fine.
</B>
<DD> Make sure that you are checking the oil on level ground, and
when the engine isn't too hot. If the level still seems okay, you
should bring your automobile in for service. It may be there is a
short in the electrical connection to the LED indicators.
<BR>
<DT><B> My automobile's battery doesn't seem to be holding a
charge. It is a new battery. </B>
<DD> Check your automobile's battery connections and clean them
off.  Make sure you are not leaving on any electrical features
(headlights, parking lights, dome light). If the problem persists,
bring your automobile in for servicing.
<BR>
<DT><B> My automobile seems to be running very rough, as if
something is holding it in place, and I have noticed a burning
smell when driving. I cannot find any fluid leaks.</B>
<DD> Check your emergency brake (also known as the parking brake).
You may be inadvertently leaving this brake on while attempting to
drive. You must release the parking brake when you want to drive
the car.
</DL>
```

The basic pattern for problem-solution pairs is:

```
<DT><B>a problem</B>
<DD>the solution to that problem
<BR>
```

The problems are listed using one of our favorite HTML tags, the definition list `<DL>`. It is easy to read because of its orderly and regular indentations.

The bold-face `<B>` tag calls extra attention to each of the problems. This makes it easier for users to locate each problem as they scan down the page.

Close

Ingredients

> If you cannot fix a problem on your own, contact us in the USA at 303-555-1234 or at
> autofix@auto.com.

```
<P>If you cannot fix a problem on your own, contact us in the USA at
303-555-1234 or at <A HREF="MAILTO: autofix@auto.com">
autofix@auto.com.</A> </P>
```

The close offers additional help. It invites the user to contact you by phone or e-mail. Even though you may have a `MAILTO` link in the signature to the page, it is wise to include one here. Making it easy to solve problems is the whole point of this page. And, the e-mail address for customer support may be different from that of the page designer.

Tips for great troubleshooting procedures

Complex remedy

If the remedy is more than a simple step or two, use the How-to procedure recipe (page 139) to create a separate Web page for the remedy. Link the troubleshooting procedure to the how-to procedure with a link something like the one shown here:

```
<DT><B>Gizmo-on indicator fails to light up</B>
<DD><A HREF="GIZONPRC.HTM>Replace the Gizmo-on light</A>
```

Complex troubleshooting procedure

If the list of possible problems is long, sort them into general categories and subcategories. Then create a cascaded series of troubleshooting pages that eventually guide the user to a specific remedy.

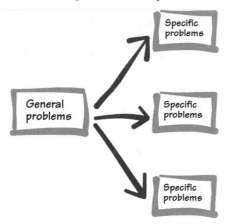

In the top-level troubleshooting procedure, give users a list of general problems to select from that will take them to a more specific troubleshooting procedure, for example:

```
<UL>
<LI><A HREF="SPECIFIC1.HTM>General problem 1</A>
<LI><A HREF="SPECIFIC2.HTM>General problem 2</A>
<LI><A HREF="SPECIFIC3.HTM>General problem 3</A>
</UL>
```

HTML code

```
<HTML>

<!----------------------------------------------->
<!--    AUTHOR:    Nancy Hoft              -->
<!--    E-MAIL:    itech@mv.mv.com         -->
<!--    CREATED:   05 APRIL 1995           -->
<!--    MODIFIED:  10 MAY 1995             -->
<!--    FILE:      trouble.htm             -->
<!--    PURPOSE:   Troubleshooting Your New -->
<!--               Automobile              -->
<!----------------------------------------------->

<HEAD>
<TITLE> Troubleshooting Your New Automobile </TITLE>
</HEAD>

<BODY>
[<A HREF="contents.htm">Contents</A>]
[<A HREF="map.htm">Map</A>]
[<A HREF="index.htm">Index</A>]
[<A HREF="comment.htm">Comment</A>]
[<A HREF="search.htm">Search</A>]
[<A HREF="myhome.htm">Home</A>]
[<A HREF="parent.htm">Up</A>]
[<A HREF="previous.htm">Previous</A>]
[<A HREF="next.htm">Next</A>]

<HR SIZE=2>

<IMG SRC="lemoncar.gif" ALT="[emblem text]"><BR>
<H1>Troubleshooting Your New Automobile</H1>

<P>Location:
[<A HREF="truehome.htm">True Auto home</A>]
[<A HREF="autofix.htm">Autofix</A>]
[<A HREF="steps.htm">Procedures</A>]
Troubleshooting Your New Automobile </P>

<HR SIZE=4>

<P> Are you having problems with your newly purchased automobile?  No
worries, we can help. That's our business.</P>

<DL>
<DT><B> My new car drove great for a few days, but then it suddenly
started sputtering, and then it just stopped.  I have been unable to
get it started since then. </B>
<DD> Have you checked the gasoline level in your new automobile?  Your
new automobile was supplied with a full tank of gasoline, but through
use, the amount of gasoline in your gasoline tank will decrease.  You
probably need to purchase gasoline for your automobile.
<BR>
<DT><B> A red LED display depicting an oil can has been showing up on
my dashboard.  I've checked the oil and the level seems fine. </B>
```

```
<DD> Make sure that you are checking the oil on level ground, and when
the engine isn't too hot.  If the level still seems okay, you should
bring your automobile in for service.  It may be there is a short in
the electrical connection to the LED indicators.
<BR>
<DT><B> My automobile's battery doesn't seem to be holding a charge.
It is a new battery. </B>
<DD> Check your automobile's battery connections and clean them off.
Make sure you are not leaving on any electrical features (headlights,
parking lights, dome light).  If the problem persists, bring your
automobile in for servicing.
<BR>
<DT><B> My automobile seems to be running very rough, as if something
is holding it in place, and I have noticed a burning smell when
driving.  I cannot find any fluid leaks.</B>
<DD> Check your emergency brake (also known as the parking brake).  You
may be inadvertently leaving this brake on while attempting to drive.
You must release the parking brake when you want to drive the car.
</DL>

<P>If you cannot fix a problem on your own, contact us in the USA at
303-555-1234 or at <A HREF="MAILTO:autofix@auto.com">
autofix@auto.com.</A> </P>

<HR SIZE=2>

http://www.autofix.com/trouble.com -- Revised: 08 MAY1995<BR>
Copyright &copy; 1995 <A HREF="page.htm"> True Auto, Ltd.</A><BR>
<A HREF="MAILTO:autofix@auto.com">autofix@auto.com </A><BR>

<HR SIZE=2>

<A HREF="contents.htm"> <IMG SRC="cntsicon.gif" ALT="[Contents]"></A>
<A HREF="map.htm">      <IMG SRC="mapicon.gif"  ALT="[Map]"></A>
<A HREF="index.htm">    <IMG SRC="indxicon.gif" ALT="[Index]"></A>
<A HREF="comment.htm">  <IMG SRC="cmnticon.gif" ALT="[Comment]"></A>
<A HREF="search.htm">   <IMG SRC="srchicon.gif" ALT="[Search]"></A>
<A HREF="myhome.htm">   <IMG SRC="homeicon.gif" ALT="[Home]"></A>
<A HREF="parent.htm">   <IMG SRC="upicon.gif"   ALT="[Up]"></A>
<A HREF="previous.htm"> <IMG SRC="previcon.gif" ALT="[Previous]"></A>
<A HREF="next.htm">     <IMG SRC="nexticon.gif" ALT="[Next]"></A>

</BODY>
</HTML>
```

COURSE DESCRIPTION

On the CD-ROM ...

The example:
examples
 chap4
  course
   course.htm

The template:
recipes
 course
  course.htm

Main Ingredients

Generic Web page, p. 105

Definition list, p. 261

Link with text trigger, p. 263

Text headings, p. 252

Inline image aligned with
 text, p. 277

Bullet list, complex items,
 p. 258

Bullet list, p. 256

Preformatted text, p. 247

Link to send e-mail, p. 267

A course description announces your training course and entices users to attend.

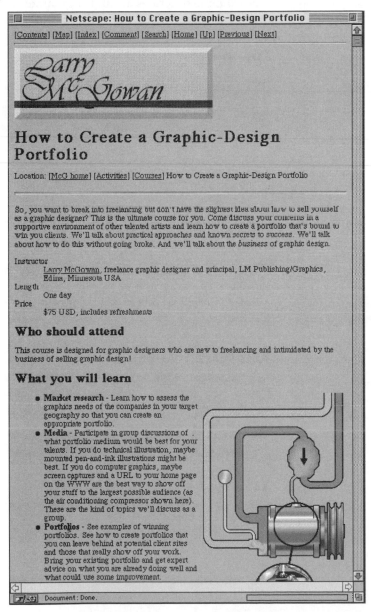

Web users will add your base course description home page to their hot lists if you continue to add new and exciting courses, and if you make it easy for them to read the description and to register.

Recipe

This recipe builds upon the Generic Web page, p. 105.

Our example describes a course in marketing for graphic designers. It is offered by Larry McGowan, who did many of the graphics in this chapter.

Opener

Ingredients

Paragraph, p. 246

> So, you want to break into freelancing but don't have the slightest idea about how to sell yourself as a graphic designer? This is the ultimate course for you. Come discuss your concerns in a supportive environment of other talented artists and learn how to create a portfolio that's bound to win you clients. We'll talk about practical approaches and known secrets to success. We'll talk about how to do this without going broke. And we'll talk about the *business* of graphic design.

```
<P>So, you want to break into freelancing, but don't have the slightest
idea about how to sell yourself as a graphic designer?  This is the
ultimate course for you.  Come discuss your concerns in a supportive
environment of other talented artists and learn how to create a
portfolio that's bound to win you clients.  We'll talk about practical
approaches and known secrets to success. We'll talk about how to do
this without going broke.  And we'll talk about the <I>business</I> of
graphic design.</P>
```

The opener is a brief marketing blurb about the course. If your course requires more than a paragraph or two of information to describe it, consider adding a link to another Web page that provides a longer, more detailed outline of the course.

Summary section

Ingredients

Definition list, p. 261

Link with text trigger, p. 263

> Instructor
> > Larry McGowan, freelance graphic designer and principal, LM Publishing/Graphics, Edina, Minnesota USA
>
> Length
> > One day
>
> Price
> > $75 USD, includes refreshments

```
<DL>
<DT>Instructor
<DD><A HREF="http://www.winternet.com/larry.htm>Larry McGowan</A>,
freelance graphic designer and principal, LM Publishing/Graphics,
Edina, Minnesota USA
<DT>Length
<DD>One day
<DT>Price
<DD>$75 USD, includes refreshments
</DL>
```

You can use the Biography recipe (p. 161) to create a biography page.

We use a definition list to structure details into a quick reference format. The name of the instructor is a link to his biography, which exists elsewhere.

Who should attend section

Who should attend

This course is designed for graphic designers who are new to freelancing and intimidated by the business of selling graphic design!

```
<H2>Who should attend</H2>
<P>This course is designed for graphic designers who are new to
freelancing and intimidated by the business of selling graphic
design!</P>
```

Ingredients

Text heading, p. 252

Paragraph, p. 246

See Bullet list, complex items, p. 258.

The Who should attend section is just a text heading and a regular paragraph, since the target audience is one group of people. If your course appeals to several different groups of people, you might use a bullet list of complex items, explaining how each group would benefit from the course.

What you will learn section

Ingredients

Text headings, p. 252

Inline image aligned with text, p. 277

Bullet list, complex items, p. 258

What you will learn

- **Market research** - Learn how to assess the graphics needs of the companies in your target geography so that you can create an appropriate portfolio.
- **Media** - Participate in group discussions of what portfolio medium would be best for your talents. If you do technical illustration, maybe mounted pen-and-ink illustrations might be best. If you do computer graphics, maybe screen captures and a URL to your home page on the WWW are the best way to show off your stuff to the largest possible audience (as the air conditioning compressor shown here). These are the kind of topics we'll discuss as a group.
- **Portfolios** - See examples of winning portfolios. See how to create portfolios that you can leave behind at potential client sites and those that really show off your work. Bring your existing portfolio and get expert advice on what you are already doing well and what could use some improvement.
- **Message** - Learn about what the business world likes and doesn't like. Learn how to start balancing business logic with good design.
- **Business Stuff** - Learn about basic business stuff. Do you want a home-based business or do you want to rent space? What about accounting? What if you have more work than you can handle?

```
<H2>What you will learn</H2>
<IMG SRC="jetlube.gif" ALT="[compressor]" ALIGN=right>
<UL>
<LI><STRONG>Market research</STRONG> - Learn how to assess the graphics
needs of the companies in your target geography so that you can create
an appropriate portfolio.
<LI><STRONG>Media</STRONG> - Participate in group discussions of what
portfolio medium would be best for your talents. If you do technical
illustration, maybe mounted pen-and-ink illustrations might be best. If
you do computer graphics, maybe screen captures and a URL to your home
page on the WWW are the best way to show off your stuff to the largest
possible audience (as the air conditioning compressor shown here).
These are the kind of topics we'll discuss as a group.
<LI><STRONG>Portfolios</STRONG> - See examples of winning portfolios.
See how to create portfolios that you can leave behind at potential
client sites and those that really show off your work.  Bring your
existing portfolio and get expert advice on what you are already doing
well and what could use some improvement.
<LI><STRONG>Message</STRONG> - Learn about what the business world
likes and doesn't like. Learn how to start balancing business logic
with good design.
<LI><STRONG>Business Stuff</STRONG> - Learn about basic business stuff.
Do you want a home-based business or do you want to rent space? What
about accounting? What if you have more work than you can handle?
</UL>
```

The advantages are formatted as a bullet list with the introductory
phrases of each item in bold type. And to liven up the display and provide
additional evidence of his talent, a graphic has been placed just after the
heading. It is aligned to the right margin so that the text flows along its
left edge.

```
<H2>What you will learn</H2>
<IMG SRC="jetlube.gif" ALT="[compressor]" ALIGN=right>
```

What you will receive section

What you will receive

- Larry's Guidelines. A booklet of helpful tips based on Larry's 15 years of graphic design experience.
- A list of organizations that can help you get started
- Larry's business card! Hey, successful business people get all of their work from referrals.

```
<H2>What you will receive</H2>
<UL>
<LI>Larry's Guidelines. A booklet of helpful tips based on Larry's
15 years of graphic design experience.
<LI>A list of organizations that can help you get started
<LI>Larry's business card! Hey, successful business people get all
of their work from referrals.
</UL>
```

This section has the same structure as the preceding one.

Ingredients

Text heading, p. 252

Bullet list, p. 256

Location and dates section

Ingredients

Text heading, p. 252

Preformatted text, p. 247

```
Locations and dates


==================================================================
Location                            Date
==================================================================
Minneapolis, MN                     12 OCTOBER 1995
------------------------------------------------------------------
Boston, MA                          13 NOVEMBER 1995
------------------------------------------------------------------
Chicago, IL                          7 JANUARY 1996
------------------------------------------------------------------
San Francisco, CA                   15 FEBRUARY 1996
==================================================================
```

```
<H2>Location and dates</H2>
<PRE>
==================================================================
Location                            Date
==================================================================
Minneapolis, MN                     12 OCTOBER 1995
------------------------------------------------------------------
Boston, MA                          13 NOVEMBER 1995
------------------------------------------------------------------
Chicago, IL                          7 JANUARY 1996
------------------------------------------------------------------
San Francisco, CA                   15 FEBRUARY 1996
==================================================================
</PRE>
```

See page 390 for information on creating real tables with HTML 3.0.

The Location and dates section is a table of when and where the course is offered. You can create such a table by formatting it manually in a monospaced font, such as Courier or Letter Gothic. To keep the browser from reformatting the table, we surround it with `<PRE>` and `</PRE>` tags.

Scheduling information section

Ingredients

Text heading, p. 252

Definition list, p. 261

Link to send e-mail, p. 267

To schedule this course

Phone
: 612-926-2838, Central Time, 11:00 a.m. to 5:00 p.m., Monday-Friday

Fax
: 612-926-8335

E-mail
: lmmcgown@winternet.com

```
<H2>To schedule this course</H2>
<DL>
<DT>Phone
<DD>612-926-2838, Central Time, 11:00 a.m. to 5:00 p.m., Monday-
Friday
<DT>Fax
<DD>612-926-8335
<DT>E-mail
<DD><A
HREF="MAILTO:lmmcgown@winternet.com">lmmcgown@winternet.com</A>
</DL>
```

In the scheduling information section, we provide a MAILTO link so that the user can register for the course right away. We also provide the telephone number and the fax number for those who have additional questions. Note that the telephone number is followed by the time zone. Remember that users are from all over the world.

Tips for a great course description

- A Web page that provides a course description is typically part of a larger cluster of course descriptions. It is very important that all these course descriptions follow the same style, both in content and in design.

- Consider adding student testimonials, either as text or as an audio clip, or both!

- Add a button that lets users add themselves to an electronic mailing list so that they are notified of new courses.

- If you supplement your online course descriptions with a printed catalog, consider providing a way for users to submit a request to be on your mailing list.

- Add a button to take users to a registration form so they can sign up for the course. Use the Registration Form recipe, page 191, as a starting point.

HTML code

```
<HTML>

<!------------------------------------------------------->
<!--      AUTHOR:   Nancy Hoft                      -->
<!--      E-MAIL:   itech@mv.mv.com                 -->
<!--      CREATED:  05 APRIL 1995                   -->
<!--      MODIFIED: 12 MAY 1995                     -->
<!--      FILE:     course.htm                      -->
<!--      PURPOSE:  How to Create a                 -->
<!--                Graphic-Design Portfolio        -->
<!------------------------------------------------------->

<HEAD>
<TITLE>How to Create a Graphic-Design Portfolio </TITLE>
</HEAD>

<BODY>

[<A HREF="contents.htm">Contents</A>]
[<A HREF="map.htm">Map</A>]
[<A HREF="index.htm">Index</A>]
[<A HREF="comment.htm">Comment</A>]
[<A HREF-"search.htm">Search</A>]
[<A HREF="myhome.htm">Home</A>]
[<A HREF="parent.htm">Up</A>]
[<A HREF="previous.htm">Previous</A>]
[<A HREF="next.htm">Next</A>]

<HR SIZE=2>

<IMG SRC="lmm_logo.gif" ALT="[emblem text]">
<H1>How to Create a Graphic-Design Portfolio</H1>

<P>Location:
[<A HREF="mcghome.htm">McG home</A>]
[<A HREF="activity.htm">Activities</A>]
[<A HREF="courses.htm">Courses</A>]
How to Create a Graphic-Design Portfolio </P>

<HR SIZE=4>

<P>So, you want to break into freelancing but don't have the slightest
idea about how to sell yourself as a graphic designer?  This is the
ultimate course for you.  Come discuss your concerns in a supportive
environment of other talented artists and learn how to create a
portfolio that's bound to win you clients.  We'll talk about practical
approaches and known secrets to success. We'll talk about how to do
this without going broke.  And we'll talk about the <I>business</I> of
graphic design.</P>

<DL>
<DT>Instructor
<DD><A HREF=" http://www.winternet.com/larry.htm>Larry McGowan</A>,
freelance graphic designer and principal, LM Publishing/Graphics,
Edina, Minnesota USA
```

```
<DT>Length
<DD>One day

<DT>Price
<DD>$75 USD, includes refreshments
</DL>

<H2>Who should attend</H2>
<P>This course is designed for graphic designers who are new to
freelancing and intimidated by the business of selling graphic
design! </P>

<H2>What you will learn</H2>
<IMG SRC="jetlube.gif" ALT="[compressor]" ALIGN=right>
<UL>
<LI><STRONG>Market research</STRONG> - Learn how to assess the graphics
needs of the companies in your target geography so that you can create
an appropriate portfolio.
<LI><STRONG>Media</STRONG> - Participate in group discussions of what
portfolio medium would be best for your talents. If you do technical
illustration, maybe mounted pen-and-ink illustrations might be best. If
you do computer graphics, maybe screen captures and a URL to your home
page on the WWW are the best way to show off your stuff to the largest
possible audience (as the air conditioning compressor shown here).
These are the kind of topics we'll discuss as a group.
<LI><STRONG>Portfolios</STRONG> - See examples of winning portfolios.
See how to create portfolios that you can leave behind at potential
client sites and those that really show off your work. Bring your
existing portfolio and get expert advice on what you are already doing
well and what could use some improvement.
<LI><STRONG>Message</STRONG> - Learn about what the business world
likes and doesn't like. Learn how to start balancing business logic
with good design.
<LI><STRONG>Business Stuff</STRONG> - Learn about basic business stuff.
Do you want a home-based business or do you want to rent space? What
about accounting? What if you have more work than you can handle?
</UL>

<H2>What you will receive</H2>
<UL>
<LI>Larry's Guidelines. A booklet of helpful tips based on Larry's 15
years of graphic design experience.
<LI>A list of organizations that can help you get started
<LI>Larry's business card! Hey, successful business people get all of
their work from referrals.
</UL>

<H2>Locations and dates</H2>
<PRE>
============================================================
Location                             Date
============================================================
Minneapolis, MN                      12 OCTOBER 1995
------------------------------------------------------------
Boston, MA                           13 NOVEMBER 1995
------------------------------------------------------------
Chicago, IL                           7 JANUARY 1996
------------------------------------------------------------
San Francisco, CA                    15 FEBRUARY 1996
============================================================
```

```
</PRE>

<H2>To schedule this course</H2>
<DL>
<DT>Phone
<DD>612-926-2838, Central Time, 11:00 a.m. to 5:00 p.m., Monday-Friday
<DT>Fax
<DD>612-926-8335
<DT>E-mail
<DD><A HREF="MAILTO:lmmcgown@winternet.com">lmmcgown@winternet.com</A>
</DL>

<HR SIZE=2>

http://www.winternet.com/lm.htm -- Revised: 12 MAY 1995<BR>
Copyright &copy; 1995 <A HREF="homepage.htm">LM
Publications/Graphics</A><BR>
<A HREF="MAILTO:lmmcgown@winternet.com">
lmmcgown@winternet.com </A><BR>

<HR SIZE=2>

<A HREF="contents.htm"><IMG SRC="cntsicon.gif" ALT="[Contents]"></A>
<A HREF="map.htm">     <IMG SRC="mapicon.gif"  ALT="[Map]"></A>
<A HREF="index.htm">    <IMG SRC="indxicon.gif" ALT="[Index]"></A>
<A HREF="comment.htm">  <IMG SRC="cmnticon.gif" ALT="[Comment]"></A>
<A HREF="search.htm">   <IMG SRC="srchicon.gif" ALT="[Search]"></A>
<A HREF="myhome.htm">   <IMG SRC="homeicon.gif" ALT="[Home]"></A>
<A HREF="parent.htm">   <IMG SRC="upicon.gif"   ALT="[Up]"></A>
<A HREF="previous.htm"><IMG SRC="previcon.gif" ALT="[Previous]"></A>
<A HREF="next.htm">     <IMG SRC="nexticon.gif" ALT="[Next]"></A>

</BODY>
</HTML>
```

BIOGRAPHY

On the CD-ROM ...

The example:
examples
    chap4
        biograph
            biograph.htm

The template:
recipes
    biograph
        biograph.htm

Main ingredients

Generic Web page, p. 105

Text headings, p. 252

Definition list, p. 261

Link to external media
    element, p. 265

A biography introduces the user to important people in your organization or to the author of your Web pages. It can add credibility and convey a more friendly, personal tone to your Web site.

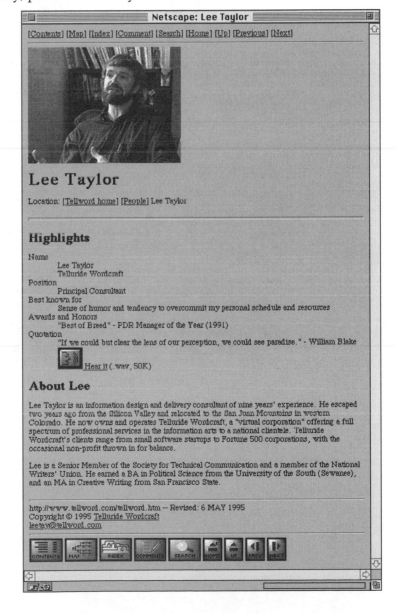

Use a biography page for

- Head honchos, key players, and other hot shots of your organization.

- Team members of a successful project.

- Designers of your organization's Web pages.

- You own biography. You're special too.

Recipe

This recipe builds upon the Generic Web page, p. 105.

This example introduces you to one of the authors of this book, Lee Taylor.

Highlights

The highlights section provides a summary of what makes the subject of the biography interesting.

Ingredients

Text heading, p. 252

Definition list, p. 261

Link to external media element, p. 265

Highlights

Name
    Lee Taylor
    Telluride Wordcraft
Position
    Principal Consultant
Best known for
    Sense of humor and tendency to overcommit my personal schedule and resources
Awards and Honors
    "Best of Breed" - PDR Manager of the Year (1991)
Quotation
    "If we could but clear the lens of our perception, we could see paradise." - William Blake

    Hear it (.wav, 50K)

```
<H2>Highlights</H2>
<DL>

<DT>Name
<DD>Lee Taylor
<DD>Telluride Wordcraft

<DT>Position
<DD>Principal Consultant

<DT>Best known for
<DD>Sense of humor and tendency to overcommit my personal schedule
and resources

<DT>Awards and Honors
<DD>"Best of Breed" - PDR Manager of the Year (1991)
```

```
<DT>Quotation
<DD>"If we could but clear the lens of our perception, we could see
paradise." - William Blake
<DD><A HREF="leequote.wav"><IMG SRC="spkicon.gif" ALT="[Lee
speaking his favorite quotation.]"> Hear it</A> (.wav, 50K)

</DL>
```

We use a second-level heading to introduce the section and then use the definition list to make the highlights stand out. We also include an audio clip of Lee saying his favorite quotation.

Details

Ingredients

Text heading, p. 252

Paragraph, p. 246

The About section offers a couple of paragraphs of detail about the subject of this biography. Interesting biographies pepper the business information with relevant personal information about the subject.

About Lee

Lee Taylor is an information design and delivery consultant of nine years' experience. He escaped two years ago from the Silicon Valley and relocated to the San Juan Mountains in western Colorado. He now owns and operates Telluride Wordcraft, a "virtual corporation" offering a full spectrum of professional services in the information arts to a national clientele. Telluride Wordcraft's clients range from small software startups to Fortune 500 corporations, with the occasional non-profit thrown in for balance.

Lee is a Senior Member of the Society for Technical Communication and a member of the National Writers' Union. He earned a B.A. in Political Science from the University of the South (Sewanee), and an M.A. in Creative Writing from San Francisco State.

```
<H2><A NAME="about">About Lee</A></H2>
<P>Lee Taylor is an information design and delivery consultant of
nine years' experience.  He escaped two years ago from the Silicon
Valley and relocated to the San Juan Mountains in western Colorado.
He now owns and operates Telluride Wordcraft, a "virtual
corporation" offering a full spectrum of professional services in
the information arts to a national clientele. Telluride Wordcraft's
clients range from small software startups to Fortune 500
corporations, with the occasional non-profit thrown in for
balance.</P>
<P>Lee is a Senior Member of the Society for Technical
Communication and a member of the National Writers' Union.  He
earned a BA in Political Science from the University of the South
(Sewanee), and an MA in Creative Writing from San Francisco
State.</P>
```

Tips for a great biography

Users are people and people want to know about other people. They want to know who the subject of the biography is and what knowledge and talents he or she offers this world. Make the biography informative and personal. Avoid being so esoteric that only a few people can identify with you.

Consider making the introduction fun for users. You can include an audio clip, a video clip, a scanned image of the subject, or, if you are daring, a cartoon or animation. Some popular biographies on the Web offer brief résumés of the subjects with samples of their work using various media (images, sound, video, illustrations).

If you include a photograph, make it clear and interesting. Try using a picture of the person doing what he or she loves and is known for.

HTML code

```
<HTML>
<!----------------------------------------->
<!--      AUTHOR:   Lee Taylor               -->
<!--      E-MAIL:   leetay@tellword.com      -->
<!--      CREATED:  03 APRIL 1995            -->
<!--      MODIFIED: 08 MAY 1995              -->
<!--      FILE:     biograph.htm             -->
<!--      PURPOSE:  Meet Lee Taylor          -->
<!----------------------------------------->
<HEAD>
<TITLE>Lee Taylor</TITLE>
</HEAD>

<BODY>
[<A HREF="contents.htm">Contents</A>]
[<A HREF="map.htm">Map</A>]
[<A HREF="index.htm">Index</A>]
[<A HREF="comment.htm">Comment</A>]
[<A HREF="search.htm">Search</A>]
[<A HREF="myhome.htm ">Home</A>]
[<A HREF="parent.htm ">Up</A>]
[<A HREF="previous.htm">Previous</A>]
[<A HREF="next.htm">Next</A>]

<HR SIZE=2>

<IMG SRC="lee.gif" ALT="[Photo of Lee Taylor]"><BR>
<H1>Lee Taylor</H1>

<P>Location:
[<A HREF="tellword.htm">Tellword home</A>]
[<A HREF="people.htm">People</A>]
Lee Taylor</P>

<HR SIZE=4>

<H2>Highlights</H2>
<DL>

<DT>Name
<DD>Lee Taylor
<DD>Telluride Wordcraft

<DT>Position
<DD>Principal Consultant
```

```
<DT>Best known for
<DD>Sense of humor and tendency to overcommit my personal schedule and
resources

<DT>Awards and Honors
<DD>"Best of Breed" - PDR Manager of the Year (1991)

<DT>Quotation
<DD>"If we could but clear the lens of our perception, we could see
paradise." - William Blake
<DD><A HREF="leequote.wav"><IMG SRC="spkicon.gif" ALT="[Lee speaking
his favorite quotation.]"> Hear it</A> (.wav, 50K)

</DL>

<H2>About Lee</H2>
<P>Lee Taylor is an information design and delivery consultant of nine
years' experience.  He escaped two years ago from the Silicon Valley
and relocated to the San Juan Mountains in western Colorado. He now
owns and operates Telluride Wordcraft, a "virtual corporation" offering
a full spectrum of professional services in the information arts to a
national clientele. Telluride Wordcraft's clients range from small
software startups to Fortune 500 corporations, with the occasional non-
profit thrown in for balance.</P>

<P>Lee is a Senior Member of the Society for Technical Communication
and a member of the National Writers' Union.  He earned a BA in
Political Science from the University of the South (Sewanee), and an MA
in Creative Writing from San Francisco State.</P>

<HR SIZE=2>

http://www.tellword.com/tellword.htm -- Revised: 6 MAY 1995<BR>
Copyright &copy; 1995 <A HREF="tellword.htm">Telluride
Wordcraft</A><BR>
<A HREF="MAILTO:leetay@tellword.com">leetay@tellword.com</A><BR>

<HR SIZE=2>

<A HREF="contents.htm"><IMG SRC="cntsicon.gif" ALT="[Contents]"></A>
<A HREF="map.htm">     <IMG SRC="mapicon.gif"  ALT="[Map]"></A>
<A HREF="index.htm">   <IMG SRC="indxicon.gif" ALT="[Index]"></A>
<A HREF="comment.htm"> <IMG SRC="cmnticon.gif" ALT="[Comment]"></A>
<A HREF="search.htm">  <IMG SRC="srchicon.gif" ALT="[Search]"></A>
<A HREF="myhome.htm">  <IMG SRC="homeicon.gif" ALT="[Home]"></A>
<A HREF="parent.htm">  <IMG SRC="upicon.gif"   ALT="[Up]"></A>
<A HREF="previous.htm"><IMG SRC="previcon.gif" ALT="[Previous]"></A>
<A HREF="next.htm">    <IMG SRC="nexticon.gif" ALT="[Next]"></A>

</BODY>
</HTML>
```

BOOK DESCRIPTION

On the CD-ROM ...

The example:
examples
   chap4
      book
         book.htm

The template:
recipes
   book
      book.htm

Main ingredients

Generic Web page, p. 105

Text heading, p. 252

Inline image aligned to text,
   p. 277

Bullet list, complex items,
   p. 258

Link with text trigger, p. 263

Pointer to page in same
   directory, p. 290

A book description both announces a book and provides information the user needs to buy it.

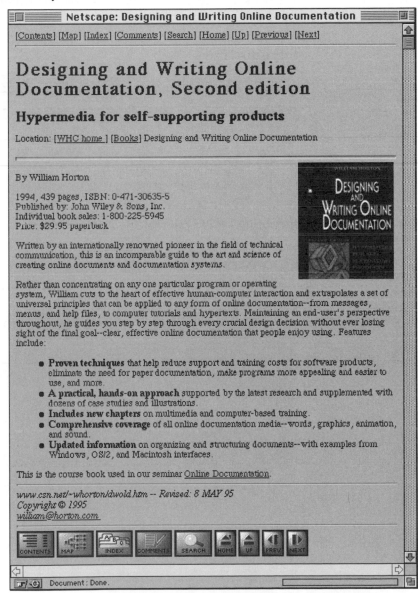

Screen shot is reprinted with permission from William Horton Consulting.

This Book Description can also serve as a book review or as a book report for a homework assignment. You can modify this recipe to promote videotapes, CD-ROMs, and related information products.

Recipe

This recipe builds upon the Generic Web page, p. 105.

The book described in this example was written by one of the authors of this book, William Horton.

Introduction

Ingredients

Text heading, p. 252

Designing and Writing Online Documentation, Second edition

Hypermedia for self-supporting products

```
<H1>Designing and Writing Online Documentation, Second edition</H1>
<H2>Hypermedia for self-supporting products</H2>
```

It boldly begins with the title and subtitle.

Summary

Ingredients

Inline image aligned with text, p. 277

Paragraph, p. 246

The actual description pairs very detailed statistics and bibliographic details with a small picture of the cover.

By William Horton

1994, 439 pages, ISBN: 0-471-30635-5
Published by: John Wiley & Sons, Inc.
Individual book sales: 1-800-225-5945
Price: $29.95 paperback

Written by an internationally renowned pioneer in the field of technical communication, this is an incomparable guide to the art and science of creating online documents and documentation systems.

Rather than concentrating on any one particular program or operating

```
<IMG SRC="dwold.gif" ALT="[cover]" ALIGN=RIGHT>

<P>By William Horton<BR>
<BR>
1994, 439 pages, ISBN: 0-471-30635-5<BR>
Published by: John Wiley & Sons, Inc.<BR>
Individual book sales: 1-800-225-5945<BR>
Price: $29.95 paperback</P>
```

This section begins with an inline image of the book's cover, aligned to the right so that the text will flow beside it. The bibliographic data are similar to what you would find in a library catalog entry for this book. We also included the toll-free telephone number in case the user wants to order a copy.

Details

The remainder of the book description engages the reader, sells the credibility of the author, and demonstrates the book's competitive advantages over other books on similar topics.

Written by an internationally renowned pioneer in the field of technical communication, this is an incomparable guide to the art and science of creating online documents and documentation systems.

Rather than concentrating on any one particular program or operating system, William cuts to the heart of effective human-computer interaction and extrapolates a set of universal principles that can be applied to any form of online documentation--from messages, menus, and help files, to computer tutorials and hypertexts. Maintaining an end-user's perspective throughout, he guides you step by step through every crucial design decision without ever losing sight of the final goal--clear, effective online documentation that people enjoy using. Features include:

- **Proven techniques** that help reduce support and training costs for software products, eliminate the need for paper documentation, make programs more appealing and easier to use, and more.
- **A practical, hands-on approach** supported by the latest research and supplemented with dozens of case studies and illustrations.
- **Includes new chapters** on multimedia and computer-based training.
- **Comprehensive coverage** of all online documentation media--words, graphics, animation, and sound.
- **Updated information** on organizing and structuring documents--with examples from Windows, OS/2, and Macintosh interfaces.

This is the course book used in our seminar <u>Online Documentation</u>.

```
<P>Written by an internationally renowned pioneer in the field of
technical communication, this is an incomparable guide to the art and
science of creating online documents and documentation systems.</P>
<P>Rather than concentrating on any one particular program or operating
system, William cuts to the heart of effective human-computer
interaction and extrapolates a set of universal principles that can be
applied to any form of online documentation--from messages, menus, and
help files, to computer tutorials and hypertexts. Maintaining an end-
user's perspective throughout, he guides you step by step through every
crucial design decision without ever losing sight of the final goal--
clear, effective online documentation that people enjoy using. Features
include:</P>
<UL>
<LI><STRONG>Proven techniques</STRONG> that help reduce support and
training costs for software products, eliminate the need for paper
documentation, make programs more appealing and easier to use, and
more.
```

```
<LI><STRONG>A practical, hands-on approach</STRONG> supported by the
latest research and supplemented with dozens of case studies and
illustrations.
<LI><STRONG>Includes new chapters</STRONG> on multimedia and computer-
based training.
<LI><STRONG>Comprehensive coverage</STRONG> of all online documentation
media--words, graphics, animation, and sound.
<LI><STRONG>Updated information</STRONG> on organizing and structuring
documents--with examples from Windows, OS/2, and Macintosh interfaces.
</UL>
P>This is the course book used in our seminar <A
HREF="online.htm">Online Documentation</A>.
```

The last line of the description is a pointer to another file in the same directory. The file is a Web page describing a course William Horton teaches in which this book is used as a textbook.

Tips for great book descriptions

Keep the book description short. Users come to a page like this to learn about a book, not to read a book. Users hope the book will teach them something or entertain them—convince them that your book will.

- Include a scanned image of the cover of the book to give users a visual idea of what the book contains.

- Provide a direct link to the publisher so that users can order the book immediately.

- Follow a style that users already understand: a catalog entry at a library, or a simple, but positive, book review.

- Offer just enough of a description so that users want to learn more. Often the description from the back cover of a paperback or from the inside flap of a hardcover's dust jacket is just right for good tickler copy.

- Enhance your description by adding links that let users jump to:
  - Table of contents or outline of the book.
  - Sample passages.
  - Examples the user can try.
  - Form for ordering the book. Use the Registration Form recipe (page 191) as a starting point.

HTML code

```
<HTML>

<!------------------------------------------------------------------->
<!--   AUTHOR:    Katherine Horton                                 -->
<!--   E-MAIL:    kit@horton.com                                   -->
<!--   CREATED:   2/14/95                                          -->
<!--   MODIFIED:  5/08/95                                          -->
<!--   FILE:      book.htm                                         -->
<!--   PURPOSE:   Description of Designing and Writing Online Doc  -->
<!------------------------------------------------------------------->

<HEAD>
<TITLE>Designing and Writing Online Documentation</TITLE>
</HEAD>

<BODY>

[<A HREF="contents.htm">Contents</A>]
[<A HREF="map.htm">Map</A>]
[<A HREF="index.htm">Index</A>]
[<A HREF="comments.htm">Comments</A>]
[<A HREF="search.htm">Search</A>]
[<A HREF="myhome.htm">Home</A>]
[<A HREF="parent.htm">Up</A>]
[<A HREF="previous.htm">Previous</A>]
[<A HREF="next.htm">Next</A>]

<HR SIZE=2>

<H1>Designing and Writing Online Documentation, Second edition</H1>
<H2>Hypermedia for self-supporting products</H2>

<P>Location:
[<A HREF="index.htm">WHC home </A>]
[<A HREF="books.htm">Books</A>]
Designing and Writing Online Documentation</P>

<HR SIZE=4>

<IMG SRC="dwold.gif" ALT="[cover]" ALIGN=RIGHT>

<P>By William Horton<BR>
<BR>
1994, 439 pages, ISBN: 0-471-30635-5<BR>
Published by: John Wiley & Sons, Inc.<BR>
Individual book sales: 1-800-225-5945<BR>
Price: $29.95 paperback</P>

<P>Written by an internationally renowned pioneer in the field of
technical communication, this is an incomparable guide to the art and
science of creating online documents and documentation systems.</P>
<P>Rather than concentrating on any one particular program or operating
system, William cuts to the heart of effective human-computer
interaction and extrapolates a set of universal principles that can be
applied to any form of online documentation--from messages, menus, and
help files, to computer tutorials and hypertexts. Maintaining an end-
user's perspective throughout, he guides you step by step through every
```

```
crucial design decision without ever losing sight of the final goal--
clear, effective online documentation that people enjoy using. Features
include:</P>

<UL>
<LI><STRONG>Proven techniques</STRONG> that help reduce support and
training costs for software products, eliminate the need for paper
documentation, make programs more appealing and easier to use, and
more.
<LI><STRONG>A practical, hands-on approach</STRONG> supported by the
latest research and supplemented with dozens of case studies and
illustrations.
<LI><STRONG>Includes new chapters</STRONG> on multimedia and computer-
based training.
<LI><STRONG>Comprehensive coverage</STRONG> of all online documentation
media--words, graphics, animation, and sound.
<LI><STRONG>Updated information</STRONG> on organizing and structuring
documents--with examples from Windows, OS/2, and Macintosh interfaces.
</UL>

<P>This is the course book used in our seminar <A
HREF="online.htm">Online Documentation</A>.

<HR SIZE=2>

<ADDRESS>
www.csn.net/~whorton/dwold.htm -- Revised: 8 MAY 95<BR>
Copyright &copy; 1995<BR>
<A HREF="MAILTO:william@horton.com">william@horton.com </A><BR>
</ADDRESS>

<HR SIZE=2>

<A HREF="contents.htm"><IMG SRC="cntsicon.gif" ALT="[Contents]"></A>
<A HREF="map.htm">     <IMG SRC="mapicon.gif"  ALT="[Map]"></A>
<A HREF="index.htm">   <IMG SRC="indxicon.gif" ALT="[Index]"></A>
<A HREF="comments.htm"><IMG SRC="cmnticon.gif" ALT="[Comments]"></A>
<A HREF="search.htm">  <IMG SRC="srchicon.gif" ALT="[Search]"></A>
<A HREF="myhome.htm">  <IMG SRC="homeicon.gif" ALT="[Home]"></A>
<A HREF="parent.htm">  <IMG SRC="upicon.gif"   ALT="[Up]"></A>
<A HREF="previous.htm"><IMG SRC="previcon.gif" ALT="[Previous]"></A>
<A HREF="next.htm">    <IMG SRC="nexticon.gif" ALT="[Next]"></A>

</BODY>
</HTML>
```

NEWS RELEASE

On the CD-ROM ...

The example:
examples
    chap4
        news
            news.htm

The template:
recipes
    news
        news.htm

Main Ingredients

A news release makes new information available to the world. It transfers private information to the realm of public knowledge. You can use it to announce your new product, new vice president, or new project.

Recipe

This recipe builds upon the Generic Web page, p. 105.

Our example news release tells about an outreach program by a Boston hospital.

Introduction

Ingredients

Text headings, p. 252

Paragraph, p. 246

> # FOR IMMEDIATE RELEASE
>
> Source: Stewart Milford, Public Relations Director, Community Health Services, Boston, Massachusetts USA
> 30 May 1995, Boston, Massachusetts USA

```
<H2>FOR IMMEDIATE RELEASE</H2>

<P>Source: Stewart Milford, Public Relations Director, Community Health
Services, Boston, Massachusetts USA<BR>
30 May 1995, Boston, Massachusetts USA</P>
```

We wanted our page to appeal to news editors, so we made it resemble a traditional press release. It begins with the tag line telling the news world who wrote the story, when the story was written, and where the story was written.

Details

Ingredients

Paragraph, p. 246

Inline image aligned to text, p. 277

The heart of the news release is a newsworthy story—factual, but told in an interesting style.

The word is out in some of Boston's gang-ravaged neighborhoods. There's a new gang out there. New colors on the street. While these members do prescribe drugs at times, they don't 'deal' and they aren't doing anything illegal. Instead of a handgun, they carry a stethoscope and a common purpose. They are members of Boston's new Community Health Services outreach group, designed to provide low-cost and mostly free health services to some of the city's poorer communities.

Besides offering medical examinations, checkups, immunization, and outpatient services, the group of physicians, nurses, emergency medical technicians, and other health care professionals talks with youths and adults about health-related topics such as nutrition and the dangers of drug and alcohol abuse.

The Community Health Services outreach group is a volunteer service funded mostly through grants from Boston-area hospitals and through personal donations.

```
<IMG SRC="picture.gif" ALT="[Image of Docs in Da Hood]" ALIGN=RIGHT>
<P>The word is out in some of Boston's gang-ravaged neighborhoods.
There's a new gang out there.  New colors on the street.  While these
members do prescribe drugs at times, they don't 'deal' and they aren't
doing anything illegal.  Instead of a handgun, they carry a stethoscope
and a common purpose.  They are members of Boston's new Community
```

```
Health Services outreach group, designed to provide low-cost and mostly
free health services to some of the city's poorer communities.</P>
<P>Besides offering medical examinations, checkups, immunization, and
outpatient services, the group of physicians, nurses, emergency medical
technicians, and other health care professionals, talks with youths and
adults about health-related topics such as nutrition and the dangers of
drug and alcohol abuse.</P>
<P>The Community Health Services outreach group is a volunteer service
funded mostly through grants from Boston-area hospitals and through
personal donations.</P>
```

As with all news stories, the copy answers the questions who, what, when, where, and why. An image of one of the Docs in Da Hood helps reinforce the content of the news story.

Offer of more information

Ingredients

Keep the news release brief, but offer complete details to news editors and others who may want them.

For more information

Stewart Milford, Public Relations Director
Community Health Services
1 Any Street
Boston, Massachusetts USA 99999
617-555-5555
CHSOR@dahood.doc.com

```
<H2>For more information</H2>
<ADDRESS>
Stewart Milford, Public Relations Director<BR>
Community Health Services<BR>
1 Any Street<BR>
Boston, Massachusetts USA 99999<BR>
617-555-5555<BR>
<A HREF="MAILTO:CHSOR@dahood.doc.com">CHSOR@dahood.doc.com</A><BR>
</ADDRESS>
```

As with all news stories, additional contact information follows. The difference from a paper press release is that a news editor or any other reader can send electronic mail directly to the author of the document.

Tips for better new releases

In the world of paper, press releases are sent to newspaper, magazine, and TV editors in the hopes that these editors will recognize the newsworthiness of the information and include it in their news coverage. The news release produced with this recipe may serve a similar role—enticing news editors. In the electronic world, however, the news-receiving public is more likely to access your news release directly. In fact, Web-based news organizations may link to your release rather than incorporating it into their own documents. This means you must decide which audience is more important, news editors or news readers, and slant the resulting Web page accordingly.

Include links to other places. This example could link to the sponsoring hospital's home page; a biography page that lists all the volunteers for this community project; a community bulletin board; a schedule of where these volunteers will be for the next month; and a form that users can complete to arrange to make donations to the project.

HTML code

```
<HTML>

<!------------------------------------------------------------------->
<!--     AUTHOR:   Nancy Hoft                                     -->
<!--     E-MAIL:   CHSOR@dahood.doc.com                           -->
<!--     CREATED:  03 APRIL 1995                                  -->
<!--     MODIFIED: 08 MAY 1995                                    -->
<!--     FILE:     news.htm                                       -->
<!--     PURPOSE:  Press Release, "Docs in Da Hood               -->
<!------------------------------------------------------------------->

<HEAD>
<TITLE>Docs in Da Hood</TITLE>
</HEAD>

<BODY>

[<A HREF="contents.htm">Contents</A>]
[<A HREF="map.htm">Map</A>]
[<A HREF="myindex.htm">Index</A>]
[<A HREF="comment.htm">Comment</A>]
[<A HREF="search.htm">Search</A>]
[<A HREF="myhome.htm">Home</A>]
[<A HREF="parent.htm">Up</A>]
[<A HREF="previous.htm">Previous</A>]
[<A HREF="next.htm">Next</A>]

<HR SIZE=2>

<IMG SRC="docshood.gif" ALT="[emblem text]"><BR>
<H1> Docs in Da Hood </H1>

<P>Location:
[<A HREF="CHSindex.htm">CHS home</A>]
[<A HREF="communty.htm">Community</A>]
[<A HREF="news.htm">News</A>]
Docs in Da Hood </P>

<HR SIZE=4>

<H2>FOR IMMEDIATE RELEASE</H2>
```

```
<P>Source: Stewart Milford, Public Relations Director, Community Health
Services, Boston, Massachusetts USA<BR>
30 May 1995, Boston, Massachusetts USA</P>

<IMG SRC="doc.gif" ALT="[text]" ALIGN=RIGHT>

<P>The word is out in some of Boston's gang-ravaged neighborhoods.
There's a new gang out there. New colors on the street. While these
members do prescribe drugs at times, they don't 'deal' and they aren't
doing anything illegal. Instead of a handgun, they carry a stethoscope
and a common purpose. They are members of Boston's new Community
Health Services outreach group, designed to provide low-cost and mostly
free health services to some of the city's poorer communities.</P>
<P>Besides offering medical examinations, checkups, immunization, and
outpatient services, the group of physicians, nurses, emergency medical
technicians, and other health care professionals talks with youths and
adults about health-related topics such as nutrition and the dangers of
drug and alcohol abuse.</P>
<P>The Community Health Services outreach group is a volunteer service
funded mostly through grants from Boston-area hospitals and through
personal donations.</P>

<H2>For more information</H2>
<ADDRESS>
Stewart Milford, Public Relations Director<BR>
Community Health Services<BR>
1 Any Street<BR>
Boston, Massachusetts USA 99999<BR>
617-555-5555<BR>
<A HREF="MAILTO:CHSOR@dahood.doc.com">CHSOR@dahood.doc.com</A><BR>
</ADDRESS>

<HR SIZE=2>

http://www.chsor.com/news.htm -- Revised: 08 APRIL 1995<BR>
Copyright &copy; 1995 <A HREF="chsor.htm">Community Health
Services</A><BR>
<A HREF="MAILTO:CHSOR@dahood.doc.com">CHSOR@dahood.doc.com</A><BR>

<HR SIZE=2>

<A HREF="contents.htm"><IMG SRC="cntsicon.gif" ALT="[Contents]"></A>
<A HREF="map.htm">     <IMG SRC="mapicon.gif"  ALT="[Map]"></A>
<A HREF="myindex.htm"> <IMG SRC="indxicon.gif" ALT="[Index]"></A>
<A HREF="comment.htm"> <IMG SRC="cmnticon.gif" ALT="[Comment]"></A>
<A HREF="search.htm">  <IMG SRC="srchicon.gif" ALT="[Search]"></A>
<A HREF="myhome.htm">  <IMG SRC="homeicon.gif" ALT="[Home]"></A>
<A HREF="parent.htm">  <IMG SRC="upicon.gif"   ALT="[Up]"></A>
<A HREF="previous.htm"><IMG SRC="previcon.gif" ALT="[Previous]"></A>
<A HREF="next.htm">    <IMG SRC="nexticon.gif" ALT="[Next]"></A>

</BODY>
</HTML>
```

ORGANIZATION PAGE

On the CD-ROM ...

The example:
examples
  chap4
    organiz
      organiz.htm

The template:
recipes
  organiz
    organiz.htm

Main Ingredients

Generic Web page, p. 105

Text headings, p. 252

Definition list, p. 261

Inline image aligned relative
  to text, p. 277

Simple inline image, p. 276

Use the Organization Page to describe your company, a club you belong to, or your university department.

An organization page focuses on the organization and its purpose, mission statement, and history. It is not the same as the home page for an organization. A home page is the top-level page at your Web site and typically contains links to other Web pages, such as an organization page.

Recipe

This recipe builds upon the Generic Web page, p. 105.

This is the Organization Page for Rustic Homes Real Estate, a part of a chain of real estate firms.

Highlights

Ingredients

Text headings, p. 252

Definition list, p. 261

The Highlights section provides a quick summary of the organization.

Highlights

Name
:   Rustic Homes Real Estate
Part of
:   The Country Life Real Estate Group
Address
:   Tangiriro Mountain Road
    Seattle, Washington USA 98116
    206-555-4444
Best known for
:   The Country Lifestyle Home Searches
    Unique Home Offerings
President
:   Lawrence Simms

```
<H2>Highlights</H2>
<DL>
<DT>Name
<DD> Rustic Homes Real Estate
<DT>Part of
<DD>The Country Life Real Estate Group
<DT>Address
<DD>Tangiriro Mountain Road
<DD>Seattle, Washington USA 98116
<DD>206-555-4444
<DT>Best known for
<DD> The Country Lifestyle Home Searches
<DD>Unique Home Offerings
<DT>President
<DD>Lawrence Simms
</DL>
```

We use a definition list to create this easy-to-read summary. Note that this layout is similar to that of the Biography (page 161).

Details

The remainder of the Organization Page provides more information about topics introduced in the Highlights section. It lends credibility to the organization by providing concrete details.

What Rustic Homes Real Estate Does

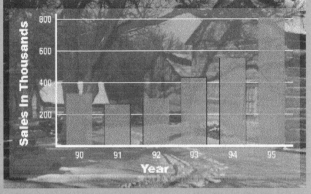

Rustic Homes Real Estate offers home buyers a wide variety of services catering to those looking for specific country and rural homes. As part of the Country Life Real Estate Group, Rustic Homes can provide a database listing of rural and country homes available throughout the United States.

Rustic Homes offers sellers nationwide visibility for their properties and a proven sales track record. As shown by this graph, the yearly sales average per agent is over $800,000!

History of Rustic Homes Real Estate

Founded in 1986 to address the growing requests for alternative country and rural real estate offerings, Rustic Homes has grown from a local real estate office to a nationwide company with over 300 agents. Its unique offerings cater to home buyers from all economic levels.

Lawrence Simms, founder and president

Lawrence Simms is one of the most successful real estate brokers in the United States. As the founder and President of the Country Life Real Estate Group, Mr. Simms has achieved a reputation for reviving the USA's rural and country homes real estate business. His firms, which include Rustic Homes Real Estate, are noted for best of class customer service.

Mr. Simms is active in community and professional associations. He is founder of the Rustic Home Owners and Builders Association of Seattle (RHOBAS) as well as honorary fellow of the International Country Living Society. He has served as an unpaid consultant to the Washington State Real Estate Commission for the past five years.

```
<H2>What Rustic Homes Real Estate Does</H2>

<IMG SRC="organiz.gif" ALT="[text]" ALIGN=RIGHT>

<P> Rustic Homes Real Estate offers home buyers a wide variety of
services catering to those looking for specific country and rural
homes.  As part of the Country Life Real Estate Group, Rustic Homes can
provide a database listing of rural and country homes available
throughout the USA.</P>
```

```
<P>Rustic Homes offers sellers nationwide visibility for their
properties and a proven sales track record. As shown by this graph, the
yearly sales average per agent is over $800,000!</P>

<H2>History of Rustic Homes Real Estate</H2>

<P>Founded in 1986 to address the growing requests for alternative
country and rural real estate offerings, Rustic Homes has grown from a
local real estate office to a nationwide company with over 300 agents.
Its unique offerings cater to home buyers from all economic levels.</P>

<H2>Lawrence Simms, founder and president</H2>

<IMG SRC="biophoto.gif" ALT="[text]">

<P> Lawrence Simms is one of the most successful real estate brokers in
the United States.  As the founder and President of the Country Life
Real Estate Group, Mr. Simms has achieved a reputation for reviving the
USA's rural and country homes real estate business.  His firms, which
include Rustic Homes Real Estate, are noted for best of class customer
service. </P>
<P> Mr Simms is active in community and professional associations. He
is founder of the Rustic Home Owners and Builders Association of
Seattle (RHOBAS) as well as honorary fellow of the International
Country Living Society. He has served as an unpaid consultant to the
Washington State Real Estate Commission for the past five years. </P>
```

Tips for great organization pages

Make your description complete. An organization page should answer these types of questions for users who visit your Web site:

- How long have you been in business?

- Are you associated with a larger business unit?

- How are you better than your competition?

- Who is in charge of your organization?

- What is your business philosophy?

The variations you use are limited only by your imagination. You could add links to the annual report, the stock market listing, the home page for the company, a family trip, and even a club conference announcement.

The HTML code

```
<HTML>

<!------------------------------------------------------------------------>
<!--    AUTHOR:   Lawrence Simms                                       -->
<!--    E-MAIL:   rustic@homes.com                                     -->
<!--    CREATED:  03 APRIL 1995                                        -->
<!--    MODIFIED: 08 MAY 1995                                          -->
<!--    FILE:     organiz.htm                                          -->
<!--    PURPOSE:  About Rustic Homes Real Estate                       -->
<!------------------------------------------------------------------------>

<HEAD>
<TITLE>Rustic Homes Real Estate</TITLE>
</HEAD>

<BODY>

[<A HREF="contents.htm">Contents</A>]
[<A HREF="map.htm">Map</A>]
[<A HREF="myindex.htm">Index</A>]
[<A HREF="comment.htm">Comment</A>]
[<A HREF="search.htm">Search</A>]
[<A HREF="myhome.htm">Home</A>]
[<A HREF="parent.htm">Up</A>]
[<A HREF="previous.htm">Previous</A>]
[<A HREF="next.htm">Next</A>]

<HR SIZE=2>

<IMG SRC="r_homes.gif" ALT="[emblem text]"><BR>
<H1> Rustic Homes Real Estate </H1>

<P>Location:
[<A HREF="clrehome.htm">CLREG home</A>]
[<A HREF="business.htm">Businesses</A>]
[<A HREF="restate.htm">Real estate</A>]
Rustic Homes Real Estate </P>

<HR SIZE=4>

<H2>Highlights</H2>
<DL>
<DT>Name
<DD> Rustic Homes Real Estate
<DT>Part of
<DD>The Country Life Real Estate Group
<DT>Address
<DD>Tangiriro Mountain Road
<DD>Seattle, Washington USA 98116
<DD>206-555-4444
<DT>Best known for
<DD> The Country Lifestyle Home Searches
<DD>Unique Home Offerings
<DT>President
<DD>Lawrence Simms
```

```
</DL>
<H2>What Rustic Homes Real Estate Does</H2>
<IMG SRC="rustic.gif" ALT="[text]" ALIGN=RIGHT>

<P> Rustic Homes Real Estate offers home buyers a wide variety of
services catering to those looking for specific country and rural
homes.  As part of the Country Life Real Estate Group, Rustic Homes can
provide a database listing of rural and country homes available
throughout the USA.</P>
<P>Rustic Homes offers sellers nationwide visibility for their
properties and a proven sales track record. As shown by this graph, the
yearly sales average per agent is over $800,000!</P>

<H2>History of Rustic Homes Real Estate</H2>

<P>Founded in 1986 to address the growing requests for alternative
country and rural real estate offerings, Rustic Homes has grown from a
local real estate office to a nationwide company with over 300 agents.
Its unique offerings cater to home buyers from all economic levels.</P>

<H2>Lawrence Simms, founder and president</H2>

<IMG SRC="larry.gif" ALT="[picture]" ALIGN=LEFT >

<P> Lawrence Simms is one of the most successful real estate brokers in
the United States.  As the founder and President of the Country Life
Real Estate Group, Mr. Simms has achieved a reputation for reviving the
USA's rural and country homes real estate business.  His firms, which
include Rustic Homes Real Estate, are noted for best of class customer
service. </P>
<P> Mr. Simms is active in community and professional associations. He
is founder of the Rustic Home Owners and Builders Association of
Seattle (RHOBAS) as well as honorary fellow of the International
Country Living Society. He has served as an unpaid consultant to the
Washington State Real Estate Commission for the past five years. </P>
<BR>
<BR>
<BR>
<HR SIZE=2>
http://www.rustic.com/organiz.htm -- Revised: 08 MAY 1995<BR>
Copyright &copy; 1995 <A HREF="page.htm">Rustic Homes Real
Estate</A><BR>
<A HREF="MAILTO: rustic@homes.com ">rustic@homes.com</A><BR>

<HR SIZE=2>

<A HREF="contents.htm"><IMG SRC="cntsicon.gif" ALT="[Contents]"></A>
<A HREF="map.htm">      <IMG SRC="mapicon.gif"  ALT="[Map]"></A>
<A HREF="myindex.htm"> <IMG SRC="indxicon.gif" ALT="[Index]"></A>
<A HREF="comment.htm">  <IMG SRC="cmnticon.gif" ALT="[Comment]"></A>
<A HREF="search.htm">   <IMG SRC="srchicon.gif" ALT="[Search]"></A>
<A HREF="myhome.htm">   <IMG SRC="homeicon.gif" ALT="[Home]"></A>
<A HREF="parent.htm">   <IMG SRC="upicon.gif"   ALT="[Up]"></A>
<A HREF="previous.htm"><IMG SRC="previcon.gif" ALT="[Previous]"></A>
<A HREF="next.htm">     <IMG SRC="nexticon.gif" ALT="[Next]"></A>

</BODY>
</HTML>
```

DOWNLOAD MENU

On the CD-ROM ...

The example:
examples
 chap4
  download
   download.htm

The template:
recipes
 download
  download.htm

Main Ingredients

Generic Web page, p. 105

Paragraph, p. 246

Bullet list, p. 256

Text and icon menu, p. 273

Retrieving file via
 anonymous FTP, p. 295

The Download Menu provides a simple, friendly interface to let customers obtain documents, software, and other materials electronically. Many companies set up computer bulletin boards like this so that their customers can download updates to computer programs, related utility programs, detailed documentation, bug fixes, and so forth.

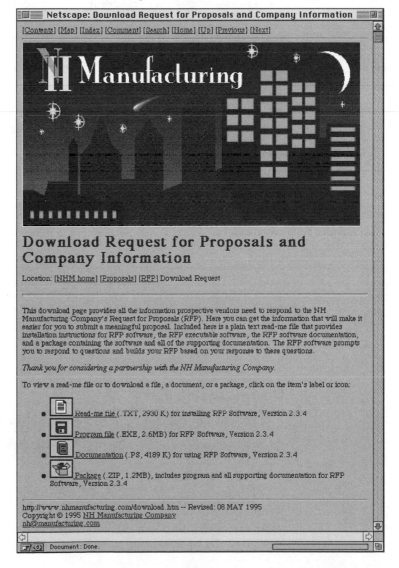

This recipe lets users download read-me files, computer programs, documents, and packages (which can include all these elements bundled as a single file). It assumes that the read-me file is a text-only file and just displays it when selected. For the other items, it downloads the file from an FTP site.

Recipe

This recipe builds upon the Generic Web page, p. 105.

Our example is for the NH Manufacturing Company. It is a download menu for vendors who want to respond to a Request for Proposals (RFP).

Introduction

Ingredients

Paragraph, p. 246

The introduction tells users what they will find on the download menu and thanks them for taking the time to use it.

> This download page provides all the information prospective vendors need to respond to the NH Manufacturing Company's Request for Proposals (RFP). Here you can get the information that will make it easier for you to submit a meaningful proposal. Included here is a plain text read-me file that provides installation instructions for RFP software, the RFP executable software, the RFP software documentation, and a package containing the software and all of the supporting documentation. The RFP software prompts you to respond to questions and builds your RFP based on your response to these questions.
>
> *Thank you for considering a partnership with the NH Manufacturing Company.*

```
<P>This download page provides all the information prospective vendors
need to respond to the NH Manufacturing Company's Request for Proposals
(RFP). Here you can get the information that will make it easier for
you to submit a meaningful proposal. Included here is a plain text
read-me file that provides installation instructions for RFP software,
the RFP executable software, the RFP software documentation, and a
package containing the software and all of the supporting
documentation. The RFP software prompts you to respond to questions and
builds your RFP based on your response to these questions.</P>

<P><I>Thank you for considering a partnership with the NH Manufacturing
Company. </I></P>
```

Downloadable files

Ingredients

Text-and-icon menu, p. 273

Retrieving file via
  anonymous FTP, p. 295

Instructions tell the user how to download the files.

> To view a read-me file or to download a file, a document, or a package, click on the item's label or icon:

```
<P>To view a read-me file or to download a file, a document, or a
package, click on the item's label or icon:</P>
```

For executable files, the browser displays a standard file menu that lets users name and choose a directory for the file on their local disk. For other file types, the browser will search for a suitable viewer depending on the file type (GIF, MPEG, PS, etc.) and display or run the file with the appropriate helper application. If users want to download the files and open them later, they must first select the download-to-disk option in their browsers and then click on the icon for the file to bring up a window allowing them to download the files to their local disk.

In our download example, each file uses an icon representing the kind of file it is. There are four icons: one for read-me files; one for executables; one for formatted documentation, which is often in PostScript format; and one for a bundled package that includes everything in a single file.

For each file type, always specify the file's format and the size of the file in bytes. Users need to know this information so that they can evaluate whether they can run or view it once they have downloaded it, how long the download will take, and how much disk space it will require.

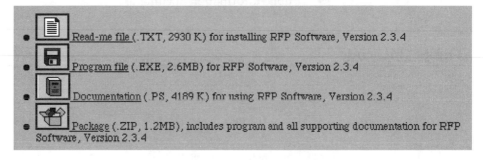

The bullets paired with the icons may not be to your liking. Try removing the <UL>, </UL> and <LI> tags, put the entire contents between <P> ... </P> tags, and add a <BR> tag after each list item.

```
<UL>
<LI><A HREF="readme.txt"><IMG SRC="readme.gif" ALT="[read me]">
Read me file </A>(.TXT, 2930 K) for installing RFP Software, Version
2.3.4
<LI><A HREF="FTP://ftp.nhmanufacturing.com/ftp/consulting/rfp.exe "><IMG
SRC="software.gif" ALT="[software]"> Program file</A> (.EXE, 2.6MB) for
RFP Software, Version 2.3.4
<LI><A HREF=" FTP://ftp.what.ever/rfp/consulting/ftp.ps "><IMG
SRC="document.gif" ALT="[document]"> Documentation</A> (.PS, 4189 K)
for using RFP Software, Version 2.3.4
<LI><A HREF="
FTP://ftp.nhmanufacturing.com/ftp/consulting/rfp.zip"><IMG
SRC="package.gif" ALT="[package]"> Package</A> (.ZIP, 1.2MB), includes
program and all supporting documentation for RFP Software, Version
2.3.4
</UL>
```

The link uses FTP (file transfer protocol) to download the file. We made both the icon and text part of the link, so users can click on either to begin the transfer.

Tips for great download menus

Use the Download Menu to make all kinds of computer media available:

- Computer games

- Homework assignments

- Scholarly notes and papers

- Speaker notes and handouts as a follow-up to a presentation

- Bug patches for computer software

- Recipes for friends in the community

- Public-information documents

The HTML code

```
<HTML>

<!------------------------------------------------------------->
<!--     AUTHOR:    Nancy Hoft                              -->
<!--     E-MAIL:    itech@mv.mv.com                         -->
<!--     CREATED:   05 APRIL 1995                           -->
<!--     MODIFIED:  08 MAY1995                              -->
<!--     FILE:      download.htm                            -->
<!--     PURPOSE:   Download Request for                    -->
<!--                Proposals and Company Info              -->
<!------------------------------------------------------------->

<HEAD>
<TITLE>Download Request for Proposals and Company Information</TITLE>
</HEAD>

<BODY>

[<A HREF="contents.htm">Contents</A>]
[<A HREF="map.htm">Map</A>]
[<A HREF="myindex.htm">Index</A>]
[<A HREF="comment.htm">Comment</A>]
[<A HREF="search.htm">Search</A>]
[<A HREF="myhome.htm">Home</A>]
[<A HREF="parent.htm">Up</A>]
[<A HREF="previous.htm">Previous</A>]
[<A HREF="next.htm">Next</A>]

<HR SIZE=2>

<IMG SRC="nhmanuf.gif" ALT="[emblem text]"><BR>
<H1> Download Request for Proposals and Company Information </H1>

<P>Location:
[<A HREF="nhmindex.htm">NHM home</A>]
```

```
[<A HREF="proposal.htm">Proposals</A>]
[<A HREF="rfp.htm">RFP</A>]
Download Request</P>

<HR SIZE=4>

<P>This download page provides all the information prospective vendors
need to respond to the NH Manufacturing Company's Request for Proposals
(RFP). Here you can get the information that will make it easier for
you to submit a meaningful proposal. Included here is a plain text
read-me file that provides installation instructions for RFP software,
the RFP executable software, the RFP software documentation, and a
package containing the software and all of the supporting
documentation. The RFP software prompts you to respond to questions and
builds your RFP based on your response to these questions.</P>

<P><I>Thank you for considering a partnership with the NH Manufacturing
Company. </I></P>
<P>To view a read-me file or to download a file, a document, or a
package, click on the item's label or icon:</P>

<UL>
<LI><A HREF="readme.txt"><IMG SRC="readme.gif" ALT="[read me]">
Read-me file </A>(.TXT, 2930 K) for installing RFP Software, Version
2.3.4
<LI><A HREF="FTP://ftp.nhmanufacturing.com/ftp/consulting/rfp.exe"><IMG
SRC="software.gif" ALT="[software]"> Program file</A> (.EXE, 2.6MB) for
RFP Software, Version 2.3.4
<LI><A HREF=" FTP://ftp.what.ever/rfp/consulting/ftp.ps"><IMG
SRC="document.gif" ALT="[document]"> Documentation</A> (.PS, 4189 K)
for using RFP Software, Version 2.3.4
<LI><A HREF="
FTP://ftp.nhmanufacturing.com/ftp/consulting/rfp.zip"><IMG
SRC="package.gif" ALT="[package]"> Package</A> (.ZIP, 1.2MB), includes
program and all supporting documentation for RFP Software, Version
2.3.4
</UL>

<HR SIZE=2>

http://www.nhmanufacturing.com/download.htm -- Revised: 08 MAY 1995<BR>
Copyright &copy; 1995 <A HREF="homepage.htm"> NH Manufacturing
Company</A><BR>
<A HREF="MAILTO:nh@manufacturing.com">nh@manufacturing.com</A><BR>

<HR SIZE=2>

<A HREF="contents.htm"><IMG SRC="cntsicon.gif" ALT="[Contents]"></A>
<A HREF="map.htm">     <IMG SRC="mapicon.gif"  ALT="[Map]"></A>
<A HREF="myindex.htm"> <IMG SRC="indxicon.gif" ALT="[Index]"></A>
<A HREF="comment.htm"> <IMG SRC="cmnticon.gif" ALT="[Comment]"></A>
<A HREF="search.htm">  <IMG SRC="srchicon.gif" ALT="[Search]"></A>
<A HREF="myhome.htm">  <IMG SRC="homeicon.gif" ALT="[Home]"></A>
<A HREF="parent.htm">  <IMG SRC="upicon.gif"   ALT="[Up]"></A>
<A HREF="previous.htm"><IMG SRC="previcon.gif" ALT="[Previous]"></A>
<A HREF="next.htm">    <IMG SRC="nexticon.gif" ALT="[Next]"></A>

</BODY>
</HTML>
```

REGISTRATION FORM

Main Ingredients

Generic Web page, p. 105

Text headings, p. 252

Form, p. 359

Preformatted text, p. 247

Text field, p. 365

Radio buttons, p. 369

Preformatted text, p. 247

Selection list, p. 374

Checkboxes, p. 371

Text area, p. 367

Reset button, p. 361

Submit button, p. 361

As with all forms, you need to provide programming to gather and process the data collected on a form. See page 376 for more information about scripting forms.

The Registration Form lets users register as the proud owners of one of your products. It also lets you capture opinions that may provide valuable insights as to how to market similar products.

Recipe

This recipe builds upon the Generic Web page, p. 105.

This example, a fill-in-the-blanks form for registering a CD-ROM collection, uses several HTML tags for creating forms.

Form

Ingredients

Form, p. 359

The form section of the page is marked with these tags

```
<FORM METHOD="POST" ACTION="http://www.cdstuff.com/cgi-bin/register1">

</FORM>
```

The METHOD and ACTION attributes say what happens when the user submits the form. The ACTION is the program that handles the results for you. Page 360 will show you how to set up such programs.

Introduction

Ingredients

Paragraph, p. 246

The form begins with a brief welcome and thank you message.

> Thank you for taking the time to register your purchase. By registering you ensure that you will be notified of new releases and special offers. Please fill in all the items below.

```
<P>Thank you for taking the time to register your purchase. By
registering you ensure that you will be notified of new releases and
special offers. Please fill in all the items below.</P>
```

Name

Ingredients

Text heading, p. 252

Text field,, p. 365

Radio buttons, p. 369

In the Name section, the user specifies—you guessed it—his or her name.

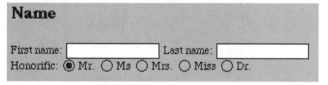

Although there is a lot of coding here, fret not. You will probably not have to change much for your form.

```
<H2>Name</H2>
First name: <INPUT TYPE="TEXT" NAME="name_first" SIZE=15>
Last name: <INPUT TYPE="TEXT" NAME="name_last" SIZE=15><BR>
Honorific:
<INPUT TYPE="RADIO" NAME="honorific" VALUE="Mr" CHECKED>Mr.
<INPUT TYPE="RADIO" NAME="honorific" VALUE="Ms ">Ms
<INPUT TYPE="RADIO" NAME="honorific" VALUE="Mrs">Mrs.
<INPUT TYPE="RADIO" NAME="honorific" VALUE="Miss">Miss
<INPUT TYPE="RADIO" NAME="honorific" VALUE="Dr ">Dr.<BR>
```

To allow more or fewer characters in a name, change the number in the SIZE= parameter. To change which honorific is the default, move the CHECKED parameter to a different line.

Address

The Address section lets users specify their address for paper and electronic mail and which to use for correspondence.

Address

Title	
Organization	
Street address	
City	
State or Prov	Postal Code
Country	
Phone	
Fax	
E-mail address	

Notify by:
(●) E-mail ( ) Fax ( ) Mail ( ) Phone

```
<H2>Address </H2>
<PRE>
Title          <INPUT TYPE="TEXT" NAME="title" SIZE=40> <BR>
Organization   <INPUT TYPE="TEXT" NAME="organiz" SIZE=40> <BR>
Street address <INPUT TYPE="TEXT" NAME="street_addr" SIZE=40> <BR>
City           <INPUT TYPE="TEXT" NAME="city" SIZE=40> <BR>
State or Prov  <INPUT TYPE="TEXT" NAME="state" SIZE=11>  Postal Code
<INPUT TYPE="TEXT" NAME="title" SIZE=14> <BR>
Country        <INPUT TYPE="TEXT" NAME="country" SIZE=40> <BR>
Phone          <INPUT TYPE="TEXT" NAME="phone" SIZE=40><BR>
Fax            <INPUT TYPE="TEXT" NAME="fax" SIZE=40><BR>
E-mail address <INPUT TYPE="TEXT" NAME="e-mail" SIZE=40><BR>
</PRE>
Notify by:
<BR>
<INPUT TYPE="RADIO" NAME="notify_by" VALUE="e-mail" CHECKED>E-mail
<INPUT TYPE="RADIO" NAME="notify_by" VALUE="fax">Fax
<INPUT TYPE="RADIO" NAME="notify_by" VALUE="mail">Mail
<INPUT TYPE="RADIO" NAME="notify_by" VALUE="phone">Phone<BR>
```

Like the Name section, this one uses labeled data-entry fields and radio buttons. The <PRE> and </PRE> tags set text in a fixed-width font so that fields and their labels line up properly.

Product

The Product section lets users specify which product they are registering.

```
<H2>Product</H2>
Which product are you registering?
<SELECT NAME="product">
<OPTION SELECTED>GIF CD-ROM collection
<OPTION> Music clips CD-ROM collection
<OPTION>Sound effects CD-ROM collection
<OPTION>MPEG clips CD-ROM collection
<OPTION>EPS CD-ROM collection
</SELECT><BR>
```

Here the `<OPTION>` tags list the user's choices. The `SELECTED` attribute marks the one that is the default.

Comments

The Comments section invites users to say why they bought the product. It lets them check off reasons from a list of common reasons and enter additional comments as well.

Comments

Why did you buy this product? (Check all that apply.)
- ☐ Quality
- ☐ Low cost
- ☐ Reliability
- ☐ Convenience
- ☐ Reputation of manufacturer

Comments on our products and services:

```
<H2>Comments</H2>
Why did you buy this product? (Check all that apply.)<BR>
<INPUT TYPE="CHECKBOX" NAME="quality">Quality <BR>
<INPUT TYPE="CHECKBOX" NAME="cost">Low cost <BR>
<INPUT TYPE="CHECKBOX" NAME="reliability">Reliability <BR>
<INPUT TYPE="CHECKBOX" NAME="styling">Convenience<BR>
<INPUT TYPE="CHECKBOX" NAME="reputation">Reputation of manufacturer
<P>Comments on our products and services:
<TEXTAREA NAME="comments" ROWS="5" COLS="65">
```

```
</TEXTAREA><BR></P>
```

The options are presented with checkboxes, allowing users to check off more than one option. The Comments section also includes a text area where users can type in free-form comments, suggestions, or off-color jokes—anything they'd like.

Action buttons

This form—and most others, too—ends with buttons to let users say what to do with the information they entered into the form. In our example the user has two choices: Process the entries or forget them.

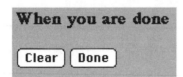

```
<H2>When you are done</H2>
<INPUT TYPE="RESET" VALUE="Clear"> <INPUT TYPE="SUBMIT" VALUE="Done">
```

Here, the Clear button erases the entries, clearing the form. The Done button submits the entries—sending them to the program listed in the ACTION= parameter in the <FORM> tag.

Tips for great registration forms

You can modify the Registration Form for other purposes. You can use it to:

- Register people for a conference.

- Make reservations at a hotel.

- Let users order products or solicit information from you.

- Build a mailing list of people interested in a particular issue.

HTML code

```
<HTML>

<!------------------------------------------------------------->
<!--    AUTHOR:   Nancy Hoft                                 -->
<!--    E-MAIL:   itech@mv.mv.com                            -->
<!--    CREATED:  14 APRIL 1995                              -->
<!--    MODIFIED: 08 MAY 1995                                -->
<!--    FILE:     register.htm                               -->
<!--    PURPOSE:  CD-ROM Collection of Stuff                 -->
<!------------------------------------------------------------->

<HEAD>
<TITLE> CD-ROM Collection of Stuff Registration Form</TITLE>
</HEAD>

<BODY>

[<A HREF="contents.htm">Contents</A>]
[<A HREF="map.htm">Map</A>]
[<A HREF="myindex.htm">Index</A>]
[<A HREF="comment.htm">Comment</A>]
[<A HREF="search.htm">Search</A>]
[<A HREF="myhome.htm">Home</A>]
[<A HREF="parent.htm">Up</A>]
[<A HREF="previous.htm">Previous</A>]
[<A HREF="next.htm">Next</A>]

<HR SIZE=2>

<IMG SRC="cd-rom.gif" ALT="[emblem text]"><BR>
<H1> CD-ROM Collection of Stuff Registration Form</H1>

<P>Location:
[<A HREF="cdsindex.htm">CDS home</A>]
[<A HREF="sales.htm">Sales</A>]
[<A HREF="customer.htm">Customer</A>]
Registration Form </P>

<HR SIZE=4>

<FORM METHOD="POST" ACTION="http://www.cdstuff.com/cgi-bin/register1">

<P>Thank you for taking the time to register your purchase. By
registering you ensure that you will be notified of new releases and
special offers. Please fill in all the items below.</P>

<H2>Name</H2>
First name: <INPUT TYPE="TEXT" NAME="name_first" SIZE=15>
Last name: <INPUT TYPE="TEXT" NAME="name_last" SIZE=15><BR>
Honorific:
<INPUT TYPE="RADIO" NAME="honorific" VALUE="Mr" CHECKED>Mr.
<INPUT TYPE="RADIO" NAME="honorific" VALUE="Ms">Ms
<INPUT TYPE="RADIO" NAME="honorific" VALUE="Mrs">Mrs.
<INPUT TYPE="RADIO" NAME="honorific" VALUE="Miss">Miss
<INPUT TYPE="RADIO" NAME="honorific" VALUE="Dr">Dr.<BR>
```

```
<H2>Address</H2>
<PRE>
Title          <INPUT TYPE="TEXT" NAME="title" SIZE=35> <BR>
Organization   <INPUT TYPE="TEXT" NAME="organiz" SIZE=35> <BR>
Street address <INPUT TYPE="TEXT" NAME="street_addr" SIZE=35> <BR>
City           <INPUT TYPE="TEXT" NAME="city" SIZE=35> <BR>
State or Prov  <INPUT TYPE="TEXT" NAME="state" SIZE=11> Postal Code
<INPUT TYPE="TEXT" NAME="pcode" SIZE=11> <BR>
Country        <INPUT TYPE="TEXT" NAME="country" SIZE=35> <BR>
Phone          <INPUT TYPE="TEXT" NAME="phone" SIZE=35><BR>
Fax            <INPUT TYPE="TEXT" NAME="fax" SIZE=35><BR>
E-mail address <INPUT TYPE="TEXT" NAME="e-mail" SIZE=35><BR>
</PRE>
Notify by:
<BR>
<INPUT TYPE="RADIO" NAME="notify_by" VALUE="e-mail" CHECKED>E-mail
<INPUT TYPE="RADIO" NAME="notify_by" VALUE="fax">Fax
<INPUT TYPE="RADIO" NAME="notify_by" VALUE="mail">Mail
<INPUT TYPE="RADIO" NAME="notify_by" VALUE="phone">Phone<BR>

<H2>Product</H2>
Which product are you registering?
<SELECT NAME="product">
<OPTION SELECTED>GIF CD-ROM collection
<OPTION> Music clips CD-ROM collection
<OPTION>Sound effects CD-ROM collection
<OPTION>MPEG clips CD-ROM collection
<OPTION>EPS CD-ROM collection
</SELECT><BR>

<H2>Comments</H2>
Why did you buy this product? (Check all that apply.)<BR>
<INPUT TYPE="CHECKBOX" NAME="quality">Quality <BR>
<INPUT TYPE="CHECKBOX" NAME="cost">Low cost <BR>
<INPUT TYPE="CHECKBOX" NAME="reliability">Reliability <BR>
<INPUT TYPE="CHECKBOX" NAME="styling">Convenience<BR>
<INPUT TYPE="CHECKBOX" NAME="reputation">Reputation of manufacturer

<P>Comments on our products and services:</P>
<TEXTAREA NAME="comments" ROWS="5" COLS="65">
</TEXTAREA><BR>

<H2>When you are done</H2>
<INPUT TYPE="RESET" VALUE="Clear"> <INPUT TYPE="SUBMIT" VALUE="Done">
</FORM>

<HR SIZE=2>

http://www.cdroms.com/register.htm -- Revised: 8 MAY 1995<BR>
Copyright &copy; 1995 <A HREF="page.htm">CD-ROM Stuff</A><BR>
<A HREF="MAILTO:cd@stuff.com">cd@stuff.com</A><BR>

<HR SIZE=2>

<A HREF="contents.htm"><IMG SRC="cntsicon.gif" ALT="[Contents]"></A>
<A HREF="map.htm">    <IMG SRC="mapicon.gif"  ALT="[Map]"></A>
<A HREF="myindex.htm"> <IMG SRC="indxicon.gif" ALT="[Index]"></A>
<A HREF="comment.htm"> <IMG SRC="cmnticon.gif" ALT="[Comment]"></A>
<A HREF="search.htm">  <IMG SRC="srchicon.gif" ALT="[Search]"></A>
```

```
<A HREF="myhome.htm">  <IMG SRC="homeicon.gif" ALT="[Home]"></A>
<A HREF="parent.htm">  <IMG SRC="upicon.gif"   ALT="[Up]"></A>
<A HREF="previous.htm"><IMG SRC="previcon.gif" ALT="[Previous]"></A>
<A HREF="next.htm">    <IMG SRC="nexticon.gif" ALT="[Next]"></A>

</BODY>
</HTML>
```

SURVEY FORM

The Survey Form is a valuable instrument for your company. With it, you can collect all sorts of data from a wide range of users from all over the world.

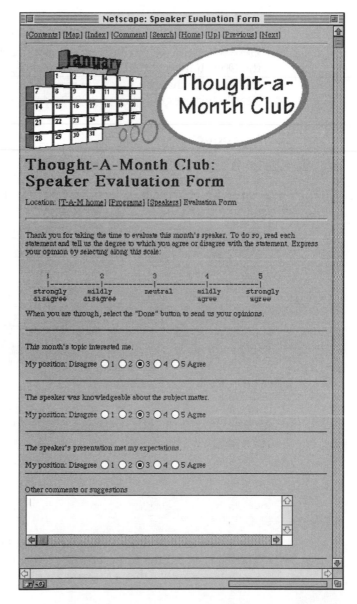

Recipe

This recipe builds upon the Generic Web page, p. 105.

Our example gathers the opinions of club members by using a rating scale to rate a speaker's presentation and a text area where members can type comments.

Ingredients

Forms, p. 359

The form portion of the page is within these tags:

```
<FORM METHOD="POST" ACTION="http://www.thoughtamonthclub.com/cgi-
bin/survey">

</FORM>
```

Here the MEHTOD= attribute specifies what happens when the user clicks the Done button at the end of the survey. The ACTION= attribute specifies the program that processes the results. You, or your service provider, must supply this program. See page 359, for more on forms.

Introduction

Ingredients

Paragraph, p. 246

Preformatted text, p. 247

Start by welcoming the survey takers, explaining the rating method, and telling the survey takers how to submit their opinions. The ratings are numeric, which will make it easy for a software program to gather, tabulate, and analyze the results.

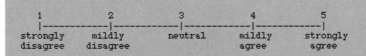

```
<P>Thank you for taking the time to evaluate this month's speaker.
To do so, read each statement and tell us the degree to which you
agree or disagree with the statement. Express your opinion by
selecting along this scale:</P>
<PRE>
      1             2             3             4             5
  |------------|------------|------------|------------|
   strongly      mildly       neutral       mildly       strongly
   disagree      disagree                    agree        agree
</PRE>
<P>When you are through, select the "Done" button to send us your
opinions.</P>
```

The rating scale is done as formatted text inside <PRE> and </PRE> tags. These tags keep the browser from reformatting the text. Why draw the scale in text rather than as a true graphic? Our main reason is to ensure that users with text-only browsers can see this scale. Being text, it also loads more quickly.

Questions

Each question in the survey has the same simple structure. Here's the first question:

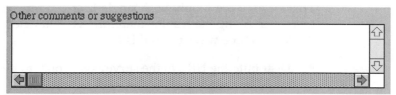

```
<HR SIZE=1>
<BR>
This month's topic interested me.
<BR>
<BR>
My position: Disagree
<INPUT TYPE="RADIO" NAME="issue1" VALUE="1">1
<INPUT TYPE="RADIO" NAME="issue1" VALUE="2">2
<INPUT TYPE="RADIO" NAME="issue1" VALUE="3" CHECKED>3
<INPUT TYPE="RADIO" NAME="issue1" VALUE="4">4
<INPUT TYPE="RADIO" NAME="issue1" VALUE="5">5
Agree
<BR>
<BR>
```

A horizontal rule `<HR SIZE=1>` separates questions from one another and line breaks `<BR>` force vertical separation between the question and the radio buttons used to enter an answer. To make the neutral opinion the default, we include the `CHECKED` parameter within its tag.

Comments

The survey form includes a text-entry area for free-form comments.

```
<P>Other comments or suggestions

<TEXTAREA NAME="comments" ROWS="4" COLS="60">
</TEXTAREA></P>
```

This free-form area complements the rating scale nicely, allowing users to enter comments that are not easily quantified or that address issues you cannot anticipate.

Action button

Ingredients:

Reset button, p. 361

Submit button, p. 361

The form ends with buttons to let the survey taker either submit the form or erase it and start over again.

```
<INPUT TYPE="RESET" VALUE="Reset"> <INPUT TYPE="SUBMIT"
VALUE="Done"><BR>
```

The Reset button lets survey takers erase all of their responses, resetting the answers to their neutral defaults. The Done button sends the answers to the program specified in the ACTION= parameter within the <FORM> tag.

Tips for great survey forms

Test your surveys before making them public on the Web. Ask seven to ten people from various parts of your company or from customer sites to take the survey. Time them. After they take the survey, query them about how the questions were phrased and if they made sense. Incorporate their feedback.

Keep survey questions brief. There are two reasons for this.

- Web users tend not to read long statements, which means that they will not complete your survey.

- If the statement is longer than the number of lines the browser can display, the user will have to scroll back and forth to comprehend the statement. Few users will do this.

This form does not identify the user so that opinions are kept anonymous. This leaves a big loophole. A single user can repeatedly fill in the form, thereby skewing the results; therefore, you may need to restrict access to the form. Three ways to do this are:

- Distribute the URL to the survey page only to the users you want to take the survey.

- Password-protect the survey page. Ask your service provider or system administrator how to do this on your server.

- Take the name of the user's machine (host attribute) from the form and limit one entry per host in the program or script that processes the form data.

Try using an image map instead of a text form to gather survey information from users. See page 383 for information on image maps.

HTML code

```
<HTML>

<!----------------------------------------------------->
<!--     AUTHOR:    Nancy Hoft                    -->
<!--     E-MAIL:    itech@mv.mv.com               -->
<!--     CREATED:   05 APRIL 1995                 -->
<!--     MODIFIED:  08 MAY 1995                   -->
<!--     FILE:      survey.htm                    -->
<!--     PURPOSE:   Survey: Speaker Evaluation    -->
<!----------------------------------------------------->

<HEAD>
<TITLE>Speaker Evaluation Form</TITLE>
</HEAD>

<BODY>

[<A HREF="contents.htm">Contents</A>]
[<A HREF="map.htm">Map</A>]
[<A HREF="myindex.htm">Index</A>]
[<A HREF="comment.htm">Comment</A>]
[<A HREF="search.htm">Search</A>]
[<A HREF="myhome.htm">Home</A>]
[<A HREF="parent.htm">Up</A>]
[<A HREF="previous.htm">Previous</A>]
[<A HREF="next.htm">Next</A>]

<HR SIZE=2>

<IMG SRC="thought.gif" ALT="[emblem text]"><BR>
<H1> Thought-A-Month Club:<BR>Speaker Evaluation Form
</H1>

<P>Location:
[<A HREF="tamindex.htm">T-A-M home</A>]
[<A HREF="programs.htm">Programs</A>]
[<A HREF="speakers.htm">Speakers</A>]
Evaluation Form</P>

<HR SIZE=4>

<FORM METHOD="POST" ACTION="http://www.thoughtamonthclub.com/cgi-
bin/survey">
<P>Thank you for taking the time to evaluate this month's speaker. To
do so, read each statement and tell us the degree to which you agree or
disagree with the statement. Express your opinion by selecting along
this scale:</P>
```

```
<PRE>
       1               2               3               4               5
       |-------------|-------------|-------------|-------------|
    strongly       mildly         neutral        mildly       strongly
    disagree       disagree                       agree         agree
</PRE>
<P>When you are through, select the "Done" button to send us your
opinions.</P>

<HR SIZE=1>
<BR>
This month's topic interested me.
<BR>
<BR>
My position: Disagree
<INPUT TYPE="RADIO" NAME="issue1" VALUE="1">1
<INPUT TYPE="RADIO" NAME="issue1" VALUE="2">2
<INPUT TYPE="RADIO" NAME="issue1" VALUE="3" CHECKED>3
<INPUT TYPE="RADIO" NAME="issue1" VALUE="4">4
<INPUT TYPE="RADIO" NAME="issue1" VALUE="5">5
Agree
<BR>
<BR>

<HR SIZE=1>
<BR>
The speaker was knowledgeable about the subject matter.
<BR>
<BR>
My position: Disagree
<INPUT TYPE="RADIO" NAME="issue2" VALUE="1">1
<INPUT TYPE="RADIO" NAME="issue2" VALUE="2">2
<INPUT TYPE="RADIO" NAME="issue2" VALUE="3" CHECKED>3
<INPUT TYPE="RADIO" NAME="issue2" VALUE="4">4
<INPUT TYPE="RADIO" NAME="issue2" VALUE="5">5
Agree
<BR>
<BR>

<HR SIZE=1>
<BR>
The speaker's presentation met my expectations.
<BR>
<BR>
My position: Disagree
<INPUT TYPE="RADIO" NAME="issue3" VALUE="1">1
<INPUT TYPE="RADIO" NAME="issue3" VALUE="2">2
<INPUT TYPE="RADIO" NAME="issue3" VALUE="3" CHECKED>3
<INPUT TYPE="RADIO" NAME="issue3" VALUE="4">4
<INPUT TYPE="RADIO" NAME="issue3" VALUE="5">5
Agree

<HR SIZE=1>
<BR>
<P>Other comments or suggestions

<TEXTAREA NAME="comments" ROWS="4" COLS="60">
</TEXTAREA></P>

<HR SIZE=1>
```

```
<BR>
<INPUT TYPE="RESET" VALUE="Reset"> <INPUT TYPE="SUBMIT"
VALUE="Done"><BR>
</FORM>

<HR SIZE=2>

http://www.thoughtamonth.com/survey.htm-- Revised: 08 MAY 1995<BR>
Copyright &copy; 1995 <A HREF="page.htm">Thought-A-Month Club</A><BR>
<A HREF="MAILTO:thinking@aboutit.com">thinking@aboutit.com</A><BR>

<HR SIZE=2>

<A HREF="contents.htm"><IMG SRC="cntsicon.gif" ALT="[Contents]"></A>
<A HREF="map.htm">    <IMG SRC="mapicon.gif"  ALT="[Map]"></A>
<A HREF="myindex.htm"> <IMG SRC="indxicon.gif" ALT="[Index]"></A>
<A HREF="comment.htm"> <IMG SRC="cmnticon.gif" ALT="[Comment]"></A>
<A HREF="search.htm">  <IMG SRC="srchicon.gif" ALT="[Search]"></A>
<A HREF="myhome.htm">  <IMG SRC="homeicon.gif" ALT="[Home]"></A>
<A HREF="parent.htm">  <IMG SRC="upicon.gif"   ALT="[Up]"></A>
<A HREF="previous.htm"><IMG SRC="previcon.gif" ALT="[Previous]"></A>
<A HREF="next.htm">    <IMG SRC="nexticon.gif" ALT="[Next]"></A>

</BODY>
</HTML>
```

CATALOG ENTRY

On the CD-ROM ...

The example:
examples
    chap4
        catalog
            catalog.htm

The template:
recipes
    catalog
        catalog.htm

Main ingredients

Generic Web page, p. 105

Text heading, p. 252

Simple inline image, p. 276

Bullet list, p. 256

Definition list, p. 261

The Catalog Entry describes one product and tells the user how to order it. An online catalog is a great idea for a company that wants to expand its sales worldwide.

Recipe

This recipe builds upon the Generic Web page, p. 105.

This catalog entry describes the Center of the World Cartography poster offering.

Slogan and motto

Ingredients

Text heading, p. 252

The content of our example begins with a memorable slogan and the company's trademarked motto.

We put your business on the map and spin the world around YOU!

We'll move latitudes and longitudes for you.®

```
<H2>We put your business on the map and<BR>
spin the world around YOU!</H2>
<I>We'll move latitudes and longitudes for you.</I>&#174;
```

Notice that we used two tricks. We used `<BR>` tag to control the line break in the slogan. Our slogan could lose its punch if the phrase broke in the wrong place.

For other special codes, see p. 315.

The second trick is the nonsensical-looking set of characters `&#174;` which HTML requires to produce the registered trademark symbol ®.

Product

Ingredients

Simple inline image, p. 276

Paragraph, p. 246

We introduce the product with a picture and a concise paragraph.

No one knows more about being lost on the map than we do. Located in the forests of Temple, New Hampshire, Center of the World Cartography struggled for years competing with big-name geographies such as Paris, France; London, England; New York, New York; and Tokyo, Japan. No more! We put our company at the center of the world map and fast became the center of attention. Center of the World Cartography wants your business to experience the same instant success we did. We create custom-designed posters that place your business at the center of the world.

```
<P><IMG SRC="map.gif" ALT="[Image of poster for Center of the World
Cartography]"></P>
<P>No one knows more about being lost on the map than we do. Located in
the forests of Temple, New Hampshire, Center of the World Cartography
struggled for years competing with big-name geographies such as Paris,
France; London, England; New York, New York; and Tokyo, Japan.  No
more! We put our company at the center of the world map and fast became
the center of attention. Center of the World Cartography wants your
business to experience the same instant success we did. We create
custom-designed posters that place your business at the center of the
world.</P>
```

Select a picture that makes the user want to know more about the product; and follow the picture with a brief marketing description—nothing too long. The description should briefly tell how the product can solve a user's problem and present information that lends credibility to both the company and the product. Keep it general because the next two sections are for all the details.

Features

Ingredients

Text headings, p. 252

Bullet list, p. 256

The Features section provides a short bullet list of what makes this product special.

```
<H2>Features</H2>
<UL>
<LI>Puts your company literally at the center of the world map!
<LI>Made of high-quality, heavyweight, recycled paper
<LI>Four-color printing with soy-based inks
<LI>Created using state-of-the-art cartographic software
</UL>
```

Specifications

Ingredients

Definition list, p. 261

Text heading, p. 252

The Specifications section is for all the technical details of the product.

```
<H2>Specifications</H2>
<DL>
<DT><B>Size</B>
<DD>11 inches x 17 inches (27.94 centimeters x 43.18 centimeters)
<DT><B>Paper</B>
<DD>Heavyweight, recycled paper made of 100% post-consumer waste
</DL>
```

Ordering Information

Ingredients

Text heading, p. 252

Paragraph, p. 246

At the end of the page, we tell the user how to order the product.

Ordering information

Poster Map, POSTER-110761
Price: $75 USD

```
<H2>Ordering information</H2>
<P>Poster Map, POSTER-110761<BR>
Price: $75 USD</P>
```

Tips for great catalogs

Remember, the Web is a multimedia environment. Don't just show users what the product looks like, but also link to an online demo. Allow users to interact with a prototype of your product. Link to a video clip that shows satisfied customers using your product.

If the technical specifications are really long and complex, consider making the main headings links to other Web pages that contain the detailed data summarized under the headings.

Some popular Web pages include customer testimonials. What do other customers say about your product? You can include just text information, or get fancy by including real audio clips from your customers. Consider showing a photograph of your customers to make testimonials more affective and credible to the user.

HTML code

```
<HTML>

<!------------------------------------------------------------>
<!--    AUTHOR:    Nancy Hoft                              -->
<!--    E-MAIL:    itech@mv.mv.com                         -->
<!--    CREATED:   03 APRIL 1995                           -->
<!--    MODIFIED:  07 MAY1995                              -->
<!--    FILE:      catalog.htm                             -->
<!--    PURPOSE:   Center of the World Cartography         -->
<!--               Poster Collection                       -->
<!------------------------------------------------------------>
```

```
<HEAD>
<TITLE>Center of the World Cartography Poster Collection</TITLE>
</HEAD>

<BODY>

[<A HREF="contents.htm">Contents</A>]
[<A HREF="map.htm">Map</A>]
[<A HREF="myindex.htm">Index</A>]
[<A HREF="comment.htm">Comment</A>]
[<A HREF="search.htm">Search</A>]
[<A HREF="myhome.htm">Home</A>]
[<A HREF="parent.htm">Up</A>]
[<A HREF="previous.htm">Previous</A>]
[<A HREF="next.htm">Next</A>]

<HR SIZE=2>

<IMG SRC="crtogrfy.gif" ALT="[emblem text]"><BR>
<H1> Center of the World Cartography<BR>
Poster Collection</H1>

<P>Location:

[<A HREF="cwcindex.htm">CWC home</A>]
[<A HREF="catalog.htm">Catalog</A>]
[<A HREF="maps.htm">Maps</A>]
Poster Collection</P>

<HR SIZE=4>

<H2>We put your business on the map and<BR>
spin the world around YOU!</H2>
<I>We'll move latitudes and longitudes for you.</I>&#174;

<P><IMG SRC="map.gif" ALT="[Image of poster for Center of the World
Cartography]"></P>
<P>No one knows more about being lost on the map than we do. Located in
the forests of Temple, New Hampshire, Center of the World Cartography
struggled for years competing with big-name geographies such as Paris,
France; London, England; New York, New York; and Tokyo, Japan.  No
more! We put our company at the center of the world map and fast became
the center of attention. Center of the World Cartography wants your
business to experience the same instant success we did. We create
custom-designed posters that place your business at the center of the
world.</P>

<H2>Features</H2>
<UL>
<LI>Puts your company literally at the center of the world map!
<LI>Made of high-quality, heavyweight, recycled paper
<LI>Four-color printing with soy-based inks
<LI>Created using state-of-the-art cartographic software
</UL>

<H2>Specifications</H2>
<DL>
<DT><STRONG>Size</STRONG>
<DD>11 inches x 17 inches (27.94 centimeters x 43.18 centimeters)
```

```
<DT><STRONG>Paper</STRONG>
<DD>Heavyweight, recycled paper made of 100% post-consumer waste
</DL>

<H2>Ordering information</H2>
<P>Poster Map, POSTER-110761<BR>
Price: $75 USD</P>

<HR SIZE=2>

http://www.worldmap.com/catalog.htm -- Revised: 07 MAY 1995<BR>
Copyright &copy; 1995 <A HREF="page.htm">Center of the World
Cartography<A><BR>
<A HREF="MAILTO:worldmap@cartography.com">worldmap@cartography.com</A>
<BR>

<HR SIZE=2>

<A HREF="contents.htm"><IMG SRC="cntsicon.gif" ALT="[Contents]"></A>
<A HREF="map.htm">    <IMG SRC="mapicon.gif"  ALT="[Map]"></A>
<A HREF="myindex.htm"> <IMG SRC="indxicon.gif" ALT="[Index]"></A>
<A HREF="comment.htm"> <IMG SRC="cmnticon.gif" ALT="[Comment]"></A>
<A HREF="search.htm">  <IMG SRC="srchicon.gif" ALT="[Search]"></A>
<A HREF="myhome.htm">  <IMG SRC="homeicon.gif" ALT="[Home]"></A>
<A HREF="parent.htm">  <IMG SRC="upicon.gif"   ALT="[Up]"></A>
<A HREF="previous.htm"><IMG SRC="previcon.gif" ALT="[Previous]"></A>
<A HREF="next.htm">    <IMG SRC="nexticon.gif" ALT="[Next]"></A>

</BODY>
</HTML>
```

MULTIMEDIA SAMPLER

On the CD-ROM ...

The example:
examples
    chap4
        mmedia
            mmedia.htm

The template:
recipes
    mmedia
        mmedia.htm

Main Ingredients

Generic Web page, p. 105

Link to external media element, p. 265

Simple inline image, p. 276

The Multimedia Sampler lets users view pictures, listen to music and sounds, and watch animation and video clips. You can use this multimedia sampler to really show off your product, to create a virtual museum, or to show users an electronic family album.

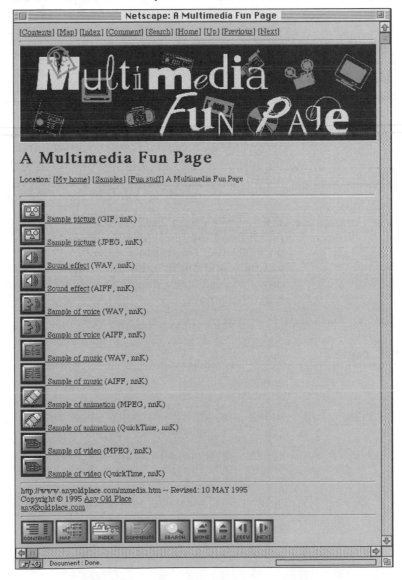

Note: To display the various media called forth by this recipe, users must have the corresponding helper application, and must set up their browsers to trigger the helper application when the media file arrives. As you can imagine, some users will not have the helper apps and will not be able to play the multimedia files. They will complain.

Recipe

This recipe builds upon the Generic Web page, p. 105.

Ingredients

Simple inline image, p. 276

Link to external media element, p. 265

This example shows a general-purpose multimedia sampler page. It is a menu of multimedia elements from which the user can select—just for fun. The entries on the sampler all have the same simple structure, for example, here's a link to a WAVE sound file.

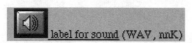

```
<A HREF="filename.wav"><IMG SRC="sndicon.gif" ALT="[sound]"> label for
sound</A> (WAV, nnK)
```

To include a multimedia object, you simply include the URL to the media file using the `<A HREF>` tag. That's it! Really! In this example, we used the ingredient for a link to an external media element, `<A HREF>`, with an `<IMG>` tag to include an inline image of the icon for that media object type.

We've included a potpourri of file formats. In every case, we indicate in parentheses the file type and the size of the file in bytes. When users click on the icon or description of the file, their browsers temporarily download a copy of the multimedia file to their disks to play locally. The temporary download can take a long time and can require a large block of memory and hard-disk space.

HTML code

```
<HTML>


<!------------------------------------------------->
<!--     AUTHOR:   Nancy Hoft                  -->
<!--     E-MAIL:   itech@mv.mv.com             -->
<!--     CREATED:  16 APRIL 1995               -->
<!--     MODIFIED: 10 MAY  1995                -->
<!--     FILE:     mmedia.htm                  -->
<!--     PURPOSE: A multimedia fun page        -->
<!------------------------------------------------->

<HEAD>
<TITLE>A Multimedia Fun Page</TITLE>
</HEAD>
```

```
<BODY>

[<A HREF="contents.htm">Contents</A>]
[<A HREF="map.htm">Map</A>]
[<A HREF="myindex.htm">Index</A>]
[<A HREF="comment.htm">Comment</A>]
[<A HREF="search.htm">Search</A>]
[<A HREF="myhome.htm">Home</A>]
[<A HREF="parent.htm">Up</A>]
[<A HREF="previous.htm">Previous</A>]
[<A HREF="next.htm">Next</A>]

<HR SIZE=2>

<IMG SRC="mfp3head.gif" ALT="[emblem text]"><BR>
<H1>A Multimedia Fun Page</H1>

<P>Location:
[<A HREF="home.htm">My home</A>]
[<A HREF="samples.htm">Samples</A>]
[<A HREF="stuff.htm">Fun stuff</A>]
A Multimedia Fun Page</P>

<HR SIZE=4>

<A HREF="gifpict.gif"><IMG SRC="picticon.gif" ALT="[picture]">
Sample picture</A> (GIF, nnK)<BR>

<A HREF="jpegpict.jpg"><IMG SRC="picticon.gif" ALT="[picture]">
Sample picture</A> (JPEG, nnK)<BR>

<A HREF="wavsnd.wav"><IMG SRC="sndicon.gif" ALT="[sound]">
Sound effect</A> (WAV, nnK)<BR>

<A HREF="aifsnd.aif"><IMG SRC="sndicon.gif" ALT="[sound]">
Sound effect</A> (AIFF, nnK)<BR>

<A HREF="wavvoice.wav"><IMG SRC="spkicon.gif" ALT="[voice]">
Sample of voice</A> (WAV, nnK)<BR>

<A HREF="aifvoice.aif"><IMG SRC="spkicon.gif" ALT="[voice]">
Sample of voice</A> (AIFF, nnK)<BR>

<A HREF="wavmusic.wav"><IMG SRC="musicon.gif" ALT="[music]">
Sample of music</A> (WAV, nnK)<BR>

<A HREF="aifmusic.aif"><IMG SRC="musicon.gif" ALT="[music]">
Sample of music</A> (AIFF, nnK)<BR>

<A HREF="mpganim.mpg"><IMG SRC="animicon.gif" ALT="[animation]">
Sample of animation</A> (MPEG, nnK)<BR>

<A HREF="qtanim.mov"><IMG SRC="animicon.gif" ALT="[animation]">
Sample of animation</A> (QuickTime, nnK)<BR>

<A HREF="mpgvideo.mpg"><IMG SRC="vidicon.gif" ALT="[video]">
Sample of video</A> (MPEG, nnK)<BR>

<A HREF="qtvideo.mov"><IMG SRC="vidicon.gif" ALT="[video]">
Sample of video</A> (QuickTime, nnK)<BR>
```

```
<HR SIZE=2>

http://www.anyoldplace.com/mmedia.htm -- Revised: 10 MAY 1995<BR>
Copyright &copy; 1995 <A HREF="page.htm">Any Old Place</A><BR>
<A HREF="MAILTO:any@oldplace.com">any@oldplace.com</A><BR>

<HR SIZE=2>

<A HREF="contents.htm"><IMG SRC="cntsicon.gif" ALT="[Contents]"></A>
<A HREF="map.htm">     <IMG SRC="mapicon.gif"  ALT="[Map]"></A>
<A HREF="myindex.htm"> <IMG SRC="indxicon.gif" ALT="[Index]"></A>
<A HREF="comment.htm"> <IMG SRC="cmnticon.gif" ALT="[Comment]"></A>
<A HREF="search.htm">  <IMG SRC="srchicon.gif" ALT="[Search]"></A>
<A HREF="myhome.htm">  <IMG SRC="homeicon.gif" ALT="[Home]"></A>
<A HREF="parent.htm">  <IMG SRC="upicon.gif"   ALT="[Up]"></A>
<A HREF="previous.htm"><IMG SRC="previcon.gif" ALT="[Previous]"></A>
<A HREF="next.htm">    <IMG SRC="nexticon.gif" ALT="[Next]"></A>

</BODY>
</HTML>
```

RESEARCH REPORT

The Research Report shares the methods, results, and conclusions drawn from experimental research. It is the electronic equivalent of a scholarly paper published in an academic journal.

Although this recipe is designed for reporting scholarly research, you can easily adapt it for:

- Corporate white papers.

- Surveys of research.

- Homework assignments.

Recipe

This recipe builds upon the Generic Web page, p. 105

Our example is the research report, "The Decline of American Long-Distance Running." It is a complete report with all the sections most common to research reports.

Title of research report and author

Ingredients

Text heading, p. 252

Beneath the title of the report is the name of the author, his affiliation, and location.

> # The Decline of American Long-Distance Running
>
> **John T. Devlin**, NH Runners Association, Temple, NH USA

```
<H1> The Decline of American Long-Distance Running</H1>
<B>John T. Devlin</B>,
NH Runners Association,
Temple, NH USA<BR>
```

The name of the author is displayed in a visually stronger font than the name of the affiliation with the use of the `<B>` tag.

The author's name and the name of the association could link to other Web pages for users who want more information about the author or organization; however, neither is important to the content of the report.

Sections of the research report

Ingredients

Text headings, p. 252

Destination marker, p. 261

Here are the most common sections included in a research report. Our example uses most of these.

- **Abstract**—consists of a single paragraph that summarizes the conclusions of the report. It is sometimes called an *Executive Summary* or *Highlights*.

- **Contents**—is the table of contents to the report.

- **Introduction**—states the research issue covered in the report. It also summarizes and critiques previous research on this subject.

- **Scope**—details and justifies the scope of the research report.

- **Method**—explains the experimental methods used in the research in enough detail that other researchers in the field can reproduce the experiment if necessary.

- **Results**—records in detail the outcome of the experiments performed. It summarizes the data and explains the statistical significance of the results.

- **Conclusions**—tells what the results mean. This section abstracts general principles from the particular results.

- **Discussion**—further elaborates on the results, pointing out areas for additional research and speculating on the applicability of the results.

- **References**—lists the references cited in the research report.

In our example, each section heading includes a destination marker. Here's the Method section heading:

```
<H2><A NAME="method">Method</A></H2>
```

The destination marker `<A NAME= ...> ... </A>` makes it possible to jump to this section from the table of contents at the beginning of this page—or from anywhere else for that matter. Using the second-level heading `<H2>` makes it easy for readers to visually scan for this section.

Abstract

Ingredients

Quotation block, p. 249

> For the better part of the last two decades, there has been a noticeable drop in the competitiveness of American long-distance runners in the international arena. This decline has been especially noticeable to the American public during Olympic years. With the 1996 Summer Olympics scheduled to take place in Atlanta, Georgia, USA, no doubt this issue will again come to the forefront.

```
<BLOCKQUOTE>
For the better part of the last two decades, there has been a
noticeable drop in the competitiveness of American long-distance
runners in the international arena.  This decline has been especially
noticeable to the American public during Olympic years.  With the 1996
Summer Olympics scheduled to take place in Atlanta, Georgia, USA, no
doubt this issue will again come to the forefront. </BLOCKQUOTE>
```

We use the `<BLOCKQUOTE>` tag to indent the abstract, thereby setting it off from the rest of the report. HTML 3.0 has an `<ABSTRACT>` tag for just this purpose. When all your users have 3.0-compatible browsers, replace the `BLOCKQUOTE` with the `ABSTRACT` tag.

Contents

The Contents previews the material in this page and lets the user jump directly to an individual section—a must for long Web pages.

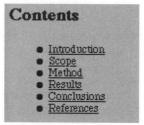

The user clicks on a contents entry and the browser scrolls to the destination marker that identifies the corresponding section.

Here are the pointers in the Contents section of our example and the corresponding destination markers within the report. Note that we put the destination markers inside their corresponding section headings.

Pointer in Contents	Corresponding destination markers

`<LI>`
`<A HREF="#intro">Introduction`
`</A>`
	`<H2><A NAME="intro">`
	`Introduction</A></H2>`

`<LI>`
`<A HREF="#scope">Scope`
`</A>`
	`<H2><A NAME="scope">`
	`Scope</A></H2>`

`<LI>`
`<A HREF="#method">Method`
`</A>`
	`<H2><A NAME="method">`
	`Method</A></H2>`

`<LI>`
`<A HREF="#results">Results`
`</A>`
	`<H2><A NAME="results">`
	`Results</A></H2>`

`<LI>`
`<A HREF="#conclusions">Conclusions`
`</A>`
	`<H2><A NAME="conclusions">`
	`Conclusions</A></H2>`

`<LI>`
`<A HREF="#references">References`
`</A>`
	`<H2><A NAME="references">`
	`References</A></H2>`

Detail sections

The Introduction, Scope, Method, Results, and Conclusions sections use a variety of common ingredients. In addition to the <P> tag, we use a numbered list <OL> twice in the Scope section to organize and sequence information.

In the Method section, we use the definition list <DL> to structure and indent the text; we use the bold <B> tag to make the categories stand out; and we use the <A HREF> tag to link each category to another page that provides the supporting details for each category—so much better than lengthy dry endnotes, don't you think?

In the Results section, to break up the long passage of text and to illustrate the report, we insert an inline image aligned to the right.

Results

In all of the racing distances studied, (5,000 meters, 1,000 meters, marathon, and road racing), there has been a decline in the effectiveness of American distance running over the study period.

It has not been a steady decline. Especially in the marathoning study group, the United States showed dominance for most of the first 10-year study period, but has suffered a steady decline since then. In marathoning, the U.S. dominance was first headed by Frank Shorter (silver 1976 Olympics after winning gold in 1972), Bill Rodgers (ranked number one in the world, numerous wins at major marathons such as Boston and Fukoka), and Alberto Salazar (ranked number one in world, major wins at Boston and New York, American Marathon Record). However, in the second 10-year study, U.S. dominance in marathoning ends, and faces a steep decline every year.

In the 5,000 meter- and 1,000 meter- track events, the United States has had few bright moments since Billy Mills's gold medal in the 1964 Tokyo Olympics. There has been no sustaining star in these distances, although there have been numerous high world rankings (such as Sydney Maree, Alberto Salazar, Bruce Bickford, Bill Pfitzenger). In the study period, the African nations, especially Kenya and Morocco, have dominated these events, especially over the second 10-year study period.

For road racing, the United States showed dominance early. Statistical research was difficult for the first 5-year study period, due to the relative lack of world-class road racing events (Tyra, 1993). The boom in road racing, especially in the United States, resulted in far more research opportunities for each subsequent 5-year study period. In road racing, the Africans, again led by Kenya, have shown dominance over the last 5-year study period.

There are some interesting statistics to go along with the above results. In the time period studied, participation in high school and college track and field programs (for this study, includes cross country, indoor, and outdoor track programs) showed an overall decline in the study period. High school track and field participation grew in the late 1970s, until it was the second most popular team sport, in terms of overall participants in the United States (Ryca, 1994). By the last 5-year study period, high school track and field participation had shown a deep decline, dropping to the fourth most popular team sport. In the study period, overall performances (in terms of times over standard high school distances) showed an overall decline in quality.

Road racing participation showed a steady increase during the study period. This was especially evident during the first three 5-year study periods. Over the last 5-year study period, road race participation numbers have shown an overall leveling off (Davidius, 7594).

During the study period, the average age of participants rose by over 5 years.

And in the Conclusions section, we use a bullet list of complex items to list reasons that are all equally important and therefore don't need the prioritization that a numbered list offers.

References (and endnotes)

Ingredients

Paragraph, p. 246

The References section lists other documents referred to in the body of the report.

> ## References
>
> Tyra, Sinotte, *History of the Olympics* (Jipcho Press, Athens, 1993).
>
> Ryca, Shih, *The Illustrated History of Track and Field* (Zatopek Publishing, Prague, Slovakia, 1994).
>
> Davidius, Victor, *Track and Field Contemporary Compendium* (Volumes 1-25, 1975-1994, Prefon Publishing, Los Altos)

```
<H2><A NAME="reference">Reference</A></H2>

<P><A NAME="tyra_1993">
Tyra, Sinotte, <I>History of the Olympics</I> (Jipcho Press, Athens,
1993).</A></P>
<P><A NAME="ryca_1994">
Ryca, Shih, <I>The Illustrated History of Track and Field</I> (Zatopek
Publishing, Prague, Slovakia, 1994).</A></P>
<P><A NAME="davidius_7594">
Davidius, Victor, <I>Track and Field Contemporary Compendium</I>
(Volumes 1-25, 1975-1994, Prefon Publishing, Los Altos) </A></P>
```

Notice that each reference item has its own destination marker `<A NAME="whatever">`, allowing users to jump to this item from the body text, like this:

> For road racing, the United States showed dominance early. Statistical research was difficult for the first 5-year study period, due to the relative lack of world-class road racing events (Tyra, 1993). The boom in road racing, especially in the United States, resulted in far more research opportunities for each subsequent 5-year study period. In road racing, the Africans, again led by Kenya, have shown dominance over the last 5-year study period.

```
<P>For road racing, the United States showed dominance early.
Statistical research was difficult for the first 5-year study period,
due to the relative lack of world-class road racing events (<A
HREF="#tyra_1993">Tyra, 1993</A>). The boom in road racing, especially
in the United States, resulted in far more research opportunities for
each subsequent 5-year study period. In road racing, the Africans,
again led by Kenya, have shown dominance over the last 5-year study
period.</P>
```

If the user clicks on the highlighted citation "Tyra, 1993," the report will scroll to the complete reference in the References section.

The way you format the citation and the complete reference will depend on your field of research. It is a religious issue. What one academic discipline decrees as the one true style another decries as blasphemy. Just figure out which style is right for your field and follow it. You want readers concentrating on your ideas and research, not on the punctuation of your references.

Notes on footnotes and endnotes

Footnotes are notes that appear at the bottom of a paper page. Endnotes are the ones that appear at the end of the whole document. Alas, HTML 2.0 does not support true footnotes and endnotes. Footnotes are impossible since the user controls the length of the display, unlike the situation on paper pages. Our advice: Forget about footnotes until your users have HTML 3.0 browsers.

You can kludge endnotes as we did for the References section. Just embed a citation in the body text and link it to a corresponding note at the end of the Web page.

Tips for great research reports

Violate the rule about short Web pages

See to page 472, which addresses this issue more thoroughly and offers some guidelines.

Most research reports are quite lengthy and often their references are as long as the body of the report. In general, a long Web page is a bad idea. But in the case of a research report, however, it is unlikely that users will read the entire report on the screen because it contains complex content and requires detailed reading—the kind of reading that a user might do after printing out the Web page. To ensure that the printout is complete, we put the whole report into one Web page, eliminating the need for users to track down and separately print all the pieces.

Respect tradition

Scholarly research has a long, abiding tradition. Put another way, academics are supremely conservative when it comes to the format, arrangement, and contents of their research papers. For acceptance, credibility, and credit toward tenure, you should make the electronic research report look like the kinds found in the most prestigious journals in your field of research.

Show, don't just tell

In most sections, include appropriate graphics, tables, and other media. If the image is small, you can include it inline, like this

```
<P> <IMG SRC="picture.gif" ALT="[text]"></P>
```

If the image is large, however, you may want to provide a button the reader can press to summon the image. Such a button would look like this:

```
<P><A HREF="extlpict.gif"> <IMG SRC="picticon.gif" ALT="[Description of
the picture]"></A></P>
```

Consider using a thumbnail image of the graphic, animation, or video as the button.

Also consider links to sounds and moving pictures. Instead of talking about a musical passage, link to a recording. Instead of describing complex motions, show them in a video or animation clip.

Link to related material

Keep your research paper concise but link to related information. Pepper your paper with click-and-jump links to:

- Raw data, tables of statistics, interviews, video clips.

- Other papers or works by the same author.

- A printable form of the research report.

- Online versions of items listed in the References section.

- The author's biography.

- Web sites and newsgroups that provide more information on this subject.

HTML code

```
<HTML>

<!------------------------------------------------>
<!--     AUTHOR: John T. Devlin                -->
<!--     E-MAIL: running@around.com            -->
<!--     CREATED:  03 APRIL 1995               -->
<!--     MODIFIED: 08 MAY 1995                 -->
<!--     FILE:     research.htm                -->
<!--     PURPOSE: The Decline of American Long- -->
<!--                    Distance Running       -->
<!------------------------------------------------>

<HEAD>
<TITLE>The Decline of American Long-Distance Running </TITLE>
</HEAD>
```

```
<BODY>

[<A HREF="contents.htm">Contents</A>]
[<A HREF="map.htm">Map</A>]
[<A HREF="myindex.htm">Index</A>]
[<A HREF="comment.htm">Comment</A>]
[<A HREF="search.htm">Search</A>]
[<A HREF="myhome.htm">Home</A>]
[<A HREF="parent.htm">Up</A>]
[<A HREF="previous.htm">Previous</A>]
[<A HREF="next.htm">Next</A>]

<HR SIZE=2>

<IMG SRC="runhead.gif" ALT="[emblem text]"><BR>

<H1> The Decline of American Long-Distance Running</H1>
<B>John T. Devlin</B>,
NH Runners Association,
Temple, NH  USA<BR>

<P>Location:
[<A HREF="index.htm">Journal</A>]
[<A HREF="year.htm">1995</A>]
[<A HREF="month.htm">May</A>]
The Decline of American Long-Distance Running </P>

<HR SIZE=4>

<BLOCKQUOTE>
For the better part of the last two decades, there has been a
noticeable drop in the competitiveness of American long distance
runners in the international arena.  This decline has been especially
noticeable to the American public during Olympic years.  With the 1996
Summer Olympics scheduled to take place in Atlanta, Georgia, USA, no
doubt this issue will again come to the forefront. </BLOCKQUOTE>

<H2><A NAME="contents">Contents</A></H2>
<UL>
<LI><A HREF="#intro">Introduction</A>
<LI><A HREF="#scope">Scope</A>
<LI><A HREF="#method">Method</A>
<LI><A HREF="#results">Results</A>
<LI><A HREF="#conclusions">Conclusions</A>
<LI><A HREF="#references">References</A>
</UL>

<H2><A NAME="intro">Introduction</A></H2>

<P> At international track meets, at marathons, road races, and team
distance relay events, the image of the American long-distance runner
is one that is rapidly fading to the background.  Where once American
runners such as Johnny Kelly, Billy Mills, Jim Ryan, Frank Shorter,
Bill Rodgers, and Alberto Salazar ruled the international long-distance
running circuit, today the African nations, led by Kenya, Morocco, and
Ethiopia rule supreme.</P>
<P>But why have American long-distance running fortunes fallen?  Over
the last decades, there has been a boom in recreational running, but
this popularity as a form of exercise has seemingly not resulted in a
growth in the long-distance running talent pool.</P>
```

```
<P>There are, of course, exceptions to this trend, such as current
world-ranked distance man Bob Kennedy, but, for the most part, American
long-distance runners have found themselves lapped by the field. </P>

<H2><A NAME="scope">Scope</A></H2>

<P>While a case can be made for the decline of world class long
distance runners in both American males and females, my research was
solely on male distance runners.  For reasons of comparative research
and statistics, I limited my research to three types of long distance
running:</P>

<OL>
<LI>Track races of 5,000 meters or longer
<LI>Road races of  10,000 meters or longer
<LI>Marathons
</OL>

<P>I chose the time period of January 1, 1975, through December 31,
1994, for this study.  For the boycotted Olympic years of 1980 and
1984, I compared national championship results with Olympic
results.</P>

<P>My research focused on these points:</P>

<OL>
<LI>Participation in long-distance running as percentage of population.
<LI>Age group participation  (Age Groups:  20 and under, 20-30, 30-40,
over 40)
<LI>World record progression over the study period.
<LI>Where different, United States record progression over the study
period.
<LI>World rankings, yearly, for the 5,000 meter-, 10,000 meter-,
marathon, and road racing categories.
</OL>

<H2><A NAME="method">Method</A></H2>

<P>My method of research can be broken down into the following
areas:</P>

<DL>
<DT><B><A HREF="backgrnd.htm">Background informational research</A></B>
<DD>I studied the race results for major races over the stated research
period.  Where available, I watched video tapes of meets and races.  My
research included sources in the United States, Canada, Europe, Africa,
Asia, Australia, and South America.  Major long-distance running
events, such as Olympics, World Cup Track Meets, the World Track and
Field Championships, and the World Cross Country Championships carried
the most weight in my statistical analysis.  For marathoning, I chose
the Boston Marathon, the New York Marathon, the Rotterdam Marathon, the
Fukoka Marathon, the World Marathon Championships, and the Olympic
Marathons to carry the most weight in statistical analysis.
<DT><B><A HREF="attend.htm">Attendance at major events over the last 5
years</A></B>
<DD>By attending these events I was able to see first hand what the
racing methods of various nations and individuals were.  I was also
able to gauge crowd participation, crowd support, and knowledge of the
long-distance running events in several countries (specifically, the
```

United States, Japan, Kenya, Germany, Finland, Australia, and the
United Kingdom).
`<DT><B><A HREF="intervw.htm">Interviews</A></B>`
`<DD>`I interviewed current long-distance runners, coaches, and fans, as
well as former long-distance running stars (including Kip Keino, Rod
Dixon, Frank Shorter, Waldmar Ciepinski, Henry Rono, and Lasse Viren).
`</DL>`

`<P>`I compiled my results and information and then, for statistical
purposes, made comparison studies of each year in the stated study
period, comparisons for every 5-year period, comparisons for every 10-
year period, and then a cumulative comparison for the 20-year study
period. `</P>`

`<H2><A NAME="results">Results</A></H2>`

`<P>` In all of the racing distances studied, (5,000 meters, 1,000
meters, marathon, and road racing), there has been a decline in the
effectiveness of American distance running over the study period.`</P>`
`<P>`It has not been a steady decline. Especially in the marathoning
study group, the United States showed dominance for most of the first
10-year study period, but has suffered a steady decline since then. In
marathoning, the U.S. dominance was first headed by Frank Shorter
(silver 1976 Olympics after winning gold in 1972), Bill Rodgers (ranked
number one in the world, numerous wins at major marathons such as
Boston and Fukoka), and Alberto Salazar (ranked number one in world,
major wins at Boston and New York, American Marathon Record). However,
in the second 10-year study, U.S. dominance in marathoning ends, and
faces a steep decline every year. `</P>`

`<IMG SRC="runner.gif" ALT="[Drawing of runner]"ALIGN=RIGHT >`

`<P>`In the 5,000 meter- and 1,000 meter- track events, the United States
has had few bright moments since Billy Mills's gold medal in the 1964
Tokyo Olympics. There has been no sustaining star in these distances,
although there have been numerous high world rankings (such as Sydney
Maree, Alberto Salazar, Bruce Bickford, Bill Pfitzenger). In the
study period, the African nations, especially Kenya and Morocco, have
dominated these events, especially over the second 10-year study
period.`</P>`
`<P>`For road racing, the United States showed dominance early.
Statistical research was difficult for the first 5 year study period,
due to the relative lack of world-class road racing events (`<A
HREF="#tyra_1993">Tyra, 1993</A>`). The boom in road racing, especially
in the United States, resulted in far more research opportunities for
each subsequent 5-year study period. In road racing, the Africans,
again led by Kenya, have shown dominance over the last 5-year study
period.`</P>`
`<P>`There are some interesting statistics to go along with the above
results. In the time period studied, participation in high school and
college track and field programs (for this study, includes cross
country, indoor, and outdoor track programs) showed an overall decline
in the study period. High school track and field participation grew in
the late 1970s, until it was the second most popular team sport, in
terms of overall participants in the United States (`<A
HREF="#ryca_1994">Ryca, 1994</A>`). By the last 5-year study period,
high school track and field participation had shown a deep decline,
dropping to the fourth most popular team sport. In the study period,
overall performances (in terms of times over standard high school
distances) showed an overall decline in quality. `</P>`

```
<P>Road racing participation showed a steady increase during the study
period.  This was especially evident during the first three 5-year
study periods.  Over the last 5-year study period, road race
participation numbers have shown an overall leveling off (<A
HREF="#davidius_1994">Davidius, 7594</A>).</P>
<P>During the study period, the average age of participants rose by
over 5 years. </P>

<H2><A NAME="conclusions">Conclusions</A></H2>

<P>The decline of American long-distance running is not one of
perception, but rather of reality.  The American long-distance running
scene is one of quantity over quality.   The United States still
produces world-class distance runners, but not at the level or in the
quantity it should.  The reasons for my findings include:</P>

<UL>
<LI><STRONG>Lack of Exposure</STRONG> - Except for the Olympics, and
some major marathons, long-distance running is not reported in the mass
media (video, audio, paper).  Long-distance running stars are not
sports celebrities, and are not as noticeable as American sports
professionals in the team sports of basketball, football, or baseball.
<LI><STRONG>The Road Race Boom</STRONG> - The backbone of the glory
years of American long-distance running was track and field.   Track
and field is an afterthought for most road racers today.   While there
are more and more participants in road racing, few have backgrounds in
track and field, or show a knowledge of track and field events.
<LI><STRONG>Big Fish in Little Pond Syndrome</STRONG> - In the years
before the start date of this study, and well into the first 10-year
study period, long-distance runners generally competed until they got
out of high school, unless they went on to compete in college.  Few
remained in competition after that, unless they were world class.
Today, road racing has changed all that.  With the advent of prize
money, it is easier for good long-distance runners to garner benefits
remaining at the same fitness level, instead of trying to move forward
to the next step of competition.
<LI><STRONG>Marathons</STRONG> - Like  the road race boom, the boom in
marathoning has not resulted in an increase in the quality or quantity
of American world-class marathoners, nor has it resulted in more
interest and appeal to the sport in general.
<LI><STRONG>Age-groups</STRONG> - Road racing also brought to the
forefront age groups.  In most races today, the winner of the over 40
age category is praised and treated the same as the overall winner of
the race.  This lessens the enthusiasm and drive to excel.  While it's
nice to know how one stacks up against participants their own age, for
development of world-class distance runners, younger runners must be
encouraged.  Finishing first in your age group, but 15th overall,
should not be treated the same as finishing first overall in the race.
If the United States is to regain competitiveness at the world-class
level, it will not do so led by 40-year-old men.
</UL>

<H2><A NAME="references">References</A></H2>

<P><A NAME="tyra_1993">
Tyra, Sinotte, <I>History of the Olympics</I> (Jipcho Press, Athens,
1993).</A></P>
<P><A NAME="ryca_1994">
Ryca, Shih, <I>The Illustrated History of Track and Field</I> (Zatopek
Publishing, Prague, Slovakia, 1994).</A></P>
```

```
<P><A NAME="davidius_7594">
Davidius, Victor, <I>Track and Field Contemporary Compendium</I>
(Volumes 1-25, 1975-1994, Prefon Publishing, Los Altos) </A></P>

<HR SIZE=2>

http://www.running.com/report.htm -- Revised: 08 MAY 1995<BR>
Copyright &copy; 1995 <A HREF="page.htm">Running Around</A><BR>
<A HREF="MAILTO:running@around.com">running@around.com</A><BR>

<HR SIZE=2>

<A HREF="contents.htm"><IMG SRC="cntsicon.gif" ALT="[Contents]"></A>
<A HREF="map.htm">    <IMG SRC="mapicon.gif"  ALT="[Map]"></A>
<A HREF="myindex.htm"> <IMG SRC="indxicon.gif" ALT="[Index]"></A>
<A HREF="comment.htm"> <IMG SRC="cmnticon.gif" ALT="[Comment]"></A>
<A HREF="search.htm">  <IMG SRC="srchicon.gif" ALT="[Search]"></A>
<A HREF="myhome.htm">  <IMG SRC="homeicon.gif" ALT="[Home]"></A>
<A HREF="parent.htm">  <IMG SRC="upicon.gif"   ALT="[Up]"></A>
<A HREF="previous.htm"><IMG SRC="previcon.gif" ALT="[Previous]"></A>
<A HREF="next.htm">    <IMG SRC="nexticon.gif" ALT="[Next]"></A>

</BODY>
</HTML>
```

INGREDIENTS

*Components for building
Web pages*

A QUICK LOOK INSIDE THE PANTRY

Here are the ingredients that you use to cook up Web pages. This chapter is not so much about the HTML tags themselves—though they are here in abundance—as it is about tags combined to form *design elements*, the chunks of stuff that you put together to make individual Web pages and whole Web sites.

As a design element, each ingredient serves a specific purpose. So instead of thinking about them as the stuff to make things *look* a certain way, think of ingredients as parts of your recipe that *do* something. Yeast makes the dough rise, and path buttons guide your users around.

The ingredients serve as templates. They contain placeholders that you replace with the real contents of your Web. Put simply, to use the ingredients:

1.   Find the one you want on the CD-ROM.

2.   Copy and paste it into your page.

3.   Replace the placeholders with your text and URLs.

4.   Test it and tweak it to make it yours.

For a little more detail about what you'll find in ingredients, read on.

About the CD-ROM

The ingredients are available on the CD-ROM in two forms:

- As individual files (`address`, `baseform`, `bgcolor`, etc.)

- As one, long file (`allinone`)

Both forms are available in two flavors: RTF and plain text.

Here's how to find them:

On the CD-ROM ...

```
ingrdnts
   as_rtf
      address.rtf
      allinone.rtf
      baseform.rtf
      bgcolor.rtf
      and many more
   as_text
      address.txt
      allinone.txt
      baseform.txt
      bgcolor.txt
      and many more
```

What you'll find for each ingredient

In this chapter, the pattern for each ingredient is as follows:

- The name of the ingredient (for example, bullet list).

- A quick reference to provide an overview of the design element.

- The HTML elements that are used.

- An example of the ingredient in use.

- Tips that will help with common problems and offer alternative ways of doing things.

Some of the simpler ingredients do not have all the items named here. For instance, if the illustration in the quick reference is complete and an additional example would only show more of the same, we left off the example. If we have no tips for you, we offer none.

If you have problems

Each ingredient has suggestions that are specific to that ingredient. Help that applies to more than one ingredient is gathered at the end of this chapter in the "Universal Problem Solving" section, page 303.

PAGE ELEMENTS

Page elements define the structure at the page level. They provide the base for almost all pages, which usually means putting them in a single file and then filling it in with other ingredients. The background elements (color and graphics) are not supported by all browsers, but are included here because they constitute page-level ingredients that are seeing increased use among Web designers.

These are the page elements:

- Page (bare bones)

- Identification block

- Banner slug

- Horizontal rule

- Signature

- Background and text color

- Background graphic

Ingredients that work closely with the page elements are:

- Identification block, which is frequently part of a page's HEAD section.

- Text headings, which also help to structure a page.

Page (bare bones)

On the CD-ROM ...

ingrdnts
   as_rtf
      page.rtf
   as_text
      page.htm

This is the minimum number of elements you should include in an HTML file. Browsers and HTML editors use the ⟨HTML⟩ tag to identify the file as an HTML file.

Quick reference

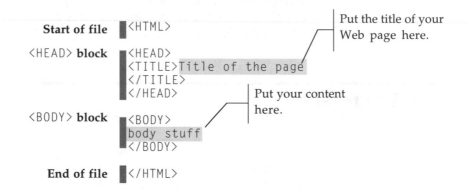

Start of file	⟨HTML⟩
⟨HEAD⟩ **block**	⟨HEAD⟩ ⟨TITLE⟩Title of the page ⟨/TITLE⟩ ⟨/HEAD⟩
⟨BODY⟩ **block**	⟨BODY⟩ body stuff ⟨/BODY⟩
End of file	⟨/HTML⟩

Put the title of your Web page here.

Put your content here.

The HTML elements

The ⟨HEAD⟩ block contains file identification information, and serves as a header whose purpose is to convey information about the file to others who might need to later do work on the file's contents. This is covered more in the description of the ingredient, Identification block.

In this most basic page, the ⟨HEAD⟩ block just contains the title of the page.

Use the ⟨TITLE⟩ tag to tell the Web browser what is to be displayed in the banner. Pay attention to the relationship between what you type here and what you place in the heading level 1. Sometimes it makes sense that the two be the same, but take a moment to consider alternatives. Make the redundancy a conscious decision. Be creative. Some Web weavers squeeze it in as another level of hierarchy, sort of a heading level 0. Others use it to sneak in off-the-wall messages.

For example, you want to make sure that your Web page lets everyone know that this is your first effort, so you proclaim it in your title as shown in the following example:

```
<TITLE> My First Web Page </TITLE>
```

By the way, if you don't use a title tag, browsers will display the HTML file's name, which is pretty lame looking. It's like a stereo without a cover with its wires hanging out—definite high-tech look, but lacking in the polish department.

In this bare bones page, text is simply typed in the section bounded by the <BODY> tags. More commonly, however, additional HTML elements are included. We'll talk more about these additional elements as we go along.

Tips

On the CD-ROM ...

examples
chap5
ingrdnts.htm

Pretty serious stuff. How about something frivolous, like cheap pyrotechnics that don't waste too much bandwidth? You can get your title bar to display more than one thing by just stacking up <TITLE> tags like this:

```
<TITLE> ******** FLASH ******** </TITLE>
<TITLE> ****** FLASH ****** </TITLE>
<TITLE> **** FLASH **** </TITLE>
<TITLE> ** FLASH ** </TITLE>
<TITLE> FLASH </TITLE>
```

Use this with caution. This kind of stuff can be attention grabbing the first time through, but after that, as much fun as fingernails on a blackboard.

Identification block

On the CD-ROM ...

ingrdnts
    as_rtf
        idblock.rtf
    as_text
        idblock.txt

The audience for the Identification block is not your users, but you and others who work on the actual HTML files. It uses HTML comment tags so browsers won't display its contents. Putting an Identification block in your HTML file helps avoid confusion and mistakes, especially when more than one person is working on a file.

Quick reference

```
<!------------------------------------------------------------>
<!--     AUTHOR:   your name goes here                    -->
<!--     E-MAIL:   your.address@whatever.domain           -->
<!--     CREATED:  date page was created                  -->
<!--     MODIFIED: date page was last changed             -->
<!--     FILE:     filename.htm                           -->
<!--     PURPOSE:  what this page provides                -->
<!------------------------------------------------------------>
```

The HTML elements

For more on comment tags, see page 314.

The actual HTML element is just the comment tag:

```
<!-- Browsers won't display this. -->
```

This is where you put information for the benefit of those people reading the HTML coding.

Using an Identification block in files is especially important for large Web sites with more than one author, as it prevents people from stepping on one another's work. It's no coincidence that the Identification block serves the same purpose as headers in computer software code. A Web site is software, and good practices in developing computer software apply.

And don't overlook Identification blocks as a low-key promotional opportunity. "Hey, that's a pretty cool page. I wonder what the coding looks like? Well, I'll just pull down the menu here and view the source file."

```
<!------------------------------------------------------------>
<!--     AUTHOR:   Arthur Ignacio Consulting             -->
<!--     E-MAIL:   art@info-design.com                   -->
<!--     CREATED:  June 15, 1995                         -->
<!--     MODIFIED: July 4, 1995                          -->
<!--     FILE:     index.html                            -->
<!--     PURPOSE:  home page containing contents list    -->
<!------------------------------------------------------------>
```

Tips

Browsers vary as to what they accept as comment tags. Some are more lenient. If the contents of your comments are being displayed by a browser, make sure that you have a closing tag `-->` in place. Also, don't leave a space between the left angle bracket and the exclamation mark `<!--`.

Banner slug

For more information on page banners, see page 414.

On the CD-ROM ...

ingrdnts
  as_rtf
    bslug.rtf
  as_text
    bslug.txt

The Banner slug is actually two HTML elements: an inline image and a level 1 heading. However, they are grouped together here as an ingredient because they are frequently combined, especially on home pages. By the way, *slug* is not the mascot. It is typesetter's lingo for a hunk of type strung together in one piece. After all, this is probably closer to typesetting than just using a word processor would be.

Quick reference

```
<IMG SRC="genbanr.gif" ALT="[emblem text]"><BR>
<H1>title of the page</H1>
```

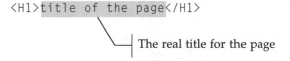

The HTML elements

To create a Banner slug, include the following elements in your HTML file:

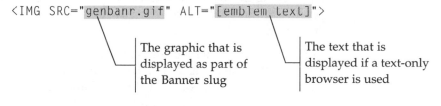

`<IMG SRC="genbanr.gif" ALT="[emblem text]">`

The graphic that is displayed as part of the Banner slug

The text that is displayed if a text-only browser is used

`<H1>title of the page</H1>`

The real title for the page

The `ALT` attribute is optional, but recommended for the benefit of text-based browsers.

Horizontal rule

On the CD-ROM ...
ingrdnts
  as_rtf
    hrule.rtf
  as_text
    hrule.txt

The Horizontal rule places a horizontal line across the page. It is frequently used as part of the Banner slug ingredient. The Horizontal rule can also be used to divide a page into zones. See page 406 for more on its use to create zones.

Quick reference

```
<HR WIDTH=75% SIZE=3 ALIGN=left>
```

The HTML elements

The Horizontal rule is produced by this HTML element:

```
<HR WIDTH=75% SIZE=3 ALIGN=left>
```

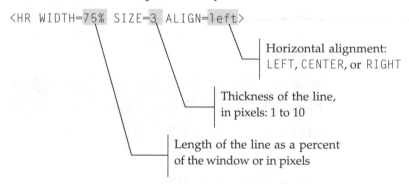

Horizontal alignment:
LEFT, CENTER, or RIGHT

Thickness of the line,
in pixels: 1 to 10

Length of the line as a percent
of the window or in pixels

The length (WIDTH) of the Horizontal rule can be specified in two ways— as a percent of the window width or in pixels. Specifying WIDTH=50% will produce a horizontal rule half as wide as the window. Similarly, specifying WIDTH=200 will produce a rule 200 pixels long.

The SIZE, or thickness, of the Horizontal rule is specified in pixels, with the default value being 2 or 3, depending on the browser. This example shows the default plus SIZE values of 5 and 10:

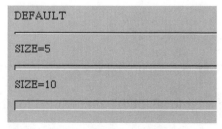

`ALIGN` means just what you might think—`LEFT`, `CENTER`, and `RIGHT`. In this example the Horizontal rule is the default `SIZE`, `WIDTH=75%`, and `ALIGN=CENTER`.

Examples of ingredients

Location: [CD-ROM Home] [Examples] Ingredients

The `WIDTH`, `SIZE`, and `ALIGN` attributes are not supported by all browsers. In those cases, the default is a line the full width of the page. And if the page is resized by the person viewing it, the line will grow or shrink accordingly.

"Hey, I've seen some horizontal rules that are in color, have owls sitting on them, and other cool stuff," you might say. Those are graphical inline images called swashes. That is, they are illustrations put in place using the `IMG` tag. And they are cool. Swashes are covered on page 407. If you use them, remember that they are graphic images and the usual cautions apply. If the person viewing your page has a text only browser, he or she won't see a line. Or if the owl is sitting on the right side of the line and the browser window is made narrower, the owl will not be seen.

Tips

Some authors get carried away with horizontal rules, be they graphical or tag-created. Maybe it's because the Horizontal rule is the only tag that looks like it might be a graphical element, but seeing several horizontal rules on one screen display seems excessive.

We've seen other authors take full advantage of the `WIDTH` and `ALIGN` attributes by specifying a series of centered, descending lengths (for example, 80 percent, 60 percent, 40 percent) to create pyramids. However, those who do this should remember that the browsers that don't support these attributes will just display a series of lines across the full screen.

Signature

On the CD-ROM ...

ingrdnts
  as_rtf
    signatur.rtf
  as_text
    signatur.txt

As used here, the Signature is an ingredient that provides basic information about the Web site. It typically appears on the home page. However, many sites have signatures on all pages, especially if they are designed to have users go directly from other locations to pages inside the site. The Signature helps these users know where they've landed. It also ensures that users who print out your page can find it *and* you again.

Quick reference

```
url of this page -- Revised: date<BR>
Copyright &copy: 1995 <A HREF="myorg.htm">name of my
organization</A><BR>
<A HREF="MAILTO:name@what.ever.domain">name@what.ever.domain</A><BR>
```

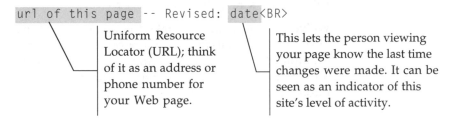

The HTML elements

The Signature is made up of several HTML elements.

```
url of this page -- Revised: date<BR>
```

Uniform Resource Locator (URL); think of it as an address or phone number for your Web page.

This lets the person viewing your page know the last time changes were made. It can be seen as an indicator of this site's level of activity.

The URL is discussed later in this chapter under "Pointers to Other Places (URLs)."

The revision date lets visitors to the page know if this Web site is fresh and dynamic or stale and dusty. This is important, especially if you want to have people come back for return visits. An evolving standard that is more direct is a "What's New" link on the home page. This tells visitors that you frequently add content that warrants return visits.

Of course, not all sites need this. For example, some sites are meant to post information about a single upcoming event. Other sites, by their nature, imply that changes are coming. A site that advertises job listings is a common example. By the way, pages that list job openings can be very popular.

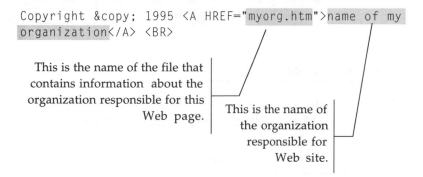

```
Copyright &copy; 1995 <A HREF="myorg.htm">name of my
organization</A> <BR>
```

This is the name of the file that contains information about the organization responsible for this Web page.

This is the name of the organization responsible for Web site.

The copyright serves two purposes. It reminds people that this is someone's intellectual property. And even though it's free for viewing, it remains the property of the organization named in the statement. The second purpose is to answer the question, "Who are these guys?" The description of the organization can range from simple to elaborate, including photographs of people, mission statements, and tours through a series of screens.

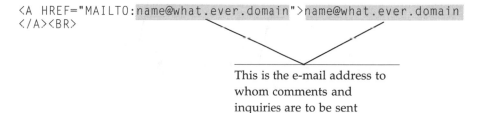

```
<A HREF="MAILTO:name@what.ever.domain">name@what.ever.domain
</A><BR>
```

This is the e-mail address to whom comments and inquiries are to be sent

It's important to have the actual e-mail address visible because not all browsers support the e-mail pop-up form required by this hypertext reference. For more information, see "Link to send e-mail" on page 267.

The <BR> tag breaks the lines, preventing them from running together into a single line when the browser displays them.

Tips

It's easy to overlook the <BR> tag. You'll know when you do because the entire page footer will be strung together, like this:

> url of this page -- Revised: date Copyright ©: 1995 name of my organization name@what.ever.domain

Background and text color

Tired of black text on a gray background? Netscape and other browsers now let you specify the color of the background and text in your Web page.

Quick reference

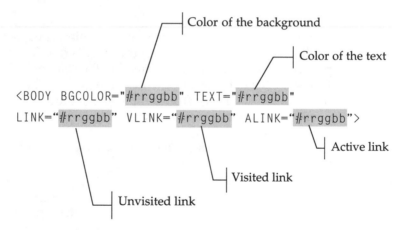

The HTML elements

To specify the color for background and text, you add attributes to the BODY tag. These attributes control the color of the background and various kinds of text:

Attribute	Controls the color of
BGCOLOR	The background—the area behind text.
TEXT	Normal body text and headings.
LINK	Text that triggers a link to a location you have not yet visited.
VLINK	Text that triggers a link to a location you have already visited.
ALINK	Text of the trigger of an active link.

Colors are specified as three two-digit numbers:

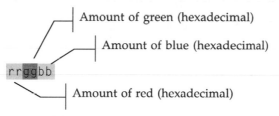

Amount of green (hexadecimal)

Amount of blue (hexadecimal)

rrggbb

Amount of red (hexadecimal)

They are in hexadecimal form. If Hex is not your native tongue, see the section "Setting Color Codes" on page 301.

For example, to have yellow text on a dark blue background, include these attributes within the <BODY> tag.

```
<BODY BGCOLOR="#0000CC" TEXT="#FFFF00"
LINK="#00DD00" VLINK="#FF0000" ALINK="#00FF00">
```

Here unvisited links are dark green, visited links are bright red, and the active link is bright green. For more about using colored backgrounds, see page 420.

Tips

Remember, not all browsers support this feature. If the colors do not change, that may be the reason. Browsers that do not support this feature use the default colors set by the user.

Remember that this ingredient is an attribute to the <BODY> tag in the Page ingredient. To use it you must put it within the regular <BODY> tag. Adding an additional <BODY> tag won't do.

Background graphic

HTML 3.0 lets you use a picture as the background of your Web page. If the picture is smaller than the browser window, it repeats like floor tiles.

Quick reference

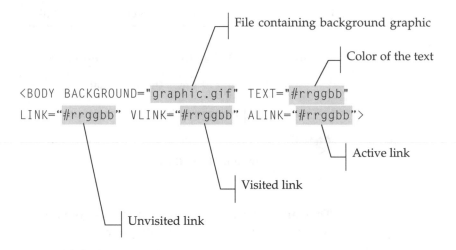

```
<BODY BACKGROUND="graphic.gif" TEXT="#rrggbb"
LINK="#rrggbb" VLINK="#rrggbb" ALINK="#rrggbb">
```

File containing background graphic

Color of the text

Active link

Visited link

Unvisited link

The HTML elements

To specify the Background graphic and the color for text, you add attributes to the `<BODY>` tag.

The `BACKGROUND` attribute specifies the URL of the graphic to use as a background. Other attributes control the color of various kinds of text:

Attribute	Controls the color of
TEXT	Normal body text and headings.
LINK	Text that triggers a link to a location you have not yet visited.
VLINK	Text that triggers a link to a location you have already visited.
ALINK	Text of the trigger of an active link.

Colors are specified as three two-digit numbers:

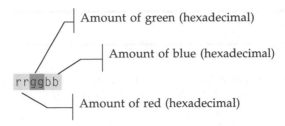

Numbers are in hexadecimal form. Need help with the hexadecimality of this tag? If so, see "Setting Color Codes" on page 301.

Here's how you might use the Background graphic. The file `logo.gif` contains a pastel image of your company's logo. You want to use this as a background for your home page, like a watermark on paper. To do this, just use this form of the `<BODY>` tag:

```
<BODY BACKGROUND="logo.gif" TEXT="#000000"
LINK="#007700" VLINK="#CC0000" ALINK="#00DD00">
```

Here, in addition to the Background Color, text is black, unvisited links are dark green, visited links are red, and active links are light green.

For more examples, see "Tiled pattern" on page 422.

Tips

Remember that this ingredient is an attribute to the `<BODY>` tag used in the Page ingredient. To use it you must place it within the regular `<BODY>` tag.

This technique is an easy way to make your pages totally illegible. Only the simplest images make a suitable background for text. And even the simplest background will not work unless you select colors that make the text clearly stand out from the background.

BLOCKS OF TEXT

This section covers blocks of text that are structural ingredients in page design. That is, while they have format characteristics, they primarily describe pieces whose content have meaning. For example, an Address block is displayed in italics, but its content is intended, as the name implies, to be an address.

The following ingredients are included:

- Paragraph

- Preformatted text

- Quotation block

- Address block

Paragraph

For more on using the paragraph tag to format text, see page 308.

On the CD-ROM ...

ingrdnts
    as_rtf
        para.rtf
    as_text
        para.txt

The Paragraph is likely to be your most extensively used block-of-text ingredient. You are likely to use it to control the formatting of not only text, but also graphical design elements—as a way of separating text from graphics and graphics from each other. When used this way, a paragraph is similar to a break
 . The main difference between a paragraph and a break is that a paragraph throws in more vertical space.

Quick reference

```
<P>This is the first paragraph. It is separated from the
following paragraph.</P>
<P> This is the second paragraph</P>
```

This is the first paragraph. It is separated from the following paragraph.

This is the second paragraph.

HTML elements

To create the Paragraph, simply place the text within the ⟨P⟩ and ⟨/P⟩ tags, like this:

```
<P>This is a paragraph of text. Replace it with your own
words. Make them more meaningful than these words.</P>
```

Tips

The most common problem is forgetting to put in paragraph tags. Paragraph returns, even multiple ones, are completely ignored by the browser. The result is that the text you enter will run together even if it is broken up by one or more paragraph returns. See page 308 for an example.

Another problem stems from variations in implementation of the paragraph tag itself by different browsers. Some assume that a single ⟨P⟩ tag appears at the end of the intended paragraph. Others assume paired start and close tags, ⟨P⟩ ... ⟨/P⟩. So, depending on the browser, the display may end up with extra spaces between paragraphs.

While the standard is heading toward paired tags, the sheer variety of browsers and versions of each browser make this difficult to work around. This is one of those situations where you have to have the wisdom not to worry about things that you can't do anything about.

Preformatted text

On the CD-ROM ...

ingrdnts
    as_rtf
        preform.rtf
    as_text
        preform.txt

Preformatted text is a straightforward ingredient. You are telling the Web browser not to change the text layout between ⟨PRE⟩ and ⟨/PRE⟩.

Quick reference

```
<PRE>
        This text                       +------+        |\
            will appear                 |      |  ------+ \
                formatted               |      |  ------+ /
                    just like this.     +------+        |/
</PRE>
```

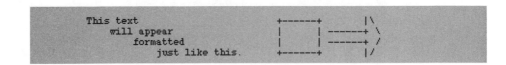

HTML elements

Preformatted text helps you get over two knotty problems:

- Controlling text appearance in a way not possible with HTML tags.

- Preventing browsers from reformatting text that you want to remain just the way it appears.

While this might sound like saying the same thing in two different ways, it really does address two different types of problems.

In the first use, you can use Preformatted text to get the text to appear on the page exactly where you desire. For example, you want the chunks of text to fall a particular way on the page. In a word processor you'd use tabs to position the text. Web browsers, however, tend to ignore tabs or interpret them in ways that you don't expect, so you must move text around by putting in spaces by hand.

The second use is commonly applied to automatically generated output, such as a database report, where you don't want the lines to wrap. You could add HTML tags to format the text, but that sort of defeats the purpose of automating the process. Of course, you could write a little C++ program to do it all, but maybe that's a little more than you want to do at the moment.

Using Preformatted text is also a way to get HTML to display a nicely aligned fill-in-the-blanks form and tables. (See page 363.) Also see how to use Preformatted text to mimic a familiar paper document on page 432.

Tips

Use a fixed-width font in your text editor for the words that you are placing between the preformatted text tags, because variable-width fonts will throw off the horizontal spacing.

Also, avoid using tab characters in your word processor. Browsers interpret them in different ways, which makes the appearance of the text unpredictable.

Quotation block

On the CD-ROM ...

ingrdnts
  as_rtf
    quote.rtf
  as_text
    quote.txt

The Quotation block sets off a special paragraph, typically a long quotation. You can use it to draw attention to any paragraph within a series of paragraphs.

Quick reference

```
<P>This is a large block of normal text. It is here so that
you can see that it goes from the left margin all the way to
the right margin. It will contrast with the following
quotation block.</P>

<BLOCKQUOTE>
This text is a quotation to be set off from regular text,
typically by being indented from the left and right margins.
</BLOCKQUOTE>
```

This is a large block of normal text. It is here so that you can see that it goes from the left margin all the way to the right margin. It will contrast with the following quotation block.

> This text is a quotation to be set off from regular text, typically by being indented from the left and right margins.

The HTML elements

The `<BLOCKQUOTE>` tag is intended, as the name implies, to set off quoted material. Browsers vary a bit as to how they display the text. Some indent from the left and right as shown in the previous example. Others indent only from the left margin.

Address block

On the CD-ROM ...

ingrdnts
  as_rtf
    address.rtf
  as_text
    address.txt

The Address block serves as an identifier of the people behind the Web site. The Address block provides the information that a user needs to communicate interest, praise, or constructive comments to those responsible for the site. It's similar in purpose to the Signature. Address blocks tend to be used only on home pages and by organizations. Individuals putting out Web sites tend to use the more anonymous Signature on their home pages.

Quick reference

```
<ADDRESS>
your name<BR>
your organization<BR>
street address<BR>
city, state or province, postal code<BR>
phone numbers<BR>
<A
HREF="MAILTO:name@what.ever.domain">name@what.ever.domain</A><
BR>
</ADDRESS>
```

The user can click here to bring up a mail form.

The HTML elements

For what it's worth, the people sponsoring the Web site are usually the folks cited in the Address block. They are not necessarily the people who authored the site, given the practice of companies hiring out the work.

The Address block is a bit of a quirky element. It is a *logical* style or element, that is, it has content *meaning*, not just appearance. If you are building a site that makes use of logical elements, then use it.

However, some Web authors have noticed that Address blocks are usually displayed as italics, which aren't always the most readable things online, and have taken to compensating for them in some way. For instance, address and phone number get displayed somewhere else in a more legible way, or they don't use the <ADDRESS> tags at all. Users can also compensate by changing the settings of their browsers and turning off italics.

Most of the elements in this ingredient are simple enough: name, address, phone number. The last line, which shows the e-mail address, is an example of one of the benefits of interactive media. Not only can your users see the address, but if they use browsers that support e-mail forms, they can fire up an e-mail session by clicking on the e-mail address:

```
<A HREF="MAILTO:name@what.ever.domain">name@what.ever.domain
</A><BR>
```

This is the e-mail address
to which comments and
inquiries are to be sent.

It's important to have the actual e-mail address visible, because not all browsers support the e-mail pop-up form required by this hypertext reference.

The e-mail form is covered later in this chapter under "Link to send e-mail," page 267.

Here is an example of the Address block in action. SK Writers is a recruitment and placement agency in Silicon Valley. The following HTML code and browser display lets users know that Shirley Krestas is responsible for her Web site and how to contact her.

```
<ADDRESS>
Shirley Krestas<BR>
SK Writers<BR>
20430 Town Center Lane, Suite 5E1<BR>
Cupertino, CA 95014<BR>
408-252-4818<BR>
<A HREF="MAILTO:shirley@skwriters.com">
shirley@skwriters.com</A><BR>
</ADDRESS>
```

Tips

One common problem is forgetting to put a break tag <BR> at the end of each line. Forgetting it causes the separate lines to string together in one long line. Maybe this is being petty, but you have to wonder why the creators of the Address tag didn't go ahead and put the pieces on separate lines.

HEADINGS

Headings on Web pages serve the same purpose as they do in books. They show your intended structure within a page and across pages. Heading levels show the hierarchy of relationships among the pieces. Combining graphic emblems with headings can provide visual cues that can make your site easier to navigate.

This section contains three ingredients:

- Text headings

- Heading with included banner

- Heading with a destination marker

For related ingredients that help give structure to Web pages and overall Web sites, see Banner slug and Horizontal rule in the "Page Elements" section of this chapter.

Text headings

For more on how to format text, see page 308.

Text headings show levels of subordination among topics. The subordination of levels is shown by changes in font size.

On the CD-ROM ...

ingrdnts
  as_rtf
    head.rtf
  as_text
    head.txt

Quick reference

```
<H1>Heading level one</H1>
<H2>Heading level two</H2>
<H3>Heading level three</H3>
<H4>Heading level four</H4>
<H5>Heading level five</H5>
<H6>Heading level six</H6>
```

Heading level one

Heading level two

Heading level three

Heading level four

Heading level five

Heading level six

The HTML elements

To use a Text heading, include the following element:

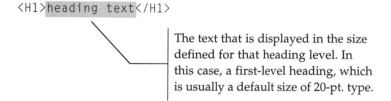

`<H1>`heading text`</H1>`

The text that is displayed in the size defined for that heading level. In this case, a first-level heading, which is usually a default size of 20-pt. type.

Tips

Because not all browsers allow you to change the size of inline text, it is tempting to use (or misuse, depending on your perspective on these things) text headings to change text sizes. No judgments here.

Heading with included emblem

On the CD-ROM ...

ingrdnts
    as_rtf
        headembl.rtf
    as_text
        headembl.txt

Combining a text heading with a graphic emblem provides visual cues that make the structure of a page or Web site easier to understand. It is similar in function to the Banner slug, but can be used on pages other than the site's home page.

Quick reference

```
<H1><IMG SRC="iconfile.gif" Alt="[text label]"> heading
text</H1>
```

The HTML elements

Use the following elements to produce a heading with an included graphic:

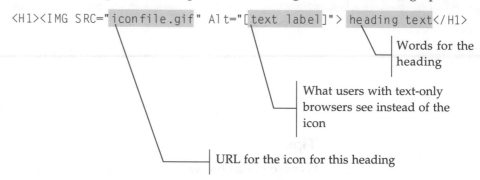

See "Pictures," page 322, for related information on including an emblem.

Heading with destination marker

When you want to let people jump directly to a particular heading within a page, include a destination marker within that heading. You must use this ingredient when your page includes the Page table of contents ingredient (see page 284).

Quick reference

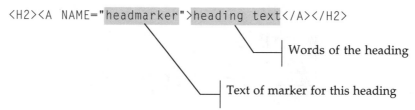

The HTML elements

This ingredient is just a Destination marker (page 268) inside of a Text heading (page 252) ingredient. From a browser,the resulting heading looks the same as one without a destination marker.

For example, to allow links to the third-level heading "Results and analysis," you could format it this way:

```
<H3><A NAME="results">Results and analysis</A></H3>
```

To provide a jump to this heading from elsewhere in the same file, you could use a link like this:

```
The <A HREF="#results">results</A> were highly encouraging.
```

For a more extensive example, see the recipe for Research reports on page 217.

Tips

Jumps to a heading can also come from

- another file in the same directory

- another file in another directory

- another Web site

For more, see "Pointers to Other Places (URLs)," page 286.

LISTS

Lists, as you might guess, are the design elements for creating lists: bulleted, numbered, and definition. Lists are good for creating structure within a page and for breaking up big blobs of text.

The lists described are the following:

- Bullet list

- Bullet list, two level

- Bullet list, complex items

- Numbered list

- Numbered list, two level

- Definition list

See the explanations for Vertical text menu and Text-and-icon menu for other ways in which lists can be used.

By the way, you can mix the elements offered here. For example, there's no reason why you can't have a numbered list with a bullet list as one of the numbered list's items.

Bullet list

On the CD-ROM ...

ingrdnts
    as_rtf
        bullet.rtf
    as_text
        bullet.txt

The bullet list, also known as an *unordered list*, displays a list of items with bullets preceding them. Use it when there is no natural sequence or ranking of the items, for example, when presenting alternatives or choices.

Quick reference

```
<UL>
<LI>first item
<LI>second item
<LI>third item
<LI>fourth item
<LI>fifth item
</UL>
```

- first item
- second item
- third item
- fourth item
- fifth item

The HTML elements

The list items, which are designated by the HTML tag `<LI>`, are placed between the start `<UL>` and end `</UL>` tags.

Some browsers support attributes on spacing, while others support attributes on the bullet's appearance. Given the inconsistency, it's probably best to resist the temptation to try to do much with the attributes.

Tips

If your text is mysteriously indented in ways that you didn't expect, you might have a Bullet list tagging problem. See the "Universal Problem Solving" section in this chapter for help, because there are several possible causes for this problem.

Some authors, apparently frustrated by the lack of control over the page appearance, simulate indented left margins by using the bullet list start and end tags. See page 410 for instructions on how to use this despicable trick.

Bullet list, two level

You can make a two-level bullet list by nesting a Bullet list inside a list item of the higher-level Bullet list. This is a good way to bring more structure to lists that are getting a bit on the long side.

Quick reference

```
<UL>
<LI>first item
    <UL>
    <LI>first sub-item
    <LI>second sub-item
    <LI>third sub-item
    </UL>
<LI>second item
    <UL>
    <LI>first sub-item
    <LI>second sub-item
    <LI>third sub-item
    </UL>
<LI>third item
    <UL>
    <LI>first sub-item
    <LI>second sub-item
    <LI>third sub-item
    </UL>
</UL>
```

- first item
  - first sub-item
  - second sub-item
  - third sub-item
- second item
  - first sub-item
  - second sub-item
  - third sub-item
- third item
  - first sub-item
  - second sub-item
  - third sub-item

The HTML elements

The elements of a two-level Bullet list are the same as those for a simple bullet list.

Tips

If you have lists that are indented in ways that you didn't expect, you might have problems with paired start and end tags either missing or not correctly nested. See "Universal Problem Solving" on page 303.

Bullet list, complex items

Use this ingredient to emphasize an item, then add more detail. It's good for items that are too complex for a standard bullet list, but too simple for a Definition list.

Quick reference

```
<UL>
<LI><STRONG>short phrase.</STRONG> more details on that item.
<LI><STRONG>short phrase.</STRONG> more details on that item.
<LI><STRONG>short phrase.</STRONG> more details on that item.
<LI><STRONG>short phrase.</STRONG> more details on that item.
<LI><STRONG>short phrase.</STRONG> more details on that item.
</UL>
```

- **short phrase**. more details on that item.
- **short phrase**. more details on that item.
- **short phrase**. more details on that item.
- **short phrase**. more details on that item.
- **short phrase**. more details on that item.

The HTML elements

To create a bullet list with complex items, include the following elements:

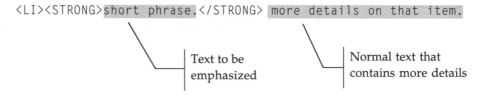

`<LI><STRONG>short phrase.</STRONG> more details on that item.`

Text to be emphasized

Normal text that contains more details

Tips

You can soften the emphasis by using a style other than `<STRONG>`. For example, you could use a physical style such as italic:

`<LI><I>short phrase.</I>more details on that item.`

Numbered list

On the CD-ROM ...

ingrdnts
   as_rtf
      numlist.rtf
   as_text
      numlist.txt

The Number list creates an automatically numbered list of items. Also known as an *ordered list*, use this design element when a sequence is numbered or the items will be referenced by number. It is ideal for step-by-step procedures or for ranked items.

Quick reference

```
<OL>
<LI>first item
<LI>second item
<LI>third item
<LI>fourth item
<LI>fifth item
</OL>
```

1) first item
2) second item
3) third item
4) fourth item
5) fifth item

The HTML elements

The list items, which are designated by the HTML tag `<LI>`, are placed between the start `<OL>` and end `</OL>` tags.

Tips

Sometimes the numbering sequence appears to misbehave. In particular, the first item doesn't contain the number one (1). Check to see if a preceding numbered list is missing its end tag `</OL>`. For more help, see the discussion of Lists in the "Universal Problem Solving" section starting on page 303.

Numbered list, two level

On the CD-ROM ...

ingrdnts
    as_rtf
        numlist2.rtf
    as_text
        numlist2.txt

You can make a two-level numbered list by nesting a numbered list inside a list item of the higher-level numbered list. This is a good way to bring more structure to lists that are getting a bit on the long side.

Quick reference

```
<OL>
<LI>first item
    <OL>
    <LI>first sub-item
    <LI>second sub-item
    <LI>third sub-item
    </OL>
<LI>second item
    <OL>
    <LI>first sub-item
    <LI>second sub-item
    <LI>third sub-item
    </OL>
<LI>third item
    <OL>
    <LI>first sub-item
    <LI>second sub-item
    <LI>third sub-item
    </OL>
</OL>
```

```
1)    first item
      1)    first sub-item
      2)    second sub-item
      3)    third sub-item
2)    second item
      1)    first sub-item
      2)    second sub-item
      3)    third sub-item
3)    third item
      1)    first sub-item
      2)    second sub-item
      3)    third sub-item
```

The HTML elements

Notice that numbered lists that are part of another numbered list must be fully contained; that is, the contained numbered lists are *nested* inside the top-level numbered list. See page 305 for more.

Tips

Surprising indenting and unexpected numbering sequences are usually caused by missing or improperly placed numbered tags. For help, see the "Universal Problem Solving" section starting on page 303.

Also, why not mix list types? For example, why not put a bullet list inside a numbered list like this:

```
<OL>
<LI>First numbered item
<LI>Second numbered item
    <UL>
    <LI>Bullet item one
    <LI>Bullet item two
    </UL>
<LI>Third numbered item
</OL>
```

Definition list

On the CD-ROM ...

ingrdnts
  as_rtf
    deflist.rtf
  as_text
    deflist.txt

Use a definition list to define a list of terms. This ingredient is useful in glossaries, short biographies of a list of people, and (if you add links) lists to other Web sites and descriptions of them.

Quick reference

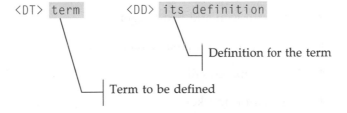

```
<DL>
<DT>first term
<DD>its definition
<DT>second term
<DD>its definition
<DT>third term
<DD>its definition
</DL>
```

The HTML elements

To add a Definition list to your page, include the following elements:

```
<DT> term          <DD> its definition
```

Definition for the term

Term to be defined

Tips

Some Web authors—no doubt frustrated by the limitations of HTML—stretch the purpose of the Definition list, using the definition term as a heading of sorts and putting full paragraphs in the definition.

Most browsers will display a definition term <DT> without a paired definition <DD>. It's a cheap way to get a bold list without bullets.

A definition list is also a good way to set up links to other Web sites:

```
<DT> <A HREF="http://www.golds-gym.com>Gold's Gym</A>
<DD>Web site for Gold's Gyms in Silicon Valley
```

As with other list ingredients, make sure that Definition list start <DL> and end </DL> tags are paired.

LINKS

This section covers hypertext links. These are the text or graphics that users click on, usually to jump to other locations. Areas in browser windows that can be clicked on to go to another location are called *hot*. Text that is hot is usually displayed by the browser in a different color and is underlined.

In addition to jumps to other locations, hot areas can also cause actions such as displaying mail forms, listing directories, and starting up helper applications.

In short, links are what make the Web interactive and, as a result, the Internet more accessible. After all, this ability to jump up, down, across, and back again is what makes it a Web.

The ingredients in this section are:

- Link with text trigger

- Link with icon trigger

- Link with icon and text trigger

- Link to external media element

- Link to send e-mail

- Destination marker

All links have at least two parts: a trigger and a destination URL. The trigger is the part that users see and click on. The URL is the destination or action that is triggered when the user clicks on the trigger.

To help users stay oriented, make the wording of the link label consistent with the title that appears in the destination page's title bar or top-level heading.

For more explanation on types of URLs, see the section later in this chapter, "Pointers to Other Places (URLs)," page 286. For specific uses of links, see the "Menus" (page 269) and "Navigation Buttons" (page 280) sections in this chapter.

Links with text trigger

On the CD-ROM ...

ingrdnts
    as_rtf
        linktxt.rtf
    as_text
        linktxt.txt

This is the basic hypertext link. This creates *hot* text that users click on to jump to other locations or trigger actions.

Quick reference

```
Link with text trigger
<A HREF="whereto.htm"> text that triggers this link</A>
```

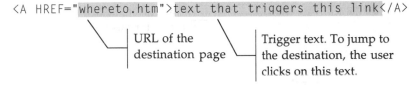

The HTML elements

To create a Link with a text trigger, include the following ingredient in your HTML file:

```
<A HREF="whereto.htm">text that triggers this link</A>
```

          URL of the destination page   Trigger text. To jump to the destination, the user clicks on this text.

For example, the following link with a text trigger jumps to the file named `about.oodb.html`, which contains information about object-oriented databases:

```
<A HREF="about.oodb.html">About Object-oriented Databases</A>
```

Link with icon trigger

Use this ingredient to create graphical images that users can click on to jump to other destinations or trigger an action. The graphical images used are usually icons.

Quick reference

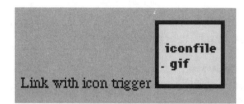

```
Link with icon trigger<A
HREF="whereto.htm"> <IMG
SRC="icon.gif"
ALT="[icon]"></A>
```

The HTML elements

To create a link with an icon trigger, include the following elements in your HTML file:

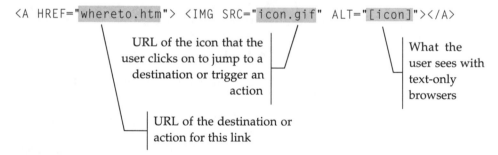

`<A HREF="whereto.htm"> <IMG SRC="icon.gif" ALT="[icon]"></A>`

URL of the icon that the user clicks on to jump to a destination or trigger an action

URL of the destination or action for this link

What the user sees with text-only browsers

Tips

If you're having trouble with your link or your graphic, see Links (page 303) or Graphics (page 304) help in the "Universal Problem Solving" section.

For graphical images that contain more than one destination to jump to, see page 383 for an explanation of image-maps.

Link with icon and text trigger

On the CD-ROM ...

ingrdnts
    as_rtf
        linkictx.rtf
    as_text
        linkictx.htm

Use this ingredient to create an icon and text link, either one of which the user can click on to jump to another location or to trigger an action.

Quick reference

```
Link with icon and text
trigger<A
HREF="whereto.htm"><IMG
SRC="icon.gif"
ALT="[icon]"> text
label</A>
```

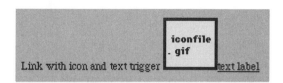

The HTML elements

To create a link with an icon and text trigger, include the following ingredient in your HTML file:

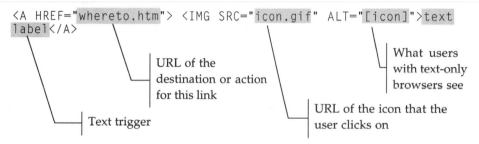

```
<A HREF="whereto.htm"> <IMG SRC="icon.gif" ALT="[icon]">text
label</A>
```

Text trigger

URL of the destination or action for this link

URL of the icon that the user clicks on

What users with text-only browsers see

Link to external media element

For more details on links to external media, see page 49.

A link to an external media element lets the user view or play media that cannot be displayed by the browser.

On the CD-ROM ...

ingrdnts
    as_rtf
        linkext.rtf
    as_text
        linkext.txt

Quick reference

```
Link to external media element<A HREF="filename.ext"><IMG
SRC="icon.gif" ALT="[icon]">label</A> (format, nnK)
```

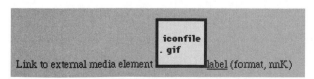

The HTML elements

To create a link to external media, put the following ingredient in your HTML file:

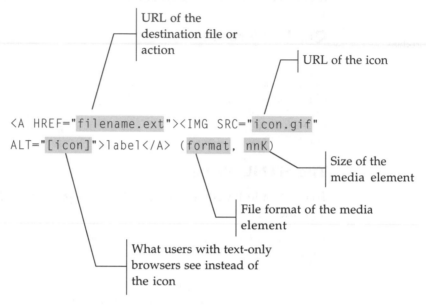

```
<A HREF="filename.ext"><IMG SRC="icon.gif"
ALT="[icon]">label</A> (format, nnK)
```

URL of the destination file or action

URL of the icon

Size of the media element

File format of the media element

What users with text-only browsers see instead of the icon

Display the file format and size as a courtesy to your users who need to know what kind of file it is and how large it is before downloading it.

For example, Barbara Heninger wants to promote her choir's recordings. She provides a sample by including the following link:

```
<A HREF="CHING.AU"><IMG SRC="EAR.GIF" ALT="[EAR
ICON]">CHING.AU</A> (AU, 277K)
```

Tips

Most user problems are related to the sheer variety of helper applications and how individual users set up their browsers to use these helper applications. Provide the file in a standard format (Chapter 6 discusses these), test the link with your helper application, and then rest easy with the understanding that you've done the best you can. The Web frontier isn't completely civilized just yet.

Link to send e-mail

Use this ingredient to bring up a mail form within the Web browser.

Quick reference

```
<A HREF="MAILTO:person@internet.mail.address">
send e-mail</A><BR>
```

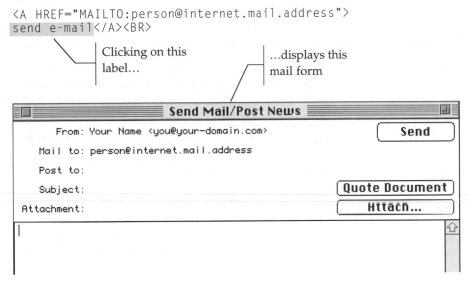

Clicking on this label...

...displays this mail form

The HTML elements

To bring up the mail form, put the following in your HTML file:

```
<A HREF="MAILTO:person@internet.mail.address">
send e-mail</A><BR>
```

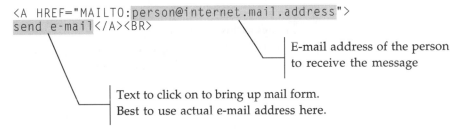

E-mail address of the person to receive the message

Text to click on to bring up mail form. Best to use actual e-mail address here.

Tips

Make sure that `MAILTO:` has no spaces between `MAIL` and `TO` and between `MAILTO` and the colon (:).

You can have the mail form addressed to more than one address by putting the addresses in the URL separated by commas. For example, the following will send mail to both e-mail addresses:

```
<A HREF="MAILTO:jimh@lucidsys.com,solution@sol-sems.com">Send
the mail</A><BR>
```

Not all browsers support this element. Because of this, it's a good practice to use the actual e-mail address as the label the user clicks on. This way, the user can have the e-mail address and send mail using another mail tool.

Destination marker

On the CD-ROM ...

ingrdnts
  as_rtf
    destmrkr.rtf
  as_text
    destmrkr.txt

Destination markers lets you create specific points inside files that users can jump to. The jumps can be from within the same file, or they can be from other files in the same directory, other files in another directory, or from another Web site.

To see how to create URLs that point to a destination marker, see "Pointers to Other Places (URLs)," page 286.

Quick reference

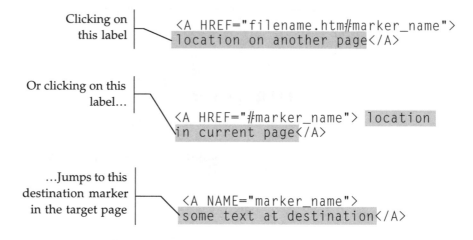

Clicking on this label

```
<A HREF="filename.htm#marker_name">
location on another page</A>
```

Or clicking on this label...

```
<A HREF="#marker_name"> location
in current page</A>
```

...Jumps to this destination marker in the target page

```
<A NAME="marker_name">
some text at destination</A>
```

The HTML elements

To create a destination marker, include the following ingredient:

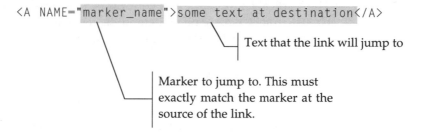

```
<A NAME="marker_name">some text at destination</A>
```

Text that the link will jump to

Marker to jump to. This must exactly match the marker at the source of the link.

For a specific use of this ingredient, see the Research Report recipe, page 217.

MENUS

Menus are ingredients that give your users an orderly choice of topics to jump to. Menus are the means by which Web authors guide their users through the information by creating structured paths.

The following menus are covered in this section:

- Vertical text menu

- Horizontal text menu

- Icon menu

- Text-and-icon menu

The basic component of menus is the Link—either a text trigger, an icon trigger, or both.

Vertical text menu

The Vertical text menu gives your users a vertical list of words or phrases to choose from. Clicking on an item in the list allows users to jump to a different page or trigger some other action.

Quick reference

```
<P>Phrase or sentence introducing the menu:</P>
<UL>
<LI><A HREF="option1.htm">first option</A>
<LI><A HREF="option2.htm">second option</A>
<LI><A HREF="option3.htm">third option</A>
<LI><A HREF="option4.htm">fourth option</A>
<LI><A HREF="option5.htm">fifth option</A>
</UL>
```

Phrase or sentence introducing the menu:

- first option
- second option
- third option
- fourth option
- fifth option

The HTML elements

You create the Vertical text menu by using a Link with text trigger within a Bullet list. A phrase or sentence introducing the menu explains the purpose of the menu to your users. Note that paragraph tags `<P>` and `</P>` set off the introductory statement.

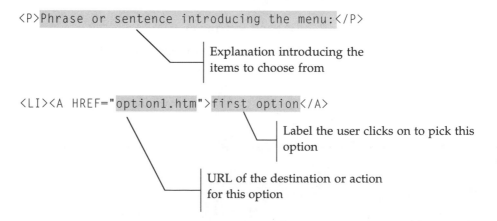

```
<P>Phrase or sentence introducing the menu:</P>
```
Explanation introducing the items to choose from

```
<LI><A HREF="option1.htm">first option</A>
```
Label the user clicks on to pick this option

URL of the destination or action for this option

Tips

If you don't want the bullets to appear, you can leave out the `<LI>` tags and place breaks `<BR>` at the end of each option item like this:

```
<P>Phrase or sentence introducing the menu:</P>
<UL>
<A HREF="option1.htm">first option</A><BR>
<A HREF="option2.htm">second option</A><BR>
<A HREF="option3.htm">third option</A><BR>
</UL>
```

For more explanation and ideas for other possible ways of listing the items in a menu, see the section on "Lists," page 255. Also see the section on "Links," page 262, for more on clickable text.

Horizontal text menu

On the CD-ROM ...

ingrdnts
   as_rtf
      menuhorz.rtf
   as_text
      menuhorz.txt

The Horizontal text menu gives your users a horizontal list of choices. Clicking on an item in the list lets them jump to a different page or trigger an action.

Quick reference

```
<P>Phrase or sentence introducing the menu:</P>

[<A HREF="option1.htm">first option</A>]
[<A HREF="option2.htm">second option</A>]
[<A HREF="option3.htm">third option</A>]
[<A HREF="option4.htm">fourth option</A>]
[<A HREF="option5.htm">fifth option</A>]
```

Phrase or sentence introducing the menu:

[first option] [second option] [third option] [fourth option] [fifth option]

See "Text navigation buttons," page 280, for a special use of this ingredient.

The HTML elements

To create the Horizontal text menu, include the following ingredient in your HTML file:

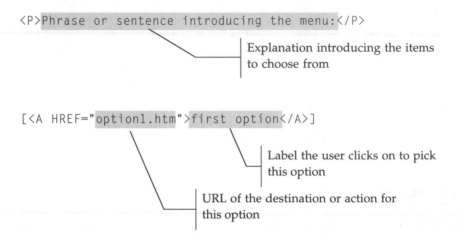

```
<P>Phrase or sentence introducing the menu:</P>
```

Explanation introducing the items to choose from

```
[<A HREF="option1.htm">first option</A>]
```

Label the user clicks on to pick this option

URL of the destination or action for this option

Tips

The text menu is displayed horizontally because browsers wrap the lines. So, some sort of divider is needed to separate the menu items from each other. In this case, square brackets ([ ]) are used. An alternative is to separate items with vertical bars (|) with a space on either side.

Icon menu

On the CD-ROM ...

ingrdnts
  as_rtf
    menuicon.rtf
  as_text
    menuicon.txt

The Icon menu gives users a graphical way of choosing from a list of items. Clicking on an icon in the list lets them jump to a different page or trigger an action such as downloading a file.

Quick reference

```
<P>Phrase or sentence introducing the menu:</P>
<A HREF="option1.htm"><IMG SRC="iconfil1.gif"
ALT="[icon1]"></A>
<A HREF="option2.htm"><IMG SRC="iconfil2.gif"
ALT="[icon2]"></A>
<A HREF="option3.htm"><IMG SRC="iconfil3.gif"
ALT="[icon3]"></A>
<A HREF="option4.htm"><IMG SRC="iconfil4.gif"
ALT="[icon4]"></A>
<A HREF="option5.htm"><IMG SRC="iconfil5.gif"
ALT="[icon5]"></A>
```

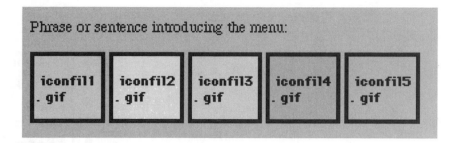

The HTML elements

To create an Icon menu, include the following ingredient in your HTML file:

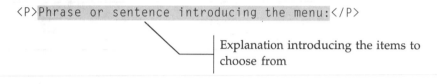

Explanation introducing the items to choose from

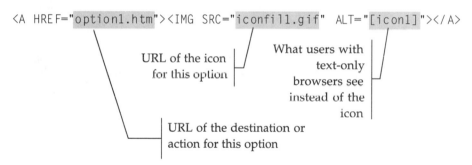

URL of the icon for this option

What users with text-only browsers see instead of the icon

URL of the destination or action for this option

Text-and-icon menu

On the CD-ROM ...

ingrdnts
    as_rtf
        menuti.rtf
    as_text
        menuti.txt

The Text-and-icon menu combines three main ingredients:

- A bullet list to create a vertical list of menu options.

- Icons to provide graphical images that can be clicked on to select an option.

- A text description of each option that can also be clicked on to select that option.

Quick reference

```
<P>Phrase or sentence
introducing the menu:</P>

<UL>

<LI>
<A HREF="option1.htm">
<IMG SRC="iconfil1.gif"
ALT="[icon1]">
first option
</A>

<LI>
<A HREF="option2.htm">
<IMG SRC="iconfil2.gif"
ALT="[icon2]">
second option
</A>
  •
  •
  •
<LI>
<A HREF="option5.htm">
<IMG SRC="iconfil5.gif"
ALT="[icon5]">
fifth option
</A>

</UL>
```

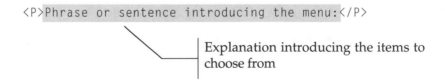

Phrase or sentence introducing the menu:

iconfil1.gif — first option
iconfil2.gif — second option
iconfil3.gif — third option
iconfil4.gif — fourth option
iconfil5.gif — fifth option

The HTML elements

To create a Text-and-icon menu, include the following ingredient in your HTML file:

```
<P>Phrase or sentence introducing the menu:</P>
```

Explanation introducing the items to choose from

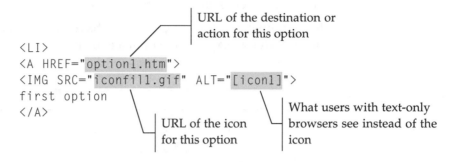

Tips

If you do not want the bullets to appear, omit the `<LI>` tags and place breaks `<BR>` at the end of each option item like this:

```
<P>Phrase or sentence introducing the menu:</P>
```

```
<UL>
```

```
<A HREF="option1.htm"><IMG SRC="iconfill.gif"
ALT="[icon1]">first option</A><BR>
```

```
<A HREF="option2.htm"><IMG SRC="iconfil2.gif"
ALT="[icon2]">second option option</A><BR>
```

```
</UL>
```

PICTURES

A lot of the Web's popularity comes from the appeal and effectiveness of graphics. This section covers how to get those catchy pictures into your Web pages, and includes these ingredients:

- Simple inline image

- Inline image aligned relative to text

- Icon link to picture (or other media)

Other ingredients make use of pictures. For instance, the Banner slug uses a picture to create that first impression for visitors to your Web site. In Headings with included emblems, a picture serves as an easily identifiable emblem that helps users recognize their current location among your pages.

And, as icons, pictures serve as easy-to-follow navigation aids when they are used in menus and navigation buttons.

For information on the pictures that have multiple clickable areas, see page 383 for an explanation of image maps.

Simple inline image

On the CD-ROM ...

ingrdnts
    as_rtf
        imginl.rtf
    as_text
        imginl.txt

Use the Simple inline image to put pictures on your Web page. All graphical browsers can display GIF graphics. Many can also display JPEG graphics. For more on these formats, see page 325.

Quick reference

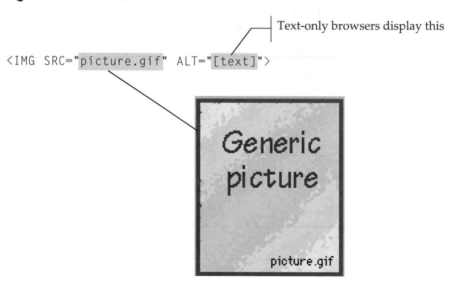

The HTML elements

Use the following ingredient to include an image in your Web page:

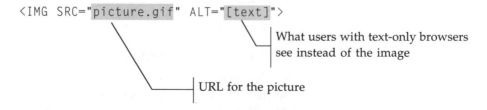

Inline image aligned relative to text

On the CD-ROM ...

ingrdnts
    as_rtf
        imagalign.rtf
    as_text
        imagalign.txt

Images can be aligned relative to text by using the ALIGN attribute for the `<IMG>` tag. A bit of variety exists among browsers when it comes to what ALIGN values are supported, so design with that in mind.

Quick reference

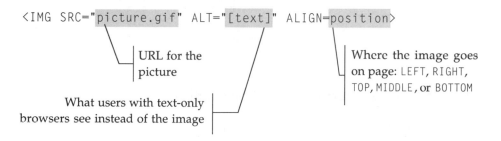

`<IMG SRC="picture.gif" ALT="[text]" ALIGN=position>`

URL for the picture

What users with text-only browsers see instead of the image

Where the image goes on page: LEFT, RIGHT, TOP, MIDDLE, or BOTTOM

The HTML elements

Most browsers support the following values with the ALIGN attribute: BOTTOM, MIDDLE, and TOP. If you don't use the ALIGN attribute, browsers will use BOTTOM.

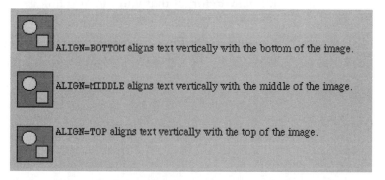

Some browsers also support the following: LEFT and RIGHT. Remember, if you use these values and your user's browser does not support them, they will be ignored.

ALIGN=LEFT places the graphic against the left margin and subsequent text to the right. Starting at the top of the graphic, the text flows around the graphic. When the lines of text reach the bottom of the graphic, they return to the margin. This effect, of course, depends on the width of the browser window. And that is under the control of the user.

ALIGN=RIGHT places the graphic against the right margin and subsequent text to the left. Starting at the top of the graphic, the text flows around the graphic. When the lines of text reach the bottom of the graphic, they return to the margin. This effect, of course, depends on the width of the browser window. And that is under the control of the user.

Icon linked to picture (or other media)

On the CD-ROM ...

ingrdnts
    as_rtf
        iconlnk.rtf
    as_text
        iconlnk.txt

Since the Web allows you to link

- Text to text

- Text to graphics

- Graphics to text

it's easy to forget that you can also link graphics to graphics (or other media). Wordless communication? What a concept!

For more on linking to external media, see the description of a Link to external media element on page 265.

Quick reference

```
<A HREF="picture.gif"> <IMG SRC="iconfile.gif"
ALT="[text]"></A>
```

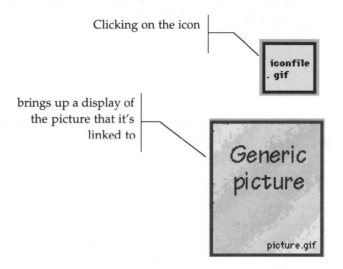

Clicking on the icon

brings up a display of
the picture that it's
linked to

The HTML elements

Use this ingredient in your HTML file to link an icon to a picture (or other media).

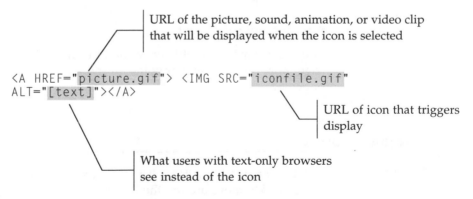

URL of the picture, sound, animation, or video clip
that will be displayed when the icon is selected

```
<A HREF="picture.gif"> <IMG SRC="iconfile.gif"
ALT="[text]"></A>
```

URL of icon that triggers
display

What users with text-only browsers
see instead of the icon

Tips

This ingredient lets you use a small graphic as a preview to a larger one. This thumbnail-enlargement combination is used for a lot of the virtual art galleries on the Web. You can also use a miniature of a frame from a video or animation clip as the icon to trigger display of the animation or video clip.

If you're having trouble with your graphic, see the Graphics help in the "Universal Problem Solving," page 303.

NAVIGATION BUTTONS

Navigation buttons give your users an on-screen way to make quick jumps to the main parts of your Web site. These can include destinations such as a contents page, a map of the site, an index, and your site's home page. Navigation buttons let users move up and down in the hierarchy or backward and forward through pages.

The following ingredients are included in this section:

- Text navigation buttons

- Icon navigation buttons

- Path buttons

- Page table of contents

The basic component of Navigation buttons is the Link, with either a text trigger or an icon trigger or both. For more on links, see the "Links" section, page 262.

Text navigation buttons

On the CD-ROM ...

ingrdnts
  as_rtf
    navtxt.rtf
  as_text
    navtxt.txt

The Text navigation buttons list locations your users can jump to. They help users quickly move around the Web site.

See "Horizontal text menu," page 271, for a related ingredient.

Quick reference

[Contents] [Map] [Index] [Comment] [Search] [My Home] [Up] [Previous] [Next]

```
[<A HREF="contents.htm">Contents</A>]
[<A HREF="map.htm">Map</A>]
[<A HREF="myindex.htm">Index</A>]
[<A HREF="comment.htm">Comment</A>]
[<A HREF="search.htm">Search</A>]
[<A HREF="myhome.htm">My Home</A>]
[<A HREF="parent.htm">Up</A>]
[<A HREF="previous.htm">Previous</A>]
[<A HREF="next.htm">Next</A>]
```

The HTML elements

To create Text navigation buttons, include the following ingredient in your HTML file:

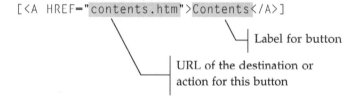

For example, the following HTML code placed on the Search page ...

```
[<A HREF="contents.htm">Contents</A>]
[<A HREF="map.htm">Map</A>]
[<A HREF="myindex.htm">Index</A>]
[<A HREF="comment.htm">Comment</A>]
[Search]
[<A HREF="myhome.htm">My Home</A>]
[<A HREF="parent.htm">Up</A>]
[<A HREF="previous.htm">Previous</A>]
[<A HREF="next.htm">Next</A>]
```

results in the following display.

[Contents] [Map] [Index] [Comment] [Search] [My Home] [Up] [Previous] [Next]

Notice that the Search button is not "hot." This tells the user that the current page *is* the Search page. By including the Search button you also ensure that all the same buttons appear in the same positions on all pages.

Tips

The navigation buttons are displayed horizontally because browsers wrap the lines. Because of this, some sort of divider is needed to separate the buttons from each other. In this case, square brackets ([ ]) are placed around each item. An alternative is to separate items with vertical bars (|) with a space on either side.

Icon navigation buttons

On the CD-ROM ...

ingrdnts
  as_rtf
    navicon.rtf
  as_text
    navicon.txt

Icon navigation buttons give your users a list of locations to jump to. Clicking on an icon propels them to a different page.

Quick reference

```
<A HREF="contents.htm"><IMG SRC="cntsicon.gif" ALT="[Contents]"></A>
<A HREF="map.htm">     <IMG SRC="mapicon.gif"  ALT="[Map]"></A>
<A HREF="myindex.htm"> <IMG SRC="indxicon.gif" ALT="[Index]"></A>
<A HREF="comment.htm"> <IMG SRC="cmnticon.gif" ALT="[Comment]"></A>
<A HREF="search.htm">  <IMG SRC="srchicon.gif" ALT="[Search]"></A>
<A HREF="myhome.htm">  <IMG SRC="homeicon.gif" ALT="[Home]"></A>
<A HREF="parent.htm">  <IMG SRC="upicon.gif"   ALT="[Up]"></A>
<A HREF="previous.htm"><IMG SRC="previcon.gif" ALT="[Previous]"></A>
<A HREF="next.htm">    <IMG SRC="nexticon.gif" ALT="[Next]"></A>
```

The HTML elements

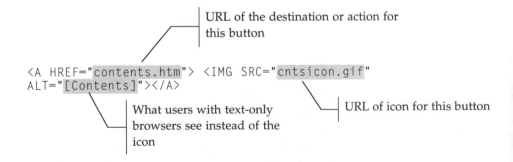

URL of the destination or action for this button

```
<A HREF="contents.htm"> <IMG SRC="cntsicon.gif"
ALT="[Contents]"></A>
```

What users with text-only browsers see instead of the icon

URL of icon for this button

For example, assume that you want to create the icon navigation buttons for the Index page at your Web site. Note that the Index icon itself does not have a hypertext link and that it uses a special faded-out version of the icon.

These icons are in the file resource icons.

```
<A HREF="contents.htm"> <IMG SRC="cntsicon.gif"  ALT="[Contents]"></A>
<A HREF="map.htm">      <IMG SRC="mapicon.gif"   ALT="[Map]"></A>
                        <IMG SRC="indxicox.gif"  ALT="[Index]">
<A HREF="comment.htm">  <IMG SRC="cmnticon.gif"  ALT="[Comment]"></A>
<A HREF="search.htm">   <IMG SRC="srchicon.gif"  ALT="[Search]"></A>
<A HREF="myhome.htm">   <IMG SRC="homeicon.gif"  ALT="[Home]"></A>
<A HREF="parent.htm">   <IMG SRC="upicon.gif"    ALT="[Up]"></A>
<A HREF="previous.htm"> <IMG SRC="previcon.gif"  ALT="[Previous]"></A>
<A HREF="next.htm">     <IMG SRC="nexticon.gif"  ALT="[Next]"></A>
```

The following display shows how the lighter version of the Index icon emphasizes that it cannot be clicked, thereby signaling that the current location is the Index page.

Path buttons

Path buttons show your users where they are in the hierarchy of pages and let them navigate back up through that hierarchy.

Quick reference

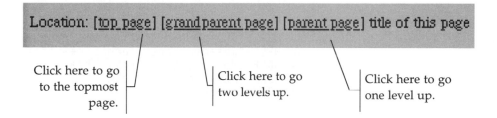

The HTML elements

To create path buttons, include the following elements in your HTML file.

```
<P>Location:
[<A HREF="toppage.htm">top page</A>]
[<A HREF="grndprnt.htm">grandparent page</A>]
[<A HREF="parent.htm">parent page</A>]
title of this page</P>
```

Label for button

URL of destination
for this button

Name of the
current page

Note: This template assumes the current page is on the fourth level of a hierarchy. If your page is deeper, add buttons; if shallower, omit some. Here's the HTML for a page at the third level:

```
<P> Location:
[<A HREF="AXZhome.htm">AXZ Home</A>]
[<A HREF="AXZprod.htm">AXZ Products</A>]
AXZacto 2000 Pro</P>
```

Page table of contents

On the CD-ROM ...

ingrdnts
    as_rtf
        pagetoc.rtf
    as_text
        pagetoc.txt

The Page table of contents lets users jump to specific headings **within** the current page. If you must have pages over a few scrolling zones long, include such a table of contents.

Quick reference

```
<P>Phrase or sentence introducing the contents:</P>

<UL>
<LI><A HREF="#headmarker1">first heading</A>
<LI><A HREF="#headmarker2">second heading</A>
<LI><A HREF="#headmarker3">third heading</A>
<LI><A HREF="#headmarker4">fourth heading</A>
<LI><A HREF="#headmarker5">fifth heading</A>
</UL>
```

Phrase or sentence introducing the contents:

- first heading
- second heading
- third heading
- fourth heading
- fifth heading

The HTML elements

This ingredient is just a special form of the Vertical text menu (page 270) where the links all point to Headings with destination markers (page 254).

```
<LI><A HREF="#headmarker3">third heading</A>
```

Corresponding markers link the table of contents entry to the corresponding heading.

```
<H2><A NAME="headmarker3">third heading</A></H2>
```

For example, suppose you have a long Web page. It has headings called "Introduction," "Research," and "Results." You want to let users jump from the start of the Web page to each of these sections. You can do this by including a table of contents like this:

```
<P>This page contains these three sections:</P>

<UL>
<LI><A HREF="#intro">Introduction</A>
<LI><A HREF="#research">Research</A>
<LI><A HREF="#results">Results</A>
</UL>
```

The Page table of contents only works if the corresponding headings have destination markers (see page 268) and the markers in the table of contents correspond exactly to those in the headings.

```
<H2><A NAME="intro">Introduction</A></H2>

<H2><A NAME="research">Research</A></H2>

<H2><A NAME="results">Results</A></H2>
```

For a full-fledged example of this technique, see the recipe for research reports on page 217.

POINTERS TO OTHER PLACES (URLs)

For the background on URLs, see page 23.

URLs are the addresses of things on the Net. URLs can be part of your public information efforts. On your Web pages, you can put in a Signature that users can use to send e-mail to you. And URLs are popping up on business cards, in employment ads in newspapers, in magazine ads and articles, and even on billboards. Understandably, they're not making much headway on radio: "Come visit our Web site at aych-tee-tee-pee-colon-slash-slash-double-you-double-you-double-you ...".

To make life easy, most URLs are built into links created by Web page authors. So, instead of users having to type in a URL—some of which can be as long as your arm and scary looking, with tildes and slashes—they just click on links.

How to use URLs in links

URLs tell links where they're supposed to go. Earlier in this chapter, we explained the basic parts of the link:

```
<A HREF="whereto.htm">trigger</A>
```

URL

User clicks on this text to jump to the destination or trigger an action.

While text triggers are the most common, graphics can also serve as triggers. And while most links jump to other Web locations, they can also jump to other Internet locations or trigger actions such as downloading files.

Format of a URL

For most authoring, you really don't need to know a lot about the parts of a URL. In practice, you can look at a URL as having three parts as shown in the following example:

The *protocol* tells the browser what Internet protocol to use to get the file. This example uses HyperText Transfer Protocol. Other protocols include FTP (File Transfer Protocol) and Gopher.

The *Web location* indicates the address on the World Wide Web. In most cases, these are Internet *domain* names, preceded by www, the standard abbreviation for the World Wide Web. Not all Web sites use www for reasons that only they can explain. Most places match location naming with protocol. For example, for an FTP site, the protocol is ftp and the Web location is something like ftp.our_domain.com.

In some unusual cases, the location will also require a port number. Then the URL might look like http://www.domain_name.edu:80. This might happen, for example, when your Internet Service Provider is about to switch servers, and they want you to test out your files on the new server before they bring it online for the world.

The *file location* tells where the destination file resides on the server. It specifies a path through the computer system's directory. What's nice is that you can use the symbol "/" across all systems, such as UNIX, Windows, and Mac. The file location can also be a link to a specific location within a Web page.

About directories

Here are a few tips that you might find useful when you set up the directories in your Web site.

Directory conventions: index.html

If the URL points to a directory, some server setups will display the file index.html or home.html from that directory. (Check with your Webmaster for the default filename at your site.) For example, if the convention is to use index.html, and you have a file by that name in the subdirectory named jobs, then the following link will open that file:

```
<A HREF="jobs">Join Us!</A><BR>
```

This convention is useful when you advertise your URL. For example, instead of advertising a URL that looks like this:

```
http://www.objectivity.com/apps/applications.html
```

you can simplify it by renaming `applications.html` as `index.html` and advertising this URL:

```
http://www.objectivity.com/apps
```

Relative paths to directories

You can also use *relative* paths to point to other directories relative to the one holding the current page. For example, suppose you have a directory structure that looks like this:

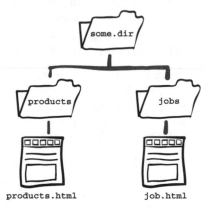

You could make a link from `product.html` to `job.html` by putting the following in `product.html`:

```
<A HREF="../jobs/job.html">Employment Opportunities</A><BR>
```

The symbol "`..`" means "go up one directory level relative to where you are now."

Relative paths make links easier to maintain. If you ever change the name of the directory `some.dir` or move it and the directories under it, you don't have to change the `HREF` path name.

Looking at a directory listing

If the URL is just the directory or subdirectory name and it does not have a default file, the browser will display the names of the files in the directory as hypertext links. Clicking on a file's name will display the contents of the file. If it is an HTML file, the tags will be interpreted by the browser. If it is a text file, then you will see the text.

Use this technique to create a low-maintenance area of your Web site: Just link to the directory once, and then keep adding plain-text files such as simple reports, meeting notes, and computer-generated files.

URL escape codes

URLs cannot include all possible characters, but can contain these standard characters:

- Letters, upper- or lowercase
- Numbers, 0 through 9
- Dollar, $
- Underline, _
- Hyphen, -
- Period, .
- Plus sign, +

But what about other characters, such as the spaces included in Macintosh filenames? Some browsers and some servers are quite forgiving, especially if the URL is within quotation marks. However, to make sure your links work on as many systems as possible, you may need to substitute special codes, called escape codes, for nonstandard characters. Here are the most common ones:

Character	Escape code
space	%20
colon, :	%3A
question mark, ?	%3f
slash, /	%2f

If you think in hexadecimal you probably noticed that the escape code is just a percent sign followed by the two-digit hexadecimal number for the ASCII character code. If the preceding sentence was gibberish, don't worry, you'll probably never have to use any of these except the %20 code for a space.

Location in current page

To refer to a location in the current Web page:

Marker to jump to

For example, you can use this URL to link a list of topics at the top of a page to their corresponding topics further down in the page. If you had a topic called "Marketing Communications," you would put this near the top of the file:

```
<A HREF="#marcomm">Marketing Communications</A><BR>
```

Then you'd put this at the destination for the jump:

```
<H2><A NAME="marcomm">Marketing Communications</A> </H2>
```

At the top of the page, users would see the Marketing Communications topic, click on it, and jump to the Marketing Communications heading.

To see how to use this URL to build a table of contents for a Web page, see page 284.

Page in same directory

To refer to a Web page in the same directory as the one holding the current page:

File to jump to

For example, the Chasm Group, a high-tech marketing consulting firm, has a page listing the firm's members. A link to the page for an individual member might look like this:

```
<A HREF="moore.html">Geoffrey Moore</A><BR>
```

Clicking on the name Geoffrey Moore tells the browser to display the contents of the file `moore.html`, which contains his picture and a short biography.

Location in page in same directory

To refer to a location in another page in the same directory:

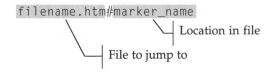

For example, to link to a point in the middle of a file named `BACKGRND.HTM` in the same directory as the current Web page, put this link in your page:

```
For more details, see <A
HREF="BACKGRND.HTM#BackgroundTarget">Background
information</A>
```

Then, in `BACKGRND.HTM`, at the place where you want the user to arrive, place this tag:

```
<A NAME="BackgroundTarget">Background information</A>
```

Make sure the file that contains the link and the destination file are in the same directory.

Page in subdirectory

To refer to a page in a subdirectory of the one holding the current page:

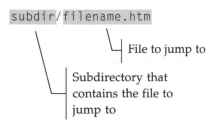

For example, suppose you have this link in your home page file:

```
<A HREF="jobs/listings.html">Employment Opportunities</A><BR>
```

Clicking on the words Employment Opportunities displays the contents of the file `listings.html`, which is in the subdirectory named "jobs."

Make sure that you do not have a "/" symbol in front of the subdirectory name.

Location in page in subdirectory

To refer to a location in a page in a subdirectory:

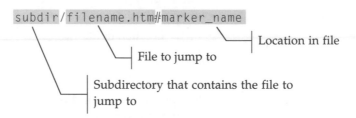

For example, to link to a point in the middle of a file named `semlist.html` that is in the subdirectory named `products`, put this link in your page:

```
For a description of this course, go to <A
HREF="products/semlist.html#robohelp">Using RoboHelp to
Develop Windows Help </A>
```

Then, in `semlist.html`, at the place where you want the user to arrive, put this tag:

```
<A NAME="robohelp"> Using RoboHelp to Develop Windows Help
</A>
```

Page in another directory

To refer to a Web page in another directory:

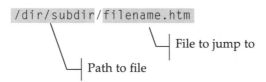

For example, you have created directories at your Web site according to the major topic areas. To make a link from your home page to one of the areas, you put the following link in your home page file:

```
<A HREF="/jobs/listings.html">Employment Opportunities</A><BR>
```

Clicking on the words Employment Opportunities tells the browser to display the contents of the file `listings.html`, which is in the top-level directory "jobs."

Make sure that you *do* have a "/"symbol in front of the directory.

Location in page in another directory

To refer to a location in a page in another directory:

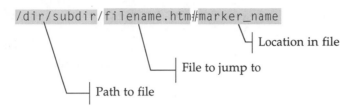

To link to a point in the middle of a file named `hobbies.html` that is in another directory at the location `/public_html/hobbies`, put this link in your page:

```
My interests include <A
HREF="/public_html/hobbies#windsurf">Windsurfing </A> on the
bay.
```

Then, in `hobbies.html`, at the place where you want the user to arrive, place this tag:

```
<A NAME="windsurf">Windsurfing </A>
```

Home page elsewhere on the Web

To refer to a home page elsewhere on the Web:

This URL triggers display of the default or home page for the named Web site. Usually this is the file named `index.html` or `home.html`.

For example, to create a link to the NCSA Home Page, include this link in your HTML file:

```
<A HREF="http://www.ncsa.uiuc.edu">NCSA Home Page</A>
```

Page elsewhere on Web

To refer to a page elsewhere on the Web:

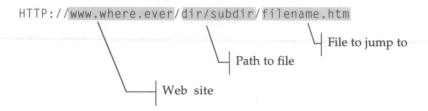

For example, to link to the file

   `otter.html`

in the directory and subdirectory

   `mammals/sea`

at the Web site

   `www.bsu.edu`

include the following element in your file:

```
Learn about<A
HREF="http://www.bsu.edu/mammals/sea/otter.html"> Sea
Otters</A> from the aquarium researchers.
```

Location in page elsewhere on Web

To refer to a location on a page elsewhere on the Web:

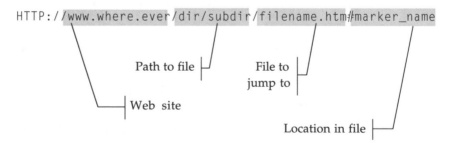

For example, to link to the location

```
<A NAME="aerobics">
```

in the file

```
powter.html
```

in the directory and subdirectory

```
training/instructor
```

at the Web site

```
www.sportscast.com
```

include the following element in your file:

```
Susan Powter's <A
HREF="http://www.sportscast.com/training/instructor/powter.html">
Aerobics Classes</A> at Gold's Gym.
```

Retrieving file via anonymous FTP

On the CD-ROM ...

ingrdnts
    as_rtf
        urls.rtf
    as_text
        urls.txt

To retrieve a file via anonymous FTP, use this URL:

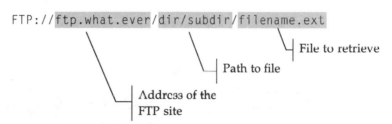

For example, to create a convenient way for your users to get a copy of the Mac file transfer utility called Fetch, include the following in your HTML file:

```
<A HREF=
"FTP://ftp.dartmouth.edu/pub/mac/Fetch_2.1.2.sit.hqx"> Get a
copy of Fetch</A> (364K, .hqx)<BR>
```

Make sure that the file that you want transferred is in an area that has *anonymous* FTP (File Transfer Protocol) service set up. Without anonymous FTP, the server will demand a user login and password.

The user's browser must be set up to save files downloaded via FTP on the user's disk rather than to display them. Since many files posted for downloading are in a special compressed file format (`.zip`, `.hqx`), the resulting display is usually gibberish.

How much you want to help depends on how you define your users. If they are primarily experienced Internauts, no problem. If your audience is likely to be thrown by this, you might design in a link to some explanations about FTP, browser setups, and helper applications.

Listing FTP directory

On the CD-ROM ...

ingrdnts
    as_rtf
        urls.rtf
    as_text
        urls.txt

To display a listing of the files and directories available at an anonymous FTP site:

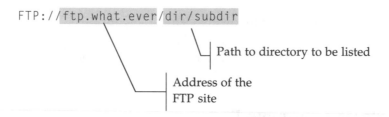

For example, to list the contents of the directory containing the Windows version of Netscape, use the following:

```
<A HREF="FTP://ftp.netscape.com/netscape1.1/windows">Netscape
for Windows</A>
```

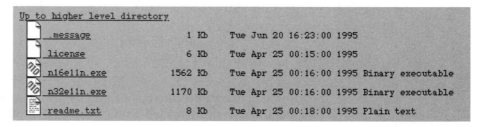

If you have problems accessing the directory, make sure that the site is an anonymous FTP site. Also, check your syntax. Because many FTP sites include FTP in their name, it's easy to forget to put in that part of the URL (FTP://).

Sending electronic mail

On the CD-ROM ...

ingrdnts
    as_rtf
        urls.rtf
    as_text
        urls.txt

For a link that brings up a form to send electronic mail, use this URL:

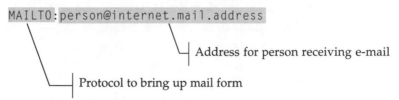

```
MAILTO:person@internet.mail.address
```

Address for person receiving e-mail

Protocol to bring up mail form

You can have the mail form addressed to more than one address by putting the addresses in the URL separated by commas. For example, the following will send mail to both e-mail addresses:

```
<A HREF="MAILTO:jimh@lucidsys.com,solution@sol-sems.com">Send
the mail</A><BR>
```

Not all browsers support this URL, so it's a good practice to use the actual e-mail address as the label the user clicks on. This way, the user can have the e-mail address and send mail using another mail tool.

Gopher server

On the CD-ROM ...

ingrdnts
    as_rtf
        urls.rtf
    as_text
        urls.txt

To link to a Gopher server site:

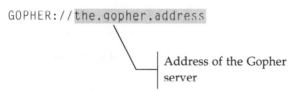

```
GOPHER://the.gopher.address
```

Address of the Gopher server

For example, to link to the U.C. Berkeley Library main Gopher menu, use the following link:

```
<A HREF="gopher://library.berkeley.edu">UC Berkeley Library
Gopher Server</A>
```

This link displays this menu:

Gopher Menu

📁 About InfoLib: The UC Berkeley Library Gopher

📁 About the Libraries (Hours, Instruction, Tours)

💻 GLADIS Online Catalog (most UCB libraries)

💻 MELVYL (tm) UC 9-Campus System

📁 Electronic Journals, Books, Indexes, and Other Sources

📁 Research Databases and Resources by Subject

📁 New in the UC Berkeley Libraries

📁 InfoCal (Class Schedule, Campus Phonebook, etc.)

Viewing Usenet newsgroup

On the CD-ROM ...

ingrdnts
    as_rtf
        urls.rtf
    as_text
        urls.txt

To refer to a Usenet newsgroup:

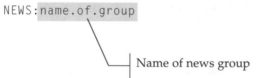

NEWS:name.of.group

                                     Name of news group

For example, to give your user a direct link to the newsgroup
`comp.infosystems.www,` use the following:

```
<A HREF="news:comp.infosystems.www>WWW News Group</A>
```

When the user clicks on the link, the browser will display the most recent articles.

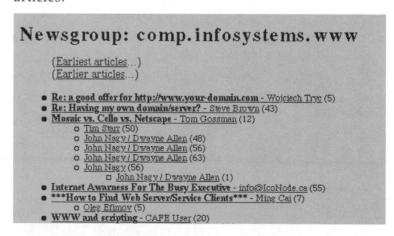

Reading Usenet newsgroup message

To display a particular Usenet newsgroup message:

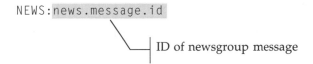

NEWS:`news.message.id`

ID of newsgroup message

For example, in mid-August 1995, to give users a link to a message pointing out a source of satellite images of Hurricane Felix, we used this link:

```
<A HREF="news:40tvmg$sqj@wn.aksi.net"> GOES 9 Rapid Scans</A>
<BR>
```

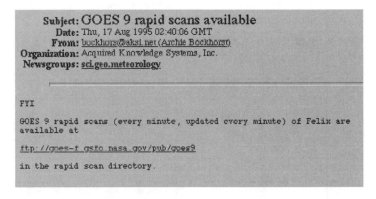

Remember, messages eventually expire and are deleted, so a link to a message will likewise expire.

URL recap

On the CD-ROM ...

ingrdnts
   as_rtf
      urls.rtf
   as_text
      urls.txt

The following table summarizes the types of pointers and the URLs to use for them.

Pointers	URLS
Location in current page	`#marker_name`
Page in same directory	`filename.htm`
Location in page in same directory	`filename.htm#marker_name`

Pointers	URLS
Page in subdirectory	`subdir/filename.htm`
Location in page in subdirectory	`subdir/filename.htm#marker_name`
Page in another directory	`/dir/subdir/filename.htm`
Location in page in another directory	`/dir/subdir/filename.htm#marker_name`
Home page elsewhere on Web	`HTTP://www.where.ever/`
Page elsewhere on Web	`HTTP://www.where.ever/dir/subdir/filename.htm`
Location in page elsewhere on Web	`HTTP://www.where.ever/dir/subdir/filename.htm#marker_name`
Retrieving file via anonymous FTP	`FTP://ftp.what.ever/dir/subdir/filename.ext`
Listing FTP directory	`FTP://ftp.what.ever/dir/subdir`
Sending electronic mail	`MAILTO:person@internet.mail.address`
Gopher server	`GOPHER://the.gopher.address`
Reading Usenet news group	`NEWS:name.of.group`
Reading Usenet news group message	`NEWS:news.message.id`

SETTING COLOR CODES

Use these codes in the ingredients for a colored background (page 242 and page 420) and for a graphic background (page 244 and page 422).

The `<BODY>` tag lets you specify the color of text and background for your Web page, using the `BGCOLOR`, `TEXT`, `LINK`, `ALINK`, and `VLINK` attributes. These attributes require you to specify colors in the format `#RRGGBB`. Here `RR`, `GG`, and `BB` are the amounts of red, green, and blue in the resulting color. The trick is that these two-digit numbers must be in hexadecimal form. That means the digits are

`0, 1, 2, 3, 4, 5, 6, 7, 8, 9, A, B, C, D, E, F`

instead of 0 through 9. That means `00` is the lowest amount of a color and `FF` is the highest.

You may want to bypass the hexadecimal arithmetic and just pick a color from this list. Try it and then finetune the individual red, green, and blue values.

Color	Code
Black	#000000
Blue	#0000FF
Slate Blue	#007FFF
Green	#00FF00
Spring Green	#00FF7F
Cyan	#00FFFF
Navy	#23238E
Steel Blue	#236B8E
Forest Green	#238E23
Sea Green	#238E6B
Midnight Blue	#2F2F4F
Dark Green	#2F4F2F

Color	Code
Dark Slate Gray	#2F4F4F
Medium Blue	#3232CC
Sky Blue	#3299CC
Lime Green	#32CC32
Medium Aquamarine	#32CC99
Cornflower Blue	#42426F
Medium Sea Green	#426F42
Indian Red	#4F2F2F
Violet	#4F2F4F
Dark Olive Green	#4F4F2F
Dim Gray	#545454
Cadet Blue	#5F9F9F

Color	Code
Dark Slate Blue	#6B238E
Medium Forest Green	#6B8E23
Salmon	#6F4242
Dark Turquoise	#7093DB
Aquamarine	#70DB93
Medium Turquoise	#70DBDB
Medium Slate Blue	#7F00FF
Medium Spring Green	#7FFF00
Firebrick	#8E2323
Maroon	#8E236B
Sienna	#8E6B23
Light Steel Blue	#8F8FBC
Pale Green	#8FBC8F
Medium Orchid	#9370DB
Green Yellow	#93DB70
Dark Orchid	#9932CC
Yellow Green	#99CC32
Blue Violet	#9F5F9F
Khaki	#9F9F5F
Brown	#A52A2A
Light Gray	#A8A8A8
Turquoise	#ADEAEA

Color	Code
Pink	#BC8F8F
Light Blue	#BFD8D8
Gray	#C0C0C0
Orange	#CC3232
Violet Red	#CC3299
Gold	#CC7F32
Thistle	#D8BFD8
Wheat	#D8D8BF
Medium Violet Red	#DB7093
Orchid	#DB70DB
Tan	#DB9370
Goldenrod	#DBDB70
Plum	#EAADEA
Medium Goldenrod	#EAEAAD
Sandy Brown	#F4A460
Red	#FF0000
Orange Red	#FF007F
Magenta	#FF00FF
Coral	#FF7F00
Yellow	#FFFF00
White	#FFFFFF

Need to see the colors before you pick? Try one of these Web sources:

- `http://www.biola.edu/cgi-bin/colorserve/colorserve.html`

- `http://www.infocom.net/~bbs/cgi-bin/colorEditor.cgi`

- `http://www.interport.net/~giant/COLOR/hype_color.html`

- `http://www.lne.com/Web/Examples/rgb.html`

UNIVERSAL PROBLEM SOLVING

These are some things to check when you run into problems with your ingredients. Some of them might seem really obvious, but in the heat of the moment, it's easy to overlook the obvious.

Links

- Make sure you have the correct filename in the `HREF` tag and that it is spelled correctly.

- If clicking on the link results in an error message, double-check the format of the URL to make sure it is right.

- If the text in the browser does not look like hot text (different color and underlined), check your typing. The problem is usually the placement of the angle brackets (`<>`).

- If the destination is a new file on a UNIX machine, and you get an error message about permissions, check the permissions to make sure the file is readable by the public.

- UNIX systems are picky about capital letters. The file `backgrnd.html` is not the same as `BACKGRND.HTML`, for example.

Links to a specific location in a file

- The target marker is not spelled exactly the same in the source and destination tags.

- The target marker and destination tags must also match upper- and lowercase letters.

- Make sure the source tag has the "#" symbol.

- Make sure the destination tag does not have the "#" symbol.

Directories and subdirectories

- If the link is to another file in a subdirectory, make sure you do *not* have the symbol "/" in front of the subdirectory name.

- If the link is to another file in another directory, make sure that you *do* have the symbol "/" in front of the directory name.

Other Web sites

- If you are making a link to another Web site, make sure you have the URL for the Web site correct by testing it interactively in your Web browser.

- Not all Web site URLs begin with WWW.

- Sometimes a trailing symbol "/" is required as part of the URL.

E-mail links

- Test the MAILTO e-mail address to make sure it actually brings up the mail form and that it sends mail to the right place.

- Make sure that "MAILTO:" has no spaces between MAIL and TO and between MAILTO and the colon (:).

- If no mail form pops up, your browser might not support mail forms.

Graphics

- If the graphic does not appear, check the filename. File converters used to create GIF format sometimes change lowercase letters to uppercase, which can be a problem on UNIX systems where picture.gif is not the same as picture.GIF.

- On UNIX systems, check permissions for the GIF file. Make sure it is set for read and execute by the public.

- In some unusual cases, browsers and servers do not recognize upper- and lowercase file extensions as the same. For example, a server may be set up to recognize files with a .gif extension as an inline graphic, and may require help from the browser to also accept a .GIF extension. If the browser is not accommodating, the graphics file is not recognized. If you run into a problem where a perfectly good GIF file refuses to display, try changing the case (i.e., from upper to lower or from lower to upper) in the filename and the reference in the HTML file.

Nested tags

You'll notice that most of the tags are paired as starting and closing tags (the ending tag is the one with a slash), and they act on everything in between them. For example, everything bounded by <TITLE> and </TITLE> will appear in the title bar of the browser.

It's a good idea to make sure that your start and end tags are "nested" correctly:

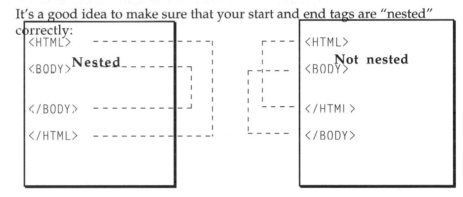

In this illustration, the example on the left is nested, and the one on the right is not. Some browsers and HTML editors are forgiving about this, and this has more visible effect on some tags than others. Overall, though, it's safest to make sure that you nest the tags.

Lists

List start and end tags should always be paired. A list start tag with a forgotten or accidentally deleted end tag causes the text to remain indented. When you see text mysteriously indented, go back and start pairing up start and end tags until you find the lonely one without a buddy.

As expected, the most common problems come from:

- Start tags without matching end tags

- Overlapped instead of nested tags

Notice that lists that are part of another list must be fully contained. The contained lists are nested inside the top-level list. For example, a numbered list nested containing other numbered lists would look like this when correctly nested:

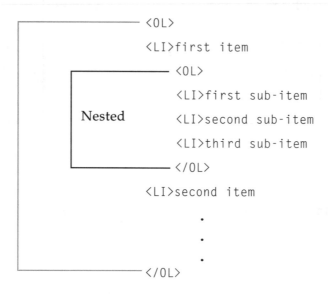

```
<OL>
<LI>first item
    <OL>
    <LI>first sub-item
    <LI>second sub-item
    <LI>third sub-item
    </OL>
<LI>second item
        .
        .
        .
</OL>
```

Nested

Indenting the second-level items makes it easier to distinguish them from the top-level items. It also makes it easier to see whether each start tag is paired with an end tag.

NUTRITION

Media and multimedia

A Web page without content is like an empty plate. It may look pretty, but it does not nourish the mind, body, or soul. In this chapter we tell you how to add content—words, pictures, icons, sounds, music, voice, animation, video, and more.

TEXT

Displayed words are the foundation of communication in Web pages. They are the most widely used medium and hence the most widely misused one. Let's take a look at some of the issues we wrestle with as authors.

Ways of formatting text

If you have worked with a modern page-layout program, or even a good word processor, you will find the typographic controls available for Web pages crude, much like those in word processors of 1979 vintage. Let's see what tags, techniques, and sleazy tricks we have to work with.

Paragraphs

On the CD-ROM ...

examples
  chap6
    text
      text.htm

Paragraphs are the baseline, the *axis mundi,* the starting point of typographic design. Without the <P> and </P> tags around blocks of text, they are not paragraphs and the browser just flows them together. For example, this text:

```
This is an example of a block of text that is NOT within a
pair of paragraph tags. In the HTML file it looks like a
separate block of text.

This is a second block of text. It is NOT within a pair of
paragraph tags. In the HTML file, it too looks like a separate
block of text. But how does it look when displayed as a Web
page?
```

gets formatted like this.

> This is an example of a block of text that is NOT within a pair of paragraph tags. In the HTML file it looks like a separate block of text. This is a second block of text. It is NOT within a pair of paragraph tags. In the HTML file, it too looks like a separate block of text. But how does it look when displayed as a Web page?

But with <P> paragraph tags:

```
</P>This is an example of a block of text that IS within a
pair of paragraph tags. In the HTML file it may or may not
look like a separate block of text.</P>

<P>This is a second block of text that IS within a pair of
paragraph tags. In the HTML file it may or may not look like a
separate block of text. But how does it look when displayed as
a Web page?</P>
```

It comes out like this.

To learn more about formatting paragraphs, see page 246.

> This is an example of a block of text that IS within a pair of paragraph tags. In the HTML file it may or may not look like a separate block of text.
>
> This is a second block of text that IS within a pair of paragraph tags. In the HTML file it may or may not look like a separate block of text. But how does it look when displayed as a Web page?

Physical character styles

On the CD-ROM ...

examples
    chap6
        text
            text.htm

Physical character styles specify what style of type to use for the included text. For example, this HTML code:

```
<P>This is normal. <B>This is Bold.</B> This is normal
again.</P>
<P>This is normal. <I>This is Italic.</I> This is normal
again.</P>
<P>This is normal. <TT>This is Typewriter.</TT> This is normal
again.</P>
```

produces this display.

> This is normal. **This is Bold.** This is normal again.
>
> This is normal. *This is Italic.* This is normal again.
>
> This is normal. `This is Typewriter`. This is normal again.

These tags are simple and reliable—all graphical browsers interpret them in the same way.

Logical character styles

On the CD-ROM ...

examples
  chap6
    text
      text.htm

Logical character styles specify the purpose or kind of information within the tags and leaves it to the browser to format the text appropriately. For example, this block of text:

```
<P>This is normal. <STRONG>This is STRONG text.</STRONG> This
is normal again. </P>

<P>This is normal. <EM>This is EMphasized text.</EM> This is
normal again. </P>

<P>This is normal. <CITE>This is CITEd text.</CITE> This is
normal again. </P>

<P>This is normal. <CODE>This is computer-CODE.</CODE> This is
normal again. </P>

<P>This is normal. <KBD>This is keyboard (KBD) text.</KBD>
This is normal again. </P>

<P>This is normal. <SAMP>This is a SAMPle computer
message.</SAMP> This is normal again. </P>

<P>This is normal. <VAR>This represents a VARiable.</VAR> This
is normal again. </P>a
```

appears like this in the Netscape browser.

This is normal. **This is STRONG text**. This is normal again.

This is normal. *This is EMphasized text* This is normal again.

This is normal. *This is CITEd text* This is normal again.

This is normal. This is computer-CODE. This is normal again.

This is normal. This is keyboard (KBD) text. This is normal again.

This is normal. This is a SAMPle computer message. This is normal again.

This is normal. *This represents a VARiable*. This is normal again.

The commonly supported logical styles include these:

Style	Tag	Typically displayed as:	Use it for text that represents:
Strong	`<STRONG>` `</STRONG>`	**bold**	Very important information. Use it to make a word or phrase stand out in a paragraph.
Emphasize	`<EM>` `</EM>`	*italic*	Subtly important information. Use it to make a word or phrase stand out but not as much as with `<STRONG>`.
Cite	`<CITE>` `</CITE>`	*italic*	Something cited, for example the titles of books, films, plays.
Computer code	`<CODE>` `</CODE>`	`fixed-width font`	Text of a computer program.
Keyboard	`<KBD>` `</KBD>`	`fixed-width font`	Input typed by a user.
Sample computer message	`<SAMP>` `</SAMP>`	`fixed-width font`	Message displayed by a computer.
Variable	`<VAR>` `</VAR>`	*italic*	Item in a syntax statement that the computer user is to replace with a specific value

Note: Not all browsers display these items the same way. Some browsers support even more logical styles. Check the documentation before using these styles and remember to test the results with a range of typical browsers.

Headings

On the CD-ROM ...

examples
   chap6
     text
       text.htm

For more on headings, see
page 252.

Headings let you make clear the organization of your Web page. They let
you show the level of importance of a block of information while providing
a prominent target for someone scanning for just this information.

Headings use the tags <H1>, <H2>, <H3> and so on to produce headings just
like those found in conventional books. For example, here's a heading
sampler:

```
<H1>Heading level one</H1>
<H2>Heading level two</H2>
<H3>Heading level three</H3>
<H4>Heading level four</H4>
<H5>Heading level five</H5>
<H6>Heading level six</H6>

<P>And just for comparison, here is a short paragraph of text.
Notice how the size and style of the text of this paragraph
contrasts with that of the headings.</P>
```

which looks like this, when displayed.

Heading level one

Heading level two

Heading level three

Heading level four

Heading level five

Heading level six

And just for comparison, here is a short paragraph of text. Notice how the size and style of the text of this paragraph contrasts with that of the headings.

Our recipes use the first-level heading <H1> to display the name of the
page, so it is probably best to use <H2> and on down for information within
pages based on our recipes.

Font size

On the CD-ROM ...

examples
    chap6
        text
            text.htm

If your users have the Netscape browser you can directly vary the size of letters of text. Netscape provides a tag to directly set the relative size of text:

```
</P>This is text at the normal size for a paragraph.<BR>
<FONT SIZE=1> This is text at a size of 1.<BR>
<FONT SIZE=2> This is text at a size of 2.<BR>
<FONT SIZE=3> This is text at a size of 3.<BR>
<FONT SIZE=4> This is text at a size of 4.<BR>
<FONT SIZE=5> This is text at a size of 5.<BR>
<FONT SIZE=6> This is text at a size of 6.<BR>
<FONT SIZE=7> This is text at a size of 7.<FONT SIZE=3></P>
```

This is text at the normal size for a paragarph.
This is text at a size of 1.
This is text at a size of 2.
This is text at a size of 3.
This is text at a size of 4.
This is text at a size of 5.
This is text at a size of 6.
This is text at a size of 7.

Note: The sizes range from 1 (smallest) to 7 (largest) and the size change stays in effect until you reset it. Don't forget to reset it to 3, the default base size.

For more on these and other Netscape extensions to HTML, see: http://home.netscape.com/ assist/net_sites/html_ extensions.html

You can use this feature for some elegant effects, like this:

Emphasizing Initial Letters

```
<P><FONT SIZE=7>E<FONT SIZE=4>mphasizing <FONT SIZE=6>I<FONT
SIZE=4>nitial <FONT SIZE=6>L<FONT SIZE=4>etters<FONT
SIZE=3></P>
```

Or you can use it the way far too many Web authors do, alas and alack:

In yOur (inter)face D-sign

```
<P><FONT SIZE=6>I<FONT SIZE=5>n <FONT SIZE=2>y<FONT
SIZE=6>ou<FONT SIZE=4>r <FONT SIZE=2>(inter)<FONT
SIZE=7>f<B>ac</B>e <FONT SIZE=7>D<FONT SIZE=4>-s<FONT
SIZE=3>ig<FONT SIZE=5>n<FONT SIZE=3></P>
```

Comments—invisible text

On the CD-ROM ...

examples
    chap6
        text
            text.htm

You can also make text in your HTML file invisible—to the user of your displayed Web page, that is. Putting text inside comment tags makes sure it does not show up in the displayed Web page though it is clearly visible when you are editing your HTML file.

```
This is the first line of text.            <BR>
<!-- This is the second line of text. -->  <BR>
This is the third line of text.            <BR>
```

Produces this display:

> This is the first line of text.
>
> This is the third line of text.

If you have written computer programs you know what we are talking about. The invisible text is called a *comment*, because we typically use it to label and annotate other text inside the HTML file.

The gods of HTML have decreed that text between the comment tags:

<!--   and   -->

is confidential and not to be mentioned to the user of the Web page. It is stuff only for us authors. At the risk of incurring the wrath of the HTML gods, though, we feel we must let you in on a little secret. Most browsers treat everything between <! and the next > as a comment and make it invisible. The hyphens are not necessary. Most browsers, we say. But not all. There are also rumors of browsers that do not let comments go on for multiple lines. That is, they require the <!-- and the --> to be on the same line. Sounds like a human-factors bug to us.

Special characters

On the CD-ROM ...

examples
    chap6
        text
            text.htm

There are some characters you cannot just type into your HTML file and have them display or work correctly. These fall into three categories:

- Special HTML characters

- ISO-Latin-1 characters

- URL escape codes

Special HTML characters

Imagine you are writing a Web page about creating Web pages. How would you mention and show examples of HTML codes? If you type them into your text, the browser would interpret them as actual HTML codes and try to act on them. A mess, believe us. So, to tiptoe around this problem, use special codes for ampersands, brackets, and quotation marks:

```
<P>This is how to include an ampersand: &amp; </P>
<P>This is how to include a less-than bracket: &lt; </P>
<P>This is how to include a greater-than bracket: &gt; </P>
<P>This is how to include a quotation mark: &quot; </P>
<P>This is how to include a nonbreaking space:
before after </P>
```

See, they work:

This is how to include an ampersand: &

This is how to include a less-than bracket: <

This is how to include a greater-than bracket: >

This is how to include a quotation mark: "

This is how to include a nonbreaking space:
before after

ISO-Latin-1 characters

The Web is international and multiplatform. That means you should be able to include all the special symbols and accented characters needed to communicate a price in pounds sterling to a Norwegian viewing your page on a Macintosh, just as you do it in dollars to an American on a UNIX system. But how can you make sure that the pounds sterling symbol (£) you enter on your PC will display correctly on a Macintosh? And where do you find those "slashed ohs" (ø) that Norwegians are so fond of? And how do you make sure these special characters do not have some different meaning on a UNIX system? You use the ISO-Latin-1 codes to represent anything but the basic letters, numbers, and typewriter symbols.

ISO-Latin-1, which is based on the ISO-8859-1 standard, is a standard for representing the letters and symbols needed for Western European languages based on the roman alphabet. Need to put something in pounds sterling? Just use the code &#163. And for the slashed oh, use &#248, or &oslash, as shown here:

```
<P>Here's the pounds sterling symbol: &#163; </P>
<P>Here are two versions of the slashed oh: &#248;  and
&oslash; </P>
```

Here's the pounds sterling symbol: £

Here are two versions of the slashed oh: ø and ø

If your browser supports HTML 3.0 style tables, you can see which of these character and entity-name codes it can display by looking on the CD-ROM:

examples
   chap6
      isolatin.htm

A complete list of the codes defined in the ISO-8859-1 standard is included here. Alas, not all browsers support all these codes. And the ability to display these characters also requires fonts that include all such characters and not all systems have such fonts.

Description	Symbols	Char Code	Entity name
nonbreaking space			
inverted exclamation mark	¡	&#161;	&iexcl;
cent sign	¢	&#162;	&cent;
pound sign	£	&#163;	&pound;
currency sign	¤	&#164;	&curren;
yen sign	¥	&#165;	&yen;
broken vertical bar		&#166;	&brvbar;
broken vertical bar		&#166;	&brkbar;
section sign	§	&#167;	&sect;
spacing dieresis	¨	&#168;	&uml;
copyright sign	©	&#169;	&copy;
feminine ordinal indicator	ª	&#170;	&ordf;
angle quotation mark, left	«	&#171;	&laquo;
negation sign	¬	&#172;	&not;
soft hyphen	–	&#173;	&shy;
circled R registered sign	®	&#174;	&reg;
spacing macron	¯	&#175;	&hibar;
degree sign	°	&#176;	&deg;
plus-or-minus sign	±	&#177;	&plusmn;
superscript 2	²	&#178;	&sup2;
superscript 3	³	&#179;	&sup3;
spacing acute	´	&#180;	&acute;
micro sign	µ	&#181;	&micro;
paragraph sign	¶	&#182;	&para;
middle dot	·	&#183;	&middot;
spacing cedilla	¸	&#184;	&cedil;
superscript 1	¹	&#185;	&sup1;
masculine ordinal indicator	º	&#186;	&ordm;
angle quotation mark, right	»	&#187;	&raquo;

Description	Symbols	Char Code	Entity name
fraction 1/4	$^1/_4$	&#188;	&frac14;
fraction 1/2	$^1/_2$	&#189;	&frac12;
fraction 3/4	$^3/_4$	&#190;	&frac34;
inverted question mark	¿	&#191;	&iquest;
capital A, grave accent	À	&#192;	&Agrave;
capital A, acute accent	Á	&#193;	&Aacute;
capital A, circumflex accent	Â	&#194;	&Acirc;
capital A, tilde	Ã	&#195;	&Atilde;
capital A, dieresis or umlaut mark	Ä	&#196;	&Auml;
capital A, ring	Å	&#197;	&Aring;
capital AE diphthong (ligature)	Æ	&#198;	&AElig;
capital C, cedilla	Ç	&#199;	&Ccedil;
capital E, grave accent	È	&#200;	&Egrave;
capital E, acute accent	É	&#201;	&Eacute;
capital E, circumflex accent	Ê	&#202;	&Ecirc;
capital E, dieresis or umlaut mark	Ë	&#203;	&Euml;
capital I, grave accent	Ì	&#204;	&Igrave;
capital I, acute accent	Í	&#205;	&Iacute;
capital I, circumflex accent	Î	&#206;	&Icirc;
capital I, dieresis or umlaut mark	Ï	&#207;	&Iuml;
capital Eth, Icelandic		&#208;	&ETH;
capital Eth, Icelandic		&#208;	&Dstrok;
capital N, tilde	Ñ	&#209;	&Ntilde;
capital O, grave accent	Ò	&#210;	&Ograve;
capital O, acute accent	Ó	&#211;	&Uacute;
capital O, circumflex accent	Ô	&#212;	&Ocirc;
capital O, tilde	Õ	&#213;	&Otilde;
capital O, dieresis or umlaut mark	Ö	&#214;	&Ouml;
multiplication sign	×	&#215;	&times;
capital O, slash	Ø	&#216;	&Oslash;
capital U, grave accent	Ù	&#217;	&Ugrave;
capital U, acute accent	Ú	&#218;	&Uacute;

Description	Symbols	Char Code	Entity name
capital U, circumflex accent	Û	&#219;	&Ucirc;
capital U, dieresis or umlaut mark	Ü	&#220;	&Uuml;
capital Y, acute accent		&#221;	&Yacute;
capital THORN, Icelandic		&#222;	&THORN;
small sharp s, German (sz ligature)	ß	&#223;	&szlig;
small a, grave accent	à	&#224;	&agrave;
small a, acute accent	á	&#225;	&aacute;
small a, circumflex accent	â	&#226;	&acirc;
small a, tilde	ã	&#227;	&atilde;
small a, dieresis or umlaut mark	ä	&#228;	&auml;
small a, ring	å	&#229;	&aring;
small ae diphthong (ligature)	æ	&#230;	&aelig;
small c, cedilla	ç	&#231;	&ccedil;
small e, grave accent	è	&#232;	&egrave;
small e, acute accent	é	&#233;	&eacute;
small e, circumflex accent	ê	&#234;	&ecirc;
small e, dieresis or umlaut mark	ë	&#235;	&euml;
small i, grave accent	ì	&#236;	&igrave;
small i, acute accent	í	&#237;	&iacute;
small i, circumflex accent	î	&#238;	&icirc;
small i, dieresis or umlaut mark	ï	&#239;	&iuml;
small eth, Icelandic		&#240;	&eth;
small n, tilde	ñ	&#241;	&ntilde;
small o, grave accent	ò	&#242;	&ograve;
small o, acute accent	ó	&#243;	&oacute;
small o, circumflex accent	ô	&#244;	&ocirc;
small o, tilde	õ	&#245;	&otilde;
small o, dieresis or umlaut mark	ö	&#246;	&ouml;
division sign	÷	&#247;	&divide;
small o, slash	ø	&#248;	&oslash;
small u, grave accent	ù	&#249;	&ugrave;
small u, acute accent	ú	&#250;	&uacute;

Description	Symbols	Char Code	Entity name
small u, circumflex accent	û	&#251;	&ucirc;
small u, dieresis or umlaut mark	ü	&#252;	&uuml;
small y, acute accent		&#253;	&yacute;
small thorn, Icelandic		&#254;	&thorn;
small y, dieresis or umlaut mark	ÿ	&#255;	&yuml;

Note: Characters are missing from the Symbol column because they cannot be displayed by the typesetting system used to produce this book.

Turn text into a graphic

If you still cannot make the text look the way it needs to, we have one last-resort solution: Make the text into a graphic. It's as simple as 1, 2, 3.

1. Use your word processor or drawing program to get the text looking exactly the way you want it to look when displayed in your Web page. Adjust fonts, sizes, styles, colors to your heart's content.

2. Capture an image of the text and save it as a GIF file. Most screen-snapshot utilities will let you do this.

3. Include the image as an inline graphic, like this:

   ```
   <IMG SRC="the_text.gif">
   ```

   Or as an external graphic like this:

   ```
   <A HREF="the_text.gif">trigger</A> (xx K, GIF)
   ```

The drawbacks, besides the time and effort required, are that the graphic may be slow to load and users who have turned off display of graphics will not see it at all. Making text into a graphic is justified, though, to create eye-popping page banners and for critical pieces of text, such as an equation, that cannot be shown otherwise.

For more advice

For more information on formatting text in Web pages, start with these sources:

- ```
  http://www.best.com/~dsiegel/tips/typography.html
  ```
- ```
  http://www.best.com/~dsiegel/tips/graphics.html
  ```
- ```
  http://info.med.yale.edu/caim/StyleManual_Top.HTML
  ```
  ```

Writing style for the Web

Spend five minutes watching someone "read" Web pages and you realize that people do not treat Web pages the same way they do paper pages. With Web pages, users skim, scan, and skip about a lot more than they do in a book. The screen lacks the crisp, sharp edges of ink on paper. These and a thousand other differences mean that we need to write Web pages in a different way from that in which we write traditional paper documents. We need to write them for the way people read them.

Simplify, simplify, simplify

Keep it simple, Shakespeare! Reading from a computer screen can be a trying, error-prone experience, especially when writers bombard readers with long sequences of convoluted, complex sentences. Use simple declarative or imperative sentences. Especially avoid compound-complex sentences with embedded clauses.

Make it shorter

Remember, Web readers are more likely to skim than read in detail. Keep your paragraphs and your sentences short and sweet. Compare the length of sentences and paragraphs in an academic tome to those in a tabloid newspaper. Make yours more like the ones in the newspaper.

Convert long paragraphs and other passages of text to a series of short paragraphs, or recast them as lists or tables. Where possible, replace blocks of text with graphics.

Speak directly to the reader

Say what you mean, simply and directly. Avoid circumlocutions, fuzzy language, and round, about explanations. Write in an active, direct style. If you want users to insert Tab A into Slot B, say "Insert Tab A into Slot B," not "Insertion into Slot B of aforementioned Tab A will effect a positive outcome."

Do not rely on punctuation

What is the difference between a comma and a period? A few pixels, perhaps. How prominent is such a difference on a glare-ridden, fingerprint-smudged screen late on a Friday afternoon? Not very. So be careful with long involved sentences where the meaning hinges on a subtle use of punctuation. Web pages are not a medium for subtlety.

Avoid the as-shown-above syndrome

The *as-shown-above syndrome* is the tendency of a writer of a series of Web pages to assume, perhaps unconsciously, that readers will read the pages in the same order they were written. You see this assumption in phrases like "as shown above" and "earlier you read that." You see it in the habit of spelling out a term or abbreviation the first time it is used, but not thereafter—even though users may read pages in any order. In truth, we must write each page somewhat as if it were the first one the reader encounters.

Link rather than include

To keep things short and simple, replace your own discussion of secondary issues with a link to some one else's explanation elsewhere on the Web. We do have a couple of provisos, though. First, only link to material that will stay at the same URL. Second, periodically check to make sure the information you referenced is still there and that its content is essentially the same.

Design tradeoffs

In using displayed text in Web pages, and other online media as well, you will need to balance three goals:

- **Legibility**. Can users read the text quickly and accurately?

- **Prominence**. Do users notice important items? Can they see the correct levels of importance among titles, headlines, headings, and body text?

- **Consistency**. Within a page and among pages, do similar pieces of information appear the same?

Watch out for conflicts among these goals. For example, often a technique that makes a piece of text stand out on the screen may make it harder to read.

PICTURES

The phenomenal success of the World Wide Web would not have occurred without its ability to display graphics—colorful, detailed, relevant pictures. Pictures, pictures, pictures. Of course, pictures come at a price. You have to create and store them. And the reader has to wait for them to display.

How to include pictures

In your Web pages you can include pictures two ways: as inline graphics or as external graphics. Inline graphics appear in the browser's window amid the text of the Web page. External graphics appear in a separate window provided by a viewer for that kind of picture.

To include an inline graphic, just call it forth with the `<IMG>` tag:

```
<IMG SRC="tiger.gif" ALT="[Picture of tiger]">
```

Here, `SRC` specifies the URL of the file to display and `ALT` specifies what users without graphical browsers see in place of the graphic.

For the background on external media, see page 44. For a template for linking to external media, see page 265.

External or linked graphics are not automatically displayed as part of your Web page; indeed, they might not even be stored on your Web server. You include external images by linking to them, like this:

```
<A HREF="diagram.pdf"> Process flow diagram</A> (140K, .PDF)
```

When your Web page user selects or clicks on a link to one of your graphics, the browser pulls a copy of the graphic file from your Web site (or wherever it's located) into the browser's memory cache. (Don't worry, it doesn't scarf up space on your hard disk unless you specifically save it to a file.)

Helper apps for displaying external graphics are often called viewers.

If the browser is properly configured, it will automatically open the appropriate viewer and display the graphic file; if not, the user may have to manually crank up the viewer and open the file. Users who don't have an appropriate viewer (or a full-blown graphics application) won't be able to see your linked graphics at all.

Viewers are designed to load quickly, using a minimum of the user's computer resources. They will normally handle most common graphic file formats—not just the inline formats of GIF and JPEG, but EPS, PCX, PICT, TIF, and XBM graphics as well. Since their primary purpose is simply to display linked graphics, they may not offer the editing or drawing power of a full-blown illustration or paint program. This is okay, since your users just want to view your linked images—in many cases, with the connect-time clock ticking rather loudly—not edit them.

As part of your own browser configuration, you should have one or more viewers installed on your own system, so that you can test the display of your linked graphics before you put them out on the Web. Of course, you'll need a viewer or two for your own Web browsing, as well. Viewers and their sources are included in "The Work Tools Shopping List" in Resources for the Web Chef.

When to use pictures

Use a picture only when you have something important to say and a picture is the best way to say it. (Same goes for other media, too.) Consider including a picture when:

- **The user will recognize the picture.** An object may be familiar but the user may not know the name of the object. This is often the case when your Web page is read by nonnative readers of English. Perhaps you want to include your photograph in your biography for people who know of your good works but have never seen your face.

- **To teach the name of an object.** If you are introducing a new object, say, your latest product, and you want users to learn to recognize it by name and appearance, a picture can speed the process.

- **Spatial relationships are important.** If the arrangement of parts is important, for instance in a repair procedure or a map, then a graphic is clearly superior to a textual description.

- **Visual appearance is the subject.** If you run an art gallery or sell cosmetics, aesthetics are a selling point, not mere decoration. Showing the beauty you create is the only way to establish your credibility.

- **To set the tone.** Pictures affect how we feel. A collection of hard-edged geometric shapes filled with primary colors and arranged in a regular pattern sets a different tone than a composition of soft-edged organic shapes in pastels and earth tones.

How do I get pictures?

Okay, you have some good reasons to include pictures. Now, where do you get them? You could hire an artist to produce the graphics. No time, no budget, you say? Okay, then consider some of these alternatives:

- **Draw them yourself**. You can pick from a wide range of computer drawing programs. Many people draw their graphics in a vector-draw program like Adobe Illustrator (Mac and Windows), Macromedia Freehand (Mac and Windows), or CorelDRAW! (Windows) before importing them into a paint-raster program like Adobe Photoshop (Mac and Windows) or Fractal Design Painter (Mac and Windows) for refinement and special effects. Keep in mind, though, that for inline display your graphics must be in an acceptable file format. Generally this means GIF or JPEG format.

- **Reengineer clip art**. Electronic clip art abounds. Most of it is pretty banal, but you can often edit it into something useful. Electronic clip art gives you at least a quick prototype to test. For Internet sources, check out `news:alt.binaries.pictures.misc`.

- **Scan in existing art**. If you scan in existing artwork, be sure to experiment and adjust settings for adequate contrast and realistic color balance.

- **Capture screens**. If you are showing computer screens or parts thereof, you can use screen-snapshot utilities to save images. Most such utilities now save in GIF format so no conversion is necessary.

- **Capture other people's pictures**. You can just find an attractive graphic in someone else's Web page and capture it. Hold on, buckaroo! That's the copyright police knocking at your door. Get permission before you use someone else's artwork.

- **Link to other's art**. Instead of copying someone else's art, just link to it on the Web. This saves you from having to maintain a duplicate copy of the art. But it does makes your page dependent on someone else to maintain the art at the same Web address. Asking permission will keep your company's lawyer happy.

Caveat copier

Copying and using someone else's words, images, or sounds in your Web page without permission is possibly immoral, definitely unethical, probably illegal, and certainly stupid. Just because people put something out on the Web does not mean they grant you permission to pirate their buttons, pictures, and other media. Don't say no one warned you when the process server arrives at your front door.

By the way, if you own this book, you do have permission to use all the examples on the CD-ROM in Web pages you create.

File formats for pictures

For inline images, two formats are common. Actually, one format is universal and the other is becoming common. These formats are GIF and JPEG. These and other formats can be used as external graphics by linking to them.

GIF (Graphics Interchange Format)

Extensions	.gif
MIME type	image/gif

Probably the most contentious issue concerning GIF files is how to pronounce GIF. Some say it like "gift," without the "t," while others pronounce it "jiff," with the "g" sounding like the one in "giraffe." We understand that the inventor of the format uses the latter pronunciation.

GIF stands for "Graphical Interchange Format." GIF is the *lingua franca* of pictures on the Web. All graphical browsers display inline GIF graphics. GIF graphics are *bit-mapped* or *raster* graphics. They can be photographs or drawings, for example:

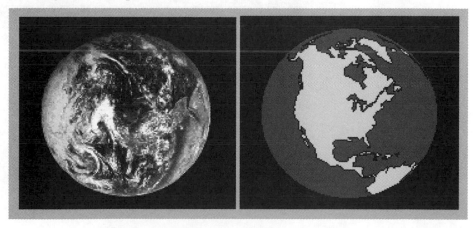

GIF graphics are stored in a compressed format that saves space. One important fact about the GIF format is that the compression is lossless. The process of compressing and uncompressing the graphic does not distort the graphic. That means that the user sees exactly the same graphic you created. This feature is especially important for line drawings, especially ones with small text, where even a small amount of distortion could render the graphic useless. GIF images are limited to 256 colors. They work well for images with large areas of solid color.

GIF images also have two special features that some browsers take advantage of, interlacing (see page 330) and transparent backgrounds (see page 334).

JPEG (Joint Photographic Experts Group)

Extensions	.jpg, .jpeg
MIME type	image/jpeg

JPEG is the name of a file format *and* the compression algorithm used in that format. Confusing, eh?

More and more browsers now let you use JPEG graphics as inline images. JPEG (pronounced "Jay-Peg") stands for "Joint Photographic Experts Group." Guess what it is best for? Photographs—how did you know?

The JPEG format can reduce the size of graphics that must be stored and transmitted over the network. But—and this is a big BUT—the compression is lossy. That means the compression–decompression process degrades the image. The picture the user sees is not quite the same as the one you created.

On the CD-ROM ...

examples
    chap6
        pictures
            pictures.htm

The degree to which the image is degraded depends on the amount of compression. Here are some examples. First, here are a photograph and drawing after being compressed and decompressed. They show the results when the compression is Best quality.

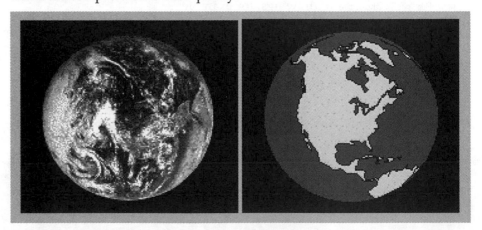

About the only difference between these JPEG images and the lossless GIF ones is that the drawing North America has a slight case of measles.

Here are the same pair of images at 50 percent quality:

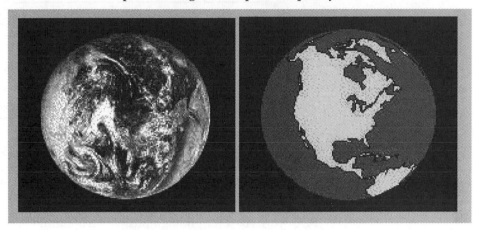

The earth is surrounded by low-flying satellites and the oceans have waves. Such features are known as *artifacts* of the compression–decompression process.

Here are the images at 25 percent quality:

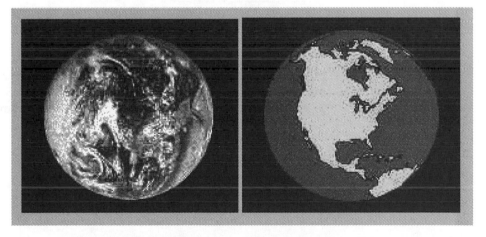

You can see a definite distortion in the cloud patterns in the photographs and the drawing has acquired an impressionistic look.

So how much did we save by compressing the images? Here are the file sizes (in bytes) of the images in different formats and different degrees of compression:

Format	Compression	Photograph (byte)	Drawing (byte)
GIF	none	10,594	9,359
JPEG	Best quality	26,510	21,295
JPEG	50%	5,620	5,472
JPEG	25%	3,784	3,839

Why, you may wonder, are the best-quality JPEG images over twice the size of the GIF images? The JPEG format stores 24 bits of color information per pixel, allowing 16,777,216 different colors, while GIF images are limited to 8 bits per pixel for a maximum of 256 colors.

JPEG works best for photographs with a continuous range of colors. It is not nearly so efficient for black-and-white images or ones with sharp edges. Its lossiness may rule it out where preserving fine detail is essential.

PICT (Macintosh PICTure)

Extensions	.pct, .pict
MIME type	image/pict

In the Macintosh world PICT is the ubiquitous, officially sanctioned, and universally supported format. PICT images can be 1, 8, 16, or 24 bits per pixel. Viewers are readily available on Mac OS systems—but only on such systems.

PostScript Page Description Language

Extensions	.ps
MIME type	application/postscript

The PostScript Page Description Language was invented by Adobe so computers could tell laser printers what to put on a sheet of paper. Just about every application can generate a PostScript file. And PostScript viewing programs exist for most systems. It is good for complex line drawings that the user will probably want to print anyway.

Adobe Portable Document Format

Extensions	.pdf
MIME type	application/pdf

Adobe's Portable Document Format is one of the new digital paper (see page 52) formats. Authors use the Adobe Acrobat writer software to create .pdf files. Users then can view the document with the Acrobat reader.

The Acrobat writer software is essentially a print driver that writes a .pdf file. Writing software is available for Windows, Mac, OS/2, and several UNIX systems.

Although this format is designed for distributing entire multipage documents, it is still an effective way to provide complex color graphics. Users see the graphic the way you "printed" it, even if they lack the fonts you used for the text in the graphic. And (here's where it gets cool) the viewer lets users zoom in on the graphic—just the ticket for viewing complicated diagrams on a small screen.

TIFF (Tagged Image File Format)

Extensions	.tif, .tiff
MIME type	image/tiff

TIFF images are popular in Mac and Windows publishing systems, especially for gray-scale photographs, although they handle color images quite well.

X Windows System Bitmap

Extensions	.xbm
MIME type	image/x-xbitmap

The X Windows System Bitmap format is used mainly for X Windows bitmaps such as icons used in interfaces. It is not widely used in other operating systems.

So which do I use?

GIF and JPEG are the most widely supported formats, especially among Windows and Macintosh systems. If you need to provide pictures for users across many platforms, use GIF for drawings and JPEG for photographs. If all of your users are on Macintosh systems, PICT is a reasonable choice for external graphics. For complex graphics involving fine lines, you may want to go with one of the "digital paper" formats, such as Adobe's PDF, or just use PostScript—provided your users have viewers for these formats.

Special techniques for pictures

In this section we will look at some techniques to improve the appearance of your graphics. These advanced techniques can make a subtle difference or an obvious one. But keep in mind that not all browsers support all these effects.

Interlaced GIF for fade-in display (Netscape)

On the CD-ROM ...

examples
  chap6
    pictures
      pictures.htm

There are several flavors of GIF, one of which is called *interlaced*. This term has to do with how the rows of pixels are stored in the file. Browsers, such as Netscape Navigator, can take advantage of the interlaced format to quickly display a low-resolution version of the image that appears to fade into focus. Let's watch as noninterlaced (on the left) and interlaced versions of the same picture load.

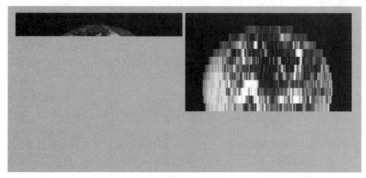

The images have just begun to display. Notice that more of the interlaced image is visible, but it is not as sharp as the noninterlaced one.

More of the noninterlaced image has formed. The interlaced image is sharper than before but still not as sharp as the noninterlaced image.

The noninterlaced image continues to paint itself onto the screen from the top while the interlaced image progressively sharpens.

The noninterlaced image is almost complete. The interlaced one is sharp throughout all but the bottom of the image.

Both images have loaded and are now identical.

Since both images required the same amount of time to finish loading, why use the interlaced format? The reasons are primarily psychological. Because it gives the user the whole image quicker, it appears to load sooner. If the intricate details of the graphic are not important, the user may be able to gather information from the graphic long before it finishes loading. Usually by the time the graphic is half loaded, the user can decide whether to wait for the other half or to move on.

To use this effect, you must save the GIF image in an interlaced format. And, the user must employ a browser that supports this effect.

Antialiasing to reduce jaggies

On the CD-ROM ...

examples
  chap6
    pictures
      pictures.htm

Antialiasing is a technique that is useful, regardless of the browser used. Antialiasing avoids the stair-step jaggedness common in bit-mapped images, especially along diagonal and curving lines. Let's look at some regular and antialiased images.

In these photographs, notice the edges of the earth:

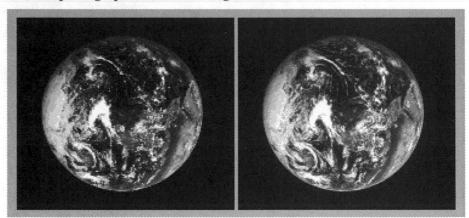

In this drawing, notice the coastlines:

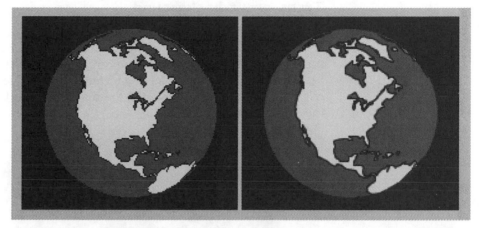

And in these logos, notice the diagonal edges of the letters.

Not all drawing programs provide antialiasing. High-end photo-editing programs such as Photoshop do. There are also utilities available that allow you to convert your vector art to antialiased bitmaps. One such utility is Adobe's ScreenReady.

Transparent background

On the CD-ROM ...

examples
chap6
pictures
pictures.htm

There are two major versions of GIF: GIF87a and GIF89a. One of the features of the GIF89a format is the ability to make one color in the image transparent. This means the image can appear as if it were directly on the browser's surface rather than in a rectangular box. Here the image on the left is on a black background. On the right, the color black was designated the transparent color:

Since not all browsers support this effect, you should make sure the graphic is not confusing when it appears on the nontransparent background. One common problem occurs when designers crop the image too tightly. The image looks okay when the background is transparent, but when the background is visible, annoying ears cling to the corners of the image:

Not all graphics programs let you designate the transparent color for GIF images. But despair not—the shopping list on page 565 includes utilities that let you set the transparent color of a GIF image.

Icons, logos, and buttons

Icons are small graphics used as emblems and buttons. They serve as visual labels and they can serve as emblems for entire pages or parts of a page. They can also serve as buttons the user clicks on to jump to another page or to activate some other function.

Make icons recognizable

Design icons so users learn them easily and remember them reliably.

Pick familiar, concrete objects

On the CD-ROM ...

examples
  chap6
    icons
      icons.htm

The best symbols are familiar, concrete objects—especially if the subject of the icon is abstract or vague. Such objects are easier to recognize and remember. Notice how these objects symbolize audio recording, photography, system error, engineering, and a dining facility by picking recognizable objects associated with those meanings.

Simplify, simplify, simplify

Keep icons simple. Remember an icon is not a picture. It is a symbol. It does not need to be totally realistic or to show intricate detail. Compare these pairs of icons.

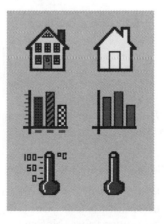

Simple icons are easier to recognize out of the corner of the eye. They remain recognizable at smaller sizes, especially by users with less than perfect vision.

Start in black and white

Get your icons working in black and white—then add color to make them work better. First design and test your icons as simple black-and-white images. When you have a set of icons that appear recognizable, try adding color to improve performance. If your icons do not work in black and white, they probably do not work in color, for several reasons:

- **Color blindness**. About eight percent of men and about one-half of one percent of women are color blind.

- **Monochrome displays**. Many users have gray-scale or black-and-white displays.

- **Contrast**. Low-contrast color combinations can make icons nearly illegible, especially for elderly eyes.

Make related icons consistent

People learn individual icons by comparing them to others on the display. Design all the icons of a single page or related series of pages to follow the same conventions of size, shape, and color coding. Compare these inconsistent icons:

To these consistent ones:

Which is easier to understand? Easier to look at? Which projects a more professional image?

Gather lots of ideas before deciding

Designing icons is tough work, especially icons for abstract concepts. Do not automatically use your first idea. Brainstorm. Doodle. Look at magazines and newspapers. Notice signs and other visual emblems. Gather as many ideas as you can before picking the one to use. Try to come up with five or six good ideas before you start drawing an icon for a concept.

Test and test again

Test your icons with actual users or people like them. Can they recognize the icons? Do they remember them well? Are they confused or offended by any of the icons? Do they have any suggestions for better icons? An icon that is perfectly clear to you and your team may baffle actual users. Better to learn that while there is still time to redesign the icon.

Labeling them

On the CD-ROM ...

examples
  chap6
    icons
      icons.htm

Label icons. Simple visual images with concise labels outperform just images or text alone. Either label the icon with text beside the icon, like this:

Or build the label into the image itself, like this:

Keep the labels short. And do not forget to proofread and test them.

Buttons versus emblems

Icons can be used for buttons and labels. Buttons do something when clicked on. Emblems merely label. It is important to communicate this distinction to users. Most browsers help by putting a colored border around images that are links but not around others. This means that icons without borders are emblems:

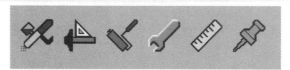

And ones with borders are buttons.

Confusion can arise when designers draw icons with borders. Are these emblems or buttons?

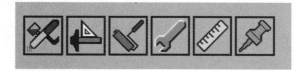

When icons serve as buttons within an image-map, you may want to put a 3-D border around them to make them look more like buttons.

For more on designing icons

Designing effective icons is not easy. To help you further in designing icons we can recommend *The Icon Book: Visual Symbols for Computer Systems and Documentation* by William Horton, published by John Wiley & Sons, Inc.

SOUNDS

Your Web pages can whistle, sing, and shout. You can make your Web pages more than mute and silent posters. To include a sound, just link to the file containing the sound, like this:

```
<A HREF="lionroar.au">Hear the new cat at the zoo</A>
(57K,.AU)
```

Such links can recite a poem, play a sonata, or give the mating call of the orange-winged hooting sparrow. You can let users hear exactly what your product sounds like. You can speak directly to users. You can also annoy users while wasting their time and filling their disks with useless megabytes. The secret to using sounds in Web pages is to use sounds that are worth the cost.

Sound file formats

There are a number of file formats routinely used for sounds on the Web. These include:

SND or AU format

Extensions	.snd, .au
MIME type	audio/basic

The SND or AU format evolved on SUN and NeXT systems and hence is most common in a UNIX environment. It is also called the Sounder/Sound tools format. These files tend to be called .au on Sun systems and .snd on NeXT systems. This format is quite basic. Hey, why do you think the MIME type is "audio/basic"? It records 8-bit samples at a rate of 8 kHz—good enough for recognizable voice but don't expect it to handle a Beethoven symphony. For you techies, it uses μ-law encoding, whatever that is.

Note, do not let the .snd extension fool you. This is not the same as the .snd format of the Amiga world and it has nothing to do with the Macintosh snd resource.

WAVE, Microsoft waveform audio

Extensions	.wav
MIME type	audio/x-wav

WAVE (.wav) is the most common format for digital sound on Windows and MS-DOS systems. It is also common on OS/2 systems.

Converters and players are widely available for Macintosh systems and some UNIX systems, at least the ones that play sound.

Technically .wav is just a form of Microsoft's Resource Interchange File Formats. These are interrelated standards for color palettes, bitmap graphics, MIDI music, and multimedia movies.

WAVE files are quite flexible. They support a range of sampling rates up to 44 kHz and both 8-bit and 16-bit depths and both mono and stereo. If your users are on Windows, this is the format to use.

AIFF, Audio Interchange File Format

Extensions	.aiff, .aif, .aifc
MIME type	audio/aiff

AIFF is the Macintosh and Silicon Graphics equivalent of Windows' WAVE format. This format supports sampling rates up to 44 kHz, 8- and 16-bit depth, and mono and stereo sound. A variant, called .aifc, adds compression. If your users are on Mac systems, you can't go wrong with this format.

Other formats

In addition, you may encounter these additional file formats, especially on FTP sites:

File format	What they are
.voc	Voice, SoundBlaster voice. Used on systems with SoundBlaster (or compatible) cards.
.sbi	SoundBlaster Instrument. Used on systems with SoundBlaster (or compatible) cards.

File format	What they are
.mod	Amiga MOD format.
.ra .ram	RealAudio files (see www.RealAudio.com)
.qt .mov	QuickTime (page 349), normally used for moving pictures, can be used to create sound-only movies.

In addition, you can include sound on the audio track of various moving-picture formats. See page 348 for a list of these formats.

Regardless of the format you choose, the user cannot play back the sound without a corresponding helper application. "The Work Tools Shopping List" (page 565) lists some of the helper applications available for various operating systems.

Recording and editing sounds

To record sounds you will need a microphone and sound-digitizing hardware. The microphone captures the sounds as analog (continuously varying) electrical signals and the digitizing hardware converts these analog signals to digital data. A sound digitizer is built into most Macintosh models, though some users upgrade to higher-performance boards. On PC platforms, popular sound boards include the SoundBlaster products from Creative Labs.

The following picture shows a typical setup for recording and editing sound:

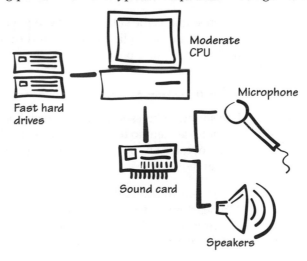

Popular sound editing programs include Sound Forge for Windows and SoundEdit 16 for Macintosh.

To edit sounds, you will need a sound-editing program. A sound-editing program may also prove handy in compressing the sound and converting it to a different file format. Here we are editing one of the sounds included on the recipe for a multimedia page:

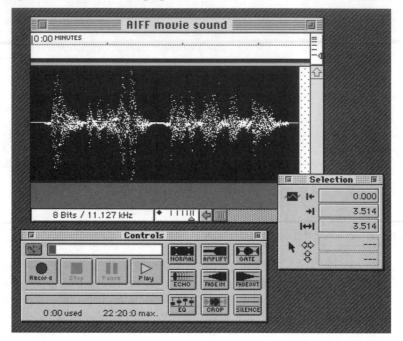

Sound as subject matter

When sound is the subject of a Web page or is important to understanding the page, include a link to the sound or incorporate the sound into the audio track of a moving picture.

When to use sound

Use sounds when sounds are a crucial part of the message of your Web page. Do not use them to be cute. The last effective use of a cute sound in Web pages occurred two years ago. Some good uses of sound as sound include these:

- **When sound is the subject**. Let surgeons listen to the sound of various heart murmurs. Bird calls may be annoying in the middle of a business report, but they are quite appropriate in a report on wildlife management for ornithologists.

- **When teaching people to distinguish between sounds**. Let mechanics and repair technicians learn the sounds made by functioning and malfunctioning devices. Teach people to recognize the Alarm and All Clear signals. Help pilots learn the many bells, beeps, and buzzes of cockpit alarm systems.

- **To represent events or objects**. Sounds can symbolize other concepts. Let computer science students listen to the rhythm of a sorting algorithm as it puts data in order. Or use cartoon sounds to mark critical events in a simulation or animation.

- **To enhance visuals**. Consider using high-quality sound with static pictures. Such sounds can inform users of what they are seeing and help them recognize critical details. You may find that the combination of a clear static picture and sound often requires less storage and performs better than the equivalent moving picture.

How to get sounds

Where do you get sounds to include in your Web pages?

You can record your own sound effects (SFX in the business) just by capturing the sounds all around you. That creaky door to your office can transport the listener to the castle of Count Dracula. A bathtub becomes an ocean and a rattling sheet of plastic, thunder. Go on a sound safari to bag sounds both exotic and mundane from your office and home.

"Too much work," you say? Need a specific sound? Consider purchasing one of the many CDs of sound effects available. These come in CD-Audio and CD-ROM formats. Since the sound is already in digital form, you can often import it directly into your sound-editing program.

If you do use sounds from a CD in your Web page, make sure you read the fine print. Just because you own the CD do not assume you can do anything you want with the sounds on it. Most CDs give you a license to use the sounds in certain ways. Make sure that including them in a Web page available to the known universe is one of those ways.

A third way to get sounds is to download them from some of the many sources on the Internet. Start with `news:alt.binaries.sounds.misc`. Again, take care that you have permission to use the sound in your Web page. Not everything available on the Internet is there with the permission of its owner.

Tips for using sounds

- **Record at the highest quality possible**. You can always downsample the sound later to save storage space, but you cannot add what the microphone did not capture initially.

- **Invest in a good microphone**. Listen with a cocked ear to sounds recorded with the microphone that came with your computer or sound board. Not too good, eh? Definitely do not rely on the microphone built into your laptop computer. You do not need to spend a fortune. Take a fifty-dollar bill to Radio Shack and don't leave until you've swapped it for a microphone that captures sounds clearly.

- **Record just the sound you want**. Remove or turn off sources of noise. That means other machines, computers, and even the air-conditioning system. Block other sources of noise. Close windows to block street noise. Put blankets over noisy objects and over walls that reflect sounds. If recording specific sounds, use a unidirectional microphone. If recording environmental sounds, use an omnidirectional microphone.

- **Don't overdo sounds**. If users do not recognize the sound or do not understand why you included it, the sound becomes *noise*! This is doubly true when they wait several minutes for the sound to download.

Voice

You are not limited to displayed words on your Web pages. Your pages can speak directly to the user.

When to use voice

- **When speech is the message**. Use voice to teach users to pronounce a technical term or to learn a foreign language. You could use voice for singing lessons and speech therapy, or to replay famous speeches.

- **To clarify meaning**. The word "ready" can be a question, a statement of fact, or a plea for action depending on how it is said, or inflected. Often the meaning of words depends on how they are said.

- **To convey emotion**. Reading the transcript of a speech, you cannot always tell whether the speaker was happy, sad, angry, impatient, skeptical, or bored. We can tell if we hear, rather than just see, the speaker's words. The tone of voice can also tell us whether to trust the speaker and whether to share the speaker's opinion of the information conveyed.

- **For complex subjects**. Voice can narrate an animation without distracting from it. Try reading instructions while watching an animation showing what to do.

Tips for using voice

We all know how to talk, but stick a microphone in front of us and our tongue ties a perfect Windsor knot. Recording the human voice takes careful design.

- **Record the voice clearly**. Place the microphone close to the mouth but out of the speaker's voice stream. Record in a quiet, echo-free room.

- **Pick a narrator with good diction** and a clear, well-modulated voice. Base the choice on what the voice sounds like coming out of the Web page, not going into it. Some voices better survive the ravages of recording, compression, decompression, and playback through the inexpensive speakers built into most computers.

- **Have the narrator pause between short segments** of narration. This will make it easier to edit the voice later.

- **Keep the quality of the sound clip high** if the voice must convey a subtle emotion. On the other hand, if recognizing the words is sufficient, then downsample the recording to save storage space and download time.

Music

Try to go through a day without hearing any music. It wafts in from the radio in the apartment downstairs. It belches from the car beside ours in traffic. It is piped into our offices and factories. It underlies almost all the movies and TV programs we watch. It is as much a part of most religious services as it is of TV commercials. (Hmmm?) And it is a part of many Web pages.

When to use music

Music is a powerful motivator. It can lead troops into battle or punctuate a sales pitch. But musical taste is highly subjective. What? You don't like my music! What's wrong with you? Let's consider whether you should use music in your Web pages. In general, use music:

- **To discuss music**. If your subject is music, don't say it, sing it. Or whistle or hum or play it.

- **To provide an emotional context**. Music can tell us how we should feel about other information. Music has been used for over seventy years to tell us how to react to scenes in movies. Use music to tell viewers how to interpret a related picture. Are they to study it, revere it, or just laugh at it? The appropriate music can lead them to the right response.

- **To maintain continuity**. If you are using moving pictures, consider adding music to smooth the flow between scenes or to bridge awkward transitions. Musical continuity can overcome visual discontinuity.

Where to get music

There are four main ways to get the music you need. Three of them are good.

- **Compose it**. With prices falling on MIDI keyboards and synthesizers, many are finding it possible to record and edit their own musical compositions. You no longer require a studio full of musicians to try out your symphony or your advertising jingle. You do require talent and persistence. You do have them, don't you?

- **Commission it**. Even if you are not a composer, perhaps someone you know is. Or you can hire someone. Many musicians compose soundtracks for training videotapes on the side. Perhaps you can hire one to score your Web pages.

- **License it**. Just as there are libraries of clip art, there are libraries of clip music. These collections of prerecorded melodies provide instant gratification. Just cut and paste. Don't forget to check the fine print about licensing to ensure that you can use the musical passages on the Web.

- **Borrow it**. The Internet landscape is dotted with caches of music for the downloading. A couple of good starting points include:

  `http://www.music.indiana.edu/misc/music_resources.html`

  `http://www.eeb.ele.tue.nl/midi/index.html`

  Do not steal it. You can easily incorporate the latest pop hit into your Web page. Think twice before you do. No, do not even think once about it. If your conscience can't tell you why this is a bad idea, the lawyers of the record company certainly can.

Tips for using music

If you use music, use it well. To make your music effective:

- **Make sure you have a good reason** for using music. Since music cannot convey any specific literal meaning, users interested in factual content may perceive music as frivolous, especially if they waited a long time for it to load and play.

- **Pick music of the appropriate tone**. Pick music that is consistent with the spirit and tone of your message. Pick music with low, somber, menacing tones to reinforce a warning. Or include a light, airy tune for a more casual subject.

- **Make the quality of the music high enough** that it has the desired effect. Poor-quality music can undercut your basic message.

- **Balance the volume level**. For background music, make the volume of the music lower than that of subject-matter sound but louder than background sounds.

MOVING PICTURES

Animation and video are both forms of moving pictures. Animation is moving drawings and video is moving photographs. Both can include a sound track. You include them by linking to the file containing the video or animation.

```
<A HREF="factory.mpg">Walk through our new factory</A> (894K,
MPEG)
```

Moving pictures can prove invaluable in explaining complex concepts. But, no mater how clever the compression algorithm, they are seldom cheap—either in terms of storage requirements or download time.

Uses for moving pictures

Moving pictures command attention and are the most direct way to show how things change and move. They fail, utterly, for static subjects. Although both animation or video could be used for many subjects, usually one form or the other performs best.

Use animation	Use video
To show movement and action by generic objects or people	To show movements by particular objects or people
To avoid distracting details	To show rich levels of detail in a scene
For a light or even humorous tone	For a serious, documentary tone
To show something that does not exist	To prove that something does exist
To show abstract concepts	For concrete objects only
For subjects too dangerous or too difficult to photograph	For objects difficult to draw but easy to photograph
To handle sensitive subjects, like sex education or race relations, where showing real people might distract from general concepts	To present specific individuals performing specific actions
	To convey emotions by showing the facial expressions, gestures, and voice of an actor

Every scene or moving segment must make an important point. Do not use moving pictures merely to set a tone.

File formats for moving pictures

Helper applications to play these formats can be found in the shopping list on page 565.

Here are the most common moving-picture file formats used on the Web:

MPEG (Motion Picture Experts Group)

Extensions	mpg, .mpeg, .mpe
MIME type	video/mpeg

MPEG, like JPEG, is both a compression algorithm and a file format that uses that algorithm. It is designed for getting VHS quality video from a CD-ROM. That means both video and audio must be compressed to 1.5 megabits per second—which corresponds to the retrieval rate of a CD-ROM. As such it is a likely candidate for users over the Internet where long download times are anathema.

MPEG achieves its high compression by using an asymmetrical lossy algorithm. Asymmetrical means that it takes a long (!) time to compress but not so long to decompress. It is lossy because video compressed and decompressed with MPEG loses something. The losses are okay if small details are not important. But if sharp edges and small details are important, MPEG ... well, it requires some getting used to. It is not ideal for animation.

The greatest recommendation for MPEG is that players are available for UNIX, Windows, and Mac systems.

QuickTime

Extensions	.mov, .qt
MIME type	video/quicktime

QuickTime is the most versatile of the many picture formats. It can contain video, animation, sound, static pictures, and, with version 2.0, MIDI music.

QuickTime provides a choice of compression schemes, including JPEG, MPEG, and others better suited for animation or static pictures.

Tools for creating, editing, and playing QuickTime "movies" are readily available for Macintosh and Windows systems—but not for UNIX systems.

For your QuickTime movie to play back on both Mac and Windows systems, users must have the QuickTime system extension or DLL and you must save your movie in a compatible format. That is, you must flatten the movie as well as make it a single-forked file.

- Flattening does not mean backing the car over the diskette. It means making sure the movie has no dependencies, or references, to other movie files. *Flattening* a movie is the same thing as making it self-contained.

- Making a movie single-forked has to do with the way the Mac saves files. Mac files have two parts: a data fork and a resource fork. DOS, Windows, and UNIX systems don't fork. So, to make the QuickTime movie playable on Windows, you must take the stuff in the resource fork and move it to the data fork.

In most editing tools you can perform these two functions by selecting the appropriate options in the Save dialog box. There are also several utilities available just for the purpose of making movies single-forked.

- Last, you must pick a compression scheme supported on the user's machine. This usually means Animation, Graphics, or CinePak.

AVI (Microsoft Audio/Visual Interleaved Format)

Extensions	.avi
MIME type	video/x-msvideo

Microsoft's AVI format, also known as Video for Windows, provides many of the same capabilities as QuickTime: inclusion of video, sound, and a variety of compression schemes for different purposes. The .avi format is universally supported on Windows systems. Players and converters for .avi are available for UNIX and Macintosh.

Other moving-picture formats

Though MPEG, QuickTime, and AVI are the big three of Web video, other formats exist, especially for proprietary animation and video formats. These include .dvi (Digital Video Interactive), .fli (Flick, Autodesk animator), and .flc (Autodesk Animator Pro).

Tips for moving pictures

- In video and animation, do not try to explain the moving picture. If your moving pictures need explanation, they would probably work better as static pictures with displayed annotation or spoken narration.

- Do not try to make your point by showing characters talking about a subject. If words are necessary, use voice-over narration to explain the concept.

- Use visual transitions (dissolves, wipes, fades, and so forth) to bridge gaps in time and location.

- For a button to activate the moving picture, use a miniature version of one frame of the moving picture. Pick a frame that is both interesting and representative of the whole moving picture.

- Experiment with different compression schemes. Some techniques allow greater compression but degrade the decompressed image somewhat. Some compression schemes work better for animation and some for video.

- Keep it simple. Keep scenes in your moving pictures clear and uncluttered. Such sequences are easier to comprehend on a grainy screen. And simpler scenes can be compressed more than complex ones. Especially avoid noisy backgrounds.

Sources of moving pictures

If you want to obtain some animation and video segments to test or to include in your own pages, check these sources:

- **Fractal Movie Archive**—http://www.cnam.fr/fractals/anim.html

- **MPEG Movie Archive**—http://w3.eeb.ele.tue.nl/mpeg/index.html

- **Multimedia resources**—http://viswiz.gmd.de/MultimediaInfo/

- **Global Village Stock Footage**—http://nbn.nbn.com/footage/

Preparing animation

To prepare your own animation for use on the Web, you must create the static pictures, put them in motion, and save the results in an appropriate file format. Sounds simple.

There are a number of tools available for creating animation sequences ranging from simple sequences of static pictures to three-dimensional models worthy of Hollywood special-effects houses. We used Macromedia Director (Mac and Windows) to prepare the animation in the Multimedia page recipe (p. 213).

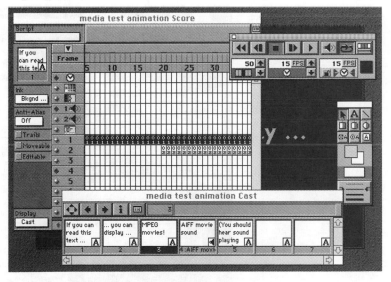

Whatever methods you use to create your animations, when the animation is done, you must convert it to one of the supported formats.

Preparing video

Preparing your own video requires capturing the video images, converting them to digital form, editing and merging the video sequences, and saving it all in the right file format. Typically this requires:

- Camera
- Videotape recorder
- Video digitizing board
- Big, fast disk or disk array

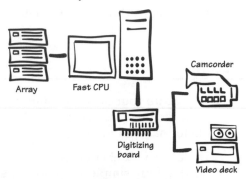

It also requires a digital video editing program such as Adobe Premiere (Mac and Windows), shown here editing one of the video sequences used in the Multimedia page recipe (p. 213).

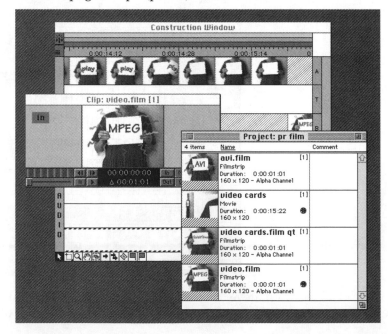

Inline animation and video?

If this whets your appetite, check out the details at http://home.netscape.com/ assist/net_sites/dynamic_ docs.html

Yes, it is possible to create inline animations and videos—ones that appear right inside the browser's window like a regular inline image. To make this happen your users must be using the Netscape browser (version 1.1 or later), which provides a feature called *server push-browser pull*. In a nutshell, this means that the server and browser talk to one another while the page is displayed. This opens up all kinds of possibilities, one of which is inline movies. You could create such a movie by writing a script on the server to feed a series of images to the browser. To trigger the animation, you'd have the <IMG> tag point to the script rather than to a static graphic.

ADDING YOUR OWN MEDIA

Before you begin, you may want to return to page 45 to make sure you understand the magic of MIME.

What if you do not find the medium you want to use listed among those supported by your browser? No problem! Well, not an insurmountable one. You can define new media types and let users download and play them.

For this to happen, you must set up your server to handle the new media type. Users must have a helper app to view or play it, and they must set up their browsers to trigger this helper app when the new media type arrives.

Getting it all working will require five steps. Let's say you want users to be able to click on buttons on your Web page to view slide shows done with a package called ZipZap Create. How might you go about this?

1. Obtain players

Unless we can obtain and distribute small, fast players to display our slide shows, there is little point in continuing. However, ZipZap Corporation provides us with their player ZipZapShow (zzshow.exe) with their blessings to distribute it freely.

2. Distribute players

Getting players to potential users may prove the most difficult step. Consider all of these approaches:

- Set up a Download Page, using the recipe on page 185.

- Post the players on your FTP and Gopher sites.

- On Web pages that use your new media type, also include a link to download the player.

- If use is restricted to a particular group of people, say the field engineers of your company, send them disks in the same envelope as their paychecks.

3. Decide MIME type and file extensions

The file extension is easy. Just use the standard one decreed by ZipZap Corporation, .zzc, for instance. The MIME type is a little trickier. First, we consult the Internet Assigned Numbers Authority to see if a MIME type already exists for this format. You can check at:

`ftp://ftp.isi.edu/iana/assignments/media-types.`

Finding no MIME type assigned, we must make up our own. Here conventions guide us. We use a main type of application since this is an application-specific format. For a subtype, we use x-zipzap. Beginning the name with x- indicates that this is an experimental, unofficial MIME type. So, we've decided:

Extensions	.zzc
MIME type	application/x-zipzap

4. Configure the server

For the server to recognize this new MIME type, it must know how to recognize files that contain this new kind of data. You must tell the server what file extensions indicate files containing data of this new type. How you so inform the server depends on the brand of server you are using. Suppose we have an NCSA-style server. To get it to recognize files with names ending in .zzc as MIME type application/x-zipzap, we'd add this line to the mime.types file in the conf directory:

`application/x-zipzap  zzc`

5. (Get users to) configure browsers

Unless the user's browser is configured to trigger the right helper app for your new media type, it will just say "Huh?" when that type arrives from the server. Here, you are at the mercy of the ignorance and indolence of individual users. Plead, cajole, beg, or bribe users to set their browsers correctly.

Prepare clear, detailed instructions, including screen snapshots showing how to fill in the corresponding dialog boxes in most popular browsers.

- Make these instructions available from Download Pages, FTP sites, and Gopher sites.

- Package them with the helper apps so that when users download the helper app they automatically get these instructions.

- On pages that include links to the new media type, add a link to download these instructions.

With a little luck and a lot of hard work, the Web can speak multimedia.

7

HAUTE CUISINE

Forms, image maps, and tables

This chapter covers some of the fancier things you can cook up—fill-in-the-blanks forms, clickable pictures called image-maps, and tables.

A lot of the sizzle of the Web comes from its ability to mimic the ways we interact with information in the physical world. When we want to give information, we often do it by filling in forms, or just writing in a blank space. And to indicate something, we point at it.

The Web has escaped the command-line-only world of interaction. Now there are fill-in-the-blanks forms. Suddenly, we have a voice, we can say something, and it's easy to do. Now, instead of plain pictures, we have pictures with multiple hot spots. (You can do some pretty interesting things with pictures you can click on.) And with HTML 3.0, you can use tables to line things up in tidy rows and columns.

These features are the ones with which Web authors and users seem to have the most fun. They're also, however, where you are once again—at least on the authoring side—reminded that you are in the world of computers and programming. Tables require extensive coding, as do image-maps. Forms and image-maps require cooperation from the keepers of the server. And you thought two-level lists were complicated.

Before you include forms and image-maps in your page, talk to the people who maintain your server. The first question you should ask is whether you are allowed to install the scripts needed by forms and the maps required by image-maps. If the answer is yes, then you can ask further how and where questions. If the answer is no, you must decide whether to forego forms and image-maps or whether to seek Internet service elsewhere.

Whether you can use forms and image-maps often depends on who owns the server.

Company owns the server

If you're in a company, and the company owns the machine with the Web server on it, chances are it's a standard setup. In this case, you'll need to find out who administers the Web server. That person is frequently known as the *Webmaster*, though at least one woman is known to have dubbed herself the *Websterina*. In some large, well-wired companies, many machines will be running Web servers. In this case, you'll need to find the machine and Webmaster for you.

Forms need small programs—sometimes referred to as *scripts*—that sometimes must adhere to naming conventions and file-directory location standards. Similarly, image-maps require access to a file that normally only the Webmaster can edit.

Server provided at a commercial site

In many cases, the cost of buying and maintaining a machine—as well as paying for the actual connection to Internet—doesn't make sense. So, people frequently go to an Internet Service Provider (ISP) and rent space. Understand, however, that not all ISPs will let you run the scripts required by forms, nor will all give you access to what you need to enable image-maps.

Some will give you some flavor of access, such as asking that you submit your scripts to them for testing before general use. You can imagine how long that takes.

And some have created nonstandard setups unique to their site that allow the individual user to do it all.

Again, you'll learn specifically what to ask during the explanation of how to implement the forms and image-maps.

In all of this, remember that there is an inverse relationship between how much you are allowed to do and the amount of handholding you can expect. The more freedom, the more you are on your own. Of course, with the freedom comes responsibility. There is a reason why ISPs are cautious: Those scripts can get away from authors sometimes. Which is not to say that ISPs are the Dodge City of the old Wild West. If the ISP doesn't have sufficient control and security, the place becomes a ghost town.

FILL-IN-THE-BLANKS FORMS

Forms let you conduct surveys, take orders for products, sign up users for training courses, gather feedback, and administer tests—all the things, in fact, that you can do with paper forms.

Forms by themselves do nothing—at least from your point of view. They gather the things that users type into the blanks, and then wait around saying, "I did my part, now who's gonna do something with all this stuff?" The something that comes along to complete the job is a small program, which likely grumbles, "Darn prima-donna form. I gotta do everything around here."

This section describes how to create forms and shows a sample script that processes the form's contents.

The format of forms

On the CD-ROM ...

ingrdnts
  as_rtf
    baseform.rtf
  as_text
    baseform.txt

A form can be simple or complex. It can fill an entire Web page, or be just a tear-at-the-dotted-line coupon at the bottom of a page. In any case, a form will likely have the elements shown in this minimalist template:

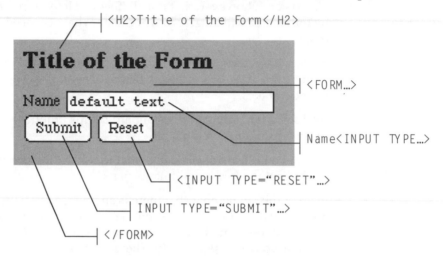

Technically, a form is everything between `<FORM>` and `</FORM>` tags. We've included a heading as a title to clearly label the form. The HTML code behind our basic form looks like this:

```
<H2>Title of the Form</H2>

<FORM METHOD="post_or_get" ACTION=url_for_processing">
Name <INPUT TYPE="TEXT" NAME="fieldname" SIZE=25
VALUE="default text"><BR>

<!--And other input elements-->

<INPUT TYPE="SUBMIT" VALUE="Submit">
<INPUT TYPE="RESET" VALUE="Reset">

</FORM>
```

The `<H2>` tag labels the form.

```
<H2>Title of the Form</H2>
```

Of course, you could make the label a `<H1>`, `<H3>`, or `<H4>` heading if that makes sense to you.

`<FORM>` and `</FORM>` tags get the browser to interpret everything in between as elements of a form.

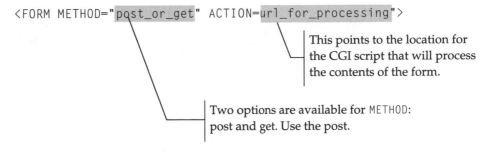

This points to the location for the CGI script that will process the contents of the form.

Two options are available for METHOD: post and get. Use the post.

In the belly of the form are form elements that let users enter information and make choices. Our absurdly simple example includes but one such gizmo: a labeled fill-in field.

```
Name <INPUT TYPE="TEXT" NAME="fieldname" SIZE=25
VALUE="default text"><BR>
```

The name that you assign to the NAME attribute will be paired with text that the user types into the blank space. This is covered further in the example below and in the discussion of the hardworking script and its handling of the content sent by the form. Here you could also include checkboxes, radio buttons, text areas, and selection lists. They are all explained later.

Once the user fills out the form, he or she can click a button either to send the contents of the form or clear the blanks and start all over:

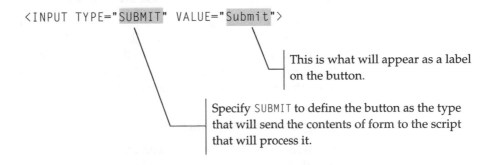

This is what will appear as a label on the button.

Specify SUBMIT to define the button as the type that will send the contents of form to the script that will process it.

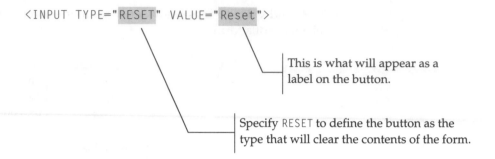

```
<INPUT TYPE="RESET" VALUE="Reset">
```

This is what will appear as a label on the button.

Specify RESET to define the button as the type that will clear the contents of the form.

With an HTML line such as the following:

```
Name <INPUT TYPE="TEXT" NAME="username"
```

If a user types George Larsen into the blank as follows:

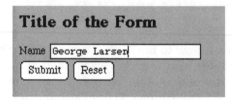

then the identifier "username" would be paired with the contents of the field (i.e., "username=George Larsen"). The two are sent as a pair to the script.

So, why does my form just sit there?

You made an example, and then you pressed the button. Nothing happened. Pretty bogus. Remember, the sending that is done by the Submit button just lets the form know that it's time to throw up for grabs all the stuff that you typed into the blanks. Something has to be there to grab all that stuff and do something with it. That's the job of the script.

Raggedy-looking blanks

In Chapter 5, something was said about the love–hate relationship that people have with HTML. Forms is an example of that. It's pretty easy to put together a form. It requires some handcrafting to get a form to look good.

Notice in this example that the blanks have ragged-left alignment:

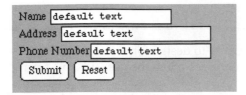

A simple way to get around this is by using the <PRE> tag, which tells the browser to display the text exactly as it is typed with a nonproportional font.

```
<PRE>

Name            <INPUT TYPE="TEXT" NAME="fieldname"
VALUE="default text"><BR>
Address         <INPUT TYPE="TEXT" NAME="fieldname" SIZE=25
VALUE="default text"><BR>
Phone Number  <INPUT TYPE="TEXT" NAME="fieldname"
VALUE="default text"><BR>

</PRE>
```

This displays as follows:

Name	default text
Address	default text
Phone Number	default text

Submit   Reset

Another technique for aligning the blanks is described in the explanation of Tables on page 399.

How forms work

To understand how to design forms and write scripts for them, you need to consider what happens when the user fills in a form.

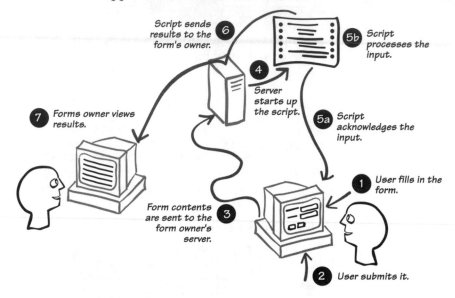

1. The user fills in the blank, clicks on checkboxes and radio buttons.

2. The user clicks the Submit button.

3. The browser sends the user's entries to the URL specified in the ACTION attribute of the <FORM> tag. Inputs are sent in NAME=value pairs.

4. The server fires up the script at the URL requested by the browser and feeds the form contents to it.

5. The script does what you have programmed it to do. It may dance a jig, make a cup of cappuccino, or just ignore the input. Most likely it will do two things:

    a) Acknowledge the input from the user. If you don't tell the user that the input was received correctly, the user may repeatedly bang the Submit button thinking nothing happened.

    b) Process the input.

6. The script may analyze the results, write them in a log file, or send them by e-mail to you, the form's creator.

7. Finally, you view the results.

Form elements

Forms can contain a variety of devices to get input from the user. These include:

- **Text field**: for entering numbers, words, and other small pieces of text.

- **Text area**: for free-form, multiple-line text entries.

- **Radio button**: for picking one item from a list.

- **Checkboxes**: for picking one or more items from a list.

- **Selection list**: for selecting one or more items from a pop-up list.

Text field

On the CD-ROM ...

ingrdnts
   as_rtf
      txtfield.rtf
   as_text
      txtfield.txt

The text field provides a blank for the user to fill in. Use it to let the user enter a name, address, phone number, or another short piece of text.

Quick reference

```
label for field <INPUT
TYPE-"TEXT"
NAME="fieldname" SIZE-25
VALUE="default text">
```

```
label for field │default text            │
```

HTML elements

The text field consists of a label and a blank for the user to fill in.

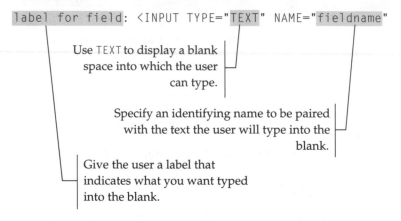

```
label for field: <INPUT TYPE="TEXT" NAME="fieldname"
```

Use TEXT to display a blank
space into which the user
can type.

Specify an identifying name to be paired
with the text the user will type into the
blank.

Give the user a label that
indicates what you want typed
into the blank.

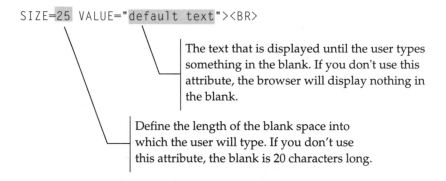

```
SIZE=25 VALUE="default text"><BR>
```

The text that is displayed until the user types
something in the blank. If you don't use this
attribute, the browser will display nothing in
the blank.

Define the length of the blank space into
which the user will type. If you don't use
this attribute, the blank is 20 characters long.

Tips

Make sure that you set a SIZE value that will handle the longest amount of text that is likely to be entered. Otherwise, your users won't be able to see what they're typing once they exceed what you specified.

You can put the label atop the field. Just put a <BR> after the label.

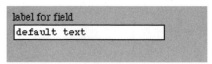

```
label for field<BR>
<INPUT TYPE="TEXT" NAME="fieldname" SIZE=25 VALUE="default
text">
```

Text area

On the CD-ROM ...

ingrdnts
  as_rtf
    txtarea.rtf
  as_text
    txtarea.txt

The text area design element lets your users type in free-form, multiple-line text. The lines they type will wrap within the text area blank. They can type full sentences and paragraphs, put in a carriage return, and type more paragraphs.

Quick reference

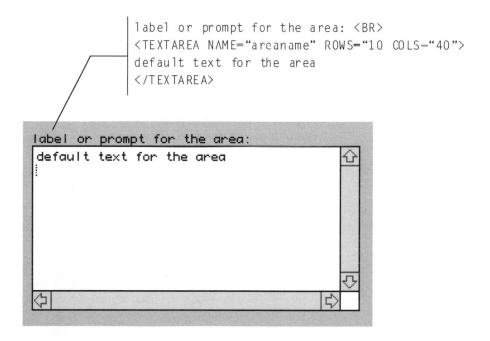

```
label or prompt for the area: <BR>
<TEXTAREA NAME="areaname" ROWS="10 COLS="40">
default text for the area
</TEXTAREA>
```

HTML elements

To display a text area, include the following elements:

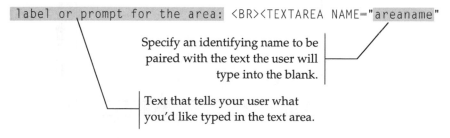

```
label or prompt for the area: <BR><TEXTAREA NAME="areaname"
```

Specify an identifying name to be paired with the text the user will type into the blank.

Text that tells your user what you'd like typed in the text area.

```
ROWS="10 COLS="40">default text for the area</TEXTAREA>
```

The text that is displayed until the user types something in the blank. If you don't use this attribute, then the browser displays a blank text area.

The width of the blank, specified in number of columns; equivalent to characters.

The height of the blank, specified in number of rows of text.

Examples

You need a form that customer support staff in your company are to complete to summarize phone calls they have had with customers. To create a blank text area that is 40 characters wide by 20 rows high, you use the following:

```
Summary of call: <BR>
<TEXTAREA NAME="Summary" COLS="40" ROWS="20">
The resolution was:
</TEXTAREA>
```

All the text typed into the text area blank will be paired with the identifier Summary when it is processed by the script handling the form's contents.

Tips

Remember that when you include a text area in a form, large amounts of information may be typed into the space. Make sure your script can process that information. In other words, you might get more than you bargained for.

Radio buttons

On the CD-ROM ...

ingrdnts
   as_rtf
      radio.rtf
   as_text
      radio.txt

Use radio buttons when you want your users to indicate no more than a single choice from a list. A user indicates his or her choice by clicking on the button next to the item. See also the related elements checkboxes (page 371) and selection lists (page 374).

Quick reference

```
label for the list:
<INPUT TYPE="RADIO" NAME="groupname2" VALUE="option 1"
CHECKED>label 1
<INPUT TYPE="RADIO" NAME="groupname2" VALUE="option 2">label 2
<INPUT TYPE="RADIO" NAME="groupname2" VALUE="option 3">label 3
<INPUT TYPE="RADIO" NAME="groupname2" VALUE="option 4">label 4
<INPUT TYPE="RADIO" NAME="groupname2" VALUE="option 5">label 5
```

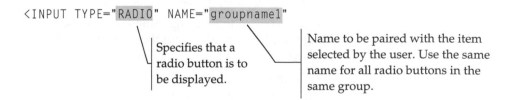

HTML elements

To display radio buttons in a form, include the following elements in your HTML file:

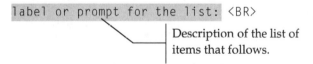

`label or prompt for the list:`

Description of the list of
items that follows.

For each item in the list include this structure:

```
<INPUT TYPE="RADIO" NAME="groupname1"
```

Specifies that a
radio button is to
be displayed.

Name to be paired with the item
selected by the user. Use the same
name for all radio buttons in the
same group.

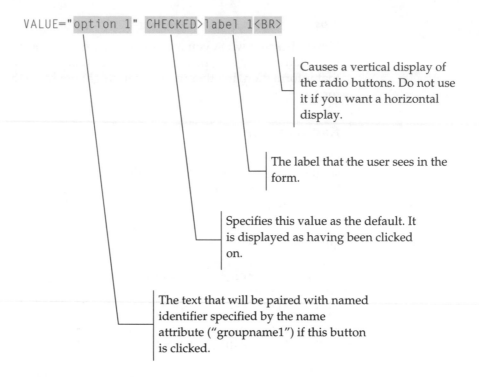

```
VALUE="option 1" CHECKED>label 1<BR>
```

Causes a vertical display of the radio buttons. Do not use it if you want a horizontal display.

The label that the user sees in the form.

Specifies this value as the default. It is displayed as having been clicked on.

The text that will be paired with named identifier specified by the name attribute ("groupname1") if this button is clicked.

Examples

Sports clothing supplier Grab-a-Hoop Troop has a Web site that lets its customers order tee shirts. The order form includes the following chunk of HTML:

```
What size do you want?: <BR>
<INPUT TYPE="RADIO" NAME="size" VALUE="small" >Small
<INPUT TYPE="RADIO" NAME="size" VALUE="med">Medium
<INPUT TYPE="RADIO" NAME="size" VALUE="large" CHECKED >Large
<INPUT TYPE="RADIO" NAME="size" VALUE="xlarge">Extra Large
```

When viewed with a browser, it looks like this:

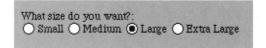

Notice that the button designating Large is checked. This was specified by using the CHECKED value with the radio button having the VALUE attribute set to large.

If this button is still selected when the form's Submit button is clicked, the value size will be paired to the value large.

Tips

Radio buttons are different from checkboxes, which allow more than one item to be selected. A radio button tends to be used for short items, especially when they're displayed horizontally. If the items to choose from are longer, and especially if vertical space on the form is a concern, then a selection list might work better.

You can also arrange the list items vertically by putting a `<BR>` after each item:

```
label or prompt for the list: <BR>
<INPUT TYPE="RADIO" NAME="groupname1" VALUE="option 1" CHECKED>label
1<BR>
<INPUT TYPE="RADIO" NAME="groupname1" VALUE="option 2">label 2<BR>
<INPUT TYPE="RADIO" NAME="groupname1" VALUE="option 3">label 3<BR>
<INPUT TYPE="RADIO" NAME="groupname1" VALUE="option 4">label 4<BR>
<INPUT TYPE="RADIO" NAME="groupname1" VALUE="option 5">label 5<BR>
```

Checkboxes

On the CD-ROM ...

ingrdnts
    as_rtf
        checkbox.rtf
    as_text
        checkbox.txt

Use checkboxes when you want your users to indicate one or more choices from a list. A user indicates his or her choice by clicking on the checkbox next to the item. See the related elements radio buttons (page 369) and selection lists (page 374).

Quick reference

```
label or prompt for the list: <BR>
<INPUT TYPE="CHECKBOX" NAME="option 1" CHECKED>label 1
<INPUT TYPE="CHECKBOX" NAME="option 2">label 2
<INPUT TYPE="CHECKBOX" NAME="option 3">label 3
<INPUT TYPE="CHECKBOX" NAME="option 4">label 4
<INPUT TYPE="CHECKBOX" NAME="option 5">label 5 <BR>
```

To arrange the list vertically, just put a `<BR>` tag after each item.

HTML elements

To put checkboxes in your form, include the following elements in your HTML file:

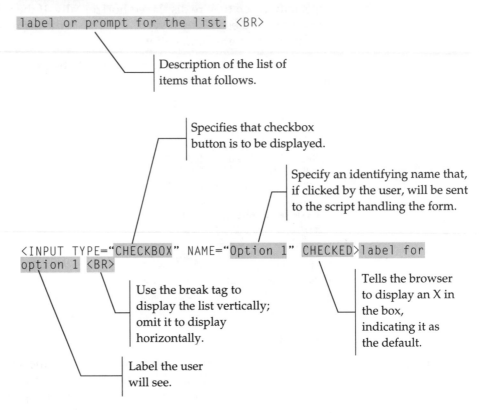

`label or prompt for the list: <BR>`

Description of the list of items that follows.

Specifies that checkbox button is to be displayed.

Specify an identifying name that, if clicked by the user, will be sent to the script handling the form.

`<INPUT TYPE="CHECKBOX" NAME="Option 1" CHECKED>label for option 1 <BR>`

Tells the browser to display an X in the box, indicating it as the default.

Use the break tag to display the list vertically; omit it to display horizontally.

Label the user will see.

Tips

```
label or prompt for the list: <BR>
<INPUT TYPE="CHECKBOX" NAME="option 1" CHECKED>label for
option 1 <BR>
<INPUT TYPE="CHECKBOX" NAME="option 2">label for option 2
<BR>
<INPUT TYPE="CHECKBOX" NAME="option 3">label for option 3
<BR>
<INPUT TYPE="CHECKBOX" NAME="option 4">label for option 4
<BR>
<INPUT TYPE="CHECKBOX" NAME="option 5">label for option 5
<BR>
```

```
label or prompt for the list:
☒ label for option 1
☐ label for option 2
☐ label for option 3
☐ label for option 4
☐ label for option 5
```

Viewing the output from checkboxes can be confusing. For example, if you were running a survey in which each question had these same choices as responses:

☐ Disgusted ☐ Displeased ☐ Neutral ☐ Happy ☒ Ecstatic

You couldn't assign NAME values using these words alone because you wouldn't be able to tell to which question your user's response was "Disgusted." So, make sure you give each value a name that can be interpreted:

```
<INPUT TYPE="CHECKBOX" NAME="Timeliness - Disgusted" >
Disgusted
```

As an alternative, you can use the syntax similar to that used in radio buttons:

```
<INPUT TYPE="CHECKBOX" NAME="Timeliness"
VALUE="Disgusted">Disgusted
```

With this, you'll get the name "Timeliness" paired with the value "Disgusted."

Selection list

The selection list normally appears as a pop-up or pull-down list from which the user selects one item. Used this way, it saves space on the page, especially for long lists.

Quick reference

```
label or prompt for the list: <BR>
<SELECT NAME="listname">
<OPTION SELECTED >first option
<OPTION>second option
<OPTION>third option
<OPTION>fourth option
<OPTION>fifth option
</SELECT><BR>
```

```
<SELECT
NAME="listname">...
```

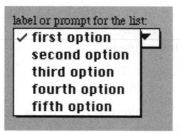

If you include the MULTIPLE attribute, users can select more than one item from the list. Browsers typically display the selections as a scrolling list.

```
<SELECT
NAME="listname
"MULTIPLE>...
```

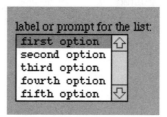

HTML elements

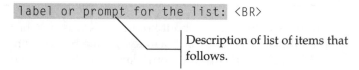

Description of list of items that follows.

An option attribute that tells the browser to display all the items in the list and allows the user to select more than one item.

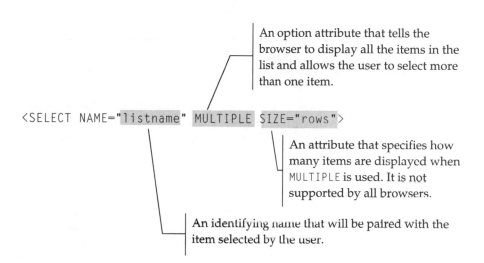

An attribute that specifies how many items are displayed when `MULTIPLE` is used. It is not supported by all browsers.

An identifying name that will be paired with the item selected by the user.

For each item in the list, include an entry like this:

The text that is displayed in the browser and is the value paired with the text specified by the `NAME` attribute.

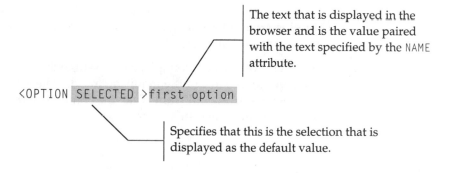

Specifies that this is the selection that is displayed as the default value.

Tips

Use the `MULTIPLE` attribute with care. Not all users know how to make more than one selection from a single list because it requires a combination of holding down a key while clicking a mouse button. Consider using checkboxes instead when you want your users to be able to make multiple selections.

Watch out for forms

Try to be conservative about your form's width. When your form is wider than the browser's display window, some browsers try to wrap the lines in the form. This means that your blanks might end up laid out in ways that you didn't quite expect.

SCRIPTS FOR FORMS

As we've been saying, the form doesn't do anything, from the user's point of view, other than serve as a place to type in information. Without a little program to do something with that information, pressing the Submit button won't accomplish much. So now it's time for the little program that we'll refer to as a *script*. Whether these things are called programs or scripts is largely convention.

In Web words, they are referred to as CGI scripts or programs. CGI is an acronym for Common Gateway Interface. You'll need to know this if you're trying to find out *where* they should be placed if you own the machine running the Web server. Usually, as a tidy way to do things, they will be placed in a directory named "cgi-bin." So, you say to your Webmaster, "Do they go in cgi-bin?"

If you get your Internet through a commercial service provider, or if you are shopping around for one that will let you do forms, you will ask, "Are we allowed to run CGI scripts?"

For the purpose of this example, we'll assume the server is a UNIX machine, which will cover most of the inquiring minds. The script itself will do what most people starting out want: Take the contents of the form and make it available to you, the form's author.

What it does, from the user's viewpoint

The user sees the following form, types the information into the blanks, and presses the Submit button which, in this case, is labeled "Send Form To Cool People Who Make Webs."

Generic Form 1

Name:
Title:
Company:
Address:
City: State: Zip:
Daytime
Phone:
Email:

[Send Form To Cool People Who Make Webs] [Reset this form]

The user then sees the following screen, which shows that everything went well and allows the user to jump back to the form:

Mail has been sent to Generic People.

Thank you for your interest.

Return to Generic Form

The HTML behind the example

On the CD-ROM ...

ingrdnts
    as_rtf
        genform.rtf
    as_txt
        genform.txt

The HTML under the form looks like the following:

```
<FORM METHOD="POST" ACTION="path/genericform1.pl">

<PRE><H2> Generic Form 1</H2>
Name:      <INPUT NAME="Name " SIZE="30">
Title:     <INPUT NAME="Title " SIZE="30">
Company:   <INPUT NAME="Company " SIZE="30">
Address:   <INPUT NAME="Address " SIZE="30">
City:      <INPUT NAME="City " SIZE="30"> State: <INPUT
NAME="State " SIZE="12"> Zip: <INPUT NAME="Zip " SIZE="10">
Daytime
Phone:     <INPUT NAME="Home Phone " SIZE="20">
Email:     <INPUT NAME="email " Size="20">
</PRE>

<P><INPUT TYPE="SUBMIT" NAME="SUBMIT" VALUE="Send Form To Cool
People Who Make Webs">
<INPUT TYPE="RESET" NAME="RESET" VALUE="Reset this form"></P>

</FORM>
```

The significant piece is the FORM line itself, which specifies the location of the script:

```
<Form method="POST"action="URL_or_path/genericform1.pl">
```

This is the path to the CGI script. It can be a full URL or UNIX path name.

If you can specify a full URL, you won't have to worry about updating what you put here if you ever decide to change the location of the form's HTML file. Heck, you can move the file to another server on the other side of the world, and this will still work. Performance might be a bit on the slow side, but it'll work. Raises some intriguing possibilities for Web design, doesn't it?

The script sends the contents of the form to you as e-mail. The e-mail arrives in your mailbox with an anonymous name as the sender of the mail. Gee, wouldn't it be good if we could get the e-mail address of the person submitting the form? Maybe, but that's a whole separate discussion about the rights of privacy.

At any rate, this is what the text of the e-mail would look like, assuming that someone actually typed responses into the blanks:

```
The following was submitted via the Generic Form

Name =Stuart Robbins
Title =Technical Marketing Manager
Company =Synopsys, Inc.
Address =700 East Middlefield
City =Mountain View
State =CA
Zip =94043
Home Phone =(415) 555-1628
email =stuart@synopsys.com
Submit=Send Form To Cool People Who Make Webs
```

From this example, you can see the pairing of the name assigned to TITLE and what was typed in. Just to be sure, here's that line of HTML code and the resulting response:

```
Title: <INPUT NAME="Title " SIZE="30">
```

Title =Technical Marketing Manager

In this example, we didn't have to be particularly careful about what we assigned to the NAME attribute because the contents were pretty obvious. For example, it would be hard to confuse the person's name with the phone number. However, this is a general purpose script and in another situation confusion could easily arise, for instance between a work phone number and a home phone number.

The first line in the e-mail text is especially important if you have more than one form on your Web pages, and you want to know what the e-mail pertains to when it arrives in your mailbox with a bunch of other e-mail sent from those other forms. This will be discussed further in the particulars of the script itself.

The script itself

Following is the top part of the script, the only part to which you need to pay attention.

```perl
#!/usr/local/bin/perl
#
# Web Cookbook script for handling forms
# The core of this script was created by
# Jeff Angwin, Webmaster for Sourcelink
# Cadence Design Systems, Inc.
# http://www.cadence.com/sneak.html
#
$mailto = "you@some_domain.com";
$message1 = "Mail has been sent to Generic People.";
$message2 = "Thank you for your interest.";
$returnpath =
"http://www.some_domain.com/some_path/genericform1.html";
$formname = "Generic Form";
$mailid = "The following was submitted via the Generic
Form";
#
# No need to change anything below this line.
#
#_____
```

The following is the rest of the script, just to be complete. The language is Perl, which has evolved as the scripting language of choice because it doesn't have to be compiled, it's relatively readable by mere mortals, and it's free.

```perl
$CONTENT_LENGTH=  $ENV{'CONTENT_LENGTH'};

read(STDIN,$inputs,$CONTENT_LENGTH);
open (MAILFILE,">/tmp/mailfile.$$");
print MAILFILE "$mailid\n\n";

@inputs=split("&",$inputs);

foreach $line(@inputs){
        $_=$line;
        tr/+/ /;
        s/%(..)/pack("c",hex($1))/ge;
        s/comments\=/\nComments:\n/g;

        print MAILFILE "$_\n";
}

close MAILFILE;
open (MAILIT, "mail $mailto < /tmp/mailfile.$$|");
close MAILIT;
system "rm /tmp/mailfile.$$";
print "Content-type: text/html\n\n";
```

```
print "<H2>$message1</H2>";
print "<HR>\n";
print "<UL>\n";
print "$message2<p>\n";
print "</UL>\n";
print "<HR>\n";
print "Return to <a href= $returnpath > $formname </a>";
```

Parts of the script that you change

If you're doing forms, you probably have some other Web pages already up and running, which means you know how to change permissions. So, be sure to change the permissions of your form's HTML file and CGI script to give read/execute privilege to everybody.

You need to modify this script to work in your environment and to reflect what you're doing. First of all, you'll need Perl available on your server. When you find it, specify its location in the first line:

```
#!/usr/local/bin/perl
```

Change the next line by putting in your e-mail address:

$mailto = "you@some_domain.com";

Now, you can customize the remaining lines. This diagram illustrates what parts to change and shows the results:

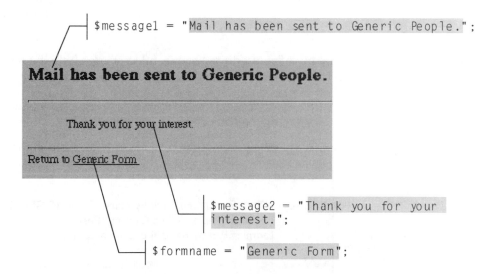

This is one of those interesting things that CGI scripts can do: build HTML displays dynamically. That is, this screen display does not exist as a real HTML file anywhere. Each time you click the Submit button, this display gets built by the script. You can see how some of the CGI whizzes can do some pretty interesting things.

The hypertext reference for the Generic Form link is also created dynamically by the script based on what you type into the following line:

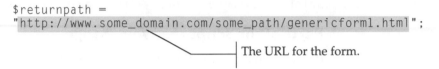

```
$returnpath =
"http://www.some_domain.com/some_path/genericform1.html";
```

The URL for the form.

So, when the user clicks on the Generic Form link, the browser redisplays the form. Giving the user this very specific link makes it easier for him or her to stay oriented and not get lost in hyperspace. You can also specify a path instead of a full URL as shown here.

Finally, you put in a little marker that gets inserted in the mail message being sent.

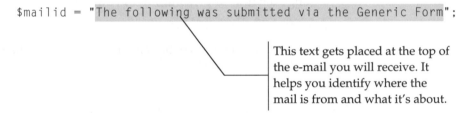

```
$mailid = "The following was submitted via the Generic Form";
```

This text gets placed at the top of the e-mail you will receive. It helps you identify where the mail is from and what it's about.

In any of your editing, be careful to change only the text within the quotes. The lines end with semicolons, which are easy to overlook, but should be left in place.

Scripting resources

CGI and scripts are not the core of this book, which is the design and implementation of Web pages. That said, here are some resources you might find useful for CGI scripting and Perl:

Books   *HTML for Fun and Profit* by Mary Morris (CGI scripting)
Perl by Example by Ellis Quigley (Perl)
Learning Perl by Randall L. Schwartz (Perl)

WWW   http://www.stars.com (This is a nice jumping-off point for scripting and tables.)

http://www.cis.ufl.edu/perl/ (The University of Florida Perl Archive)

IMAGE-MAPS

Suppose you want to include a photograph of your company's board of directors so that users can click on a board member to jump to a biography of that member. Or, say you want to use a map of Canada to let users click on a province to learn about its environmental regulations. Or, you want a flowchart to present an overview of your manufacturing process and also serve as a menu for detailed information on each step in that process. Image-maps let you do these things with Web pages. Here, for example, is the image-map used on page 418:

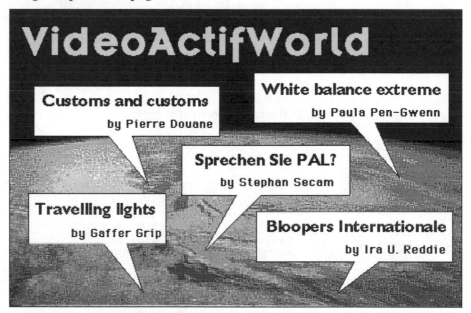

Image-maps are also called *clickable pictures* or *graphical maps*. They appear in your Web page like normal pictures, but image-maps have hot spots. No, you won't feel a temperature difference. The term *hot spot* means that if the user points the cursor in this area and clicks the mouse, the Web page associated with that area appears. The hot spot works like a hypertext link.

To use an image-map in your Web page, you must:

1. **Create the image.**
2. **Create the map file** that defines hot spots in the image.
3. **Specify the locations** of the image, program, and map file to process the image-map.
4. **Install these pieces** on the server and set their permissions.

Quick Reference

On the CD-ROM ...

ingrdnts
    as_rtf
        imagmapn.rtf
    as_text
        imagmapn.txt

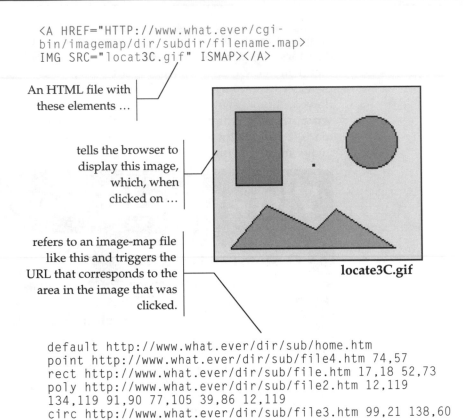

```
<A HREF="HTTP://www.what.ever/cgi-
bin/imagemap/dir/subdir/filename.map>
IMG SRC="locat3C.gif" ISMAP></A>
```

An HTML file with these elements ...

tells the browser to display this image, which, when clicked on ...

refers to an image-map file like this and triggers the URL that corresponds to the area in the image that was clicked.

locate3C.gif

```
default http://www.what.ever/dir/sub/home.htm
point http://www.what.ever/dir/sub/file4.htm 74,57
rect http://www.what.ever/dir/sub/file.htm 17,18 52,73
poly http://www.what.ever/dir/sub/file2.htm 12,119
134,119 91,90 77,105 39,86 12,119
circ http://www.what.ever/dir/sub/file3.htm 99,21 138,60
```

filename.map

1. The user clicks on the image.

2. The browser sends the position of the click to the server with the image-map program.

3. The server starts up the image-map program.

4. The image-map program consults the map file to find out where to go next.

5. The image-map program tells the server the URL of the new destination.

6. The server fetches and displays this new destination.

Here's a graphic overview of the process:

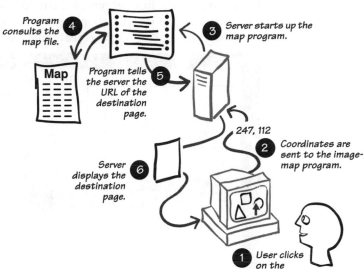

Create the image

Creating or selecting the image to use is part of the graphic design work of building your Web site. The image must be in GIF format. See page 324 for information on creating graphics.

Create the map file

Once you have created or selected the image, you'll need to map the different areas of the image to separate URLs. The actual mapping is a pairing of coordinates that describe the area to the URL that you assign to that area. These coordinates and paired URLs are put into a plain-text file that is referred to, surprisingly enough, as a *map file*.

The coordinates that describe the areas in the image are in pixels. They start in the upper-left-hand corner with the coordinates (0,0), with the X coordinates extending to the right and the positive Y coordinates going down. A clickable area can be a point, rectangle, circle, or polygon. In addition, any area not explicitly defined is assigned to a *default* URL.

With that said—and if you're still awake—it's likely that you won't have to know any of this. Just get one of the map-making tools suggested in Resources for the Web Chef on page 565, and map away. Here, for example, you see us using WebMap to create this example:

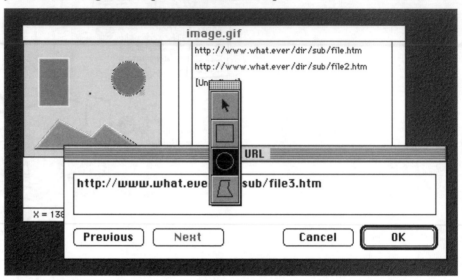

As we said, map files come in two flavors: NCSA and CERN. Your service provider or system administrator can tell you which to use.

On the CD-ROM ...

ingrdnts
    as_rtf
        ncsamap.rtf
    as_text
        ncsamap.txt

Just so you know the difference, this is what an NCSA image map looks like:

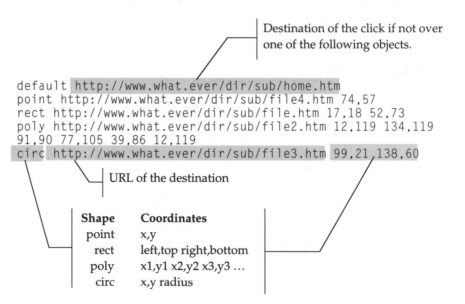

Destination of the click if not over one of the following objects.

```
default http://www.what.ever/dir/sub/home.htm
point http://www.what.ever/dir/sub/file4.htm 74,57
rect http://www.what.ever/dir/sub/file.htm 17,18 52,73
poly http://www.what.ever/dir/sub/file2.htm 12,119 134,119
91,90 77,105 39,86 12,119
circ http://www.what.ever/dir/sub/file3.htm 99,21 138,60
```

URL of the destination

Shape	Coordinates
point	x,y
rect	left,top right,bottom
poly	x1,y1 x2,y2 x3,y3 ...
circ	x,y radius

And this is one for a CERN image-map.

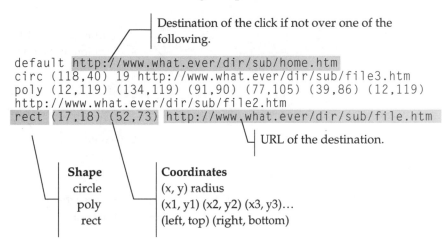

Destination of the click if not over one of the following.

```
default http://www.what.ever/dir/sub/home.htm
circ (118,40) 19 http://www.what.ever/dir/sub/file3.htm
poly (12,119) (134,119) (91,90) (77,105) (39,86) (12,119)
http://www.what.ever/dir/sub/file2.htm
rect (17,18) (52,73) http://www.what.ever/dir/sub/file.htm
```

URL of the destination.

Shape	Coordinates
circle	(x, y) radius
poly	(x1, y1) (x2, y2) (x3, y3)…
rect	(left, top) (right, bottom)

Notice that all lines that start with the "#" symbol are comment lines.

Specify the locations of the image, program, and map file within the HTML file

These elements that you specify in the HTML file do the following:

- Display the image.

- Tell the browser that this is an image-map.

- Tell the location of the image-map program.

- Tell the location of the map file that you created.

For image-maps, include the following element in your HTML file:

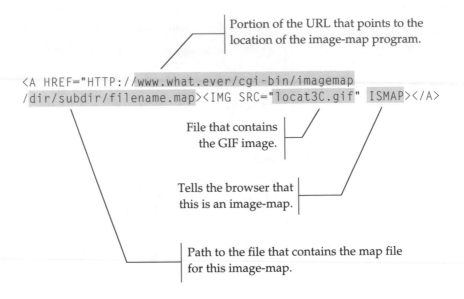

Portion of the URL that points to the location of the image-map program.

File that contains the GIF image.

Tells the browser that this is an image-map.

Path to the file that contains the map file for this image-map.

Install the pieces

The final step in making your image-map work is to install all the pieces on your server and set their permissions. In general, the GIF image file and the HTML file go in the same directory you are using for your other Web pages. Depending on the setup of your server, the map file may go in the same directory as the Web page or it may go into a command directory. Usually the GIF image file and the map file should have permissions set to readable and executable by the public (chmod 655 *filename*). Your service provider or system administrator can give you more explicit instructions.

Tips for image-map makers

Get the facts first

Before you begin slinging pixels, gather the facts you will need later. Check with your service provider or system administrator. Do they have an FAQ or read-me file telling how to use image-maps? Consult a local Web newsgroup by posting questions such as "Should the map file be NCSA or CERN format?" To use image-maps you need to know:

- Do I use CERN or NCSA format for the map file?

- In which directory do I store the map file?

- What permissions do I give it?

- What permissions do I give the image file?

- What is the URL for the program that processes image-maps?

Test and debug

After you have installed the files, test your image-map as a user. If you encounter problems, check these possible causes:

- Wrong type (NCSA or CERN) map for a particular server.

- Inadequate permissions for the image or map file—probably need to be executable by the public.

- Map file is in the wrong directory.

- URL or path to image file, map file, or image-map program is incorrect.

- URLs in map file are incorrect.

Consider the GUI-less

Image-maps don't work too well for users with text-only browsers or who have turned off graphics. To let such unfortunates use your pages, supplement your image-map with a compact text menu that presents the same choices.

For examples of image-maps combined with text menus, see pages 418 and 430. For a template of a text menu, see page 271.

Use 'em and reuse 'em

Once you have an image-map working, you can include it in several different Web pages without having to redefine the image or map files. Give you any ideas?

TABLES

In the early days of the Web, formal tables did not exist. The only way to display information in columns and rows was by physically placing it there by hitting the spacebar on the keyboard and using the `<PRE>` tag. Some got around it by taking screen shots of the table and making GIF images, which, given the size of some tables, made viewing them an exercise in patience. Even through much of the first half of 1995, you still couldn't be sure that a significant number of your users had browsers that supported tables.

Now, though, you can be fairly confident about using tables. After all, this is not a "would-be-nice" such as colored backgrounds. This is honest-to-goodness useful functionality.

However, the Web author's desire to stretch HTML's capabilities applies no less to tables. Some authors are using tables in ways that folks didn't exactly have in mind when they were writing the specifications for table tags. Some really creative types, for example, are using tables to simulate multicolumn layouts. (See page 412.) Others have found that tables are a good way to get fill-in-the-blanks forms to line up nicely without using a `<PRE>` tag. That is covered on page 400.

This section starts with the basics of a table, which is then followed by a series of variations. Each variation assumes that you have the basic table elements under your belt.

In the WYSIWYG world, building tables feels like a real throwback, almost like arts and crafts. It's like you're laying down the structure, one row at a time, from the top down. And it's no wonder that it feels this way because that is what you're doing.

Basic table

On the CD-ROM ...

ingrdnts
    as_rtf
        t3by2.rtf
    as_text
        t3by2.txt

The basic table is a simple two-row, three-column grid capped with a caption. Once you understand how it's made, you can easily add rows and columns. It looks like this from the outside:

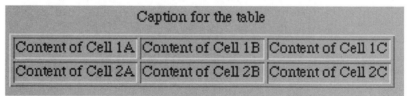

Caption for the table		
Content of Cell 1A	Content of Cell 1B	Content of Cell 1C
Content of Cell 2A	Content of Cell 2B	Content of Cell 2C

And from the inside, it looks like this:

```
<TABLE BORDER>
<CAPTION ALIGN=TOP>Caption for the table</CAPTION>
<TR>     <! ---- starts a row          >
    <TD>Content of Cell 1A</TD>
    <TD>Content of Cell 1B</TD>
    <TD>Content of Cell 1C</TD>
</TR>  <! ---- ends a row               >
<TR>
    <TD>Content of Cell 2A</TD>
    <TD>Content of Cell 2B</TD>
    <TD>Content of Cell 2C</TD>
</TR>
</TABLE>  <! ----- ends the table      >
```

Looks complex! It is complex. And it only gets more so for more sophisticated tables. Let's go through it a bit at a time and work from the outside in.

A table is everything between `<TABLE>` and `</TABLE>` tags.

Within the `<TABLE>` tag you put attributes that control the appearance of the whole table. Adding `BORDER` …

```
<TABLE BORDER>
```

says to draw borders around all the cells of the table.

`<CAPTION>` — Caption for the table

The optional `<CAPTION>` tag adds a caption to the table. The text of the caption goes between the `<CAPTION>` and `</CAPTION>` tags. Within the opening `<CAPTION>` tag the `ALIGN` attribute specifies where to put the caption. For example,

```
<CAPTION ALIGN=TOP>Caption for the table</CAPTION>
```

puts "Caption for the table" atop the table. `ALIGN=BOTTOM` would put it below the table.

`<TR>` — Table rows

Each row of the table appears between `<TR>` and `</TR>` tags.

<TD> — Table data (cell contents)

The content for each cell in a row is surrounded by <TD> and </TD> tags. For example, the first row of the basic table contains three cells:

```
<TR>      <! ---- starts a row              >
   <TD>Content of Cell 1A</TD>
   <TD>Content of Cell 1B</TD>
   <TD>Content of Cell 1C</TD>
</TR>  <! ---- ends a row                  >
```

So, this means <TD> and </TD> tags only appear within <TR> and </TR> tags.

To border or not to border

Should you draw your table with borders (<TABLE BORDER>), like this:

Caption for the table		
Content of Cell 1A	Content of Cell 1B	Content of Cell 1C
Content of Cell 2A	Content of Cell 2B	Content of Cell 2C

Or without (<TABLE>), like this:

Caption for the table		
Content of Cell 1A	Content of Cell 1B	Content of Cell 1C
Content of Cell 2A	Content of Cell 2B	Content of Cell 2C

Throughout this chapter, we included borders to show the structure of the tables more clearly. In practice, though, we often omit the border to reduce visual clutter. It's your choice.

Table with column headers

On the CD-ROM ...

ingrdnts
    as_rtf
        tcol.rtf
    as_text
        tcol.txt

You can emphasize the heads of columns in your tables.

Caption for the table			
Head A	**Head B**	**Head C**	**Head D**
Content of Cell 1A	Content of Cell 1B	Content of Cell 1C	Content of Cell 1D
Content of Cell 2A	Content of Cell 2B	Content of Cell 2C	Content of Cell 2D

To add column headers to your tables use the `<TH>` tags in place of the `<TD>` tags in the first row.

```
<TABLE BORDER>
<CAPTION ALIGN=top>Caption for the table</CAPTION>
<TR>
    <TH>Head A</TH>
    <TH>Head B</TH>
    <TH>Head C</TH>
    <TH>Head D</TH>
</TR>
    <TD>Content of Cell 1A</TD>
    <TD>Content of Cell 1B</TD>
    <TD>Content of Cell 1C</TD>
    <TD>Content of Cell 1D</TD>
</TR>
<TR>
    <TD>Content of Cell 2A</TD>
    <TD>Content of Cell 2B</TD>
    <TD>Content of Cell 2C</TD>
    <TD>Content of Cell 2D</TD>
</TR>
</TABLE>  <! ----- ends the table        >
```

Text for column heads

Table with row and column headers

On the CD-ROM...

ingrdnts
    as_rtf
        trowcol.rtf
    as_text
        trowcol.txt

You can add both row and column headers to your tables.

Caption for the table				
	Head A	**Head B**	**Head C**	**Head D**
Head 1	Content of Cell 1A	Content of Cell 1B	Content of Cell 1C	Content of Cell 1D
Head 2	Content of Cell 2A	Content of Cell 2B	Content of Cell 2C	Content of Cell 2D

Create column headers by placing the `<TH>` tags in a row. Create the row headers by placing the `<TH>` tags at the start of the row to which they correspond.

Quick Reference

Places a blank cell above the row headers.

Creates the headers for the columns. Displays them as emphasized text.

Header for the first row. Displays it as emphasized text.

Header for the second row. Displays it as emphasized text.

```
<TR>
    <TH></TH>
    <TH>Head A</TH
    <TH>Head B</TH>
    <TH>Head C</TH>
    <TH>Head D</TH>
</TR>
    <TH>Head 1</TH>
    <TD>Content of Cell 1A</TD>
    <TD>Content of Cell 1B</TD>
    <TD>Content of Cell 1C</TD>
    <TD>Content of Cell 1D</TD>
</TR>
<TR>
    <TH>Head 2</TH>
    <TD>Content of Cell 2A</TD>
    <TD>Content of Cell 2B</TD>
    <TD>Content of Cell 2C</TD>
    <TD>Content of Cell 2D</TD>
</TR>
```

Table with headers spanning rows and columns

On the CD-ROM ...

ingrdnts
  as_rtf
    tspan.rtf
  as_text
    tspan.txt

You can create headers that span two or more rows or two or more columns. This is useful for creating groupings in your tables.

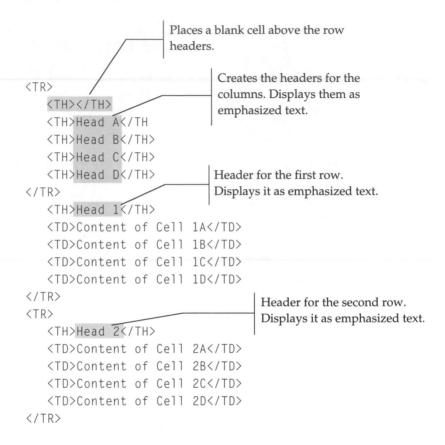

Caption for the table					
		Head A-B		Head C-D	
		Head A	Head B	Head C	Head D
Head 1-2	Head 1	Cell 1A	Cell 1B	Cell 1C	Cell 1D
	Head 2	Cell 2A	Cell 2B	Cell 2C	Cell 2D
Head 3-4	Head 3	Cell 3A	Cell 3B	Cell 3C	Cell 3D
	Head 4	Cell 4A	Cell 4B	Cell 4C	Cell 4D

In the introduction to this section on tables we made the suggestion that you construct tables by layering them one row at a time, starting at the top. It might help to remember this when you create tables with headers spanning rows and columns. If you're familiar with the computer game Tetris, it has a similar feel.

For example, creating a heading cell that spans two rows and has two rows joined to it would be constructed in the following sequence:

```
<TH ROWSPAN=2>label</TH>
```

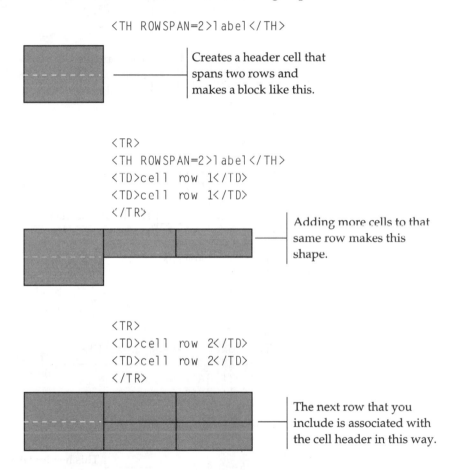

Creates a header cell that spans two rows and makes a block like this.

```
<TR>
<TH ROWSPAN=2>label</TH>
<TD>cell row 1</TD>
<TD>cell row 1</TD>
</TR>
```

Adding more cells to that same row makes this shape.

```
<TR>
<TD>cell row 2</TD>
<TD>cell row 2</TD>
</TR>
```

The next row that you include is associated with the cell header in this way.

Here's the HTML code that created the table at the beginning of this section:

```
<TABLE BORDER>
<CAPTION ALIGN=top>Caption for the table</CAPTION>
<TR>
    <TH ROWSPAN=2 COLSPAN=2></TH>
    <TH COLSPAN=2>Head A-B</TH>
    <TH COLSPAN=2>Head C-D</TH>
</TR>
<TR>
    <TH>Head A</TH>
    <TH>Head B</TH>
    <TH>Head C</TH>
    <TH>Head D</TH>
</TR>
    <TH ROWSPAN=2>Head 1-2</TH>
    <TH>Head 1</TH>
    <TD>Cell 1A</TD>
    <TD>Cell 1B</TD>
    <TD>Cell 1C</TD>
    <TD>Cell 1D</TD>
</TR>
<TR>
    <TH>Head 2</TH>
    <TD>Cell 2A</TD>
    <TD>Cell 2B</TD>
    <TD>Cell 2C</TD>
    <TD>Cell 2D</TD>
</TR>
</TR>
    <TH ROWSPAN=2>Head 3-4</TH>
    <TH>Head 3</TH>
    <TD>Cell 3A</TD>
    <TD>Cell 3B</TD>
    <TD>Cell 3C</TD>
    <TD>Cell 3D</TD>
</TR>
<TR>
    <TH>Head 4</TH>
    <TD>Cell 4A</TD>
    <TD>Cell 4B</TD>
    <TD>Cell 4C</TD>
    <TD>Cell 4D</TD>
</TR>
</TABLE>
```

Creates a blank cell that is two columns wide by two rows deep.

This header spans two columns.

This header spans the next two columns.

These are the headers for the four columns.

This header spans two rows.

This header labels the first row of data.

This header labels the second row of data.

This header spans two rows.

This header labels the third row of data.

This header labels the fourth row of data.

Table with contents aligned differently

You can specify how the contents of a cell are aligned.

Caption for the table		
This text is aligned to upper left.	This text is aligned to upper center.	This text is aligned to upper right.
This text is aligned to center left.	This text is aligned to center.	This text is aligned to center right.
This text is aligned to bottom left.	This text is aligned to bottom center.	This text is aligned to bottom right.
Everything in this row is aligned the same.	Everything in this row is aligned the same.	Everything in this row is aligned the same.

To control how items are aligned within their cells, include `ALIGN` and `VALIGN` attributes with the `<TR>` or `<TD>` tags.

```
<TABLE BORDER>
<CAPTION ALIGN=top>Caption for the table</CAPTION>
<TR>
    <TD VALIGN=top ALIGN=left>This text is aligned to upper left.</TD>
    <TD VALIGN=top ALIGN=center>This text is aligned to upper
center.</TD>
    <TD VALIGN=top ALIGN=right>This text is aligned to upper right.</TD>
</TR>
<TR>
    <TD VALIGN=center ALIGN=left>This text is aligned to center
left.</TD>
    <TD VALIGN=center ALIGN=center>This text is aligned to center.</TD>
    <TD VALIGN=center ALIGN=right>This text is aligned to center
right.</TD>
</TR>
<TR>
    <TD VALIGN=bottom ALIGN=left>This text is aligned to bottom
left.</TD>
    <TD VALIGN=bottom ALIGN=center>This text is aligned to bottom
center.</TD>
    <TD VALIGN=bottom ALIGN=right>This text is aligned to bottom
right.</TD>
</TR>
<TR VALIGN=top ALIGN=left>
    <TD>Everything in this row is aligned the same.</TD>
    <TD>Everything in this row is aligned the same.</TD>
    <TD>Everything in this row is aligned the same.</TD>
</TR>
</TABLE>
```

Use `ALIGN` and `VALIGN` attributes to control the alignment of the content of cells. `ALIGN` controls the horizontal alignment and `VALIGN` controls the vertical alignment. Put them within `<TD>` tags to control alignment of individual cells or within <TR> tags to control the whole row.

```
<TD VALIGN=align_val ALIGN=align_val> Cell contents to be
aligned</TD>
```

Vertical alignment of cell contents. Can be TOP, CENTER, or BOTTOM.

Horizontal alignment of cell contents. Can be LEFT, CENTER, or RIGHT.

Cell contents.

```
<TR VALIGN=align ALIGN=align>
    <TD>Everything in this row is aligned the same.</TD>
    <TD>Everything in this row is aligned the same.</TD>
    <TD>Everything in this row is aligned the same.</TD>
</TR>
```

Note: Putting the VALIGN or ALIGN attributes in the table row element saves the effort of including them in every cell definition for that row.

Table with different kinds of content

On the CD-ROM ...

ingrdnts
    as_rtf
        tcontent.rtf
    as_text
        tcontent.txt

The contents of cells can be more than just text. You can also include graphics and even other tables.

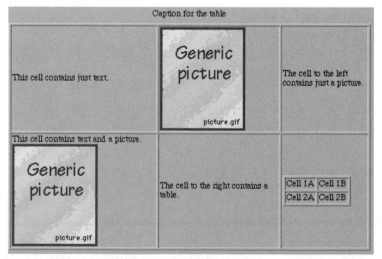

To create a table with different kinds of content, include the content within the <TD> tags for individual cells.

```
<TABLE BORDER>
<CAPTION ALIGN=top>Caption for the
table</CAPTION>
<TR>
    <TD>This cell contains just text.</TD>
    <TD><IMG SRC="picture.gif"></TD>
    <TD>The cell to the left contains just a
        picture.</TD>
</TR>
<TR>
    <TD>This cell contains text and a
        picture. <IMG SRC="picture.gif"></TD>
    <TD>The cell to the right contains a
        table.</TD>
    <TD>
            <TABLE BORDER>
            <TR>
                <TD>Cell 1A</TD>
                <TD>Cell 1B</TD>
            </TR>
            <TR>
                <TD>Cell 2A</TD>
                <TD>Cell 2B</TD>
            </TR>
            </TABLE>
    </TD>
</TR>
</TABLE>
```

Puts a graphic into a cell.

Puts text and a graphic into a cell.

Puts a whole table into a cell.

Formatting fill-in-the-blanks forms

Elements other than simple text can be table data. You can use tables as an alternative to using the <PRE> tag to align the contents of a fill-in-the-blanks form.

For example, let's say that your Web site is a way for your clients to order copies of presentations from talks that you have given. Include the following between your <FORM> tags:

```
<H3>Presentation Overheads</H3>

<TR>
<TABLE BORDER>
<TH>Speaker</TH>
<TH>Date of Event</TH>
<TH>Location of event</TH>
<TH>Qty</TH>
</TR>

<TR>
<TD>  <INPUT NAME="Speaker "      SIZE="20"> </TD>
<TD>  <INPUT NAME="Date "         SIZE="14"> </TD>
<TD>  <INPUT NAME="Location "     SIZE="15"> </TD>
<TD>  <INPUT NAME="Qty "          SIZE="3">  </TD>
</TR>

<TR>
<TD>  <INPUT NAME="Speaker "      SIZE="20"> </TD>
<TD>  <INPUT NAME="Date "         SIZE="14"> </TD>
<TD>  <INPUT NAME="Location "     SIZE="15"> </TD>
<TD>  <INPUT NAME="Qty "          SIZE="3">  </TD>
</TR>

<TR>
<TD>  <INPUT NAME="Speaker "      SIZE="20"> </TD>
<TD>  <INPUT NAME="Date "         SIZE="14"> </TD>
<TD>  <INPUT NAME="Location "     SIZE="15"> </TD>
<TD>  <INPUT NAME="Qty "          SIZE="3">  </TD>
</TR>

</TABLE>
```

The browser will display the following:

Presentation Overheads

Speaker	Date of Event	Location of event	Qty

8

PRESENTATION

Visual design of Web pages

In cooking, the term *presentation* refers to how the food appears to the diner. Presentation covers such issues as the mixture of colors on the plate, the shape of individual items, and their arrangement.

In Web page design, *presentation* concerns the layout of pages, the use of page banners and swashes, the integration of text and graphics on the page, and the design of buttons and emblems—how it looks.

In this chapter we have not included a separate section on the process of visual design, not because it is unimportant, but because it is not a separate process from the design of other aspects of the page and of related pages. The presentation of the page must fit the larger purposes of the page. The visual design of an individual page must fit in with that of other related pages. And you must test the visual design, just as you test the links and content.

This chapter will help produce pages that encourage people to read and view what you present—and make them smile.

HTML, especially early versions, provides few tools to control the exact appearance of information on the page. In a way this is a blessing, because it removes the temptation to endlessly tweak font sizes and nudge graphics one way or another. But it leaves the designer with precious little control over what the viewer sees. In this chapter we will show you how to take control of how your pages appear to Web readers.

Consider the digital paper alternative

If, after perusing this chapter, you feel you cannot make your page look the way it should, consider preparing your information using one of the digital paper systems, such as Adobe Acrobat, and then using the Web to transport the resulting page images to your users. For more on the digital paper alternative, turn to page 52.

PAGE LAYOUT

When people first encounter a Web page they see the whole page before they attend to the details. People do not start in the upper-left corner of the Web page and proceed down the window line by line. They first see the page as a whole and their eyes flit and skip to examine visually attractive elements. The arrangement of elements on the page is the biggest factor in determining what people notice and read—or whether they abandon the page and surf on to someone else's page.

Let's look at some of the ways of controlling where graphics and blocks of text appear on the Web page.

Go with the flow

Web page browsers by default flow graphics and lines of text against the left margin. This can result in left-heavy pages. Such pages look unbalanced, waste space, and require the user to scroll vertically to read the whole page.

On the CD-ROM ...

examples
  chap8
    lefthevy
      lefthevy.htm

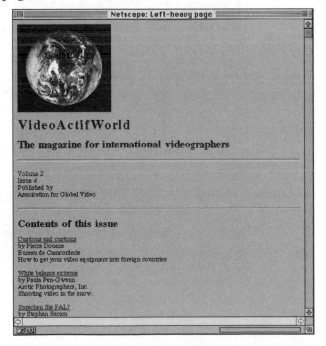

The biggest problem with such pages is that they violate our expectations of balance and symmetry. We are used to seeing paper pages and screen displays that balance information evenly across the display. Before we present techniques to position items horizontally on the page, let's consider what we can do to improve left-aligned pages.

- **Avoid a long series of short lines of text**. Can you double up lines of text without making the text harder to scan or read? Perhaps you can use the available horizontal space to spell out an abbreviation or define a term.

- **Use wide rather than tall graphics**. Choose graphics that are wide rather than tall. Rather than a series of three tall graphics, can you consolidate them into one wide graphic? Or can you just put all the graphics on the same line?

- **Use swashes to point to the left margin**. A bar that fades out to the right will draw attention back to the left margin thereby making the left alignment of text and graphics appear intentional, not accidental. (For more on swashes, see page 407.)

Here we see how some of these techniques lessen the imbalance of the page.

On the CD-ROM ...

examples
   chap8
      lefthevy
         lefthvfx.htm

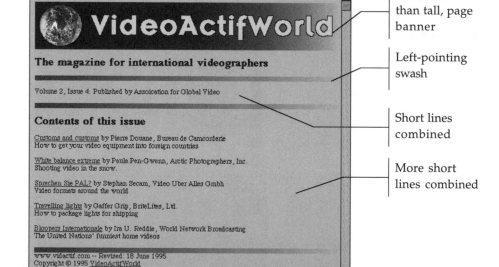

Wide, rather than tall, page banner

Left-pointing swash

Short lines combined

More short lines combined

Although accepting the default, left alignment may not always produce the most effective page layout; however, it is safe. Your pages will appear much the same on all browsers. You need not lose sleep worrying about how it looks to someone running version 0.9 beta of GlobalGazer.

Dividing the page vertically into zones

To avoid overwhelming readers of complex pages, many designers divide the Web page into distinct zones. Each zone contains one type of information. For example, this page has five zones separated by horizontal rules.

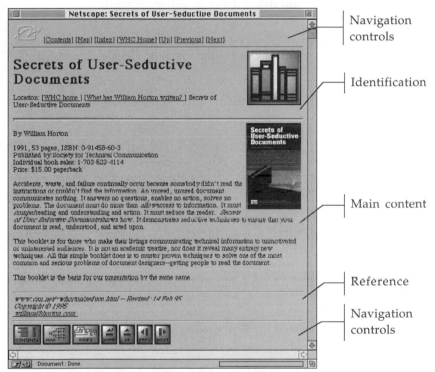

Screen shot is reprinted with permission from William Horton Consulting.

Dividing a complex page into zones lets users quickly identify which zone to scan. Then they confront the five to ten items within that zone, rather than the 25 or 30 pieces of information in the page as a whole. Dividing the page into specific zones is especially important in a related series of pages. Readers quickly learn what kind of information each zone contains and where it appears on the page. Such knowledge makes navigating and reading Web pages more predictable and more fun.

In general, divide the page into three to five zones vertically—no more than seven, certainly. Arrange the page so that each zone contains no more than five to seven graphics or blocks of text. If you have more than seven or so blocks of information in a zone, divide them up with blank space, color coding, boxes, or other graphical techniques.

There are three ways to divide the page into zones: rules, swashes, and breaks. Let's look at each one in turn.

Horizontal rules

For more on horizontal rules, see page. 238.

Horizontal rules are Web-speak for horizontal lines. You produce them with the HTML <HR> tag. Netscape Navigator and some other browsers let you define rules of different widths.

On the CD-ROM ...

examples
  chap8
    zones
      zones.htm

> The following rule is the standard 2-pixel rule:
>
> _____
>
> The following rule is three pixels thick:
>
> _____
>
> The following rule is four pixels thick:
>
> _____
>
> The following rule is five pixels thick:
>
> _____
>
> The following rule is six pixels thick:
>
> _____

```
<P>The following rule is the standard 2-pixel rule:</P>
<HR>

<P>The following rule is three pixels thick:</P>
<HR SIZE=3>

<P>The following rule is four pixels thick:</P>
<HR SIZE=4>

<P>The following rule is five pixels thick:</P>
<HR SIZE=5>

<P>The following rule is six pixels thick:</P>
<HR SIZE=6>
```

You can use different thicknesses to signal major and minor divisions. However, do not use more than three different thicknesses in a page and make sure that there is at least a 30 percent difference between the thicknesses you use.

Swashes

You can also separate zones with colorful swashes. Swashes are stripes extending horizontally across the page. To the browser they are just wide graphics. Here are some examples.

On the CD-ROM ...

examples
  chap8
    zones
      zones.htm

The following swash fades from blue to the background gray in color. It is in the file "swash1.gif."

The following swash fades vertically from light gray to dark gray. It creates the appearance of a bulge in the surface. It is in the file "swash2.gif."

The following swash is like the previous one except that it is blue instead of gray. It is in the file "swash3.gif."

The following swash fades from red to blue horizontally. It is in the file "swash4.gif."

The following swash spans the colors of the spectrum from left to right. It is quite colorful, perhaps too colorful. It is in the file "swash5.gif."

For more on how to include graphics, see page 322.

To include a swash, you first create the graphic and then you embed the tags to display the graphic, like this:

```
<IMG SRC="swash1.gif"><BR>
```

Swashes can add a dash of color to an otherwise gray page. By repeating a color or texture from the page banner, they can make the page more cohesive.

Swashes are graphics and as such must be fetched and loaded separately. This can delay display of the whole page, especially when accessed by modem. To minimize this delay:

- Keep the swashes as small as possible The smaller the graphic, the quicker it loads.

- Reuse the same swash throughout a page or a series of pages. Many browsers cache loaded items so that subsequent displays of the same item do not require reloading it over the network.

But what about poor souls with text-only browsers? They won't see your colorful swashes. To make sure that text-only users see the same zones, you can include text dividers as ALT attributes in your <IMG> tags, like this:

```
<IMG SRC="swash1.gif"
ALT="-------------------------------------------------------------------"><BR>
```

Here are some other text swashes you can use:

```
ALT="===================================================================="

ALT="++++++++++++++++++++++++++++++++++++++++++++++++++++++++++++++++++++++"

ALT="********************************************************************"

ALT="%%%%%%%%%%%%%%%%%%%%%%%%%%%%%%%%%%%%%%%%%%%%%%%%%%%%%%%%%%%%%%%%%%%%%%"

ALT="!!!!!!!!!!!!!!!!!!!!!!!!!!!!!!!!!!!!!!!!!!!!!!!!!!!!!!!!!!!!!!!!!!!!!!"
```

Breaks

Breaks are just blank lines used to vertically separate paragraphs of text or other items on the page.

On the CD-ROM ...

examples
  chap8
    zones
      zones.htm

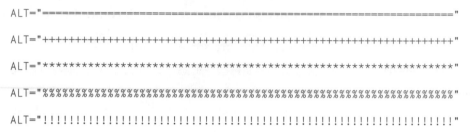

There are no extra breaks or paragraphs between this paragraph and the next one.

Between this paragraph and the next one is a single break tag.

Between this paragraph and the next one are two break tags.

And between this paragraph and the next are (you guessed it) three break tags.

Do you see how the break tags add extra vertical space between paragraphs?

Here's what the HTML looks like behind the scenes:

```
<P>There are no extra breaks or paragraphs between this paragraph and
the next one.</P>
<P>Between this paragraph and the next one is a single break tag.</P>
<BR>
<P>Between this paragraph and the next one are two break tags.</P>
<BR>
<BR>
<P>And between this paragraph and the next are (you guessed it) three
break tags.</P>
<BR>
<BR>
<BR>
<P>Do you see how the break tags add extra vertical space between
paragraphs?</P>
```

Breaks are not as distinct or prominent as rules or swashes. They work best for separating items within a zone while rules and swashes work best to separate zones.

Positioning text and graphics horizontally on the page

Positioning items horizontally is a lot harder than positioning them vertically. It requires ... er ... uh ... What it requires is cheating. Until most of the features of HTML 3.0 are supported by all browsers, we will have to kludge and hack to position things on the page. We must use existing features in unorthodox ways. We may choose to use features not found in all browsers.

Using preformatted text to force positions

One way to control format is to use preformatted text. We can produce this layout:

On the CD-ROM ...

examples
   chap8
      horizpos
         horizpos.htm

```
This is a paragraph of preformatted text.
It is aligned against the left margin.

              This is another paragraph of text. It is indented
              15 spaces from the left margin.



                        This paragraph is indented 25 spaces from
                        the left margin. It has 3 blank lines above
                        it and three blank lines below it.

This paragraph is back at the left margin
like the first.
```

with this HTML code:

```
<PRE>
This is a paragraph of preformatted text.
It is aligned against the left margin.

              This is another paragraph of text. It is indented
              15 spaces from the left margin.



                        This paragraph is indented 25 spaces from
                        the left margin. It has 3 blank lines above
                        it and three blank lines below it.

This paragraph is back at the left margin
like the first.
</PRE>
```

For more on preformatted text, see page 247.

It's not elegant. In fact, it's ugly. The monospaced font of preformatted text looks crude. And, because the line endings are fixed, this text is time consuming to revise. But it appears just like you told it to.

Using list tags to indent text

If you find yourself craving a simple INDENT command, despair not. Since most browsers indent lists, you can use a list construction to force indentation. You can do something like this:

On the CD-ROM ...

examples
  chap8
    horizpos
      horizpos.htm

This paragraph is a regular paragraph. Notice that it is not indented.

> This paragraph is indented because it is within a single pair of list tags. It is not formatted as a list item, because it does not begin with a list-item tag.

> This paragraph is also indented because it is within the first pair of list tags.

>> This paragraph is even further indented because it is within the second pair of list tags.

> This paragraph is back at the first level of indentation because it follows the end-list tag that closed the inner list.

This paragraph is back at the left margin because it follows the end-list tag that closed the outer list.

Just put regular blocks of text between the start `<UL>` and end `</UL>` of the list. Here's the HTML behind the example:

```
<P>This paragraph is a regular paragraph. Notice that it is not
indented.</P>

<UL>

<P>This paragraph is indented because it is within a single pair of
list tags. It is not formatted as a list item, because it does not
begin with a list-item tag.</P>

<P>This paragraph is also indented because it is within the first pair
of list tags. </P>

<UL>
<P>This paragraph is even further indented because it is within the
second pair of list tags.</P>
</UL>

<P>This paragraph is back at the first level of indentation because it
follows the end-list tag that closed the inner list.</P>

</UL>

<P>This paragraph is back at the left margin because it follows the
end-list tag that closed the outer list.</P>
```

For more on lists, see page 255.

This is not an officially sanctioned use of list tags, but street-wise HTML coders resort to it in a pinch.

Flowing text around graphics

Netscape Navigator, and a few other browsers, allows text to flow around graphics on the page, like this:

On the CD-ROM ...

examples
  chap8
    horizpos
      horizpos.htm

Notice that text wraps to the right of this picture because the IMG tag for the picture included ALIGN=LEFT. Browsers, such as Netscape Navigator, that recognize this feature will place the image on the page and then fit the text between the graphic and the right margin.

This paragraph of text wraps to the left of the second picture because the IMG tag for that picture included ALIGN=RIGHT. Browsers that recognize this feature will place the image on the page and then fit the text between the graphic and the left margin.

To trigger this, you include an ALIGN attribute within the image tag. ALIGN=LEFT anchors the graphic to the left margin and ALIGN=RIGHT anchors it to the right. Succeeding text and graphics merrily flow around the margin-bound graphics, as shown. Here is the HTML behind this example:

```
<IMG SRC="picture.gif" ALIGN=LEFT>
<P>Notice that text wraps to the right of this picture because the IMG
tag for the picture included ALIGN=LEFT. Browsers, such as Netscape
Navigator, that recognize this feature will place the image on the page
and then fit the text between the graphic and the right margin.</P>
<BR><BR><BR>
<IMG SRC="picture.gif" ALIGN=RIGHT>
<P>This paragraph of text wraps to the left of the second picture
because the IMG tag for that picture included ALIGN=RIGHT. Browsers
that recognize this feature will place the image on the page and then
fit the text between the graphic and the left margin.</P>
<BR><BR><BR><BR><BR>
```

For more on the <IMG> tag, see page 276 and page 322.

Browsers that do not recognize the ALIGN attribute just drape paragraphs and graphics in sequence against the left margin.

Using tables to position text and graphics

The most sophisticated way to position text and graphics involves the use of borderless tables. HTML 3.0 defines tables whose cells can contain text and graphics. The content of cells can be aligned within the cell. This means you can arrange information like this:

On the CD-ROM ...

examples
    chap8
        horizpos
            horizpos.htm

For more about using HTML 3.0 style tables, see page 390.

Wow! That's almost as sophisticated as a 1979 word processor. How'd we do it? We defined a 2-row-by-3-column table. Each block of text occupies one of the corner cells. The graphic sprawls over the two cells of the middle column. We used vertical and horizontal alignment attributes to point the text in the right direction. Here's the HTML code:

```
<TABLE>

<TR>
<TD ALIGN=RIGHT VALIGN=TOP>This paragraph of text is to the upper left
of the picture.</TD>
<TD ROWSPAN=2><IMG SRC="picture.gif"></TD>
<TD VALIGN=TOP>This paragraph of text is to the upper right of the
picture.</TD>
</TR>

<TR>
<TD ALIGN=RIGHT VALIGN=BOTTOM>This paragraph is to the lower left of
the picture.</TD>
<TD VALIGN=BOTTOM>This paragraph is to the lower right of the
picture.</TD>
</TR>

</TABLE>
```

Unfortunately, tables are not backward compatible. Browsers that do not support tables just string out the text and graphics along the left margin. The results are seldom satisfactory.

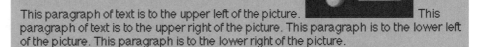

This paragraph of text is to the upper left of the picture. This paragraph of text is to the upper right of the picture. This paragraph is to the lower left of the picture. This paragraph is to the lower right of the picture.

A tabular format works well for catalogs, brochures, data sheets, and specifications that tightly couple text and graphics.

How big is a page?

How much of your page does the user see at a time, that is, without having to scroll the browser window? The answer depends on the size of the user's screen, how much of that screen the user is willing to cover up, and how much of the browser's window actually shows the page and how much is covered with buttons and icons and scroll bars.

Of course, if your users have 1274 x 1024-pixel displays, page area is probably not at the top of your worry list. But let's look at a worst-case, cold-sweats-in-the-night scenario. Say your users have garden variety 640 x 480-pixel monitors. Here are some measurements we took with the browser window as large as possible. If the browser lets you turn off some of its buttons to see more of the display, we measured height with the buttons showing and hidden. Here are the results.

Browser	Width	Height, maximum buttons	Height, minimum buttons
Netscape 1.0N for Windows	610	305	395
Netscape 1.1N for Macintosh	610	320	410
MacWeb 1.00ALPHA3.2 for Macintosh	600	375	375
Mosaic 2.0.0 for Macintosh	590	340	360

Note: Anything over about 600 pixels wide and 250 pixels high requires the user to scroll.

PAGE BANNERS

Most Web pages start with a page banner across the top of the page. Page banners combine text and graphics to immediately orient the reader to the purpose and content of the page. They come in a wide variety. Some even work.

To make sure that your page banner serves its purpose, first decide what the page banner must accomplish. It can answer many of the user's initial questions. A page banner can do several things for you and for your reader:

- **Identify the subject**. What is this page about? That is the reader's first question.

- **Show its importance**. Within a cluster of related pages, you may have major and minor topics. Which is this one?

- **Indicate location**. Where am I? Users get lost. Your page banner can tell them where they are on the Net and where they are within a cluster of related pages.

- **Impress the user**. Wow! Cool! That's neat! A good page banner may so impress the user that the user actually decides to read something.

- **Express your corporate identity**. Who are you? What organization published this page? Is it the same organization that published another page I saw recently?

- **Set the tone**. How am I to interpret this page? Is it serious or is it a joke? The page banner should set a tone that tells the user whether the page is a video game or a safety warning.

Keep in mind, however, that no page banner can do everything equally well. As a designer it is your job to decide which purposes are most important.

Formats

On the CD-ROM ...

examples
   chap8
     banners
       banners.htm

There are as many different kinds of banners as there are designers. It is a uniquely individual activity. Some general categories are more common than others. Let's take a look at them, starting with the economical and ending with the elaborate.

Text with colorful underline

One of the simplest just combines the title, usually as a level-one heading, and a colorful swash, like this:

VideoActifWorld

```
<H1>VideoActifWorld</H1>
<IMG SRC="swash4.gif">
```

Or, the swash may be above the text.

Since the only graphics are the swash, this page banner loads relatively quickly. It is appropriate for a low-level topic in a cluster, especially if the swash echoes a color or texture from the page banner of the top-level topic.

Icon with text beside it

Another common page banner, especially where loading times are a concern, merely combines a colorful icon or emblem with the words of the title, like this:

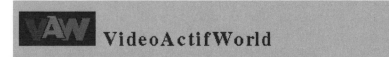

```
<H1><IMG SRC="banner2.gif" ALT="[VAW]"> VideoActifWorld</H1>
```

Because the graphic is small it loads rapidly.

Graphic and stylized text

A simple, tasteful banner often results from combining a small graphic or emblem with stylized text on a filled rectangle, like this:

```
<IMG SRC="banner1.gif" ALT="[VideoActifWorld]">
```

Such a page banner is moderate in size and in prominence. It is, thus, appropriate for topics at a middle level of importance between the high-level home page and low-level details.

Text and graphic on gradient

A simple, easy to create page banner consists of a small graphic plus the title of the page on a gradient, like this:

```
<IMG SRC="banner6.gif" ALT="[VideoActifWorld]">
```

Such page banners are not flashy, but are tasteful and restful to the eye. They are appropriate for mid- and low-level topics, especially where users are looking at detailed information and may be viewing several such pages at a sitting.

Photographic background to text

You can often produce a visually attractive heading by superimposing the title on a relevant photographic background, like this:

```
<IMG SRC="banner3.gif" ALT="[VideoActifWorld]">
```

Take care, though, that the title stands out from the background and that the title does not so obscure the photograph that the reader cannot recognize it.

Square graphic with text beside it

Another economical design combines a slightly larger graphic with text. It uses the ALIGN=LEFT attribute to lodge the image to the left, while the text flows around it to the right, like this:

```
<IMG SRC="banner5.gif" ALIGN=LEFT
ALT="[VideoActifWorld]"><H1>VideoActifWorld</H1>
<BR><BR><BR><H2>The magazine for international videographers</H2><BR
CLEAR=ALL>
```

One advantage of this format is that it allows room for a subtitle. The subtitle might look better aligned with the lower edge, but positioning it there would run the risk that in other browsers it would slide beneath the graphic image.

If your users have a browser that supports HTML 3.0 tables, make the banner a table with cells for the graphic, the title, and the subtitle.

For more about using HTML 3.0 style tables, see page 390.

```
<TABLE>

<TR>
<TD ROWSPAN=2> <IMG SRC="banner5.gif" ALT="[VideoActifWorld]"></TD>
<TD VALIGN=TOP> <H1>VideoActifWorld</H1> </TD>
</TR>
<TR>
<TD VALIGN=BOTTOM> <H2>The magazine for international
videographers</H2> </TD>
</TR>

</TABLE>
```

Integrated text and graphic

Other page banners integrate the title of the topic into a colorful graphic, something like this:

Such an approach is appropriate for a home page or introductory menu where the user first enters a related cluster of topics.

If you take this approach, make sure that the text remains legible and that the page banner is no larger than necessary.

Title and map all in one

The most elaborate, eye-popping, and expensive page banner presents the user with a bright, colorful painting.

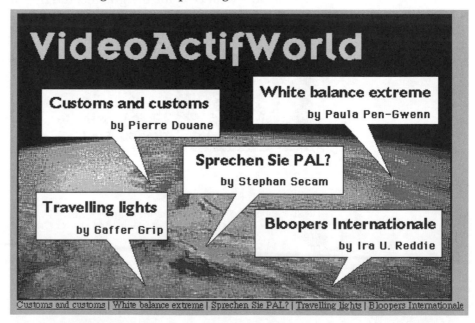

```
<A HREF="HTTP://www.wherever.com/cgi-bin/imagemap/vaw.map>
<IMG SRC="banner7.gif" ISMAP></A><BR>

<A HREF="customs.htm"> Customs and customs</A>       |
<A HREF="whitebal.htm">White balance extreme</A>  |
<A HREF="sprechen.htm">Sprechen Sie PAL?</A>           |
<A HREF="lights.htm">  Travelling lights</A>          |
<A HREF="bloopers.htm">Bloopers Internationale</A>
```

To see how to use image-maps, see page 383. For another example of an image-map used as a page banner, see page 430.

Such a painting is also an image-map so that the user can jump directly to subtopics by clicking on objects in the painting.

Such large graphics work well only when the user is connected through a high-speed network. Also consider the needs of users who have graphics turned off. One solution is to make the same choices of subtopics available through a text menu just below the graphic, as we did in this example.

How large?

How large should you make the page banner? Larger banners can contain more information and can appear more impressive. But the larger the banner, the slower it loads. For a group of related pages arranged in a hierarchy of topics and subtopics, you may want to use larger page banners for major topics and smaller banners for minor subtopics.

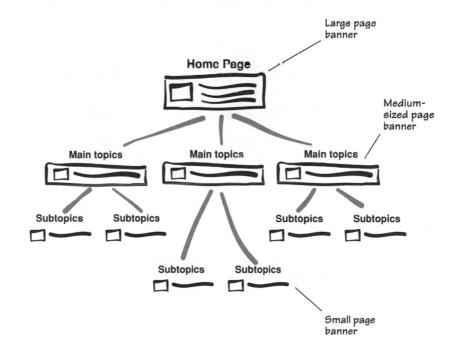

GRAPHIC BACKGROUNDS AND COLORED TEXT

On the CD-ROM ...

examples
  chap8
    backgnds
      bkgnds1.htm

Most browsers display the text of the page in black on a gray background, something like this:

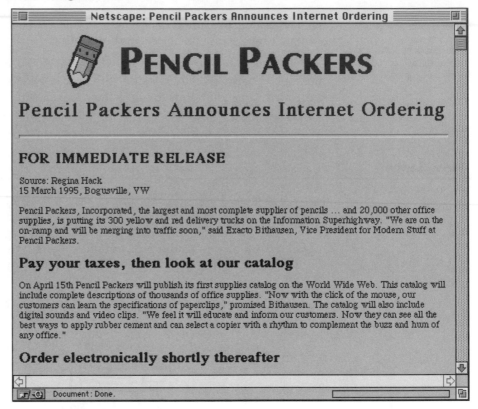

This combination is simple, legible, and just what Web users are accustomed to. It is like speaking in a normal tone of voice. But sometimes you want to shout. HTML 3.0 and Netscape extensions let you shout.

Color background

Netscape has introduced extensions that let you specify the background color, as well as the color for text, links, active links, and visited links. Here we made the background blue and the text yellow.

On the CD-ROM ...

examples
    chap8
        backgnds
            bkgnds2.htm

For more on this
extension, see page 242.

The color combination was triggered by this form of the BODY tag:

```
<BODY BGCOLOR="#0000CC" TEXT="#FFFF00"
LINK="#00DD00" VLINK="#FF0000" ALINK="#00FF00">
```

If hexadecimal is not your
native language, consult
page 301 which lists the
codes for common colors.

The BGCOLOR parameter sets the color of the background and TEXT sets the color of the body text. Colors are specified as amounts of red, green, and blue in two-digit hexadecimal numbers (00 = minimum amount, FF = maximum amount). Deep blue is #0000CC and light yellow is #FFFF00. (We had to change the color of the text in the page header manually so it would not blend into the background.)

Tiled pattern

HTML 3.0 lets designers designate a graphic to be repeated as a tile behind text and graphics of the page. For example, the legal-pad background of this display was produced by just such a tile:

On the CD-ROM ...

examples
  chap8
    backgnds
      bkgnds3.htm

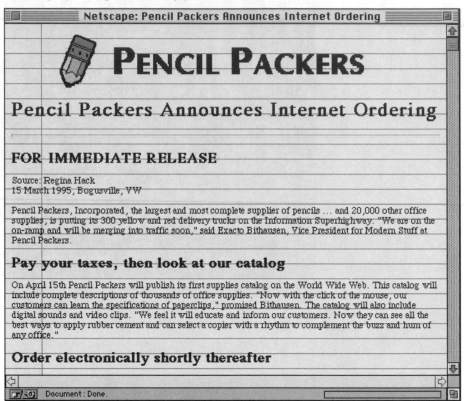

The tile is a simple graphic that when repeated forms the overall pattern. In this case the tile was this image:

For more on this
extension, see page 244.

The magic is done by this form of the BODY tag:

```
<BODY BACKGROUND="legalpad.gif" TEXT="#0000CC"
       LINK="#007700" VLINK="#CC0000" ALINK="#00DD00">
```

For help setting colors, see
page 301.

The BACKGROUND parameter just specifies the file containing the image to use as a tile. The TEXT, LINK, VLINK, and ALINK parameters set the colors of text, links, visited links, and active links, respectively. Colors are specified as amounts of red, green, and blue in two-digit hexadecimal numbers (00 = minimum amount, FF = maximum amount). Deep blue is #0000CC and light yellow is #FFFF00.

We have seen several Web pages that use a tiled background to put an embossed logo behind the text, such as a watermark on fine paper, something like this:

On the CD-ROM ...

examples
  chap8
    backgnds
      bkgnds4.htm

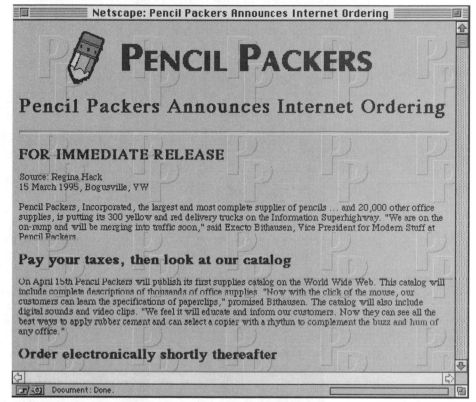

Yet another good use is to put a textured background, such as old paper or stucco, behind the page. Whatever texture you pick must not make the text on the page illegible. Have someone wearing bifocals give you an opinion.

Photograph

You are not limited to small graphics for a background tile. You may even be tempted to use a large photograph. Do not do it. First, the photograph may take a long time to load, and your page will end up looking something like this:

On the CD-ROM ...

examples
  chap8
    backgnds
      bkgnds5.htm

Photographs almost never work well as a background to detailed text. The detail of the photograph renders the text illegible. (Yes, we **did** try it with dark text. That made it even worse.)

If you must use a photograph for a background, choose a simple one and either lighten or darken it so that text stands out and remains legible.

DESIGN CASE STUDIES—PUTTING IT ALL TOGETHER

In this section we look at six design studies. These studies present prototypes for Web pages for different people and organizations. These prototypes integrate many of the techniques presented in this chapter.

These studies take a conservative approach. As a rule, they require only common HTML 2.0 features. The exceptions to this rule rely on widely supported extensions that are cleanly ignored by browses that do not support them.

Keep in mind that these design studies are not complete examples. We left off extensive navigation buttons and items to keep the studies simple and to focus attention on the visual design. To complete them you would need to add signatures and navigation buttons.

Automotive electronics firm

Hautomotive Electronics sells electronic components to the automotive industry. These components go into luxury and sports cars. The decision to incorporate Hautomotive components into a car's design is made by the engineers designing the car. Hautomotive does not sell to the general public.

Because their audience is mostly engineers and purchasing managers, Hautomotive wants its Web pages to look objective and precise, with just a pinch of technology and a dash of excitement.

This design illustrates the mechanical style. This style employs gridlike layout, dominated by vertical and horizontal lines. The only curving lines are those of the perfectly cylindrical tire. Pictures are all of inanimate manmade objects. They are photographs or highly realistic drawings. The only color is in the cool green of the circuit board. For cohesion a small square of the circuit board is repeated beside each menu selection. Overall the style is conservative and restrained. The only areas of special visual interest are the wheel and the circuit board, items of great interest to the audience of engineers.

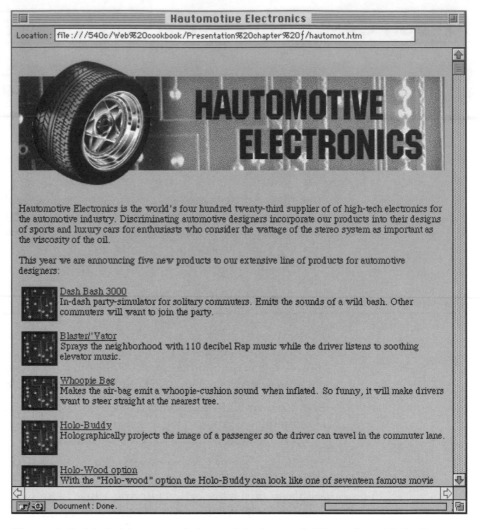

The code behind this example is straightforward. The only trick is the use of the `ALIGN=LEFT` attribute to make the selectable item and its description perch beside the square pieces of circuit board rather falling below them.

```
<HTML>

<!------------------------------------------------------------->
<!--       FILE:      hautomot.htm                         -->
<!------------------------------------------------------------->

<HEAD>
<TITLE>Hautomotive Electronics</TITLE>
</HEAD>

<BODY>

<IMG SRC="hautembl.gif" ALT="[Hautomotive Electronics]"><BR>
```

```
<P>Hautomotive Electronics is the world's four hundred twenty-third
supplier of high-tech electronics for the automotive industry.
Discriminating automotive designers incorporate our products into their
designs of sports and luxury cars for enthusiasts who consider the
wattage of the stereo system as important as the viscosity of the
oil.</P>
<P>This year we are announcing five new products to our extensive line
of products for automotive designers:</P>

<A HREF="nowhere.htm"><IMG SRC="hauticon.gif" ALIGN=LEFT ALT="[Dash
Bash 3000]">
Dash Bash 3000</A><BR>
In-dash party-simulator for solitary commuters. Emits the sounds of a
wild bash. Other commuters will want to join the party.
<BR CLEAR=LEFT><BR>

<A HREF="nowhere.htm"><IMG SRC="hauticon.gif" ALIGN=LEFT ALT="[Blaster-
Vator]">
Blaster-Vator</A><BR>
Sprays the neighborhood with 110 decibel Rap music while the driver
listens to soothing elevator music.
<BR CLEAR=LEFT><BR>

<A HREF="nowhere.htm"><IMG SRC="hauticon.gif" ALIGN=LEFT ALT="[Whoopie
Bag]">
Whoopie Bag</A><BR>
Makes the air-bag emit a whoopie-cushion sound when inflated. So funny,
it will make drivers want to steer straight at the nearest tree.
<BR CLEAR=LEFT><BR>

<A HREF="nowhere.htm"><IMG SRC="hauticon.gif" ALIGN=LEFT ALT="[Holo-
Buddy]">
Holo-Buddy</A><BR>
Holographically projects the image of a passenger so the driver can
travel in the commuter lane.
<BR CLEAR=LEFT><BR>

<A HREF="nowhere.htm"><IMG SRC="hauticon.gif" ALIGN=LEFT ALT="[Holo-
Wood option]">Holo-Wood option</A><BR>
With the "Holo-wood" option the Holo-Buddy can look like one of
seventeen famous movie stars. Watch other cars get out of your way when
Dirty Harry rides shotgun.
<BR CLEAR=LEFT><BR>

<P>If you're reading this Web Page in your car, hit the brakes, pull
over, and gives us a call on your Hautomotive cellular phone at 1-800-
555-7272.</P>

<P>At Hautomotive we like to say:</P>
<BLOCKQUOTE>
Without electrons, a car is just sculpture.
</BLOCKQUOTE>

</BODY>
</HTML>
```

Day-care centers

Brats-R-Us chain is a nationwide chain of day-care centers. Their customers are almost all working parents of infants and toddlers.

Brats-R-Us wants to use the Web to entice new customers. However they are concerned about appearing machinelike. They want to keep their image kind, caring, and friendly. They want a look that is soft and warm, yet clean and professional.

On the CD-ROM ...

examples
  chap8
    bratsrus
      bratsrus.htm

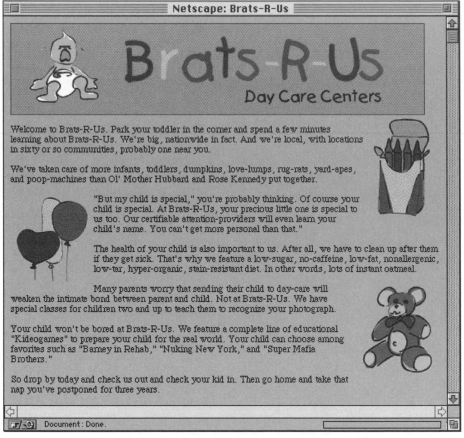

This design embodies the organic style. It is dominated by bright, warm colors, rounded shapes, and objects with positive associations. The primary graphic is of an infant. The graphics are more like cartoons than mechanical drawings or photographs. The layout is informal, with text flowing around casually scattered graphics.

Unity is provided by repeating colors from the page banner in the objects on the page and by selecting objects closely associated with children. The size and position of the teddy bear echoes that of the infant in the page banner.

The HTML code uses only one trick. To force text to flow around the images of the crayons, balloons, and the teddy bear, the <IMG> tag for those graphics includes an ALIGN=LEFT or ALIGN=RIGHT attribute.

```
<HTML>

<!------------------------------------------------------------------>
<!--       FILE:       bratsrus.htm                            -->
<!------------------------------------------------------------------>

<HEAD>
<TITLE>Brats-R-Us</TITLE>
</HEAD>

<BODY>

<IMG SRC="babyembl.gif" ALT="[Brats-R-Us Daycare Centers]"><BR>

<IMG SRC="babypic1.gif" ALIGN=RIGHT ALT="[Crayons]">

<P>Welcome to Brats-R-Us. Park your toddler in the corner and spend a
few minutes learning about Brats-R-Us. We're big, nationwide in fact.
And we're local, with locations in sixty or so communities, probably
one near you.</P>

<P>We've taken care of more infants, toddlers, dumpkins, love-lumps,
rug rats, yard-apes, and poop-machines than Ol' Mother Hubbard and Rose
Kennedy put together.</P>

<IMG SRC="babypic2.gif" ALIGN=LEFT ALT="[Balloons]">

<P>"But my child is special," you're probably thinking. Of course your
child is special. At Brats-R-Us, your precious little one is special to
us too. Our certifiable attention-providers will even learn your
child's name. You can't get more personal than that."</P>

<P>The health of your child is also important to us. After all, we have
to clean up after them if they get sick. That's why we feature a low-
sugar, no-caffeine, low-fat, nonallergenic, low-tar, hyper-organic,
stain-resistant diet. In other words, lots of instant oatmeal.</P>

<IMG SRC="babypic3.gif" ALIGN=RIGHT ALT="[Teddy Bear]">
<P>Many parents worry that sending their child to day-care will weaken
the intimate bond between parent and child. Not at Brats-R-Us. We have
special classes for children two and up to teach them to recognize your
photograph.</P>
<P>Your child won't be bored at Brats-R-Us. We feature a complete line
of educational "Kideogames" to prepare your child for the real world.
Your child can choose among favorites such as "Barney in Rehab,"
"Nuking New York," and "Super Mafia Brothers."</P>
<P>So drop by today and check us out and check your kid in. Then go
home and take that nap you've postponed for three years.</P>

</BODY>
</HTML>
```

Artist

Edouard DeGauss is a computer artist, more at home with pixels than paint, more comfortable with Phong shading than with felt-tipped markers. Edouard wants his Web page to serve as a résumé and a notice to the world that Edouard is indeed an artist to be reckoned with.

On the CD-ROM ...

examples
  chap8
    degauss
      degauss.htm

The look is deliberately flamboyant and frenetic. Creativity is more important than factual content. Aesthetics (or Edouard's idea of aesthetics) dominate. The layout is free-form and dynamic.

The code is as simple as the resulting layout is exotic. The entire content is just an image-map and, for those not displaying graphics, an equivalent text menu.

```
<HTML>

<!-------------------------------------------------------------->
<!--      FILE:      degauss.htm                            -->
<!-------------------------------------------------------------->

<HEAD>
<TITLE>Edouard DeGauss, Computer Artiste</TITLE>
</HEAD>

<BODY>

<A HREF="HTTP://www.artcoop.com/cgi-bin/imagemap/degauss/home.map>
<IMG SRC="degauss.gif" ISMAP ALT="[There is not alternative to
art.]"></A><BR>

 [<A HREF="degaubio.htm">DeGauss</A>]
 [<A HREF="dropshad.htm">Shadows</A>]
 [<A HREF="selfport.htm">Portraits</A>]
 [<A HREF="montages.htm">Montages</A>]
 [<A HREF="fauxreal.htm">Faux reality</A>]
 [<A HREF="ransomty.htm">Typography</A>]

</BODY>
</HTML>
```

Law firm

Connem, Bilkem, and Gottcha, PC, is a law firm and wants to look like one. They are conservative and want to protect that image. No new-fangled gadgetry, please. Just a calling card.

On the CD-ROM ...

examples
chap8
lawfirm
lawfirm.htm

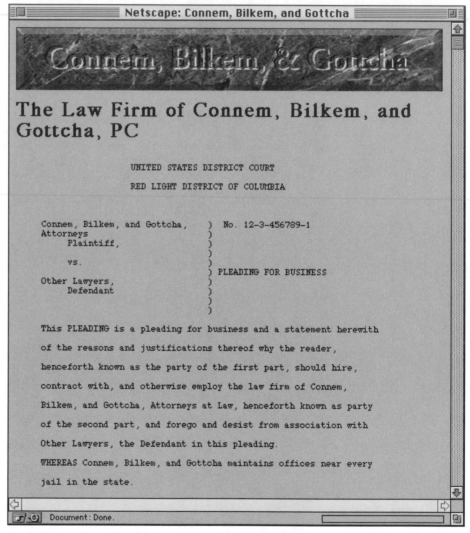

This design is an example of the corporate style. It is a constrained, conservative layout. It consists of mostly vertical and horizontal lines, square edges, and stable shapes. Colors are cool and calm, or else just black and white. The message is conveyed in text rather than in graphics.

The page banner just engraves the company name into a marble plaque of the kind associated with wealthy corporations. The one innovation is that the sales pitch is formatted in the distinctive style of a legal pleading.

The only trick in this HTML code is the simplest one possible. The body text is formatted entirely between a <PRE> tag and its corresponding </PRE> tag. Fortunately the typewriter-like typeface used by the <PRE> tag resembles that used in legal pleadings.

```
<HTML>

<!------------------------------------------------------------------>
<!--      FILE:      lawfirm.htm                                 -->
<!------------------------------------------------------------------>

<HEAD>
<TITLE>Connem, Bilkem, and Gottcha</TITLE>
</HEAD>

<BODY>

<IMG SRC="lawembl.gif" ALT="[Connem, Bilkem, and Gottcha]"><BR>
<H1>The Law Firm of Connem, Bilkem, and Gottcha, PC</H1>


<PRE>
                        UNITED STATES DISTRICT COURT

                        RED LIGHT DISTRICT OF COLUMBIA



        Connem, Bilkem, and Gottcha,   ) No. 12-3-456789-1
        Attorneys                      )
              Plaintiff,               )
                                       )
                                       )
              vs.                      )
                                       ) PLEADING FOR BUSINESS
        Other Lawyers,                 )
              Defendant                )
                                       )
                                       )

This PLEADING is a pleading for business and a statement herewith

of the reasons and justifications thereof why the reader,

henceforth known as the party of the first part, should hire,

contract with, and otherwise employ the law firm of Connem,

Bilkem, and Gottcha, Attorneys at Law, henceforth known as party

of the second part, and forego and desist from association with

Other Lawyers, the Defendant in this pleading.

WHEREAS Connem, Bilkem, and Gottcha maintains offices near every
```

```
jail in the state.
WHEREAS Connem, Bilkem, and Gottcha continuously monitors all
radio channels dispatching ambulances.
WHEREAS Connem, Bilkem, and Gottcha makes generous donations to
all major political candidates.
WHEREAS Connem, Bilkem, and Gottcha is winner of the 1994 Bail
Bondsman's Appreciation award.
WHEREAS the reader does not want to sit in the witness box and be
asked, "When did you stop beating your spouse?"
THEREFORE Let it be ordered that the reader will immediately and
forthwith, without any reservation or undue delay, contract with
Connem, Bilkem, and Gottcha for legal services.
</PRE>

</BODY>
</HTML>
```

Community bulletin board

The Community Bulletin Board is sponsored by the city government of a small city. Its charter is to keep the citizens informed about goings-on in the city.

The Community Bulletin Board will serve the role of an old-fashioned bulletin board where citizens and government officials can post announcements of interest to the public. It will be accessed primarily by individual citizens from their homes or small businesses. Since many have limited computer experience, the Community Bulletin Board should be simple and friendly.

On the CD-ROM ...

examples
  chap8
    bullbrd
      bullbrd.htm

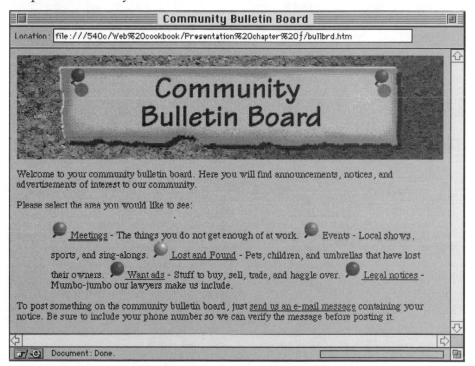

The Community Bulletin Board uses the metaphor of a physical bulletin board. The page banner looks like a yellowing announcement tacked onto a cork board. Each category of announcements is marked by a colorful push-pin.

Rather than march in military regularity down the page, the announcements run together producing a free-form pattern of pins, just the way they would appear on a bulletin board. There was another reason for not using a conventional bullet list. Many of the users have low-cost monitors, which could not display a long vertical list in one scrolling zone.

The only nonstandard aspect of the HTML code is the list without list items. The result is to indent the content between the <UL> and </UL> tags. Because no <LI> tags are used to mark individual items, they all flow together like a paragraph of text.

```
<HTML>

<!------------------------------------------------------------------>
<!--        FILE:      bullbrd.htm                                -->
<!------------------------------------------------------------------>

<HEAD>
<TITLE>Community Bulletin Board</TITLE>
</HEAD>

<BODY>

<IMG SRC="bbrdembl.gif" ALT="[Community Bulletin Board]"><BR>

<P>Welcome to your community bulletin board. Here you will find
announcements, notices, and advertisements of interest to our
community.</P>

<P>Please select the area you would like to see:</P>

<UL>

<IMG SRC="pinorang.gif" ALT="[Meetings]"><A HREF="nowhere.htm">
Meetings</A> - The things you do not get enough of at work.

<IMG SRC="pinaqua.gif" ALT="[Events]"><A HREF="nowhere.htm">
Events</A> - Local shows, sports, and sing-alongs.

<IMG SRC="pinyellw.gif" ALT="[Lost and Found]"><A HREF="nowhere.htm">
Lost and Found</A> - Pets, children, and umbrellas that have lost their
owners.

<IMG SRC="pingreen.gif" ALT="[Want ads]"><A HREF="nowhere.htm">
Want ads</A> - Stuff to buy, sell, trade, and haggle over.

<IMG SRC="pinred.gif" ALT="[Legal notices]"><A HREF="nowhere.htm">
Legal notices</A> - Mumbo-jumbo our lawyers make us include.

</UL>

<P>To post something on the community bulletin board, just <A
HREF="MAILTO:sysop@internet.mail.address">
send us an e-mail message</A> containing your notice. Be sure to
include your phone number so we can verify the message before posting
it.

</BODY>
</HTML>
```

Investment briefing

The offices of Knearly Brokerage maintain a vast library of information of interest to the individual investors who make up most of its customer base. Clerks and brokers at Knearly Brokerage spend a lot of time retrieving reports and faxing them to customers. Knearly Brokerage wants to make the entire library of information available over the Web. They have arranged all the information in a vast four-level hierarchy of cabinets, drawers, folders, and individual documents. They want users to be able to navigate this hierarchy reliably.

This design shows the page for an individual document at the bottom level of the hierarchy:

On the CD-ROM ...

examples
  chap8
    invest
      invest.htm

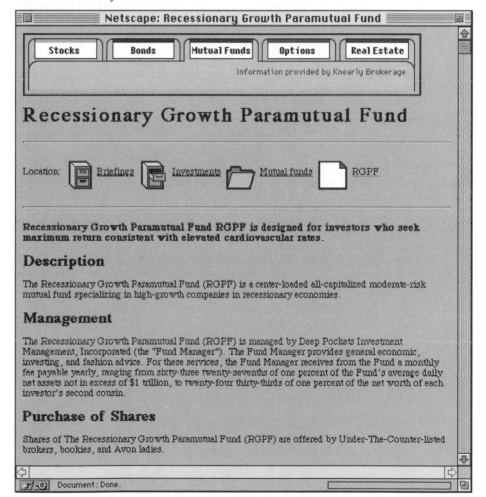

Because this page occurs four levels deep in a hierarchy, it does not need to introduce Knearly Brokerage or try to impress the reader. At this point the reader just wants information.

The page banner follows the filing-cabinet metaphor by showing the tabs of file folders for related categories of information. Notice that the tab for Mutual Funds is to the front, indicating that this page shows a document from that folder. These tabs are also part of an image-map so the user can click on a tab to see a list of the documents in that folder. Below the title are icons and labels showing the current document's location in the hierarchy. The user can click on one of the labels to jump to that level.

The only formatting trick in the HTML code is the use of the ALIGN=MIDDLE attribute in the IMG tags for the icons. This centers them vertically with their labels.

```
<HTML>

<!------------------------------------------------------------------->
<!--        FILE:        invest.htm                               -->
<!------------------------------------------------------------------->

<HEAD>
<TITLE>Recessionary Growth Paramutual Fund</TITLE>
</HEAD>

<BODY>

<A HREF="HTTP://www.what.ever/cgi-bin/imagemap/dir/subdir/filename.map>
<IMG SRC="invest.gif" ALT="[RGPF]" ISMAP></A><BR>

<H1>Recessionary Growth Paramutual Fund</H1>
<HR SIZE=2>

<P>Location:
<IMG SRC="cabinet.gif" ALIGN=MIDDLE ALT="[Cabinet]"><A
HREF="nowhere.htm">Briefings</A>

<IMG SRC="drawer.gif" ALIGN=MIDDLE ALT="[Drawer]"> <A
HREF="nowhere.htm">Investments</A>

<IMG SRC="folder.gif" ALIGN=MIDDLE ALT ALT="[Folder]"> <A
HREF="nowhere.htm">Mutual funds</A>

<IMG SRC="document.gif" ALIGN=MIDDLE ALT ALT="[Document]"> <A
HREF="nowhere.htm"> RGPF</A></P>

<HR SIZE=2>

<P><B> Recessionary Growth Paramutual Fund RGPF is designed for
investors who seek maximum return consistent with elevated
cardiovascular rates.</B></P>

<H2>Description</H2>
```

<P>The Recessionary Growth Paramutual Fund (RGPF) is a center-loaded all-capitalized moderate-risk mutual fund specializing in high-growth companies in recessionary economies.</P>

<H2>Management</H2>

<P>The Recessionary Growth Paramutual Fund (RGPF) is managed by Deep Pockets Investment Management, Incorporated (the "Fund Manager"). The Fund Manager provides general economic, investing, and fashion advice. For these services, the Fund Manager receives from the Fund a monthly fee payable yearly, ranging from sixty-three twenty-sevenths of one percent of the Fund's average daily net assets not in excess of $1 trillion, to twenty-four thirty-thirds of one percent of the net worth of each investor's second cousin.<P>

<H2>Purchase of Shares</H2>

<P>Shares of The Recessionary Growth Paramutual Fund (RGPF) are offered by Under-The-Counter-listed brokers, bookies, and Avon ladies. </P>

<H2>Redemption of Shares</H2>

<P>Shares of The Recessionary Growth Paramutual Fund (RGPF) may be redeemed at the net asset value determined by the Fund Manager, after a request in writing in green ink on crinkly mauve paper. </P>

<H2>Expenses</H2>

<PRE>
```
                                      Percentage of net assets
     Management fees ........................    .45%
     12bK2j.3 fees ..........................    .21%
     Lawyers' fees ..........................    .62%
     Vacations for management ...............    .12%
     Bail for management ....................    .23%
                                              ==========
     TOTAL FUND OPERATING EXPENSES ..........   1.63%
```
</PRE>

</BODY>
</HTML>

RECAP

Designing attractive and effective Web pages is not hard when you keep in mind the main lessons of this chapter.

- Design the presentation of the page to accomplish the overall goals of the page. Design for its own sake is bad design.

- Use a consistent presentation style for a group of related pages.

- Divide complex pages into distinct zones, each featuring a particular kind of information, such as navigation controls, identification, or main content.

- At the top of the page, include a prominent page banner to identify the page and entice the user to read it.

- Use a colored or patterned background to make the page look more interesting, but take care to keep text legible.

- Test your page with people different from you. Test with people who like different colors. Test with someone wearing bifocals and someone who is color blind.

- Don't forget the needs of nongraphical users—those using text-only browsers and those who have turned off graphics. If you use image-maps, make the same choices available through a text menu. Use the ALT attribute in <IMG> tags to provide textual descriptions of critical graphics—such as close-captioning a TV program.

9

INTERNATIONAL CUISINE

Designing for the whole world

It is called the *World Wide* Web. Your Web pages will be read by users from all over the world whose cultural expectations and languages are different from your own. They want to understand your Web pages as much as you want them to read them. So, plan your Web pages—text, graphics, and design—with international users in mind.

HELP THIS WEB PAGE OBTAIN ITS PASSPORT!

On the CD-ROM ...

examples
chap9
before.htm

Can you design Web pages for the whole world? Here's your chance. List the ways to improve this Web page to make it communicate better with a worldwide audience. See the section "Before and After" on page 466 for our recommendations.

Netscape: FlameCloth Pyrolon 34

[Contents] [Index] [Home] [Up] [Previous] [Next]

FLAMECLOTH

Pyrolon 34 flame-resistant fabric

When it's hot Hot HOT!

We mean hot. H Oh Gawd T. Hotter 'n Houston in August Hotter than where you wish your inlaws would go. We're talking O'Leary's-barn hot. That's the kind of heat our agency-approved, lightweight, puncture-resistant, flame-proof Pyrolon 34 industrial fabric takes in stride.

Let's see how it stacks up against the competition:

Characteristic	Pyrolon 34	Ash-best-Os	Krash N
Flame resistance	👌	👌	👌
Puncture resistance	👌	👎	👎
Acid resistance	👌	👎	👎
Price	$10.34 per sq ft	$13.00 per sq ft	$18.00 per sq ft

If you'd like a free sample, give our sales office a call at 1-800-BUY-OURS during office hours. Or fill in this Internet "Q-pon":

Name
Organization
Street
City   State   Zip

[Oh forget it] [Send the sucker]

FlameCloth Corporation, Revised: 4/7/95

THE FIRST TWO WS IN WWW ARE REAL

The WWW is truly global. Users can connect to it via modem, a LAN, WAN, cellular network, or via a satellite dish. There's even a WWW browser for the Apple Newton. And they can read your Web pages from the middle of the Sahara desert, from atop Mt. Fuji, and even from inside their automobiles (not while driving, we hope). It really doesn't matter where they are.

The internationality of the Web builds on the global span of the Internet. While most users are accessing the Internet from the United States, the rest of the world is also getting on board the Internet. According to a February '95 press release by the Internet Society, access to the Internet increased 26 percent in just the fourth quarter of 1994. This brought the total number of Internet host computers to almost five million! The Internet hosts were distributed as shown in the following table:

Note: The press release included no figures for Central and South America.

Region	Internet hosts	Growth
North America	3,372,551	26%
Europe, West	1,039,192	22%
Asia	151,773	19%
Europe, East	46,125	40%
Africa	27,130	29%
Middle East	13,776	33%

The Graphics, Visualization, and Usability (GVU) Center's Second WWW Survey (10 October 1994–16 November 1994) and Third WWW Survey (10 April–10 May 1995) offer these figures on WWW use. Note that the figures reflect the number of survey respondents and not the actual number of WWW users. (http://www.cc.gatech.edu/gvu/user-surveys)

*Numbers were supplied by James Pitkow at GVU.

| Region of the world | Number of WWW users* | | |
	Survey 2 (Oct–Nov '94)	Survey 3 (Apr–May '95)	Growth rate
North America: United States	2,306	6,978	203%
Europe	823	1,276	55%
North America: Canada, Mexico	213	688	223%

Region of the world	Number of WWW users*		
	Survey 2 (Oct–Nov '94)	Survey 3 (Apr–May '95)	Growth rate
Oceania	120	291	143%
Asia	29	146	403%
Middle East	8	30	275%
Africa	7	23	229%
South America	8	20	150%
Antarctica	3	5	67%
West Indies	2	5	150%
Central America	3	4	33%

Though North America dominates usage of the Internet and the Web, usage in Europe is substantial and growing most rapidly in Asia.

ENGLISH GOOD SPOKEN HERE

The world regions with the fastest growth have one thing in common: English is not an official language in any of these regions. And yet English remains the *lingua franca* of the WWW. Why?

There are several reasons why English is the language of choice.

- The common language among the users in the early days of the WWW was English.

- Most Web servers run on a UNIX platform and the language of UNIX is still predominately English.

- There was much controversy (and there still is) over what character set should be used to support multiple writing systems.

- Even though English is not the first language of all Web users, it is an almost universal second language of people in large and medium-sized businesses.

For whatever reasons, English is the writing system and the language of the WWW. Yet more and more WWW users and Web page authors are not native readers or speakers of English.

MODIFY YOUR RECIPES FOR INTERNATIONAL PALATES

Because your audience is truly global, you will need to modify your Web page recipes for international palates. Language is only part of the challenge of a global audience. The other challenge is culture.

Hence the purpose of this chapter: recipes to make your Web pages more appealing to users around the world. We talk about both language and cultural issues here.

We provide four recipes for the global success of your Web pages on the WWW.

1. How to write in English for non-native readers of English
2. How to create graphics for global appeal and comprehension
3. How to create multimedia objects for global appeal and comprehension
4. How to test Web pages for global content

We'll also give you some idea of developments that may make the WWW more global than it currently is.

In general, all the recipes in this chapter will help you to communicate with the largest possible audience of users connected to the WWW. Otherwise, you throw away one of the main reasons for publishing on the WWW. You can target specific local audiences using traditional communication vehicles such as newspapers, magazines, marketing literature, video, television, printed product documentation, and non-Web online documentation. However, none of these media make reaching a global market as easy as does the World Wide Web.

What if my Web pages don't follow the recipes of international cuisine?

Good question. Most likely your Web pages will be read by many users from around the world anyway. The issue here is: If your pages offend or confuse your primary audience, they will leave and not come back. So, what constitutes an effective Web page is defined by who you consider to be your primary audience.

- If your intent is to address a truly global audience, then you need to consider using all the recipes here.

- If your intent is to address an audience of users in English-speaking countries such as the United Kingdom, Australia, New Zealand, and the United States, then the recipe for writing in English for non-native readers of English may not be helpful.

- If your intent is to address only users whose language and culture are the same as your own (and you do not care if you unintentionally offend or confuse others who may stumble upon your Web page), then skip this chapter and move along. But consider this: Even within your own country there are a variety and diversity of ideas, cultural backgrounds, and languages. View it as an opportunity.

Should I translate my Web pages?

Translation is expensive and difficult—and often necessary. Consider these issues when deciding whether to translate:

- What percentage of your users cannot read English?

- How often will your content change? (This might necessitate frequent translation.)

- How many languages do you need to support?

- What is the cost of translation?

- Will more and better graphics obviate the need for translation? (What drain will more graphics have on the time it takes for a user to load a Web page?)

- Are Web browsers and servers available for the target language? (More on this issue in the next section.)

What if my Web pages need to be translated?

If you decide you do need to translate your pages you must still confront two issues:

- The different character sets required

- The way English text expands when translated

Depending on the language you need to support, you may have trouble finding acceptable browsers and servers. For example, English is fully supported. Most Western European languages are supported. But languages in Central and Eastern Europe that use the Roman alphabet (Polish, Czech, Slovak, Croat, and Turkish) and languages with other alphabets, such as

Japanese, Chinese, Arabic, Greek, and Russian, are currently not supported by all Web servers and browsers. The reasons are technical and we explain them a bit in "Toward a More Global WWW" on page 465.

Some work-arounds, in case the target languages are not supported, include creating audio clips of someone reading the text in the target language and including a series of inline images of text in the target language.

If you do have your Web pages translated, consider the effect that translation has on your page design—expanding or contracting text altering its appearance—and design accordingly. Don't forget the text in graphics and in icons; text expansion can be a real problem there, too. You may need to redesign such graphics so that they do not include text.

For example, text translated from English to German or Spanish often requires as much as 30 percent or more space to express the same thought. Here is a table and chart to help you calculate expansion rates.

Characters in English	Characters in other European languages
5	10–13
10	18–24
15	26–32
20	33–39
25	39–45
30	44–50
35	49–55
40	55–61
45	61–66
50	66–71
55	72–77
60	77–83
65	82–88
70	88–95

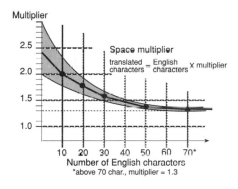

From *Illustrating Computer Documentation* by William Horton, published by John Wiley & Sons, Inc.

RECIPE: ENGLISH FOR NON-NATIVE READERS

Among spoken and written languages, English is about as flexible as a contortionist. You can play with words that sound the same but are spelled differently ("The king is going to knight him tonight.") and with words that are spelled the same but sound different ("The court ruled invalid the claim that the plaintiff was an invalid."). You can drop all those connection words such as articles and conjunctions and still make sense ("~~After~~ I came ~~and~~ I saw ~~the~~ painting, I ~~then~~ went to a bar ~~and~~ ordered a lemonade."). You can combine parts of words with relative ease to make up new words ("Webpageoholic"). You can even use the same word as different parts of speech to mean something completely different each time. ("To improve the display of data on the display monitor, display the Display Control Panel and adjust the Display Frequency control until the display monitor displays correctly.") Pretty cool, eh? Not if your grasp of English is minimal.

As a writing system, English has a teeny, tiny alphabet—26 characters, or 52 if you count upper- and lowercase. Tiny!

And the spelling of certain words in English can vary throughout the English-speaking countries. For example, *color* and *colour* are each valid spellings, but the former is the proper spelling in the United States and the latter is the proper spelling in the United Kingdom, Australia, New Zealand, and many other countries that are, or once were, part of the British Commonwealth. Here's a short quiz that lets you see for yourself how the way we write varies even among English-speaking countries.

QUIZ: Identify the country or countries that these authors are mostly likely from. Each correct answer is worth 20 points. The answers are on page 454.

1. To telephone us, just dial 1.800.555.5555.

2. It's fair dinkum, mate!

3. Come and join us on Boxing Day!

4. The deadline for entering this contest is 11/07/95.

5. Our organisation was founded in 1455.

So, how did you do? Chances are you got most of these correct, but if you didn't, just imagine how your users feel when they try to understand text that hasn't been written with non-English readers in mind. And if they don't understand, then your Web pages cease to be as effective as they could be.

Notes from International Cuisine 101: Simple changes to text

Oops! First blunder. International Cuisine 101. Most Americans understand this to be an introductory course at the college level. But course numbering systems are different around the world. So, how many people will understand this reference?

Here is a list of simple ways to make the text in your Web pages more global.

Note that for some of these issues, there are international standards that you might find useful. Most are published by the International Organization for Standardization (ISO). We provide their contact information in the "Recommended Reading" section on page 470.

Potentially confusing information	How to make this information work for non-American readers of English
Telephone numbers	Include the country code, the area code (if applicable), and the telephone number. If some users can take advantage of 800 numbers and the like, include these too, but provide the general telephone number so that everyone can contact you. In general prefix the national number with a plus and the country code, for example, +1-303-555-5555 for a number in the United States and +81-3-5421-7698 for one in Tokyo.
Date formats	Spell out the name of the month. 11 November 1995 and November 7, 1995, are unambiguous to users worldwide. However, 11-7-95 is 7 November 1995 in some places and 11 July 1995 in others. ISO 8601 specifies date formats.
Time formats and time zones	The proper way to designate time differs around the world. In most of Europe and Asia, for example, time is designated using the 24-hour clock. And don't forget about time zone differences. If it is 8:45 PM in New York City, it is 02:45 in Paris, France. For universal time, state the time on a 24-hour clock set to the London time zone. This is called UTC (Universal Time Coordinated) and replaces the old GMT. ISO 8601 also specifies time formats.

Potentially confusing information	How to make this information work for non-American readers of English
Number formats	Numbers are written using different syntax around the world. For example, in the United States we write 1,033.41. In France we write this number as 1 033,41. And in Germany we write this number as 1.033,41. Obviously you can't write the same number in all the formats of the world. So what format do you use? Again, provide some clue on your Web page indicating the country you are from. Your users will figure out the rest.
Units of measurement	The United States does not use the metric system, which is used throughout most of the rest of the world. Provide both the U.S. measurement and also the metric equivalent.
Currency	If you are selling products via the WWW, consider showing the price of the product in more than one currency. Always use proper syntax and indicate the currency units. ISO 4217 specifies the codes (e.g., USD for U.S. dollars) for currency units.
Addresses	When creating forms that require users to type in their addresses, consider that postal address formats differ from country to country. For example, in Switzerland, the format of an address looks like this: M. P. Delmas 20, rue de la Poste CH-1211 Geneva Suisse The number of the building is followed by a comma. There is no zip code. There is a country code (CH) followed by the postal code (1211). Contact your post office for assistance in writing addresses properly. Always indicate the country in the address. When you include the address for your company, if it has offices or distributors in other countries, consider providing these addresses. Users much prefer to deal with people in their own countries, and often language barriers are the main reason. Give your users options.

Potentially confusing information	How to make this information work for non-American readers of English
Addresses (continued)	Tell users worldwide how to purchase your product. Link to a page that lists all the addresses, telephone numbers, and business hours of distributors worldwide that market and sell your company's products. It is often less expensive for users to purchase in their own or neighboring countries than to order products from a country far away.
Electronics	Indicate voltages, fuse types, plugs, and amperages for major target countries if you are selling or describing electronic equipment. In photographs, avoid showing power plugs and other details that vary from country to country.
Legal information	There are many differences here, since laws differ around the world. In all cases, you are wise to consult legal counsel if you are unsure about any legal issues. For example, is your warranty the same in all countries? What about intellectual property? Is your copyright protection the same worldwide?
Nationally bound miscellany	If you are from the United States, do you have references in your Web pages to Social Security, Medicare, Internal Revenue, FDIC, or the FCC? Such references may be useless and meaningless to non-Americans. If you are from another country, consider any references in your Web pages to things that only make sense to people from your country. The British know and loathe VATs; Americans think vats are used to make beer. Either remove this information from your Web page, or move it to a page for users who are from your country.
Page sizes	Paper page sizes differ around the world. In the United States, the common size is called letter size, which is 8.5 x 11 inches. In Europe and many other regions, the common size is called A4, which is 210 x 297 millimeters. If possible, reference both page size standards in instructions on setting up a printer or fax machine. You may need to take paper page size into account if you want your Web page to fit on a single paper page when printed out. The German Industry Standard (DIN) for most paper sizes used throughout Europe is DIN 66008.

Notes from Advanced International Cuisine: Too much spice is not so nice

Writing creatively to hold a user's attention is truly a good idea. However, writing that is packed with references to things that only a particular group of people will understand is ineffective. If users cannot understand your references, you lose them completely.

Here are some advanced topics in communicating with a worldwide audience that most translators and non-native speakers of English say add ambiguity in English prose.

Quadruple-deckers

A triple-decker is tough enough to get your teeth around, but a quadruple-decker is nearly impossible. Here is an example.

The command module reaction control system adjusts the attitude of the spacecraft.

A quadruple-decker is a logjam of nouns, the first four of which modify the fifth. You could rewrite the sentence this way to avoid adding ambiguity.

The reaction-control system of the command module adjusts the attitude of the spacecraft.

Though rewriting quadruple-deckers may add a few words, it will make sentences easier for non-native readers of English to understand.

Same spice, different dish

A spice is not limited to one dish. You can put cinnamon in your pastry dough, but you can also put cinnamon in your coffee. And depending on your preferences, you can use cinnamon in all sorts of other dishes, as in Mexican and Thai cuisine. The list might be endless if we all sat down and compared notes. Same spice, different dish.

The analogy is particularly true when you have many authors writing and creating Web pages; you find that you all use the same word in different ways. Here are some examples of the word *display* used differently each time.

*The **display** flickers when we have thunderstorms.*

*Monica **displays** the charts.*

*The **display** option is turned on.*

For a non-native reader of English, the word *display* is confusing. What does it really mean? Here, *display* has three distinctive meanings. Too much, declares the non-native reader of English, too much!

All uses of *display* here are correct. So how do you eliminate confusion for the non-native reader of English? Choose one definition of the word and use the word that way every time. Create a rule for using that word and make sure that all Web authors know about and abide by that rule. One word, one meaning, all the time throughout your Web pages.

DDT

To see how to link to an entry in a glossary, see page 268.

Don't Do This. Few users will know what acronyms mean unless they are explained or are so common that the world understands them (unlikely) or unless they are linked to a glossary page providing explanations. First, try avoiding acronyms. Do you really need to abbreviate? Second, link acronyms to a glossary page or explain them in the context of each Web page every time. Users may access only a few of your Web pages and probably won't do so sequentially.

Blunders in the kitchen

Everybody makes mistakes. Most can be corrected if you go back and review your work. Some examples of writing mistakes on Web pages include spelling mistakes, incorrect punctuation, and incorrect word usage. If these occur, non-native readers of English are going to have a very hard time understanding what you are trying to say. Native readers of English will grudgingly figure out what you mean, but it's extra effort for them, too. Review your work. Get friends and colleagues to read your Web pages and find errors before users do.

Here are some more tips to make sure you are understood:

- Use spelling checkers and grammar checkers to catch simple errors.

- Write simple, short, and direct sentences. Avoid complicated passives, such as "should by now have been created."

- Use unambiguous verbs. Avoid conditional, vague verbs such as "may," "should," "might," and "could."

- Use standard punctuation.

- Avoid contractions such as "can't," "isn't," and "it's." Spell everything out.

- Sidestep politically charged writing, such as the use of personal pronouns, "s/he" and "he/she," or using "she" as the generic form. Such usages confuse non-native readers of English. Instead use "they" or "you."

- Forego humor. The lighthearted tone of this book, for example, may not be appropriate for Web pages that are designed with an international audience in mind.

Don't mistake a lack of command of English for a lack of knowledge. The barrier is one of language, not of intelligence.

Pleasing the international palate

There's one given when cooking to please the international palate: Everyone has different preferences. Some people like Thai cuisine, others like fast food, some like French cuisine, others like health food. You just never know ... unless you ask.

And so it is with writing. References to Murphy's law, the Golden Rule, sports analogies and phrasing, and so on, clearly require that users be familiar with these things. Analogies, idioms, metaphors, slang, and jargon all make assumptions about the reader's cultural background, preferences, lifestyle, profession, knowledge.

To appeal to the widest audience:

- **Carefully choose your words**. Question whether something will really make sense to a global audience. Your references don't have to thrill the whole world, but try and meet the needs of your most important market.

- **Test your information before it's published** on the WWW by having people from different countries take a look at it.

- **Consider having your information translated and customized** for target audiences. Since translation and customization cost more to do, choose the target audience based on market research. For instance, if you log accesses to your Web site, check to see what countries users are from.

Answers to the quiz on page 448

1. The United States only or the United States and English Canada, depending on the particular arrangement with the telephone company.
2. Australia and New Zealand.
3. Australia, New Zealand, Canada, and the United Kingdom.

4. Who knows? In Europe this date is July 7, 1995. In the United States and Canada this date is November 7, 1995.

5. The United Kingdom most likely. There are two clues here: the spelling of the word *organisation* and the date, 1455. Not many countries were established in 1455 and therefore not many organizations were in existence, making it bloody likely that this sentence was written by someone from the United Kingdom.

RECIPE: GRAPHICS FOR GLOBAL APPEAL

Graphics can make text easier to understand—especially by non-native readers of English. They can ease learning, reduce the need for translation, and give your Web pages an international look. But graphics are not a universal language unless you design them for use globally.

How do I make a "global" graphic, you may ask? It's not hard. Just follow these simples guidelines:

Avoid culture-specific images

Images may be universal, but their meanings are not. Avoid using images whose meanings vary from country to country. For instance:

- **Puns and verbal analogies**—They are impossible to translate and require a subtle knowledge of the language. Puns and verbal analogies may prove very difficult for users who read your language as a second language. Look at these examples:

Graphic	Intended meaning	Problems
	Scale of a map	The words for balance scale and the relationship between distances in the world and the map are not the same in all languages.
	Post entries in an accounting program	Posting a package means mailing it but posting data means writing it into a ledger. Such different concepts will not have the same name in all languages.

Graphic	Intended meaning	Problems
	Oncology department of a hospital	Oncology is made of the Greek words for "study of" and "cancer." Cancer is the Latin word for crab. Few know Latin and Greek. Anyway the image looks like a malignant growth.

- **Gestures**—Trust us on this, there is almost no configuration of the human hand that is not considered obscene, rude, or impolite somewhere in the world. Here are some gestures commonly used in the United States:

If you must use a hand, use a right hand and show it holding, pressing, or moving something.

Graphic	Meaning in U.S.	Problems
	Yes, OK	In Sicily, this is an invitation to insert the thumb into a private part of the anatomy.
	Precisely, yes	In France this means zero or worthless. In Japan it is a reference to money. In South America it means that the viewer is a part of the anatomy of this shape.
	Stop, halt	In Greece, this gesture, which goes back to Byzantine times, means, "Here's excrement in your face."

- **Mythological and religious symbols**—Here's a news flash: We do not all share the same religious or mythological symbology. The easiest way around this problem is to simply avoid using such symbols in your Web pages. If you don't get the picture, here are a few rather bad examples:

Graphic	Intended meaning	Problems
	Fatal error	Would someone raised a Hindu, Buddhist, or Zoroastrian recognize the grim reaper?
	Minor glitch	Some may not recognize this as a gremlin, but see instead a bat with a long tail. A gremlin can be a symbol of a minor problem or a satanic cult.
	First aid	Images incorporating crosses and six-pointed stars can offend in Arabic countries. In such countries, the local version of the Red Cross is known as the Red Crescent.

- **Totems (animals as symbols)**—Images of animals are often used to represent those characteristics or traits commonly associated with that animal—for instance, the ferocity of a tiger, the swiftness of a falcon, or the wisdom of an owl. And *there* is the problem. Many of these associations are culture-specific. Take a look at these examples:

Graphic	Intended meaning	Problems
	Loyalty Search, re-trieve	To Americans, dogs are pets or hunting companions; to many Asians, they are food. In some Islamic countries dogs are viewed quite negatively.
	Wisdom Expert system Training	In southeast Asia, the owl is considered a particularly brutal and stupid bird.
	Copy, reproduce rapidly	Rabbits are also symbols of sexual promiscuity. In many parts of Europe, rabbit is a dinner entrée. In Australia, rabbits are vermin.
	Savings account	To Muslims and many Jews, the pig is considered unclean and unholy.

- **Colors**—Yes, oh yes. You can get into trouble with colors, too! For instance, in the United Kingdom, first place is often awarded a red ribbon; in the United States, first place earns a blue ribbon. The use of green to symbolize money works in the United States, but would that convention work in Germany, France, or Canada? Remember that colors have associations, but your associations may not be your reader's.

Here are some tips to keep you from stepping in the paint pot:

- Use color only to reinforce the primary message.

- For Web pages used in business and technical settings, use color where the context does not suggest symbolic or religious interpretations.

- Clearly define your color codes and make the color scheme explicit.

- Test with typical users and revise colors that are misinterpreted.

Consider reading and scanning direction

The accustomed reading direction of the reader influences the interpretation of the sequence of events in a graphic, the relative importance and virtue of objects in a graphic, and the recognition of objects representing text. Western cultures, which write left to right, draw charts and graphs with time flowing from left to right. They write numbers with the most significant digits on the left. The left knob of a faucet controls the hot water and the right controls the cold. In religious art and drama, good is most often on the right and evil to the left.

These conventions are *just* conventions and not shared by the whole world, especially countries whose languages are traditionally written right to left or in columns top to bottom. For instance, in the Middle East, an advertisement for laundry detergent presented dirty clothes on the left, clean clothes on the right, and the box of detergent in between. It confused Arabic readers who read text right to left. Here are some simple tips that will help avoid this kind of confusion:

- Show sequence with arrows if you must arrange objects left to right.

✗ No   **✔ Yes**

Warming   Warming

- Use vertical sequence because all languages read from top to bottom on a page:

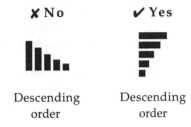

✗ No   ✔ Yes

Descending   Descending
order   order

Generalize images

Go into any modern business office around the world and you will find more familiar sights than unfamiliar ones. On desks you might see a telephone, a typewriter or computer, file folders, a ruler, a calculator. You might also see people attending meetings where they sit around tables and listen to one another talk. The image of business is similar around the world—provided you don't look too closely.

When you do, you find many differences. Common office objects look and work differently. The shape and ring of the telephone is not exactly what you are familiar with. Clip boards, thumb tacks, and file folders have a different shape than the ones in your office. The rulers measure in different units than yours and power plugs have a different configuration of prongs than the ones back home.

Highly realistic graphics draw attention to such details and can confuse and mislead. To avoid this confusion, maintain a soft focus so that your images are understood by business users around the world. Here are some suggestions:

- **Suppress unimportant details**—Just the facts!
  - Draw your graphics in a simplified style, showing the object from a viewpoint that hides unnecessary detail or national differences such as power plugs and on–off switches.
  - Remove as much text as possible. For instance, show keyboards with blank keys. Indicate buttons and function keys by position instead of name.
  - Use inanimate objects instead of people as symbols. Unless the subject is a person, *do not* show a person.
  - If you must use people, draw them as simple line drawings, cartoons, or stick figures. Forego realistic details.

- For actions, show just the hands of the person performing the action.
- If a procedure can be performed easily with either right or left hand, show it being performed with the right hand.
- Do not indicate skin color. Pure white and pure black better represent generic skin than gray, tan, or brown.

- **Show the best-known version**—Many objects come in several versions. If one version of an object is more common throughout the world, use it. This is not the time to be parochial.

For an automobile, select a small boxy model like the Honda Accord or Ford Escort, which are sold in many different countries. For a truck, show a typical delivery truck rather than a pickup truck, which is not as common in Europe as in America. Show 10 or 5 divisions per unit in a measuring ruler rather than 12 or 4. The divisions can thus represent millimeters or tenths of an inch:

If there is no international version, then pick the most common version familiar to the largest number of users. Look at these examples. Although these versions are not universal, they are quite common:

Checklist for global differences

Here's a troubleshooting guide for global graphics. Use it to put the *World Wide* into your Web pages.

Difference	What to do
Racial characteristics	Use simple, abstract figures, devoid of recognizable bone structure or hair style. Use unshaded line drawings of people. Omit any indication of skin color.
Relations between sexes	Use simple unisex cartoons or stick-figure drawings of people, hands, and faces. Show no one in a demeaning or degrading condition.
Clothing	Simplify drawings of clothing to omit seams, folds, buttons, and belts.

Difference	What to do
Modesty	Do not show bare arms, shoulders, legs, or feet.
Gestures	Avoid hand gestures. If you show a hand, show the right hand holding or pressing something.
Color associations	Define and explain color symbology. Use colors in a technical or business context only.
Familiarity with graphical formats	Limit yourself to common, well-established formats.
Sense of humor	Avoid heavy-handed humor, especially puns.

RECIPE: MULTIMEDIA FOR WORLDWIDE AUDIENCES

Choose multimedia objects— sound effects, voice, music, and video—with care when communicating with a worldwide audience. Here are some tips.

Sound effects

Sound can certainly add to the experience of using a computer. Modems may beep when the connection is successful, sound clips may execute when the operating system performs a particular task, and certainly game software blasts you with noises every time you press a key on the keyboard or point and click on something with the mouse. Sound makes interaction seem more real. It can also make it a real nuisance.

Choosing appropriate sounds and using them at appropriate times requires some cultural research. For example, the sounds that software makes when a user makes a mistake might cause the user great embarrassment in some countries. Also, the sounds of animals and violence might be humorous in one country but offensive or considered inappropriate in others.

Tips on using sound effects

- **Use sound functionally**—Use sounds that people need to do their jobs. For example, use sound clips to teach physicians to recognize heart disorders through a stethoscope.

- **Use realistic sounds**—Use sounds to denote concrete objects and actions, such as a phone ringing. Avoid using sounds for vague symbolic meanings, for example, a low rumbling noise to connote a sense of danger.

- **Set the context in which the sound occurs**—If users see a picture of a telephone and then hear a ringing sound they are likely to interpret the sound as coming from the phone, even through phones might make a different sound in their countries.

- **Pick common stereotypical sounds**—Use sounds as they appear in movies seen around the world—for instance, a creaking door in a horror movie or the roar of an airplane landing.

Voice

Voice used for narration, teaching, or storytelling requires careful thought to be effective in global Web pages. Pick a narrator with these characteristics.

- **Clear diction**—Separates rather than slurs words. Pauses between sentences. Speaks at moderate rate of speed.

- **Free of a strong accent**—Avoid accents that distract from the message. Unless they are relevant, regional, ethnic, or social-class accents will confuse or annoy the listener. Forego the Boston brogue, Southern drawl, or Midwestern twang. Keep in mind that English speakers around the world do not all speak American English and most hear all Americans as speaking with an accent. If your organization is American, use an American narrator speaking American English. If Australian, use an Australian speaking Australian English.

- **Moderate pitch**—Squeaky falsettos and booming basses are hard to understand after being sampled, compressed, decompressed, and played back through the inexpensive speakers attached to most computers.

- **Appropriate gender**—In the United States, Canada, and most of western Europe, you can make use of female voices with about equal effect. In much of Asia, Africa, and South America, where business decisions are made mostly by men, a female voice may lack authority. Remember, what's politically correct in Northern California may be blasphemous in Saudi Arabia. Know your market, know your goals, then decide.

  Okay, here's a sleazy trick. Pick a high-pitched male (a tenor, not a bass) or a low-pitched woman (a contralto, not a soprano), and electronically alter the voice so it is not clearly male or female.

Music

Your choice of music can also be a cultural concern. Certain composers or types of music may be symbolic of religious or political activities. For example, John Philip Sousa's compositions usually invoke a patriotic response from many people living in the United States because his compositions are usually played on national, or political, holidays such as July 4th, Independence Day. Not all users will understand the significance of Sousa's compositions and may not understand how and why you chose them for your Web page.

Watch out for specific cultural associations. The melody known as "God Bless America" on one side of the Atlantic is "God Save the Queen" on the other where it serves as the British national anthem. The fluid melody that evokes a river in Smetana's *The Moldau* also serves as the core of the Israeli national anthem. And in Israel many older citizens cannot abide the music of Wagner because Hitler claimed to draw inspiration from Wagnerian operas.

Video

Video makes it easy to show people, places, things, and action. Many multinational companies, for example, include in their introductory videos shots of corporate sites and employees from around the world to convey the idea that they are truly international. These videos can also help the international user feel more at home.

Keep in mind, however, that people don't all dress the same way, buildings don't look the same, and some cars have the steering wheel on the left and some on the right. If those differences are not part of your message, don't show them.

Video is expensive to shoot, edit, revise, and localize. Use it when nothing else can as effectively communicate your intent.

RECIPE: TESTING FOR GLOBAL CONTENT

To reach the widest audience possible, think about having your Web pages tested for global appeal. Here are some easy ideas for doing this:

- Send the URLs of your Web pages (or fax printouts of them if the recipients don't have WWW access) to people in your company who work in other countries. Non-native readers of English who are bilingual are good choices. Ask them whether there is anything in the tone, wording, or graphics that is not appropriate for readers in their countries. Is the writing easy for a non-native reader of English to understand?

- Ask the distributors of your company's products throughout the world to review the Web pages for language and cultural issues.

- Hire a team of expert reviewers. Consider usability consultants, cross-cultural communication consultants, cultural anthropologists, and ESL (English as a Second Language) instructors to test the pages for language and cultural content.

A tip for collecting feedback

One way to collect feedback from these sources is to create a home page with a feedback form and a MAILTO link. See page 267 for more information.

Once your Web pages are reviewed for language and cultural content, make all feedback visible to your Web page authors so that everyone learns.

TOWARD A MORE GLOBAL WWW

As we mentioned at the beginning of this chapter, the WWW does not at present support all writing systems. The reasons are mostly technical, but there are some political reasons as well. Suffice it to say that the WWW consortium is aware of the need to support more writing systems.

The main issue has to do with character sets. A character set is the alphabet for a language that is stored in and used by a computer to display symbols, messages, and so on. Think of a character set as containing all the keys on your keyboard plus a few more. Most computers rely on one of two character sets: ISO-LATIN-1 or its subset, ASCII.

There are other technical issues involved here, too, but we refer you to the "Recommended Reading" section on page 470 if you'd like more information.

The drawback is that ASCII supports a maximum of 128 characters and ISO-LATIN-1 supports a maximum of 256 characters. Both character sets let computers handle English, for example, very well. English has 26 lowercase letters and 26 uppercase letters, the numbers 0-9, and some characters such * and %, punctuation marks, and mathematical symbols. These characters don't add up to 256. However, in Japanese, Chinese, and Korean, for example, many more characters are required to communicate. In Japanese, basic literacy makes use of 2,000 characters.

There are ways to jump between and among character sets on a computer, but it's tedious work. To address this and related problems, a group of computer companies formed the Unicode Consortium. The Unicode Consortium created Unicode, which is a character set that supports many writing systems simultaneously. Unicode has also been accepted as a standard of the International Organization for Standardization (ISO). Not everyone thinks Unicode is a perfect solution to the world's language problems, though, so it has not been adopted by many companies to date.

In the interim, HTML supports character entities that let you display characters found in ISO-LATIN-1. Refer to page 442 for the current list of HTML-supported character entities.

Other solutions exist, too. The Netscape browser, for example, is available in Japanese. CompuServe, which owns the rights to the Air Mosaic browser, offers its products in some other languages and boasts a machine translation service for multilingual communication. Alis Technologies, Inc., in Montreal, Canada, has announced a browser, called WorldNet, that will be fully multilingual. Alis promises the browser will be available in the fall of 1995.

And on goes the multilingual evolution of the WWW.

DOES THIS WEB PAGE GET ITS PASSPORT?

Remember the "before" Web page on page 442? Here are the changes we'd make for this Web page to get its passport.

The problems

Nonstandard English

The before version uses colloquialisms, sentence fragments, and nonstandard spellings with abandon. These might amuse a native speaker of English, but they could also confuse someone with English as a second language. Some examples:

> When it's hot Hot HOT!
>
> H Oh Gawd T.
>
> Hotter 'n ...
>
> Q-pon
>
> Send the sucker

And do not forget this quadruple-decker:

> ... our agency-approved, lightweight, puncture-resistant, flame-proof Pyrolon 34 industrial fabric ...

We rewrote the text to be less bombastic, using more conventional English.

References to things unique to America

The before version refers to things that only an American could be expected to understand. Few outside the United States know where Houston is or grasp the effect of its combination of heat and humidity. In many countries, inlaws are valued, not candidates for Hades. And for obscurity, little can top the allusion to the O'Leary's barn, where the Chicago fire started.

We replaced all these with just one reference to noon in the Sahara, which is something all geographically knowledgeable readers can understand.

Obscene gestures

The icons used to mean "yes" and "no" are unfortunately obscene or impolite gestures in parts of the world. We just replaced them with the plus and minus signs.

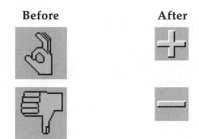

The danger that someone will misinterpret the plus sign as a Christian cross is mitigated by its use with the minus sign. The context makes the meaning clear.

Units of measurement

In the before version, units are in square feet only and prices are not clearly U.S. dollars. After all, other countries use "$" to mark currency. To fix this, we flag the currency and repeat the price for a metric unit:

Before	After
$10.34 per sq ft	$10.34 USD per sq ft ($113 USD per sq meter)

Time and dates

Since the before example does not tell where the company has its offices, the office hours listed are ambiguous—even for readers from the United States. We fixed this by stating that the office was in New York and by repeating the hours in Universal Time Coordinated (UTC).

Before	After
8AM and 5PM	8 AM and 5 PM New York time (13:00 to 22:00 UTC)

The revision date is also ambiguous since some countries put the month first and others put the day first.

Before	After
4/7/95	7 April 1995

Phone number

The 800 number is convenient for users in the United States and Canada but not elsewhere. To fix this we added the general number, complete with country code.

Before	After
1-800-BUY-OURS	1-800-BUY-OURS
	+1-212-555-4435

Address format

The fill-in-the-blanks form only works for United States' addresses.

Name

Organization

Street

City   State   Zip

We added a field for country. We renamed "Zip" as "Postal code" and "State" as "State or province," and we made the fields larger to accommodate longer names than are common in the United States.

Name

Organization

Street

City

State or Province

Country

Postal code

After

And what does the updated, passport-worthy Web page look like?

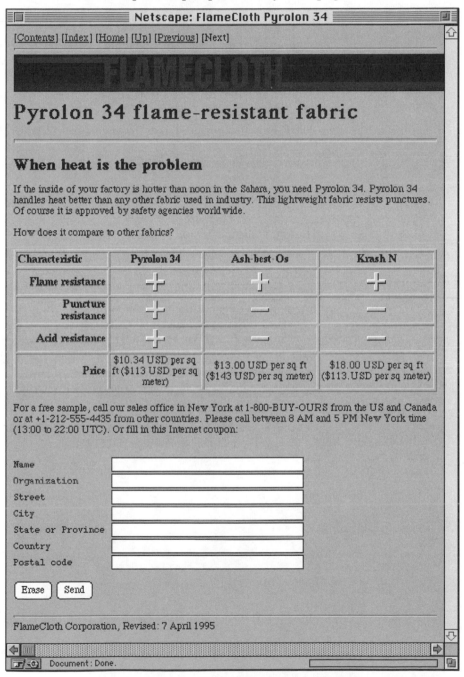

RECOMMENDED READING

Here are some additional references on publishing globally.

American National Standards Institute (ANSI) publishes standards for the United States that you might find useful. Write to them at: ANSI, 11 West 42nd Street, 13th Floor, New York, NY 10036, USA.

Apple Computer, Inc. *Guide to Macintosh Software Localization*. Reading, MA: Addison-Wesley, 1992.

Axtell, Roger E. *Do's and Taboos Around the World. 3rd Ed*. New York: John Wiley & Sons, 1993.

————. *Do's and Taboos of Using English Around the World*. New York: John Wiley & Sons, 1995.

Hoft, Nancy L. *International Technical Communication: How to Export Information about High Technology*. New York: John Wiley & Sons, 1995.

Horton, William. *The Icon Book*. New York: John Wiley & Sons, 1994.

————. *Illustrating Computer Documentation*. John Wiley & Sons, 1991.

IBM Corporation. *National Language Support Reference Manual, Volume 2*. IBM Corporation. Order number SE09-8002. Updated periodically.

International Organization for Standardization (ISO). Various international standards are published by ISO. To learn more, write to them at: ISO, 1, rue de Verambe, Postal Box 56, CH-1211, Geneva 20, Switzerland.

Jones, Scott, Cynthia Kennellyijn, Claudia Mueller et al. *Developing International User Information*. Bedford, MA: Digital Press, 1992.

Morris, Desmond. *Manwatching: A Field Guide to Human Behavior*. New York: Harry N. Abrams, 1977.

O'Donnell, Sandra Martin. *Programming for the World: A Guide to Internationalization*. Englewood Cliffs, NJ: Prentice Hall, 1994.

ASK THE MASTER CHEFS

Answers to your most vexing questions

Dear Master Chefs,

Why does my page look different on other people's computers?

— Screens of Confusion

The World Wide Web is not a WYSIWYG system. In fact it's WYSINWIS (What You See Is Not What I See). The reasons are many. Some you control and some you do not:

- **Different browsers format pages differently**. One browser may make <H2> headings 14-point Helvetica bold while another makes them 18-point Times Roman. Remember, HTML is a mixture of structural codes (<H1>, <P>, <LI>) and formatting codes (
, <B>, <I>). There is no absolute consistency in the format for structural codes—or even formatting codes.

  Tip: Recommend or supply a particular browser to your users.

- **Users have a say**. Some browsers let users specify what fonts and colors to use for various components of the page. Some users just can't leave the defaults alone. Some users make the browser window wide, some make it narrow. Some users turn off the display of graphics.

  Tip: Tell users how to set up their browsers to best view your pages. You could put these instructions in a How-to page (see page 139 for recipe) and let your users jump to this page from your home page.

- **Not all browsers understand all tags**. There are many versions, iterations, and interpretations of the official HTML specification. Most browsers politely ignore any tags they do not support. Also, not all users have the latest version of the browser.

  Tip: Aim for a middle ground, not the latest and greatest and not the lowest common denominator. Use features supported by the browsers of a majority of your users.

  Tip: Test your Web pages with a variety of browsers.

- **The computer makes a difference**. The browser must display the page in the fonts and colors available on the user's computer. The size and resolution of the user's monitor can vary too.

  Tip: Specify a minimum configuration and design for the middle ground.

> Dear Master Chefs,
>
> Should I use a few big pages or lots of short ones?
>
> — King of Scrolls

There's no right answer to this question, so we'll share with you the rationale for choosing one method over another.

One long page		Lots of short pages	
Pros	**Cons**	**Pros**	**Cons**
Users can print the whole page and get a mini book.	Long pages take a long time to load.	You can create modular topics and use links to support free-form learning.	For the Web page author, it becomes difficult to remember what page contains what information.

One long page		Lots of short pages	
Pros	Cons	Pros	Cons
Users with slow modems can avoid delays when clicking on links to other Web pages.	Long pages make it difficult for users to find the information they need. Users need to read through a lot of information they don't care about. Shorter pages can break up the informa-tion more intelligently, letting the users choose the topics they want to view.	Users can find the information they need more quickly. Break up the information into logical modules of information that are topic specific and provide navigational aids.	It can take too long for users to read through all the pages, especially if loading is slow.
All the information on a topic is right there, making it easier for the Web page author to maintain the Web page.	Long pages can require perpetual scrolling to read through to the end. Perpetual scrolling, unfortunately, does not burn calories!	Users can read the information they need more quickly. Shorter pages that are topic specific provide all the information the user needs to know.	Too many short pages might overload users. The user might get tired of learning so little in one page and move on to another Web site.

Dear Master Chefs,

How do I make long topics more palatable?

— Paging Downer

Take a peek at the Research Report example on page 217. This is the longest Web page example we provide. Printed, it is about four pages long. To the printed world, that's not very long. To the online world, it's a drag.

We created a table of contents (TOC) at the top of the Web page. Each entry in the TOC links to a heading later in the page.

For more on the page table of contents, see page 284.

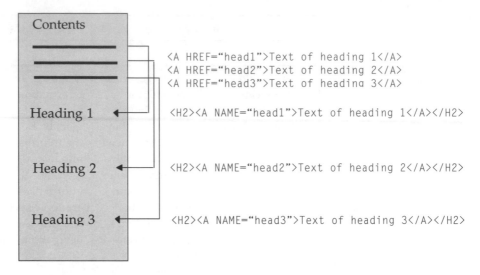

Some Web pages even have text buttons or icons at each heading that users can click on to jump back up to the TOC when they finish reading that section.

```
<A HREF="#contents">[Back to Contents]</A>
```

Dear Master Chefs,

Why do users complain my page is too slow? It seems fast enough to me.

— T1-2-Me

Here are the most common causes of slow Web pages.

- **The Web page contains many graphics inline**, or it contains a very large, complex graphic inline. Each graphic requires another complete Internet access even when the graphic is stored in the same directory as the HTML for the page.

  Tip: Reduce the number of graphics. Shrink large graphics. Also consider replacing a row or grid of individual buttons with a single image-map.

- **Users have slow modems**. Compared to a T1 line, all modems are slow. Dial-up users typically communicate through 9600- or 14.4K-baud modems, which transfer 9600 or 14,400 bits per second respectively, give or take a little depending on compression and other tricks. A T1 line, which many corporations use to connect their major sites to the Internet, transmits data at a rate of 1.544 million bits per second.

Wow, you say? Well, when you call your telephone company and ask about the cost of a T1 line, we think you'll say Wow to that, too.

Tip: Test your pages from a dial-up line with a slow modem. This won't make your pages any faster but it will sensitize you to the plight of many users.

- **You developed and tested your pages on a fast, local hard disk** but not over the Internet.

  Tip: See the previous tip!

- **The pages are very popular** and everybody is trying to fetch them at the same time.

  Tip: This is a good problem! Become a Web page design consultant. Also consider setting up mirror sites duplicating your Web pages on other servers.

- **The pages are housed on an overloaded server.**

  Tip: Change to a different Internet service provider. Have your own Web server. Set up mirror sites for your pages.

- **Pages take a roundabout route.** Consider how many hops a message has to go through to get to your user. Maybe your user is in San Francisco, United States, but your pages are in Geneva, Switzerland. Your user's host computer (your Internet service provider's computer) has to talk to a bunch of other host computers to find the particular host computer that can serve it a copy of the page you want to see. Then it has to find its way back to you. Then the browser you're using has to interpret the HTML code and display it on your computer screen. And if there are graphics to be displayed, your host computer has to go back to Switzerland a few times to get everything your user needs to see the whole Web page.

  Tip: Minimize the number of files the user's browser has to load to construct a page.

- The speed of the user's computer might be another factor.

  Tip: There's not much you can do about this. At least test your pages on a system similar to those of your users.

There are all sorts of other technological factors that influence the speed at which data are transmitted. But until everybody has T1 lines to lightly loaded servers:

- Use fewer and smaller graphics.

- Make pages smaller.

- Test your pages the way users access them: slow modem from real server.

- Mirror your pages at multiple sites.

- Instead of multiple buttons, use a single image-map.

Dear Master Chefs,

Should I include images inline or let users jump to them?

— Look before You Leap

That depends on how large (in bytes) the graphics are and how many of them there are. It also depends on what the graphics contribute to the content of the page.

- If an image is just nice to have and it's a big file, link to the graphic rather than include it. This way users focus on the primary content and there's no forced feeding of graphics. If they're curious, they can bop off to your graphic if they want to.

- If the page is your home page, go ahead and include your logo and a banner to set the tone of pages to come and give your Web site its identity. Such graphics are important to the content of the page, so include them inline.

- If the Web page discusses an important topic that can be shown in a graphic, then supplement the discussion with an inline graphic.

- If the graphic serves as a navigation aid, as in an image-map, then it's important and users need to see it.

- If there are lots and lots of graphics on a Web page and the page takes a long time to load, link to those inline images of secondary importance.

> Dear Master Chefs,
>
> How do I make the text size larger?
>
> — Headliner Headaches

There are a variety of answers to this question.

If you have a small piece of text to make bigger, consider making it a heading with the <H1>, <H2>, and so forth. See page 312 to learn how.

If only a few users are complaining that the text is too small, suggest that they change the default text size in their browsers.

If all of your users have a browser, such as Netscape, that supports a font-size command (<FONT SIZE=4>, for example), use it. It won't do any harm since most browsers ignore tags they do not understand. See page 313, to learn how this command works.

> Dear Master Chefs,
>
> How many links is too many?
>
> — Chain Linked and Fenced In

The correct answer to this question is annoying: The right number of links is the right number of links. Yuck!

To determine the number of links you need, consider the content and purpose of your page. A table of contents page is all links. A page in a tutorial that covers only one step might have one link back and one link forward. A home page's links will always vary.

Users who access the Web over slow modems will resent the time wasted following links that provide information of only secondary value. Casual Web explorers and those accessing the Web for entertainment or to pass time, will appreciate lots of possible destinations. However, a lot of links present a lot of opportunities for a casual user to get distracted or lost.

Don't close your eyes to the visual design issues. Links are visual design elements. Most often they appear as underlined words. This affects how your page looks. If your page is covered with underlined words, it's going to look like a skin rash!

So, consider each of these perspectives and come up with a sense of what makes sense. Don't start following hard-and-fast rules, though. Every page is unique. Feel it out. Ask users what they think. Test. Whatever. Refine your sense of what's right.

> Dear Master Chefs,
>
> No one really reads my Web pages. What can I do?
>
> — Is Anybody Out There?

Hey, we're here! Our first question is how do you know no one reads your Web pages? If you have a statistical program running on your Web server that truly indicates that no one is accessing your Web pages, then, okay, we need to talk. If you don't have a statistical program running, talk to your Internet service provider or system administrator and find out if they can set you up with one of the many programs available that record the number and Internet address of users who access your Web site.

To stay competitive on the WWW, you need to:

1. **Give value**. WWW users insist on getting value for their time. Content! Content! Content! If your page provides has-been links to overreferenced Web sites (such as Yahoo), or links to Web pages that newbies link to (pages that talk about HTML tags), then users are going to get tired of your page quickly. There's nothing of value. Also, if your page is a billboard of self-promotion, well, you'll lose lots of folks really quickly. They're there to learn something, or tickle their neurons, or whatever. They want to get something out of their experience at your Web site. So provide content, make your site interesting, design meaningful Web pages. Nothing is more seductive than the solution to a user's problem. What may seem dry and boring to one person may make another pant with desire—if he or she recognizes it.

2. **Don't waste time**. WWW users care about their time. If your page is wallowing in big graphics files, or if you've overloaded your pages with links to external objects that require the user to have special hardware and software, then few users will want to take the time and visit. Your site is a drag on their time. But before you eliminate content, think about your audience and the purpose of your page. What is the value to my user?

3. **Associate your Web page with others**. Link from your page to others providing additional information on the same subject. And ask the authors of those pages to link to your page. Doing so makes both your pages more valuable.

4. **Publicize**. Tell your co-workers, your relatives, your friends, your pen pals, your distributors, your customers, your professional organizations, and any one else who will listen about your Web pages. How? Perhaps you should write the Master Chefs and ask.

5. **Forget the numbers**! Concentrate on quality, not quantity. If your company's product is a surgical tool for repairing damaged nerves, you are more concerned with attracting the attention of a few thousand

neurosurgeons than millions of electronic joy riders with nothing better to do than flit from Web page to Web page. If you design a Web page for your public library, do you really want Russian scientists and Pakistani manufacturers wasting their time and clogging your server? We thought not.

> Dear Master Chefs,
>
> How do I publicize my Web site?
>
> — Self-Published

To promote your Web pages, you can:

- Add your URL to all your printed promotional material: business cards, brochures, printed catalogs, letterhead, press kits, newsletters, and any gizmos such as pens and T-shirts that you give away.

- Add your URL to your e-mail signature file. A signature file contains text you want tacked on to the end of all of your e-mail messages. This signature typically provides the name and address of the sender. On UNIX systems, this signature if often stored in a file `names.signature`.

- Write up a brief e-mail announcement to these sites:
  `net-happenings@is.internic.net` and `www-announce@www0.cern.com`
  `javiani@rns.com`

- Register your Web site with the WebCrawler, Lycos, and ALIWEB search services:
  `http://webcrawler.cs.washington.edu/WebCrawler/SubmitURLS.html`
  `http://fuzine.mt.cs.cmu.edu/mlm/lycos-register.html`
  `http://web.nexor.co.uk/aliweb/doc/aliweb.html`

- Post a brief announcement, beginning with the word ANNOUNCE to the `comp.infosystems.www.announce` newsgroup.

- Register your URL with these announcement sites:

Site name	URL to site
Yahoo	`http://akebono.stanford.edu:8000/yahoo/bin/add`
NCSA	`http://www.ncsa.uiuc.edu/SDG/Software/Mosaic/Docs/whats-new-form.html`
Aliweb	`http://web.nexor.co.uk/aliweb/doc/aliweb.html`
Mother of all BBS	`http://www.cs.colorado.edu/home/mcbryan/public_html/bb/add.html`
BizWeb	`http://www.bizweb.com/InfoForm/infoform.html`
Cern	`http://info.cern.ch/hypertext/DataSources/WWW/Geographical_generation/new.html`
Open Market	`http://www.directory.net/dir/submit.cgi`

> **Dear Master Chefs,**
>
> My users complain that they can't see the whole Web page on the screen. How can I change this?
>
> — Furiously Fragmented

Your users may be suffering from a visual disorder called *Low-cost VGA monitor disease.* (Technically this is called *640x480 tunnel vision syndrome.*)

- Use smaller graphics, especially for the page banner.

- Replace inline graphics with a link to external graphics.

- Break your long topic into multiple topics.

- Edit, edit, edit, edit! Make your Web page more concise.

> **Dear Master Chefs,**
>
> I notice you sometimes use `<B>` instead of `<STRONG>`. Isn't that considered bad technique?
>
> — Structural Purist

Yes we did use `<B>` where we could have used `<STRONG>`. And, yes, it is generally better to use a structural tag that tells what a piece of text is rather than a formatting tag to specify what it is to look like. And, yes, we are ashamed of ourselves. But, no! We will not change it.

Why? Do you mean besides our customary arrogance? The reason is a sad one. When we began testing our templates we discovered that some browsers (we won't name names, but you know who you are) formatted the `<STRONG>` in italic rather than bold type. Italic? Text in italic is not easy to read and actually looks <WEAK> rather than <STRONG>. At least with <B>, you know what you're going to get.

When the browsers fix it, we'll fix it. Till then we kludge.

> Dear Master Chefs,
>
> How do I make my HTML code prettier and easier to read?
>
> — Optically Challenged

Here are a few tips that should save a few diopters on your next eyeglass prescription:

First, let your HTML code breathe. Give it some space—or spaces, we should say. Since in most places extra blank spaces and lines have no effect on the resulting page display, you can usually add space freely. The exception is between <PRE> and </PRE>.

To start, put blank lines before and after units of information such as lists, headings, groups of related buttons, and so forth. Some people put a blank line after each paragraph. Others put an extra blank line before each top-level heading.

To further divide a long file, insert a horizontal line between logical units. To keep this line from showing up on the browser, make it a comment:

```
<!------------------------------------------------------------------->
```

If you have a series of repeated items, such as items in a list or a series of related buttons, insert spaces so that corresponding parts line up. For example, add spaces to this:

```
<A HREF="contents.htm"><IMG SRC="cntsicon.gif" ALT="[Contents]"></A>
<A HREF="map.htm"><IMG SRC="mapicon.gif" ALT="[Map]"></A>
<A HREF="myindex.htm"><IMG SRC="indxicon.gif" ALT="[Index]"></A>
```

So that it looks like this:

```
<A HREF="contents.htm"><IMG SRC="cntsicon.gif"  ALT="[Contents]"></A>
<A HREF="map.htm">     <IMG SRC="mapicon.gif"   ALT="[Map]"></A>
<A HREF="myindex.htm"> <IMG SRC="indxicon.gif"  ALT="[Index]"></A>
```

Also break lines so that complete tags stay together. Look at this complicated list item with icon, text, and hypertext link:

```
<LI><A HREF="option1.htm"><IMG SRC="iconfill.gif"
ALT="[icon1]">first option</A>
```

See how much easier it is to understand, when broken into meaningful parts?

```
<LI>
<A HREF="option1.htm">
<IMG SRC="iconfill.gif" ALT="[icon1]">
first option
</A>
```

Finally, comment your code. Perfectly obvious HTML code can turn to hieroglyphics overnight. Imagine what six months can do. Imagine what reading some one else's code is like.

A few labels and notes will inoculate your code against this linguistic deterioration. For example:

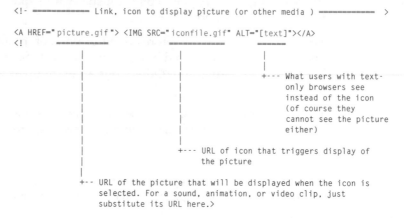

<table>
<tr><td style="border:1px solid black; padding:8px;">
Dear Master Chefs,

What are the most common mistakes by Web authors?

— Wannadoit Right
</td></tr>
</table>

You've come to the right place. We've seen 'em all. We've made 'em all.

1. **Trying too hard to be "way cool!"** The Web is a medium for creative expression. Unfortunately some Web authors take the need for creative expression too far, putting it above their users' needs for information. Often Web readers would rather be informed than entertained, would rather have their questions answered than their senses dazzled. As psychologist Abraham Maslow said, "A first-rate soup is more creative than a second-rate painting."

2. **Failing to test**. Nothing you fail to test will ever work. Even things you do test will sometimes go haywire. So test. Test again. Test your test. Test locally. Test remotely. Test at midnight. Test at high noon. Above all, test your pages the way users will access them.

3. **Not maintaining their Web pages**. Are links still valid? Is the content stale? Is the last revised date in the signature more than six months ago? If you don't maintain your Web pages, you can expect a thin guest book.

4. **Trying too hard to self-promote**. Users want content! They want to know about you, too, but give them more than a sales pitch. Give them reasons to come back to your site and read on. Give them reasons to want to learn more about you and your company. Give them something of value to take away with them.

5. **E N O R M O U S   G R A P H I C S**. Hey, we're really glad you have a 100-dpi, 19-inch monitor and a fiber-optic line (actually, we're jealous). But give a thought to the poor user struggling on a 640 x 480 VGA monitor who dials in over a 14.4K modem. What would you say if you waited three minutes for a graphic to load and it was so big you had to scroll to see all of it? And what if the graphic told you nothing you did not already know?

6. **Words, words, words**. Just as bad as enormous graphics are pages that are nothing but wall-to-wall words. Web pages are not paper pages. Expectations for Web pages are set more by TV and video games than by novels. If you have a lot of words, turn them into tables and lists that users can skim and scan, without having to read in detail. Include meaningful, appropriately sized graphics too.

7. **Thinking locally, publishing globally**. What's a Parisian fashion designer to make of this sales pitch: "Bottom of the ninth. Trailing by three. Bases loaded. Two out. You're up. You're cool because you're decked out in Dylan." Or what's a petroleum engineer in Rio to make of a page that begins with the American okay gesture (circle formed by thumb and forefinger), which in South America has an obscene meaning? Chapter 9 will help you avoid blunders such as these.

8. **Learning too little**. Knowing five HTML tags no more qualifies someone to author Web pages than possessing a typewriter makes someone a best-selling author or owning a camcorder qualifies someone to direct the remake of *Citizen Kane*. Yet many Web page authors stubbornly refuse to learn.

11

COMPLETE MEALS

*Creating effective
Web page clusters*

Up 'til now, you've been primarily concerned with displaying
and delivering your content through individual Web pages.
The tools and guidelines we've offered so far should be pretty
useful in helping you do this. (No false modesty here!) Using
our examples from Chapters 4, 5, 6, and 7 as templates, for
instance, you can whip up some fairly tasty dishes in short
order. By following our presentation suggestions from Chapter
8, you'll create content that is both visually appealing and
considerate of the user's resources.

But now it's time to move to the next level, to go beyond crafting well-tempered Web pages, to become more user-centered. In this chapter, we'll focus on the art of linking your Web pages with premeditated intent, combining them into logical structures that we call *Web clusters*.

An effective Web cluster is more than just great pages clumped together with some go-to links; it's a cohesive whole designed to maximize usability while providing clear benefits to you or your organization. If you link pages ad hoc without building in this cohesion, your structure may be more effective at chasing users away than addressing their needs or your objectives. Without sufficient forethought, your Web site and its various clusters can become merely a time-consuming hobby—or worse, if you're developing it on company time.

STRUCTURE = CONTEXT = MEANING

Here's why we believe the structure of your Web clusters—as expressed in the links among your pages and resources—is critical:

- **Your links define the paths that users follow to navigate among your Web pages and other resources**. We mean navigation in its largest sense here, so it includes running CGI applets, performing scripts, downloading files, and so forth—anything that your Web pages offer your users.

- **This navigation, in turn, defines the relationship between pages (and other resources)**: That video clip explains this procedure because its link is here; this link calls up that reference list because it is related to this topic.

- **These relationships define the context of your Web pages and their content**. To a large degree, context is meaning; users will interpret and understand your Web content based on the context in which they receive it.

In short, your linking structure creates the context in which your users will understand your Web content. If you are casual about the way you define this structure, then your results will probably be equally indifferent; if you pay careful attention to the context that your links create, you can increase the payback for your Web development efforts—not to mention the delight with which your users access your Web site.

And lest you think we're overcomplicating things, keep in mind that while the Web as it exists today is largely built of text-based pages and supporting resources, that won't always be the case: The widespread use of 3-D and virtual reality is just around the corner, and eventually you'll be developing Web worlds instead of Web pages. If you think a poorly organized cluster of Web pages is a problem, imagine how disorienting it would be in virtual reality!

Caveat Webster

Any Web cluster with more than three interlinked pages is by BWSS (Because We Say So) definition a potential cybermaze that must be structured with care and forethought to achieve maximum effect and highest and best use.

WHAT'S IN STORE

This chapter, then, is your implementation guide, provided to help you stitch together your Web pages (and other resources, of course) into coherent Web clusters, so that you and your users get the most out of your hard work. The rest of the chapter is organized like this:

1. We start with some **guidelines** for designing effective clusters—a seven-step process that will help you define and hit your target. (It may be tempting to skip this part, just to get your Web content out there a little bit sooner, but you increase your chances of a haphazard or ineffective structure if you do.)

2. Then we move on to a **chart** that shows what kind of clusters work well to meet various objectives of different kinds of organizations; once you've worked through the guidelines, you'll be able to find yourself on the chart and see what kinds of clusters we think are your best bet.

3. We close with a series of **examples** of Web clusters of distinction. While they may not be Web sites that will climb onto the "cool" charts with a bullet (or vanish just as quickly), they will create a groundswell of satisfied (read *repeat*) users who get what they need from your pages with a minimum of fuss, muss, and access time.

So, let's step ahead to the objective-setting process.

SEVEN STEPS TO STRUCTURAL HAPPINESS

It's no revelation that you have to plan a structure before you can build it; it is certainly not news that you have to define a target before you can expect to hit it with any regularity. Even so, in the workplace (known as *real life* in some circles) we frequently don't play by this simple rule.

You'd be surprised how many Web authors can tell you how they created some fancy effect or where they found some obscure URL to link to—even though they can't tell you, in convincing terms, why they created their pages in the first place, or what their users are supposed to get out of them. (Their users probably can't tell, either.) This is okay for college students with time on their hands, but "because it's there" is probably not good enough for those of us who have added Web development to an already teeming plate of things to do.

To make a coherent Web presence happen, you need three things:

1. A process for developing your Web content and structure.

2. Content and development resources to work with.

3. Not quite enough time or resources to do the work required.

Thank-you to Len Scrogan of the Boulder Valley Schools in Boulder, Colorado, for this turn of phrase.

We can't do much to help with the second item, and the third is pretty much a given—so we'll concentrate here on the essential process. Here's an overview of how we see it working:

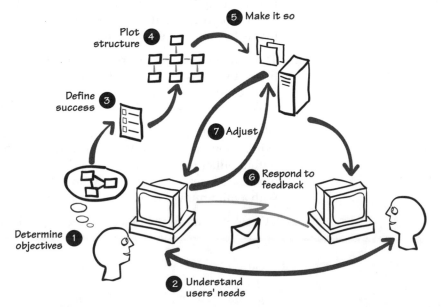

So, put away your HTML crib sheet, sharpen your pencils, step back from the world of links and URLs for a moment, and look at your own version of the Big Picture while we humbly offer the following guidelines to structural happiness.

Step 1: Determine your objectives.

To get the best return from the sweat equity you're investing in your Web pages, you must be specific and knowledgeable about what you are trying to accomplish. Targeting your objectives is probably the most important step in designing or choosing a Web page structure; you gotta know where you want to go before you know which map to use.

For example, here's our goal for writing this book and developing the CD-ROM of goodies:

> Whether you are developing your Web site just for fun or for competitive survival, we want your Web presence to be a paragon of clean design and usability, a source of delight to your clients and users, and jealously duplicated by your competition. (Especially since you're using our book!)

Business and organizations typically want to get on the Web for a combination of the following reasons (YMMV, Your Mileage May Vary, remember?):

- Information gathering, surveys, and research.

- Global exposure and/or market presence.

- Online ordering and delivery of goods, services, and information.

- Interaction with members, participants, customers, and clients.

Where do your own needs fit in? To answer that question, we suggest you sketch out in written or diagram form a picture of what you want your Web site to do and be. Nothing complicated, no big research effort, no task force or tiger team needed—just some thoughtful reflection in a quiet place over a stimulating beverage of your choice.

Here are a few pump primers to help you get the juices flowing:

- Why are you creating this Web site?

- What, in general terms, do you want it to be used for? Write your goal down in 50 words or less—a quick-and-dirty mission statement, if you will.

- What do you want to get out of it? For example, are you looking for:

  - Feedback and discussion from users about your content, your creations, or your comments?

  - Customer queries about your products, services, or offerings—in short, self-qualified marketing leads?

  - The warm glow of making the world a better place by providing valuable information, free software, or a centralized location for specialized resources?

  - Actual orders from actual customers?

  - A showcase of your talents or knowledge?

  - An Internet presence to raise your organization's hipness/coolness rating?

  - A cost-effective way to electronically distribute products, technical information, or services?

Once you give these questions some thought, you'll probably find that you have several objectives, so you'll have to prioritize them. Try weighing them in this order:

- What's going to give you the biggest return (however you've defined it) for the least amount of work?

- What's going to generate measurable or tangible results immediately?

- What's going to generate results (positive, we hope) that are of interest to: your Web development funding source; your management; your critics or naysayers; sources of potential support (peers, customers, and colleagues); and your users?

Okay, that's the hard part. Now let's go on to the next challenge.

Step 2: Understand your users' needs.

Once you have an idea of what you (or your organization) want to get out of your Web page development effort, you need to line up that target with what your users need and want. (We know, we know, but it's a startling concept to some.)

For example, you may want to generate prospects and leads for your private airplane brokerage business while your users are looking for inside info on the aviation world, such as, say, tips on small airports located near Disneyland. By providing this kind of content as a public service—in exchange for having a user fill out a registration or survey form—your Web site can become middle ground where you can reach your objectives while providing users with something of value that meets their needs.

Some questions for your consideration:

- Who are your users? What base of users are you hoping to attract?

- What do your users want? Why did they link to your pages?

- Do they expect direct benefits from your Web pages—such as software or information content to download—or more indirect gains, such as bibliographies or referrals to sources?

- How frequently will your users want or need to return to your pages?

- Do you, in fact, have to attract an audience, or are you creating Web pages for use within your organization, or by users who are self-motivated (such as people seeking software upgrades or technical support)? In other words, do you have a built-in or otherwise captive audience?

- How are most of your users accessing your Web pages? Are they dialing into SLIP accounts, or linking from a corporate network T1 link? What kind of bandwidth can you assume they have access to? Do you know what kind of platform they are on or what kind of helper applications they'll have on hand?

- How important are drop-in users—or will most of your Web page visitors be referred or otherwise subscribed?

It's critical for you to give some thought to the agendas your users are bringing to the table. If you don't address your users' needs at some level—whether it's through information, results, access, or even entertainment—they won't stay long, and they won't come back.

Step 3: Define success.

The next step is to give yourself some specific, quantifiable results with which to measure your success. Try combining your objectives with your users' interests and whip together several informal scenarios that describe a successful visit to your Web pages by your typical user. For example:

> My Web page is successful when my user keeps the URL for my Web page in his or her hot list, checks my Web site every other week, and orders at least three information products over the next twelve months.

Be sure not to get too formal or fancy with your scenarios; they're for your benefit, not Hollywood's. All you're trying to do is express your objectives in terms of actual results or events. Any scenario that takes you more than ten minutes to prepare is probably overdone. Here's a few icebreakers to help you define these target results:

- How many users visit your Web pages in a typical week?

- What do your users do while visiting your Web site?

- How long do your users stay linked to your pages?

- How many links within your Web page structure will your users activate in a typical session? That is, how many of your pages or resources will your users visit during a typical session?

- How often do you want your users to come back?

You'll probably come up with some combination of these three types of success factors:

1. **Raw results** that can be measured by the Web server software, such as usage statistics and daily hit counts. These will be particularly useful in measuring the effect of refinements to your Web pages, and in throwing around impressive-sounding numbers at budget time.

2. **Internal consequences** that indicate the impact that your Web site is having on your organization, such as fewer calls to technical support or an increase in international contacts. These are your bread-and-butter benefits, so be sure to set some realistic targets here.

3. **External consequences** that illustrate the impact your Web presence is having outside the organization, such as changes in government actions, media coverage of a new service or product, or public discussion of a particular issue. While these kinds of results are typically more ego-boosting than directly beneficial, that's okay: Boosting the right egos in appropriate ways is a good thing.

Step 4: Plot your structure.

Now that you have a clearer idea of where you're going with your Web pages—and how to tell when you get there—you'll need to decide what Web structure best suits your objectives. To make this task easier, we've prepared a chart called "Guidelines for Selecting Cluster Types," which maps your objectives to effective structures. Later in the chapter we diagram and describe each structure, so when you're ready to do this step, browse the chart (see page 496) to figure out which structures you're interested in, then look them up further in the chapter.

In real life you'll probably use a combination of structures, so don't get too hung up on the categories we've offered in the guidelines. We know our sample structures are effective, but you know best what structure will work for your users. (That's why you got the Web page assignment, right?)

For example: Suppose you have a Web cluster for company and product information that you expect will be mostly visited by newcomers. You might want to create a guided tour as your default structure for most users, using linked Web pages that display in this sequence:

1. A stop in your corporate "lobby" to meet your friendly guide and see what's new at the company.

2. A map, animation, or video showing your manufacturing locations.

3. A catalog or showroom of products made at each location, linked to those locations.

4. A general product index available in either alphabetic or product category order.

5. A tutorial on how to place an order via your new computerized ordering system.

6. The ordering system itself.

That's a great structure for users who want to know about your company and your products, but for your repeat customers you should also layer in a set of links that creates a fast path directly to your index or your ordering system. (And since links are free, why not both?)

That's what we mean by combining and refining our sample structures.

Step 5: Make it so.

Well, you can't get through the process without actually developing Web resources and putting them into your chosen structure, can you? Once you've figured out which pages and page clusters will work best for you and your users, it's time to get to work, following the steps that we've elucidated in Chapter 3 and elsewhere:

1. Copy resources and source files from the CD-ROM as you need them.

2. Create and incorporate your new content.

3. Link and load.

4. Test, test, and then test some more.

5. Publish and publicize.

Step 6: Track results and respond to feedback.

Once your Web pages are public, you'll start getting hits, responses, and e-mail about them. Depending on the Web server choices that you've made, the responses that you'll receive can give you both direct feedback—e-mail from users themselves—and indirect feedback—typically demographics, hit counts, and other objective information that will tell you who are accessing your Web pages, and what they're doing when they get there.

Naturally, you'll compare these results with your objectives and success targets on a regular basis.

No matter what Web clusters or pages you offer, your Web presence is going to generate some kind of responses (e-mail, orders, whatever), so your organization has to be prepared to deal with them. Remember, too, that every contact is a potential customer, member, or participant; if someone e-mails you complaining about the background color on your pages, use that opportunity to ask if he or she has entered the product-naming contest.

The key thing to remember is that the speed of electronic communication sets up user expectations for instant gratification. You can handle user feedback manually or automatically, but don't dilly dally about it. The user who e-mailed you asking for more information about your organization generally expects a response within 24 hours—and has probably contacted your rivals as well.

Step 7: Adjust, adjust, adjust.

The good thing about the Web's electronic medium is that changes and updates are relatively easy to make (you won't need to make any fixes, of course, since you used our templates):

- Change a file, add an image, update a video clip, retest your changed pages, and you're off and running.

- Analyze the pattern of user hits for feedback on which pages are working and which ones aren't pulling their weight. Then revise your Web pages and their links accordingly.

    For example, are your users missing your cool graphical index, and using the slower search button instead? Make the index link more prominent, and move the search to the end of your structure.

- If you have volatile content (in terms of it being constantly updated, not necessarily flammable), then consider setting up automatically generated pages (like cranking out a weekly catalog from a product database), so you can have your system do these updates for you.

The bad news is that this continual improvement and currency is expected by your users. To keep your active users (those who have responded in some way) happy, you have to respond quickly to their comments and concerns. To keep the lurking traffic (those who admire your pages silently without placing orders, offering comments, or downloading your content) flowing past in a steady stream, you have to keep your content fresh.

GUIDELINES FOR SELECTING CLUSTER TYPES

The following table maps your organization type, your objectives, and your users' needs to suggested cluster structures. Find yourself in the chart, examine the suggested structures and pick the ones that are best for your needs, and then refer to the samples of those structures later in this chapter.

If you are ...	And your main Web objectives are ...	And your users' objectives are to ...	We suggest the cluster(s):
Small consultancy or service business	Increase name recognition. Position your expertise in your field.	Find specialized resources in your particular field.	Newsletter/ Magazine (page 522) Online Reference (page 530)
	Open new national and international markets.	Obtain unique goods or services. Reduce geographic isolation.	Catalog (page 517)
	Generate business leads. Build prospect database.	Find out about your company, your field, or your industry. Get something free or cool.	Sequential (page 502) Grid (page 508) Newsletter/ Magazine (page 522)
	Support customers at low cost. Maintain large company presence.	Obtain product upgrades, technical support, order status, etc. In short, customer service.	Online Reference (page 530) How-To (page 526) Training Lesson (page 534) Grid (page 508)

If you are ...	And your main Web objectives are ...	And your users' objectives are to ...	We suggest the cluster(s):
Community or issue-centric organization	Increase name recognition. Generate interest in programs, issues, efforts.	Explore giving financial or volunteer support. Apply for assistance.	Newsletter/Magazine (page 522) Catalog (page 517) Hierarchical (page 505)
	Educate or persuade the public. Educate internal/private membership.	Get information, news, the inside scoop on topical events. Research issues.	Newsletter/Magazine (page 522) Online Reference (page 530) Training Lesson (page 534)
	Support your community base at low cost. Maintain presence outside the community. Provide public services.	Find information and resources in your area of geography or expertise. Obtain services and resources.	Online Reference (page 530) Hierarchical (page 505) Sequential (page 502) Training Lesson (page 534)
Public agency	Provide administrative and information services at low cost. Speed up internal processes.	Find information and resources. Answer questions. Complete applications, forms, surveys, and returns.	Online Reference (page 530) How-To (page 526) Sequential (page 502) Training Lesson (page 534)
	Receive bids, specifications, and otherwise support expenditure process.	Find government purchasing contacts. Respond to government RFPs.	Catalog (page 517) Online Reference (page 530) How-To (page 526)

If you are …	And your main Web objectives are …	And your users' objectives are to …	We suggest the cluster(s):
Public agency (continued)	Poll public opinion.	Vote or express opinions.	Hierarchical (page 505)
	Educate or persuade the public.	Research public decisions and actions.	Newsletter/ Magazine (page 522) Hierarchical (page 505)
Personnel or training department	Reduce Q&A and policy reference tasks. Standardize policy & procedure revision levels and access. Improve internal processing of forms and paperwork.	7 x 24 access to accurate policies and procedures. Faster response to information and approval requests. Equal access to knowledge and resources needed for advancement.	Online Reference (page 530) How-To (page 526) Sequential (page 502) Training Lesson (page 534)
	Provide simple content training on topics such as safety, legal or environmental requirements, or technical knowledge basic to your business.	7 x 24 access to accurate policies, procedures, and technical references. Nonthreatening, nonjudgmental training resource. Spare-time learning.	Training Lesson (page 534) How-To (page 526) Newsletter/ Magazine (page 522)

If you are ...	And your main Web objectives are ...	And your users' objectives are to ...	We suggest the cluster(s):
Customer or Technical Support group	Reduced stress and time pressure. Happier users. Faster response time. Online product and warranty registration. Improved filtering of basic calls.	Obtain upgrades, fixes, and patches. Review FAQs and other resources to solve their problems themselves. Find out about product changes. File complaints or compliments.	Online Reference (page 530) How-To (page 526) Hierarchical (page 505) Sequential (page 502)
	Opportunity to respond in more depth.	Post complicated questions and get answers someday.	Hierarchical (page 505) Grid (page 508)
Marketing, advertising, or sales group or agency	Leads, leads, and more leads! Improve competitive positioning. (Everybody else is doing it!) Improve hipness quotient for company. Drive Internet demographic group to other marketing options. Perform polls and surveys.	Find information on specific product, service, industry, or company. Be amused or impressed with online presence. Browse well-designed sites for Web page ideas. Respond to surveys, contests, or giveaways.	Newsletter/ Magazine (page 522) Sequential (page 502) Grid (page 508) Hierarchical (page 505)
	Generate online sales.	Obtain sample products, demos, beta copies, up-grades, and fixes.	Sequential (page 502) Grid (page 508) Hierarchical (page 505)

If you are ...	And your main Web objectives are ...	And your users' objectives are to ...	We suggest the cluster(s):
Individual, personal Web chef	Attract attention to yourself, your cause, or your group. Provide access to resources you deem worthy or interesting. Connect with new friends, colleagues, or partners.	Find out about you or your organization. Find kindred spirits. Be amused or impressed with online presence. Browse well-designed sites for Web page ideas.	Newsletter/ Magazine (page 522) Hierarchical (page 505) Sequential (page 502)

SAMPLE CLUSTER STRUCTURES

Now that you have an idea of what kind of Web clusters you want to create, browse through this section to pick our collective brains on their effective arrangements and uses. For those of you who want to explore all the options, we've arranged the sample structures into two groups:

1. **Generic clusters** which can be used in a variety of ways, and should appeal to you home-improvement types. The three generic clusters (sequential, hierarchical, and grid) are ordered from simple to complex; think of these as structural templates, if you will.

2. **Specific clusters**, which are intended to meet certain needs common to businesses and organizations; the five clusters in this group are ordered from the basic to the (relatively) esoteric. We think of these as application clusters, FWIW.

For each cluster:

● We offer a quick overview diagram of the cluster (so you can picture it in your mind), then describe the best uses of that structure.

● We describe and illustrate the cluster's structure in some detail.

● We list the most likely navigation links for pages in that cluster.

- We offer some observations on the difficulty of creating and maintaining the cluster, and give each one a rating we call the "Sweat Equity Index." This is a number that rates the difficulty (on a scale of 1 to 10) of four tasks:

  1. Original development of the Web cluster structure.

  2. Testing and debugging of links.

  3. Revisions and additions to the cluster's structure.

  4. Revisions and additions to the cluster's content.

BTW ...

A template for each cluster is replicated on the CD-ROM, in the Meals subdirectory (or folder). When you're ready to stop reading and start building, head there first; placeholder files for the cluster structure (say that three times fast!) are stored in the familiar RTF color-coded format.

The location of the starting page for each template is listed at the beginning of the template description.

Generic clusters

In this section we'll describe three types of generic clusters:

1. Sequential clusters (immediately following).

2. The common hierarchical cluster, which starts on page 505.

3. The more challenging grid cluster, which begins on page 508.

We think that these generic clusters can be pretty useful, especially if you're just getting started in building your Web site, or if you want to take a fairly quick-and-dirty route to establishing your Web presence. If you don't have any clear and compelling objectives that drive you into one of the specific clusters discussed later, then you can probably mold one of these three classics into a workable Web site.

Sequential cluster

On the CD-ROM ...

meals
  sequence
    start.htm

One of the most common Web clusters follows a fairly generic sequential pattern. It has a primary, author-defined path, typically set by some form of next and previous links that lead the user through a specific sequence of pages, each of which covers one topic. Some versions offer side trips to related information or media content, as well. The sequential structure is the one most familiar to many users, since it essentially follows a page-turning "book" metaphor.

Here's an overview of what a sequential cluster looks like:

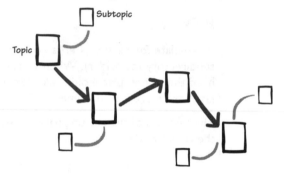

When to use it

Use this structure when you need to control or guide the sequence in which information is revealed to the user. Presumably, this is when you know better than your users what sequence your pages should follow. (This may not be as often as you might think!)

Some of the best uses for the generic sequence are for:

- Limited tutorials.

- Guided tours.

- Depictions of timelines and event-based sequences.

- Descriptions of linear processes.

Some of the worst uses are for:

- Arbitrary sales pitches—forcing your user into a marketing trap is bad for business and your karma.

- Research or reference works—confining your reader in a predetermined sequence.

- Unrelated or nonsequential information, of course.

How to build it

By definition, a sequential structure has a beginning and an end, and goes to additional places in between. A few detours are a good idea, too, if you have content that is related but not essential to the main topic; by using detours, you can provide a fast track through your sequence for experienced users, while still providing enough background for the newbies. (See, hypertext is your friend!)

The diagram below illustrates what a generic sequential cluster looks like.

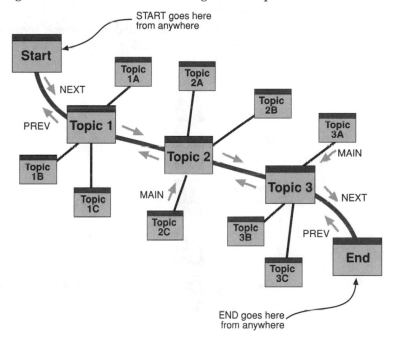

Here's what we mean by the components in this diagram:

- **Start page**—This is your welcome/introduction page; it establishes the general topic and instructs the user how to proceed (and what to expect). Since each sequence has a fairly fixed path and length, you should provide either a screen count (something like: "This topic is discussed in the next seven pages ...") or an estimated completion time. If appropriate, make note of any shortcuts or unusual navigation tricks that you've included.

- **Topic pages**—Individual pages or other resources that display, demonstrate, describe, or otherwise cover a specific related topic.

- **Subtopics/Detours**—Individual pages or resources that cover related but minor topics. Typically these will be dead ends off the main topic sequence; users are expected to explore the occasional subtopic, then return to the main road.

- **End page**—Your closing page that sums up or concludes the topic. Usually you'll want to include links back to the start page or over to other related topics. If appropriate to your users, you can include a survey or registration form, too, especially if completing the sequence qualifies them for something.

Navigation

Since it's so straightforward, the generic sequence cluster doesn't need much more than the most basic navigation palette. Pages in this structure have the following buttons:

Start		Jumps back to the start page in the sequence
End		Jumps to the end page in the sequence
Previous		Jumps to the previous topic page
Next		Jumps to the next topic page
Main		Jumps back to the main sequence from a subtopic

The subtopic pages are accessed through text or graphic links incorporated into the topic page content.

Sweat equity index

How tough is it to develop and maintain a Web cluster based on this sequential structure? Well, we give it a medium score of 5.5, slightly tougher than average. (A score of 10 indicates extreme difficulty.) The main challenge is to keep the sequences coherent and, when revising content, to keep links intact—particularly if you've attached multiple links to a page or resource that's under revision.

Hierarchical cluster

Another common Web cluster uses a familiar tiered hierarchical structure. A hierarchical structure usually features a series of author-defined paths, branching off from a common starting point—typically your home page. This structure is both simple and flexible, and can be used for almost any business application.

Here's an overview of what a hierarchical cluster looks like:

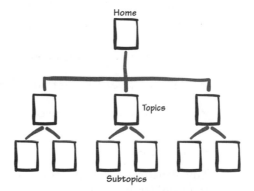

The general pattern of a hierarchy provides links downward, from general information to specific information to details. If you're object-oriented (or genealogically inclined), think of it as a grandparent-parent-child pattern. As a general rule, a hierarchical structure does not need to provide a lot of lateral movement between peer items on the second and third tiers. You certainly can, of course, but then you're moving more into the grid model—which is fine if it delivers your content more effectively.

Remember the Webmaster's motto: Do what works!

When to use it

Use this structure when you need to deliver multiple levels of detail or complexity on more than one or two topics. If there's an implicit or explicit hierarchy in your content, then this is the structure for you. Likewise, if you cannot decide which cluster structure to use, then try this one first.

You can use a hierarchical structure to present:

• A series of guided tours, all emanating from a single departure point. Each tour is self-contained, but also relates to an overall geography lesson.

- A corporate-like org-chart with branches based on topics, responsibilities, territories, or other content-driven categories.

- A telescoping view of an event, a collection, or a resource. This works like a zoom feature, so that your user can click from, say, a weekly community calendar listing to zoom in on a page describing a particular event (including ticket information and order form), and then zoom in further to a profile of the performing artist—complete with a video clip of a sample performance, of course.

Think twice before using a hierarchy to deliver:

- Information for which you need to control the sequence.

- Flat or superficial data that do not have multiple levels of detail.

- Unrelated or disparate content.

How to build it

The structure of a hierarchy cluster is pretty straightforward: It follows the familiar inverted-tree pattern (trunk-branch-twig) that we use for all sorts of information. It does not necessarily have a defined sequence, although you certainly can include lateral links between topics as appropriate.

This structure will typically look something like this:

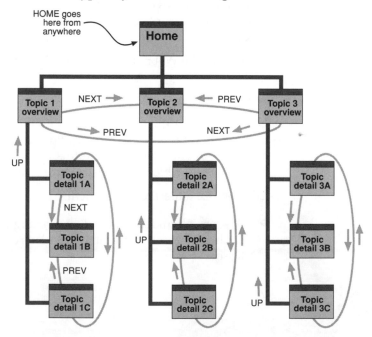

We only show three topics in our diagram, but you could just as easily have thirty, or even three hundred. If you have more than, say, a dozen topics, then you may want to insert an index or table of contents that categorizes your topics by source, media, subject matter, or some other criteria. Doing so gives users an intermediate step, making it easier for them to find what they're looking for.

Here's what the diagram components represent:

- **Home page**—This is the point-of-departure page where you establish the presence of your company or organization, and provide a context for the topics that are accessible through this page. This could be your ultimate home page, or it could be a lesser home base from which your users can explore a series of topics

- **Topic overview**—Individual pages or other resources that display, demonstrate, describe, or otherwise provide general information about a particular topic.

- **Topic detail**—Multiple individual pages or other resources whose content provides a closer examination of the topic.

Keep in mind that hierarchical clusters also nest well; that is, you can combine several cluster groups into one or more superclusters, if your content or your users' needs warrant.

Navigation

The generic hierarchy cluster needs only basic navigation elements. Each page in the hierarchy cluster sports these buttons:

Home Jumps back to the home page from anywhere in the cluster.

Up Jumps up a level to the more general page related to the current page. For example, when your user is on topic detail page 3B, the Up link jumps to topic overview page 3.

Next Jumps to the next page in the sequence at the current level. For example, when your user is on topic detail page 3B, the Next link jumps to topic detail page 3C. Or, if your user is on topic 1 overview, the Next link jumps to topic 2 overview.

Previous Jumps to the previous page in the sequence at the current level. For example, when your user is on topic detail page 3B, the Previous link jumps to topic detail page 3A. Or, if your user is on topic 3 overview, the Previous link jumps back to topic 2 overview.

Links to navigate down the structure—proceeding from the general to the specific for a particular topic—are provided as text or graphic links incorporated into the topic page content.

Sweat equity index

We give this cluster a midrange sweat equity index score of 5—halfway up the difficulty ladder. Developing and maintaining a hierarchical structure requires a series of fairly easy discrete tasks, but keeping track of those tasks can become a bit of a burden. So, the initial development requires some thought, but more-than-occasional revisions require some pretty good bookkeeping. (Note how William Horton Consulting, in the example in Chapter 3, uses a spreadsheet to keep track of pages, resources, and links—not a bad idea!)

Grid cluster

On the CD-ROM ...

meals
  grid
    topic1A.htm

The grid cluster is the most complex of the structures that we've designed for you, but it's also the one that offers your users the most freedom to navigate among your Web pages and resources. (Not to mention the most tempting opportunity to get lost in cyberspace!) The grid is also the most egalitarian of structures: Every topic carries the same weight as its compatriots, and there is (at best) only an implied sequence or hierarchy.

Here's an overview of what a grid cluster looks like:

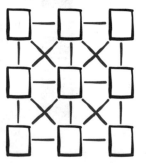

When to use it

You could use the grid cluster effectively for:

- **Supporting a large map or other graphic** that serves as a menu for navigation (technically, these are known as *image-maps*). These image-maps are very powerful tools that can be used in a variety of ways, from highlighting regional service areas to providing a graphical interface to repair and troubleshooting information.

- **Technical information** that is best presented in complex tables, such as charts of technical specifications or product options.

- **Information that is two-dimensional in nature**—that is, content such as financial or statistical data that is arranged around X and Y axes.

- **Adventure or learning games** or multidirectional tours that don't follow a single sequence.

- **Content that lends itself to a two-dimensional presentation**, such as an architectural tour through an office building, or a corporate organizational chart.

These are only a few of the potential uses, of course; generally any collection of Web resources whose content components are richly interconnected is a likely candidate for some form of a grid cluster. About the only content that you wouldn't consider for this structure is anything that must be presented in a particular sequence, such as specific how-to procedures or guided tours.

How to build it

The grid structure is somewhat unique in that it provides a high degree of *lateral linking*—that is, links between related topics—as well as the familiar vertical linking from general-to-specific-to-detailed content. It also supports *diagonal linking*, in which a topic page written at a general level of detail may be linked to a page or resource prepared at the specific level below a related topic page. (Lateral and diagonal linking are not technically precise terms, by the way, so be careful about throwing them around in newsgroups and conversations.)

As you can see from the diagram below, each topic is linked laterally, vertically, and diagonally to all the topics to which it is related in some way. (Of course, there's no literal direction in Web space, but we have to represent the structure on the page somehow.)

Your cluster structure will look something like this:

Topic 1A	Topic 2A	Topic 3A	Topic 4A	Topic 5A
Topic 1B	Topic 2B	Topic 3B	Topic 4B	Topic 5B
Topic 1C	Topic 2C	Topic 3C	Topic 4C	Topic 5C
Topic 1D	Topic 2D	Topic 3D	Topic 4D	Topic 5D
Topic 1E	Topic 2E	Topic 3E	Topic 4E	Topic 5E

Don't get too worked up about making the diagram of your cluster structure too symmetrical; it's more likely than not that your real-world grid will have some ragged edges and frayed fringes. (And don't even try to create a grid cluster without diagramming it out on paper first!)

The components in the diagram tell their own story: Each component is a topic unto itself, with links to nearby related topics. There may be some sequence implied or expressed, but there's no requirement for it.

All well and good, but it's still a little abstract, isn't it? To illustrate this structure more effectively, let's revisit the grid diagram with some sample content.

Example

The Park Nursery wants to put up a Web site that helps potential customers select native Southwestern plants for their landscaping projects. Their experience tells them that there are two main criteria involved: the altitude of the area to be landscaped, and the amount of sunshine that area gets. They decide to use a grid structure to provide this information.

Here's what this grid cluster might look like in real life:

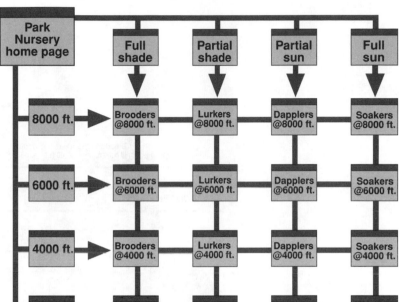

And here's how these pages could be structured and linked. We won't go into full-blown detail since this is just an example, but you'll get enough content to follow along:

- **Park Nursery home page**—Gives background information about the company, provides sufficient navigation tools to get your users to any page in the grid, and describes how to use them.

  These navigation tools could simply be text or button links, but we've got a better idea: Since we're talking about the great outdoors here, let's get a little advanced and use an image-map to provide navigation in a visual and compelling way. Visualize something like this on the home page:

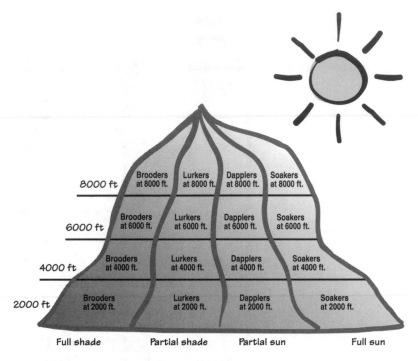

The image-map shows a mountain divided into 2000-foot altitude zones and into four grades of sunlight exposure.

Each of the altitudes (6000 ft., for example), each of the grades of sunshine (Partial shade), and each of their intersections (Lurkers at 6000 ft.) is a link to a more detailed page.

Here's where users can go from the home page (hang with us here!):

- Users who select one of the altitude zone numbers (which are coded on the map as links) jump to the corresponding Altitude page. For example:

4000 ft.	links to the page ...	**Native Plants at 4000 ft.** There are a variety of native plants that thrive happily on the climate they enjoy at 4,000 feet, even in the dead of winter. The list below is ...

- Users who select one of the sunshine grades ("Full sun," "Partial sun," etc.), jump to the corresponding Exposure page:

Partial sun	links to the page …	**Native Plants for Partially Sunny Areas**
		Many native plants prefer partial sun during growing season. The list below is …

- Users who select one of the intersecting altitude and sunshine zones on the mountain, jump to more detail on the specific "Exposure-at-Altitude" page.

Dapplers at 4000 ft.	links to the page …	**Native Plants for Partially Sunny Areas at 4000 ft.**
		There are a variety of native plants that thrive happily in partially sunny locations at 4000 feet…

- **Altitude pages**—These are the Web pages shown on the left column, or Y-axis, of the diagram. Each page describes, in general terms, the kinds of native plants that grow at that altitude, and lists regional places of interest at that altitude where such plants are thriving.

  Each Altitude page also includes links so users can jump laterally to any Exposure-at-Altitude page at this same altitude.

- **Exposure pages**—These are the Web pages shown at the top (or at the bottom, in the case of the image-map), or X-axis, of the diagram. Each page describes, in general terms, the kinds of native plants that thrive in that level of sun exposure.

  Each Exposure page also includes links, so that users can jump vertically to any of the Exposure-at-Altitude pages for this degree of sunshine.

- **Exposure-at-altitude pages**—These are the pages where the X- and Y-axes meet. Here you find information about the native plants that thrive at this particular combination of altitude and sun exposure. Each of these pages includes navigation buttons to jump to adjacent pages to see plants for a higher or lower altitude or for more or less sunshine.

This nursery example illustrates the use of a grid cluster for two-dimensional, tabular data. Granted, it doesn't take full advantage of the diagonal navigation that a grid can support; looking at the actual context, there's not a lot in common between plants with different sun exposure requirements that live at different altitudes, and we didn't want to push the example too far. Needless to say, your grid content may require a different linking structure and emphasis.

That's probably enough fertilizer for thought for the time being; our intention was to flesh out the idea of a grid structure with enough detail so that the concept would take root. At this point we'd better leave well enough alone.

Navigation

As with any Web structure, your users can enter a grid cluster at any point. Unlike more orderly structures, however, a grid may not make it evident by context just where they are and how they got there. That's where effective navigation aids become critical to the grid structure.

The rich interlinking of Web pages and resources in a grid structure calls for some heavy-duty navigation functions. Check out these mondo-buttons:

All of these navigation aids are in the grid cluster pages at:

meals
   grid
      topic1A.htm

You-are-here map

This is an image-map that tells your users where they are in the grid, and allows them to jump directly to any other page in the grid. Each Web page shows the same map, but substitutes the image that highlights its location. The example at left is the image for the page located in the second row, fourth column.

(Looking at our mountain map, this would be the page "Dapplers at 6000 ft.")

NavButton map

This image-map navigates to a neighboring page relative to your current Web page. It's a Zen thing, sort of: Where you go depends on where you are. The map consists of one image with nine hotspots; each hotspot links to the page located one slot over in the grid, in whatever direction that hotspot points to.

(On each and every Web page displaying the map, the nine hotspots have to be hard-coded to go to the proper page: That's nine changes times the number of Web pages in your grid, to get the pages fully linked. Whew!)

For example, if your users are on the page located in the second row, fourth column, and they click on the right diagonal down map segment, they'll go to the page located in the third row, fifth column of the grid. (In terms of our nursery example, they'd go from "Dapplers at 6000 ft." to "Soakers at 4000 ft.")

Nav icons

(All nine of them)

If you can't use or don't want to deal with image-maps, you can also assemble a cluster of icon buttons. The navigation button at left looks and acts very much like the image-map above, but it's actually made up of nine tiny GIFs manually coded to link to the proper page.

If you can't do image-maps, or if you (or your users) can't handle the loading time for nine GIFs, you can create the same navigational structure using text links. Using essentially the same HTML coding as the Nav icons described above—but leaving out the IMG codes that embed the tiny GIFs—you can create a text version that looks like this:

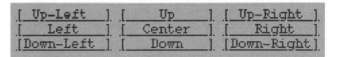

Web chef hint:

Remember that templates for all of the structures we describe here are included on the CD-ROM, in the `meals` directory. This includes the image-map navigation buttons and the HTML coding necessary to make them work. (Remember, too, that your Web server has to support image-maps, or you can't use them.)

Sweat equity index

The grid structure makes for pretty diagrams, but it also makes updating and revising the content of a grid cluster not so pretty:

- The initial effort is fairly sizable; you'll probably go through several design iterations before you are satisfied with the results—and then you can start coding.

- Changes to content down the line aren't so bad if you preserve your page-naming conventions (so that you don't have to change the navigation links).

- Changes to structure are rife with possible errors and will probably take twice as long as you'd like.

- Estimate sufficient time to test after each round of changes—and then double that estimate.

We gave the grid structure a hefty 8.5 score out of a possible 10 (most difficult).

Application-specific clusters

Now let's move on to some more specialized Web structures that many businesses and organizations will find of value:

- The catalog cluster explained on page 517 is useful for a variety of description-and-ordering applications—and not just software products, either.

- Nearly every organization that has a presence on the Web should have some form of newsletter/magazine cluster on their Web site. See page 522 for a description of this type of structure.

- If you have to deliver specific procedures either in house or out, check out the how-to cluster that we explore on page 526.

- Got a large volume of detailed, segmented information that you want to distribute via the Web? That's what our online reference cluster is for—to give you an efficient structure for making referential information available. Our description begins on page 530.

- Although extended training is not a good idea over today's limited Web bandwidth, there are some ways to offer basic training over a wide range of topics. See page 534 for details.

We think you'll find these application-specific clusters helpful in addressing your own particular needs and objectives. Keep in mind that you can also combine these structures with each other, or with the generic templates, in some pretty interesting and effective ways. These templates are just your starting point, so don't stop here!

Catalog cluster

On the CD-ROM ...

meals
  catalog
    catalog.htm

If you're publishing Web pages for an organization that sells products or services, then the catalog cluster is probably the first structure you're interested in. It's a familiar and comfortable mechanism for both parties: The seller provides pictures, descriptions, and specifications about the product he or she offers, and the buyer browses or searches through them, selects the product(s) he or she wants, and orders it or them. Catalogs are effective, cheap, and relatively simple to produce in either online or hard-copy form.

Here's an overview of what a catalog cluster looks like:

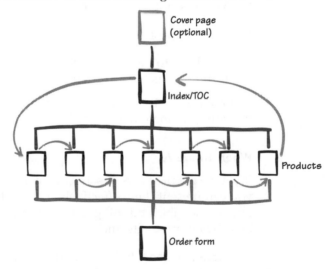

Catalogs are intended to create commerce, of course, and commerce on the Web is a relatively new and unproven thing. If you've gone so far as to buy this book and develop Web content, then you've probably already made the decision to at least try it. We say good for you, and don't forget to market the existence of your Web catalog heavily: Issue press releases, put it on your cards, letters, and other print material, include it in your telemarketing sales pitches, and talk it up by any other method you can imagine.

We can't do a full-scale business case here—there are whole books for that, and we list what we think are the best ones on page 615—but we know that putting your catalog on the Web does have some advantages over hard copy:

- You save trees and postage costs.

- You can continually update the catalog contents to reflect changes in pricing or specifications—and with the right systems, you can even do this automatically.

- You can accept orders and provide customer service online—cutting costs in both areas while keeping your electronic doors open 24 hours a day.

- Your users can't lose your catalog at the bottom of the bathroom reading pile.

There are also some big disadvantages to Webcasting your catalog:

- You may not reach your customers.

- You will probably reach your competitors.

- You have to deal with the security issues involved in taking and fulfilling electronic orders.

Our advice: Put up a basic catalog and see how it works for you—but don't use your printing budget to do it.

When to use it

If you've got products or services that somebody else on the Web wants, then you can present them effectively in a catalog structure. This includes the obvious tangible and soft goods from anoraks to software, as well as some less obvious products, such as:

- Access or consultations (think in terms of fund raisers, here).

- Demos and prototypes.

- Gift certificates.

- Publications and reprints.

- Service contracts.

Of course, it can work the other way, too: If you're a big enough buyer, you can prepare a catalog of things that you want, and let suppliers come to you. This works particularly well for government agencies and other organizations that do major purchasing through a bid process; there's no reason why you can't catalog your Requests for Bids online, too.

In fact, at least one organization has done just that: ABAG (the Association of Bay Area Governments) in California has a version of an online contracts catalog at:

`<http://www.abag.ca.gov/bayarea/commerce/ace/ace.html>`

BTW ...

For brevity's sake, we'll use the term *products* in this section to refer to all manner of catalog contents.

Since a catalog structure is primarily a series of product or service descriptions accessible through some form of index or topic listing, you can present almost anything within its format. Of course, there is some content for which it's not appropriate, such as:

- Hierarchical content that requires multiple levels.

- Scholarly, technical, or scientific content not conducive to the thumbnail-sketch treatment.

- Tutorials, procedures, and other sequence-based content.

How to build it

The structure of a catalog cluster is pretty straightforward: It follows the familiar index-thumbnail-order pattern of the glossy stuff that we're accustomed to finding choking our mailboxes.

The basic structure will typically look something like this:

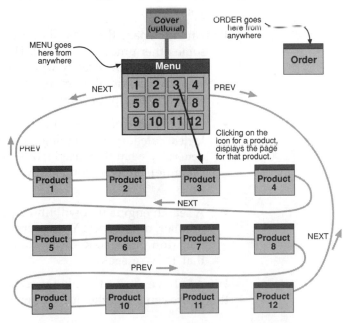

Here's the breakdown on the catalog cluster's components:

- **Cover page**—This is an optional introduction to your organization and its product line. The cover page is typically designed to maximize visual impact; it's also a good idea to use it to emphasize time-critical or featured products that you want to call to your users' attention.

  The cover page can be coded either as a table (if your users are thought to have capable browsers) or as a full-page image-map (if your users have sufficient bandwidth).

  Our catalog cluster on the CD-ROM does not include a cover page, but you can use the cover page from the newsletter/magazine cluster as a template if you wish.

- **Menu/Index/TOC**—Given the highly graphical content of most catalogs (not to mention those pesky bandwidth limitations), it's unlikely that most users will take the time to browse through your catalog page by page. To make your catalog effective (and your effort worthwhile), you must therefore include some form of organized access to the various categories and products it contains.

  You already know what your four choices are, but we'll cover them briefly anyway:

  - A menu page that shows thumbnail-sized images of your product line, arranged into some logical categories. This will be valuable for users who know what something looks like but don't know what you call it.

  - An index page that lists all products by name or part number (or some other unique identifier). This will be a blessing for your users when they know exactly what model or part they need, and don't want to wear out their mouse buttons scrolling through pages of product descriptions they're not interested in.

  - A TOC (table of contents) that lists all products according to some logical category or grouping. This works best for users who know generally what they need (software versus plumbing supplies, for example), but who don't know what products you offer along those lines.

  - A search engine that will find a product based on its name, part number, or category. Your users will like this one best, because then they don't have to know anything except the name of the thing that they're seeking.

  Want to have the best catalog you can? Provide all four mechanisms, so that users can select the one that works best for them.

- **Product pages**—Each product page supplies details about a single product. Include in here one or more pictures, a list of features and benefits, technical specifications, sample contents, a demonstration or prototype—essentially whatever content it takes to convince your users to buy the product.

  A well-designed product page will include buttons (backed by appropriate scripts) to select product factors, such as size, color, pattern, version, or options. These buttons allow your users to build a specification of the product they want to buy—and the scripts pass the specs along to the order form.

  All product pages are, of course, linked to the order form described below. There's also usually a default sequence through the product pages, just in case some users with a T1 connection and time on their hands want to page through your catalog. Depending on your product line, it can also be a good idea to include a `MAILTO` link that allows your users to request additional information about a specific product.

- **Order form page**—Here's where the housefly of commerce (escaping from the ointment, no doubt) hits the Web. Since a catalog cluster is designed to generate orders, you gotta have some place to take 'em. The order form page gathers the necessary product and payment information from your users—and product specifications from the various product page scripts—and processes it through a CGI script or some other means external to the order page.

  We won't go into the specifics of creating forms in this section: If this is new territory for you, see page 359.

Navigation

The navigation functions of the catalog are intended to drive users toward the order form. (Well, that is the whole point of a catalog, isn't it?) The mechanisms themselves aren't complex, however: Each product page in the cluster includes these buttons:

Cover   Jumps back to the cover page from anywhere in the cluster

Menu   Jumps back to the menu page from anywhere in the cluster

Next   Jumps to the next page in the default sequence through the catalog

Previous		Jumps to the previous page in the default sequence through the catalog
Order Form		Jumps to the order form page from any page in the cluster (including the cover and menu pages)

Pretty much every element on the cover and menu pages—whether graphic, headline, or text—is linked to the corresponding product page. Cross-references between related or complementary products ("Ordering shipping boxes? Stock up on tape and utility blades, too!") are expressed in text links incorporated into the product page content.

Sweat equity index

The linking structure in a catalog is fairly easy, so once you get the CGI scripts and order form up and running, you'll spend most of your time developing and updating product content. Since this product information is usually highly structured, a catalog cluster is a good candidate for automation, in which an independent application—usually a database of some sort—generates coded HTML files on the fly whenever you tell it to.

Anyway, we give the catalog cluster a sweat equity score of 4 (out of a possible 10).

Newsletter/magazine cluster

On the CD-ROM ...

meals
   newsmag
      cover.htm

The newsletter/magazine cluster—another of the more common structures in use on the Web today—is based on the tabloid model. For those of you who don't read (much less buy!) those magazines at the grocery check-out line, tabloids generally cover themselves with a series of catchy headlines (supported with out-of-context quotations and horrific photos), that lead to articles within. (And then again, maybe not.)

Here's an overview of what a newletter/magazine cluster looks like:

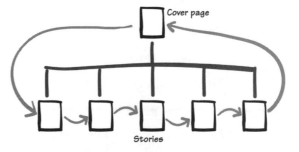

The online equivalent is the Web newsletter/magazine: you display a set of headlines with enticing hints of detail that are linked to more complete treatments of the topic.

When to use it

The news/mag (for short) structure is popular because it is both a familiar interface and an effective vehicle for various forms of media. Use this structure when you want to make information available about yourself, your organization, or your chosen issues or events. In short, it serves the same purpose as a newsletter, newspaper, press release, or news broadcast.

You can use a news/mag structure to present:

- **Your résumé or work experience** as a series of news stories. This is kind of cute, but it's also effective, because it allows you to represent yourself in terms of your accomplishments.

- **Your organization's activities and accomplishments**, in much the same way as the personal résumé described above. This is the same rationale behind most company newsletters that are printed on paper. On the Web, of course, you can do more with it in terms of media and linking structure.

- **A series of profiles of any subject**, from personnel to political issues. Let your customers know who they're talking to on the phone, and let your staff express themselves (within reason and good taste, of course!).

- **A collection of technical or conceptual white papers**. Pull those puppies out of the dusty reference library and jazz them up with an improved presentation and a focus on results. Think *Scientific American Enquirer*, and you'll get the picture.

You can present almost anything in news/mag format, but of course there is some content for which it's not appropriate:

- Tutorials, procedures, and other sequence-based content.

- Hierarchical content that requires multiple levels.

- Scholarly, technical, or scientific content that derives no benefit from a more casual presentation.

How to build it

The structure of a news/mag cluster is pretty straightforward: It follows the familiar headline-lead-article pattern that we're accustomed to receiving from our news media. It may have several layers of detail, and makes good use of hypertext linking to call in resources from outside the cluster itself. It does not necessarily have a defined sequence, although you can create an implied priority with visual emphasis and placement: Big, bold headlines in the top left corner will probably attract the most attention. You certainly can also include lateral links between topics as appropriate.

Technically, there's no limit to the number of stories you can include in each news/mag issue. For practical purposes, however, we recommend that you limit yourself to eight stories, max—and we think five is about the right number. The main limitation is in the size, legibility, and usability of your cover design.

The basic structure will typically look something like this:

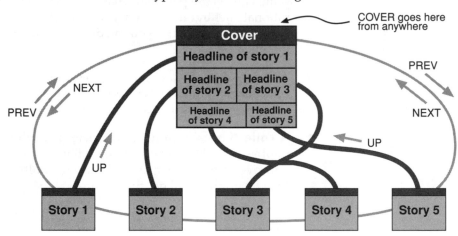

Here's the breakdown on the news/mag cluster's components:

- **Cover page**—Introduces the stories or articles in a beguiling manner using graphics, headlines, and text to entice your users into delving into the related content. To preserve the analogy to the print version, the cover page is typically laid out in columns of various shapes and sizes, just like a front page.

  The cover page can be coded as a table (if your users are thought to have capable browsers), as a full-page image-map (if your users have sufficient bandwidth), or a grouping of graphics as we have used in the template on the CD-ROM.

- **Articles/Stories**—Individual pages or other resources that describe and display narrative content related to a particular topic. Stories may be linked laterally to other related stories, and will often contain links to media objects that supplement the text. You'll typically define a default article-to-article sequence too, so that your users can page through the entire cluster one story at a time.

Navigation

There aren't too many places to go in a news/mag cluster, so the navigation elements are pretty basic. Each article page in the cluster sports these buttons:

Cover Jumps back to the cover page from anywhere in the cluster.

Next Jumps to the next article page in the default sequence. On the last article page, jumps to the cover page.

Previous Jumps to the previous article page in the default sequence. On the first article page, jumps to the cover page.

Pretty much every element on the cover page—whether graphic, headline, or text—is linked to the article page that holds the corresponding content. Cross-references between stories are expressed in text links incorporated into the article page content.

Sweat equity index

Thanks to its splashy beginnings and familiar structure, the newsletter/magazine cluster seems more like fun than work. The flat linking structure is a piece of cake, so we suggest you spend most of your time on developing an attractive design and compelling content. Our score for this cluster is a gentle 1.75 out of a possible 10 (most difficult).

How-to/procedure cluster

On the CD-ROM ...

meals
  howto
    how2menu.htm

The self-contained how-to or procedure cluster is one of the most finite and efficient Web structures around. It's very effective at presenting task-oriented content, and is one of the structures that benefits most from including nontext media such as video and animation. Clean and compelling, how-to clusters stand up very well on their own digital feet; but, they also can easily be linked into other, larger structures with no loss of clarity or context.

Here's an overview of what a how-to cluster looks like:

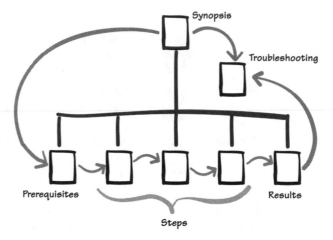

When to use it

The how-to cluster can be used to effectively deliver any set of fixed instructions. These instructions will probably be technical (such as software configuration tasks), mechanical (hardware or infrastructure maintenance), or procedural (filling out forms, and so on). The instructions don't have to be related to your core business or organizational charter, either; they can be marketing-oriented, administrative in nature, or even whimsical.

Some potential uses include:

- Publishing warranty claim procedures for your product dealers and customers.

- Providing instructions on how to use your organization's resources—for example, a task-based user's guide to a library's online services.

- Providing a form of online help to improve an offline process. For example, you could speed up registration for extension classes by showcasing the registration process on your campus Web site.

- Arguing a rhetorical point by presenting an opposing viewpoint as a how-to procedure that results in an undesirable outcome. For example, you could take issue with, say, your state's income tax level with a satirical procedure titled "How to Bankrupt All State Businesses." (This is a purely theoretical example, of course.)

Naturally, you don't want to use a how-to cluster for presenting conceptual information, or for exploring reference resources. In fact, that's probably the toughest thing about developing a how-to cluster; keeping the content tight and focused on the task at hand, and not adding content that's nice to know but not essential. Resist the temptation to provide background or reference information as best you can; when you have to succumb, add links to this information, and keep any actual background or reference content out of the procedure.

How to build it

The how-to structure is similar to a training lesson in that it begins with a synopsis, has a specific sequence and conclusion, and includes some form of testing or validation of learning at the end. The similarities end there, however; by being task based instead of conceptually based, the how-to cluster remains leaner and more straight-lined, with fewer side trips to related topics than the training lesson might take.

The typical how-to structure will look something like this:

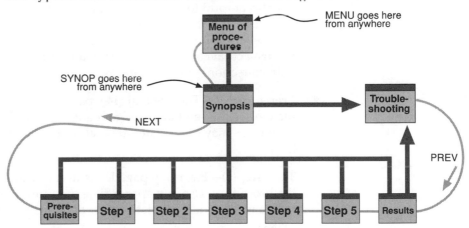

Here's how the components of a typical how-to structure are used:

- **Menu of procedures**—The menu is the entry point for all of the procedures developed for a particular topic or category. It may have a brief introduction on the general subject matter, and should summarize the content or intent of each procedure it lists.

   Note: If you have stitched your individual how-to clusters directly to various pages in a larger, umbrella structure, then you may not need this Menu.

- **Synopsis**—The synopsis page for each procedure provides an overview of the procedure and describes its objectives and prerequisites. The overview should be complete enough so that experienced users can perform the procedure without having to read further; for the less experienced, it serves to preview the procedure thoroughly. Every task step in the procedure is listed and summarized; each item in the task list contains a text link to the page for that task step.

   Depending on the length of your synopsis, you can include the procedure's objectives (expressed in terms of the desired outcome) and prerequisites (which can be anything from specific tools to skills to materials) on the synopsis page, or you can shift them to a separate page that follows the synopsis in the sequence. (Our template on the CD-ROM has a separate prerequisites page.)

   It's also helpful to include estimates of the length of time necessary to complete both the procedural review and the task itself. For example: This seven-step review will take you approximately 15 minutes; filling out the actual claim form will take an estimated 45 minutes, including data collection and calculations.

- **Prerequisites**—The prerequisites page begins the procedure by listing the tools, skills, and knowledge required to perform the procedure. If your users may need more preparatory information, provide those links here.

- **Task step(s)**—Each step page leads users through one task or phase of the procedure. Use any appropriate medium to explain or illustrate the task, and show how it relates to (or depends on) previous and following tasks.

- **Results**—The results page helps users evaluate their results by showing (or describing) the typical or desired outcome of the procedure. It includes a link to the troubleshooting page, in case users miss the target in some way.

Troubleshooting—This page helps users diagnose and correct problems or unexpected results. It usually contains a list of symptoms and their remedies; if a remedy represents another complete procedure, it may contain links to another how-to cluster. For example, you could present a troubleshooting page that includes inline links to how-to pages elsewhere in your Web site.

Navigation

Since you're building your how-to cluster with a specific sequence in mind, its navigation needs are fairly basic. Each page includes these buttons:

Menu Jumps back to the menu of procedures (if used).

Synopsis Jumps to the synopsis from anywhere within the procedure.

Next Jumps to the next page in the default sequence through the procedure.

Previous Jumps to the previous page in the default sequence through the procedure.

The synopsis page contains a list of all the steps necessary to complete the procedure; each step in the list contains a text link to the corresponding step page, so that your users can look up a specific step if needed.

Sweat equity index

The simple sequential structure of a how-to cluster makes it a breeze to develop and maintain (assuming, as always, that your actual content has already been created). To keep from losing the user, your structure must be simple and straightforward, anyway; given bandwidth limitations, you won't be tempted to go too crazy with interlinking content. We give the how-to a mere 2.5 rating out of a possible 10 in difficulty.

Online reference

On the CD-ROM ...

meals
   onlinref
      refmenu.htm

If you have a sizable body of information that's structured into lots of small segments—such as a programming command reference for a software product, for example, or a set of corporatewide personnel procedures—you can distribute this content very effectively in an online reference cluster. The online reference's highly segmented structure makes revisions fairly easy, and supports automated updates (that are typically generated by database applications) quite well.

Here's a high-level fly-by of this segmented structure:

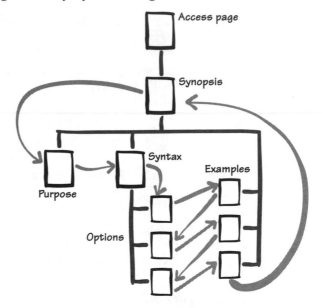

Whether your users are potential customers out there somewhere on the Internet, or co-workers visiting your in-house Web site, you can use the online reference structure to give them 7 x 24 access to the most current information available, using a very efficient structure that allows them to get in and get out with a minimum of browsing, searching, or otherwise mucking around.

When to use it

Use an online reference cluster to deliver a few levels of detail or explication on a wide scope of topics. If you have lots of short information segments—less than two pages' worth, let's say—on more than, oh, a half-dozen topics, then you can effectively use the online reference structure.

You can use an online reference structure to effectively present:

- Hardware or software documentation, particularly command or function references.

- Technical, operating, or procedural specifications.

- Operating or personnel procedural references.

- Structured FAQ-style references.

You can also use an online reference as an effective shell to allow your users to download resources in a variety of media. Even with limited bandwidth, your users can harvest a wealth of riches from your online gold mine. Within a reference structure, you can offer downloads of:

- Digital paper versions of research reports, presentations, and support materials.

- 3-D tours of related places and concepts.

- Platform-specific help files, such as Windows help.

- FrameViewer, WorldView, and other browseable online documents.

In short, don't let the limitations of the Web (in its current incarnation, anyway) hobble your own creative thinking. If it's digitized, you can move it—and the online reference structure offers you just the library structure you need.

You probably don't want to use an online reference cluster to deliver sequential or structurally shallow information; this is not the place for electronic billboards, roadsigns, or long-winded training sessions.

How to build it

An online reference cluster is essentially a specialized form of a hierarchical structure; unlike the more classic configurations, however, it tends to be broader and shallower. Think of an online help system, such as OS/2's Help Manager, as an example: It features a series of short, lightly layered topics, typically accessed through either a table or an index of topics. With an online reference, speed is of the essence, so the flatter and broader the structure, the better.

Let's say that you want to create an online reference of the standard programming commands used by your firm's service technicians to configure equipment installed in the field. (Thereby replacing a van full of manuals with one laptop computer—a startling concept in some quarters.) Your online reference cluster would take something akin to the following form:

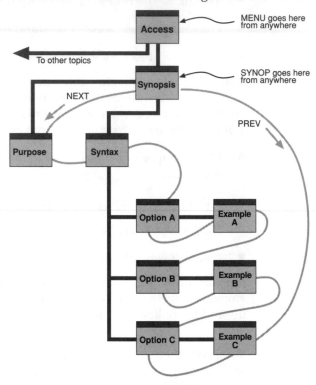

And here's the key to the diagram components:

- **Access page**—This serves as your user's entry point to your online reference. It can be a standard table of contents, an alphabetical index to topics, a listing of error codes generated by the equipment, or simply a search field that searches the topic table for the user. Its purpose is to allow your field tech to select and proceed directly to his or her topic of choice, without having to tunnel down through layers of information.

- **Synopsis page** —The synopsis page provides an overview of the command or feature. For the novice it is a preview of more detailed information. For the expert it is a quick reference. It provides jumps to more detailed information.

- **Purpose page**—The purpose page answers the question, "Why use this item?" It tells the reader what the command or feature can do and when to use it.

- **Syntax page**—The syntax page shows the correct format and variations of the command or statement. It provides more detail than the synopsis page. It includes links to even more detailed explanations of individual options or parameters.

- **Option page**—The option page explains one option or parameter in great detail. It tells what values the user can specify for this option and what results to expect. The option page is linked to an example page that shows the option in use.

- **Example page**—The example page shows one option in action. It is linked to the page for the option used in the example.

Navigation

Since the essential navigation for the online reference cluster is vertical, a basic navigation palette will suffice. Reference pages include the following buttons:

Menu Jumps back to the access page from anywhere in the cluster.

Synopsis Jumps back to the synopsis page of the current topic from anywhere in the cluster.

Next Jumps to the next page in the default sequence through the cluster. For example, when your user is on the syntax page, the Next link jumps to option A; or, if the user is on example B, the Next link jumps to option C.

Previous Jumps to the previous page in the default sequence through the cluster. For example, when your user is on the syntax page, the Previous link jumps to the purpose page; or, if the user is on example B, the Previous link jumps to option B.

Links to navigate down the structure—proceeding from the synopsis to the syntax, options, and examples for a particular topic—are incorporated into the Web page content with text or graphic links.

Sweat equity index

How tough is it to develop and maintain this online reference sequence? Given its broad, shallow structure, we think this is one of the easiest: We rated it at a mere 3.5 in difficulty (10 is the toughest). The real struggle will be in wrestling the mass of your reference information—which, by its nature, is often somewhat voluminous—into submission so you can stuff it into your structural container.

Training lesson

On the CD-ROM ...

meals
   training
      lssnmenu.htm

So, can you think of uses for an electronic training network that provides (essentially) free distribution, on demand, in real time, to a global audience of public or internal users? (Hmmmmm—is this a trick question?)

A training lesson cluster can provide your Web audience with relatively painless access to quick lessons on topics of importance to you. Think of it as a series of electronic flash cards offering your users brief lessons on discrete topics or tasks.

We can assume that your training lesson will look something like this:

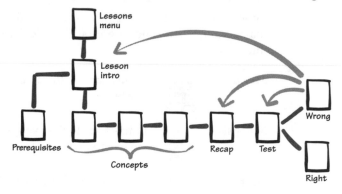

When to use it

Due primarily to technical and bandwidth limitations, the Web is not ideal for delivering detailed training; computer-based training resources on a desktop or LAN offer more options, more control, and better response time.

You certainly can and should use your Web pages to offer basic training or brief refresher courses, however. Remember the Internet's share-and-share-alike perspective; it's a good thing to offer pro bono training in your area of technology or expertise—particularly when it's within the context (and within link's reach) of your products, services, or people that relate to that technology or subject. No matter what business you're in or what cause you support, it's in your best interests to educate your users (and good for your karma, too).

You can also overcome the Web's bandwidth limitations by using your training cluster as a front end to a wide range of training support materials, from take-home lessons (in the wordprocessing format of your choice) to downloadable training modules written in Authorware, Quest, IconAuthor, Toolbook, or some other CBT format. Keep in mind that you can both distribute training (in downloadable form) and deliver training (in real time)—and that both mechanisms have a time and a place.

Some potential uses include:

● A series of earth science lessons (à la "Dr. Science"), offered as a public service by an environmental action group.

● Procedures for filling out complicated and invasive forms, made available by a friendly government bureaucracy.

● Background lessons on video digitizing concepts and terminology, published online by a high-end monitor manufacturer.

● A printer manufacturer could link out from its online product catalog to a short, cogent technical discussion about printer drivers and their role in successful output (not to mention their impact on the language used by product developers during beta tests).

How to build it

The training lesson is essentially a merging of sequence and hierarchical clusters; it's really more of a difference in application than in actual structure. Think of a training cluster as a structure that provides hierarchical access to a series of sequential topic chains. (Or, if you prefer, as an electronic workbook with a table of contents and a series of lessons, each of which you go through in sequence.)

The generic training structure will look something like this:

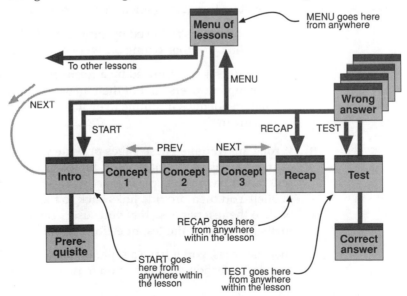

Here's the blow by blow on the components of the previous diagram:

- **Menu of lessons** —The menu is the entry point for all of the lessons. It may have a brief introduction on the general subject matter, and should summarize the content or intent of each lesson it lists.

- **Lesson intro** —The introduction page for each lesson describes the objectives and prerequisites for that lesson. On this page you'll list the concepts, skills, or knowledge that your users will gain from completing the lesson; be sure to include lesson length or anticipated completion time.

- **Prerequisites**—The prerequisites page lists the skills and knowledge necessary for the particular lesson with clarity and brevity.

- **Concept**(s) —Each concept page teaches one main idea of the larger lesson. Use any appropriate medium to explain or illustrate the idea, and show how it relates to previous or following ideas.

- **Recap** —This page summarizes the main lesson and calls out the important points covered on the separate concept pages. This page is included to reinforce your users' learning and give them a final overview of the lesson before testing.

- **Test**—The test page gives your users the opportunity to demonstrate their mastery of the concepts and details taught in the lesson. The actual testing mechanisms can consist of:

  - Test questions followed by text menus or bullet lists where choices link to either wrong answers or correct answers.

  - Test questions followed by simple multiple-choice radio buttons that link to either wrong answers or correct answers.

  - Test questions followed by a forms interface that accepts input. When your users submit their answers, the form calls an independent CGI routine to evaluate the results and respond accordingly.

- **Wrong answer**(s)—These pages provide your users with a second chance to master the material. If linked to a specific wrong answer, a reiteration page can explain exactly why the answer is wrong. (Be gentle!) You then provide links back to the original concept page or back to the test page, so that your users can decide whether to study further or answer the test question again.

  In some cases, you'll have a separate page for each wrong answer to each test question. In others, you may want to link instead to a generic "wrong answer, buddy" page that simply lets your users return to the concept page applicable to that question.

- **Correct answers**—These pages provide positive feedback to your users, briefly congratulating them on selecting or entering the correct answer. You'll probably want to link back to the test page at the end of this page, so that your users can forge ahead with their lesson.

  In some cases, you'll have a separate page for each right answer. In others, you may want to link instead to a generic "way to go, pal" page that simply lets your users return to the test page to continue with testing.

Navigation

The hop-and-skip linking required to make the testing mechanism work gives the training cluster some unique navigation needs. Each lesson page comes equipped with these buttons:

Menu Jumps back to the lesson menu page from anywhere in the cluster. For serious training, you may want to remove this button from the concept and test pages, so that your users have to completely "pass" the current lesson before they can select another one.

Start Jumps to the lesson intro from anywhere within the lesson

Next Jumps to the next page within the lesson.

Previous Jumps to the previous page within the lesson.

Recap Jumps directly to the recap (summary) page from anywhere within the lesson.

Test Jumps to the test page from anywhere within the lesson.

Links to navigate through the test-reward-reiteration loop are provided in the content of those pages, using text or graphic links.

Web chef hint

As a general rule you should probably determine your testing mechanism first, and then plan your cluster structure to support that mechanism.

Sweat equity index

Assuming you have mastery and ownership of its content, the concepts and specific messages of a training lesson cluster are not that hard to develop and maintain: The testing-feedback loops require a bit more effort, and will probably require some CGI development to be really effective.

We give it a slightly higher-than-average rating of 6.5 on the 10-point sweat equity scale.

In Closing . . .

At this point, you've probably had your fill of structures and clusters and other words difficult to pronounce when you're tired. Congratulations on sticking with it; this was not as glamorous or as fun a chapter as, say, "Nutrition," but we think it's essential to the success of your Web site as a whole.

The key thing to remember is that you have to strike a balance between what you want and what your users want—then create the Web environment and content that supports that balance. Flashy and cool isn't really enough for most of us; we have to offer some dull but pragmatic benefits through our Web pages, in order to make our effort worth it.

Here's a few last-minute reminders of all we've been through:

- **If in doubt, keep it simple**. In fact, keep it as simple as you can, anyway.

- **Use the templates and our attempts herein at clarity to your own advantage**, and don't hesitate to mold them to your own needs; we're offering experience and knowhow here, not omniscience or clairvoyance.

- **Know what you want**, and design toward it.

- **Make your links and structure count**; be aware that the whole of your Web presence is greater than the sum of its parts.

- **Give your users value**, content, and feedback.

CORDON BLEU

Web publishing on a corborate scale

Once people begin understanding the capabilities of the Web, they begin considering how it might be put to use in larger, industrial-strength settings. Inevitably, this leads to concerns about scaling up in size. How can we make authoring easier? What do we do about all the current information that we have? Should we use public-domain tools or should we buy commercial products? Which commercial products are best?

Despite what the vendors will tell you and sell you, there is no easy answer. Two factors tell us so:

- The tools are in transition.

- The Web is in transition.

This chapter will not give pat answers. It will provide a framework to help you think about your own situation. With such a framework, you can better sort through the barrage of rapidly changing information.

WHAT ARE YOU DOING?

We sometimes overlook the most obvious questions. One of the most obvious questions is, "What are we trying to accomplish here?" A clear answer to that question goes a long way toward deciding the best methods and tools for your project.

Let's assume that you are trying to apply the Web within a company that produces a product. Forget for the moment that we are talking about the Web, and just consider how information is created and distributed in such a company. This perspective shows you the relationship between what you want to do and what else is going on in your company. This way you won't put too much emphasis on the one goal that you have in mind at the cost of other things you might want to do later. Also, it might bring to mind uses that you hadn't considered.

The following generic model shows how information is created and distributed, particularly in technology-based companies:

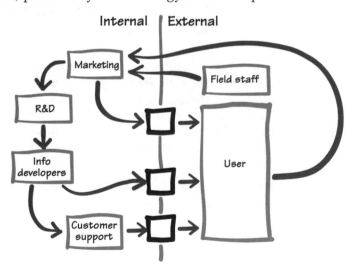

In this illustration, the arrows show the cyclical flow of information. Unless it is a new company that has not yet shipped a product, there is no starting point. So, let's dive in at an arbitrary point and follow the flow through a complete cycle.

- Marketing receives information from external sources and generates requirements. Marketing also begins developing collateral material to support the sales of the product.

- Research and Development (R&D) responds by specifying the implementation of the next product.

- Information developers (usually writers and trainers) prepare manuals, online documentation, training materials, and so forth.

- Customer support responds to customer inquiries

- The user requests corrections and enhancements to the product, and around we go again.

The three boxes on the line between external and internal activities represent the three areas where companies are using the Web to deliver information to their customers:

- Marketing—Corporate Web site, largely marketing communications.

- Info developers—Web site to deliver user documentation and training.

- Customer support—Web site to deliver product problem work-arounds, frequently asked questions, unique applications of the product.

Beyond these areas, companies are sprouting internal Webs for distribution of information, both in support of product development and in simply running the company. In turn, customer companies are also developing Web sites, mirroring the vendor company. In this context, information actually flows and, when consciously planned, can flow smoothly.

Delivering marketing communications

The box connected to the marketing area is the standard company Web site. It is what you will likely see when you string together "HTTP//www." to a company's domain name (e.g., apple.com, hp.com, ibm.com). Included at the site are things such as company location (including maps), corporate backgrounds, product data sheets, job openings, and press releases. Marketing communications organizations employ company Web sites as delivery vehicles that complement their other forms of delivery, such as mailers and other materials.

The biggest concerns in this type of Web site are common to almost anyone using a new information delivery vehicle:

- Presentation of company image.

- Converting existing materials.

- Effect on process of authoring.

The implications for a company Web site add their own unique spin. Company image becomes very important. Frequently, this is manifested in the balance between the desire for a big graphical splash and what current communications bandwidth can handle. Simply put, it would be nice to have a full-screen graphical image, but users viewing it through a 14.4 modem might lose patience waiting for the image to display.

The biggest challenge in converting existing marketing materials is usually layout-dependent materials, such as data sheets. Part of the problem is getting the content at all because this type of material is frequently authored using a page layout tool with a closed, proprietary file format.

Conversion usually requires extracting the text in some way and converting the images to GIF format. You may have to cut-and-paste from one window to another on your computer. If you don't have access to the electronic source files, you may have to scan in printed data sheets and run an optical character recognition (OCR) program on it.

HTML, alas, provides only limited control over the format of the displayed page. If you need more precise control you can create two versions of the document: one as a Web page and the other in a page-layout format. On the Web page you can include a link to download the page-layout format from an FTP site (see page 295).

For the page-layout version you'll need to determine the following:

- File format (e.g., Microsoft Word, RTF, PostScript, Adobe PDF).

- Platforms (e.g., UNIX, Mac, PC).

- Whether to compress and, if so, which format to use (e.g., tar, zip, hqx).

While converting existing documents can be time consuming, once a company Web site is established, ongoing maintenance is less complicated than for other sources of information. Polished data sheets are not produced often enough to warrant elaborate authoring systems. Just make sure that when new data sheets and other materials are authored, the text and graphics are available in electronic form for conversion.

Generally speaking, press releases, announcements, new job listings, and other simple materials can be converted using translators. (In this chapter the term *translator* means software that converts information from one file format to another, rather than a person who converts English into French or Chinese. In this field, alas, the term has two meanings.)

Translators minimize the disruption to authors and existing processes. People in marketing will appreciate your efforts to keep things simple for them, which increases the chances that they will add new Web site content on a regular basis.

The conversion approach imposes two requirements on authors: They must

- Use tagging elements, such as styles, consistently.

- Run a translator after the document is written.

Tagging elements are like the styles in Microsoft Word and the tags in FrameMaker. You must use them consistently and thoroughly. Translators depend on style tags to decide what HTML elements to wrap around pieces of text. That means you must restrict yourself to the styles the translator recognizes and you must do all formatting via styles. No using tabs and carriage returns to get things to look right.

Translators may be separate programs that read in a wordprocessing file and spit out an HTML-coded text file. Increasingly they are "Save as HTML" commands built into wordprocessing and page-layout programs.

The Marketing department will also need to know how to move files to the server that houses the Web site and how to set the correct permissions for them. Transfer usually requires a datacommunications or FTP program, such as Fetch on the Macintosh or WinFTP on the PC. Putting files in the correct directories and setting permissions typically require a handful of UNIX commands (see page 97).

After the conversion of existing material has been accomplished, unobtrusive processes put in place, and the fear of distinctly unfriendly UNIX commands overcome, company Web pages become just another accepted vehicle for marketing the company and its products.

Customer-support Web sites

If you've ever worked as a hotline-support technician, or if you've ever known anyone who has, you know that these people need help. The phones ring incessantly. Questions ranging from the mundane to the mind bending stream through unendingly. Burnout is high, and anything that can help lighten the load is welcomed. It's easy to see why customer-support organizations love anything that resembles an electronic bulletin board for answering customers' questions. Web sites can do this well.

This type of Web site needs:

- *Live* information.

- Information searches.

- Controlled access.

Direct access for customers

Customer-support organizations began using bulletin boards so customers could serve themselves. Instead of calling the hotline and having a customer-support person query the information base, now customers could get the information directly.

Customers like the direct access, too. If you've ever been put on hold or needed an answer at an hour that didn't correspond with the hotline's business hours, you understand the appeal of this self-service approach.

While this is the general idea, the reality is that Web implementations vary as to the amount of direct access afforded customers.

On one end of the spectrum, there really is no direct access to the actual information base. In this case, database reports are generated in electronic form and then HTML tags added. What is actually published is a snapshot of the database's contents. Thus the reports must be published at regular intervals.

Companies usually start with this kind of system, since it requires only the information systems already in place. For example, while a software company with a bug-tracking system may want to provide their customers access to information about bugs, they do not want to give them direct access to the tracking system. Bug-tracking systems are typically for use *within* the company and their content requires some screening.

Because your goal is to provide a timely snapshot of information, translators are acceptable for this type of publishing. In a sense it is no different from creating a printed book. While the contents can be updated more frequently and at less expense, the information provided is essentially static.

As we move along the spectrum toward direct access, we increase the frequency at which the Web pages are updated. Automating the process so that Web pages are updated daily will meet most needs. The other end of the spectrum is direct access to database contents. To use some computer jargon, this is access to *live* information with *real-time* access. That is, if information is added to the database, the next request for information will display that new content immediately. This is accomplished through the Common Gateway Interface (CGI) and programs or scripts that make use of

CGI. A CGI script can be triggered by your user simply visiting your Web page or by clicking on a link or button on that page.

For example, if it is important that customers know how much inventory of a particular item is available, a CGI program can search the inventory database, request a report, automatically add HTML tags, and then display the results in the browser. Here's a diagram to illustrate what we mean.

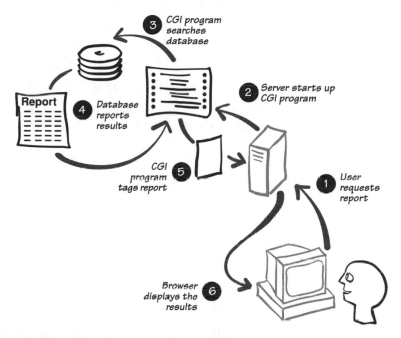

Searching for information

Whether the Web site provides snapshots or live information, some sort of search mechanism is needed. Any search engine–database combination can be constructed, but it will usually require some programming and UNIX skills.

The most common is the Wide Area Information Server (WAIS), which allows you to set up searches across the contents of the Web site—that is, you don't have to have a formal database because the pages themselves are the source for information. Several implementations are available, ranging from public-domain versions to commercial applications.

The basic principles are similar to search engines in general. An index is derived from the contents. When your user types entries on a fill-in-the-blanks form and submits a request for a search, the search engine consults the index. The process to create the index can take quite some time to run and is usually automated as an off-hours job, which in UNIX is referred to as a *crontab job* (the UNIX command that sets up the process).

Access control

Often you want to restrict access to information. For example, you may want to limit access to customer-support Web pages to those users who have purchased a maintenance agreement.

Two levels of access control can be used. The simplest is the UNIX file directory *user authentication* described in NCSA's Mosaic User Authentication Tutorial at the following URL:

```
http://wintermute.ncsa.uiuc.edu:8080/auth-tutorial/tutorial.html
```

You might recognize this level of access control. It's usually the kind behind the dialog boxes that pop up and ask you for your name and a password.

This low level of access control is acceptable because, under the terms of the maintenance policy, attempting to break in is illegal. Customer companies have too much to lose by knowingly doing something illegal.

A tighter level of security can be achieved by setting up what's called a "firewall." To do this, a company segregates a network (including, perhaps, a Web server), eliminating contact with other networks within and without the company. To gain access to this network requires a password and is normally restricted to certain company personnel. This is obviously not the approach to use if you are going to allow public access to the Web server; doing so would let people who are not employees into the inner sanctum. An example of a more appropriate use for this tighter level of security is distributing company-sensitive information to the field sales force.

Making user documentation available

More and more organizations are using the Web to distribute their owner's manuals, reference guides, tutorials, and other forms of user documentation. Tools and techniques used for these endeavors run the gamut from simple Save-as-HTML translators to elaborate automated production methodologies. If you just need a way to get existing manuals to users, then translating may do the job. But, if you want to go after bigger enterprise-sized informational development and delivery problems, translators alone lack the firepower you need.

Where translators don't work

Translators can help you deliver information until you develop a bigger, better solution—but translators have their limits. They merely buttress the existing book-printing model.

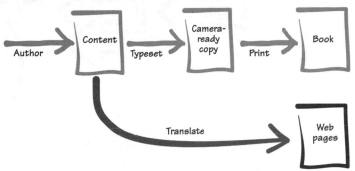

That is, translating the source document and making it available on the Web is like typesetting and printing. In industry, this is sometimes called a *back-end* process, as opposed to something built into the main process.

Although the user documentation may look different, the authoring processes are pretty much the same—that is both the blessing and the curse of translators. Their blessing is that they do not disrupt existing workflows. Their curse is that they discourage developing new workflows more suited to electronic media.

So, why would you need a new workflow? Perhaps you want to design *true online information*, not just *books dumped online*. This means breaking the content into smaller chunks, making the information more modular and easier to access.

For small Web sites created and maintained by a single author, this isn't a problem. When you get into larger sites, with more than one author, there are a lot of little pieces to track. Nasty things can happen if you don't use formal methods that employ real tracking tools.

So, that's why programmers do that

When information is designed for online display and distribution, it's a good idea to emulate the way programmers develop computer software. It makes sense when you think about it. Authoring online information is more like programming than writing. The thing that you're creating is honest-to-gosh software. And when you come right down to it, there must have been a reason why programmers came up with their way of doing things—no doubt based on experiences, some of them probably bad enough to make programmers want to do something better.

The following flowchart is a simple model for creating software:

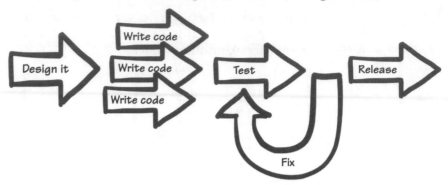

What the flowchart doesn't show are all the different people scurrying back and forth (some completing their assignments on time while others are late), last-minute design changes, not enough time for testing, and one wild postrelease party. In other words, instead of an orderly march, it's more like a herd heading roughly east. This is the basis for the joke applied to programmers and technical writers: Managing them is like herding cats.

It is this messiness that causes problems, and that's where tools come in. They help you follow the right steps by making it easier to do so. But more on that when we get into tools.

When you try to do more

Okay, so far we've seen that the Web can be used to

- Deliver marketing communications.
- Serve as a bulletin board for customer support.
- Deliver user documentation.

<EDITORIAL> When you see how much of the work in companies is about information flow, you gotta wonder why they don't spend more thought, time, and money on the plumbing? </EDITORIAL>

But this is a frozen picture of things. Remember that information *moves* and moves in a big, roughly circular, flow. Information is created at one spot and used at another. If the information moves along smoothly, then people whose work it is to receive information—and create more information out of it—are efficient, productive, and happy. If the pipes are clogged, then not-so-good things happen.

Information clogging in high-tech

There is a common problem in high-tech companies churning out products at a torrid pace, trying to hit those market windows of opportunity that the sales department guarantees will help them make their quotas. Marketing writes specifications, which Engineering uses to write other specifications, which in turn are used by others such as Quality Assurance, Training, Technical Publications, and Customer Support. Each depends on the supplier of information upstream. If that information supplier doesn't provide information that meets the needs of the information consumer, time is wasted and mistakes made.

For years, companies solved the problem by adding more information creators. Cost-saving measures (downsizing, rightsizing, dumbsizing) quickly put an end to throwing bodies at the problem, reducing information output. Companies then discovered that putting out less information increased customer-support problems and decreased customer satisfaction. Costs were not reduced, just delayed and shifted from one department to another.

When companies provided better ways for their customers to get information, a curious thing happened: After a period of satisfaction, the customers demanded even more.

Getting help from information databases

Companies are now coming around to looking broadly at the way the information gets created and distributed. They are looking at their information as one big pool, instead of a lot of individual documents. This leads them to think about information databases. One model looks like this:

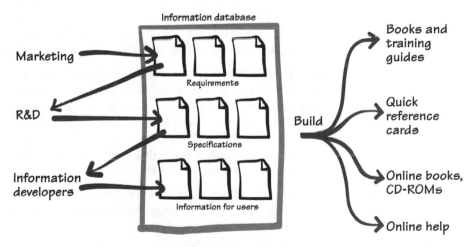

This model shows only one database as an illustration. Sometimes it makes sense for different areas to have their own databases.

In this model, authors create the content and then put it in an information database. Once there, the content is available for others to use. The system includes safeguards so owners of the individual pieces of content are the only ones who can make changes although others can read them. For example, a marketing analyst may list requirements for a new product. An engineer in R&D may use these requirements when specifying the product. The technical writer writing the user's guide for the product may start by consulting the engineer's specification.

Database tools can help to author a complex Web site—or any online delivery system. Authors can check information in and out of the database. This is a big help on a large Web site created and maintained by a continually changing cast of characters.

However, setting up large, formal databases can be expensive and getting all the participants synchronized can be such an effort that sometimes it doesn't seem worth the aggravation. So, instead, companies are looking for other ways to get some of the benefits of a database. Interestingly enough, this is another area where the Web has come into use.

Internal Webs as alternatives to databases

Companies are experiencing explosive growth on their internal Webs. The reason is that it is pretty simple and inexpensive—like free—to get a Web server running. These internal Webs are usually several times larger than the ones the companies make available to the public.

How simple can it be? Imagine that your company has Macintoshes hooked up to your UNIX network. To get a Web server running, you get a copy of MacHTTP in the public domain, put it on one of the Macs, and double-click on the icon. That's it. If your company also has PCs on the network, you will suddenly have the ability to share information across all three platforms.

In this environment, just about anybody can become an information provider. No need to put proposals together and give presentations to the bigwigs. If you're in Engineering, and you think it's a good idea to make your specifications available, you just do it. If you're a technical writer who thinks trainers might benefit from the user guide you're writing, you figure out how to use one of the public-domain translators, HTMLize the thing, and put it on the internal Web.

There are problems with this freewheeling approach, though. If you want anything that even resembles standards, you'll need to have meaningful dialogs with lots of people.

Then there's a question about where your content goes. For example, if you're an engineer and you have made a change to your specification, it's a good bet that a trainer or technical writer has content from the previous version somewhere.

One of the subtle problems with Web publishing is something called *source control*. If you author with a word processor and use a translator to make the HTML version, you need to decide which is the *source file*—the file that you'll make changes to. It's really tempting to go into the HTML file and make changes. But, if you do that, you will lose all those changes if later you rewrite the wordprocessor version, do another translation, and then replace the HTML file that you edited earlier. It's a common error when you have even one overworked author. It's guaranteed to happen when two people work on the same set of files.

None of this should stop you from using the Web in this way. The benefits are worth the risks. You just need to be careful and compensate by using a little *humanware*. For example, if you're an engineer, each time you change a specification, call or send e-mail to those who rely on your specs. Or, if you're a marketeer responsible for white papers on the external Web site, you take a sacred oath to make all changes to the Microsoft Word source file that is kept on a colleague's Mac, not to your private copy and not to the HTML version derived from the source file.

Getting even more out of the system

On the bleeding edge is an approach that takes the information database one step farther. Instead of putting *whole* chapters and Web pages into the database, the pieces are broken down, down, down into even smaller, subdocument chunks. As the following illustration shows, the pieces then can be reassembled in different ways through *builds* to construct books, quick reference cards, Web pages, and other information delivery vehicles.

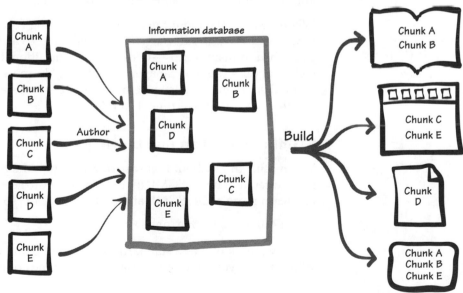

With this scheme, you'd produce Web pages by using a fill-in-the-blanks template. For example, if we were to divide this book's Chapter 4 into smaller chunks for a database, we'd have a page that would have the following structure:

We could then do a build from the database that assembles the pieces as shown to make a printed book. We could also make a little reference booklet of just the page name and the HTML code. With some programming help, we could make an online help system or Web site with each chunk as a separate screen.

This beats making copies for each document because you don't have to keep track of which documents make use of which pieces. One piece is updated, and all documents are automatically updated during the build.

When people talk about the benefits of creating content this way, they use terms such as *reuse* and *retargeting*. A single piece can be authored once and published in many forms—without much additional effort. Where once a technical publications manager would say, "I can deliver a reference manual *or* an online help system with my current staff," now they say, "With a wee bit of overtime, I can do both."

SGML: More than just tagging

When folks think about this way of authoring, the technology that pops up more often that not is SGML (Standard Generalized Markup Language). You can learn more about SGML at the *SGML Open* Web site:

```
http://www.sgmlopen.org
```

For now, think of it as a standard for describing and tagging information. With SGML, you make clear exactly what types of information are included in your various documents. Without such clarity, you end up writing random pieces into your database—garbage in, garbage out.

While some describe HTML as a subset of SGML, SGML purists will disagree. They'll tell you that HTML tags have a similar appearance, but they do not support *structure*, at least not to the extent that SGML does. And that's the real point of doing SGML.

Using SGML is a BIG deal. It requires an investment in effort that will not see returns for a few years. It is expensive and requires a change in the perspective of information developers.

But the potential benefits, especially across departments and company-wide enterprises, are great. This explains why virtually all the information technology vendors pay some sort of homage to SGML in their product lines.

You don't have to go whole hog into SGML just yet. As with informational databases, you can use Web technology to test the waters. You can build little SGML-like prototypes using the Web and experiment in structure and reuse. Scale these experiments up slowly until you can make a business case for SGML with your company's decision makers.

Position to be portable, be portable to be in position

Another potential benefit of SGML—or even moving in the direction of SGML—is as an insurance policy. By following a true ISO standard such as SGML, you make your information portable. That is, if you need to migrate to other authoring tools or to the next generation of whizbang technology, all the structuring and preparation work that you will have done will not be wasted. Somebody will offer an inexpensive translator from SGML to the new technology. In other words, if you make your information portable, you will be in a better position to respond to changing technology.

POSITIONING OF THE VENDORS' TOOLS

Now we finally get to how to look at the vendors' tools. Whew. We've presented a lot of technical information up to this point. But this background is needed because without it, you're looking at the tools like the proverbial blind men and the elephant. Your point of view when grabbing a tail is a lot different than when you're grabbing a trunk. And there's a big difference in what you choose if you're doing just a small Web site by yourself, or if you're setting up an enterprise-wide information database.

The following drawing shows where various tools can help.

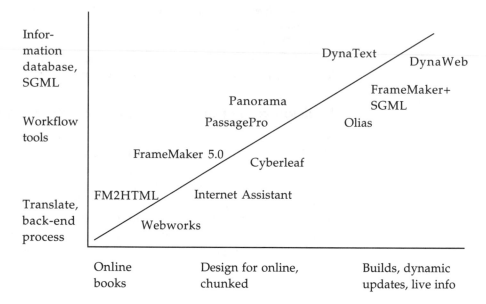

The vertical axis shows the progression in technology, and the horizontal axis shows increasingly ambitious things that you can try.

The tools listed are a mix of authoring, delivery, and management tools. It is far from being a complete list. These are just examples that illustrate where tools can help out in the information development and delivery schema you're putting together.

Authoring tools, including translators, are the things that you use to create the documents. *Delivery tools* are viewers, which include Web browsers and, for the purposes of this model, search engines and information servers.

Management tools are database and workflow tools that help keep track of where a document is in its development process.

You can use this model in different ways. Use it to go window shopping—you don't know what it is that you want to get, but you just want to look around and learn. Use it to prepare a grocery list, then go shopping for the items on that list.

Working with the tool vendors

When you talk to vendors about their products, the model will help you understand their tools. By asking questions about their line of products, you can get a sense of how they define their market. You'll see whether they focus on one area or if they cover a range. If they focus on one area, such as translators or SGML authoring, then you know that you'll need to think about integrating their tools with those from other vendors, especially if you're "trying to get more out of the system."

If the vendor covers a range of areas, you can ask questions to see how well integrated the tools are. Often, technology vendors grow their product lines through partnerships and acquisitions. If they don't do a good job of integrating the tools, or if you buy the tools too early—when they're still trying to figure out what to do—the burden of integration will be on you.

To learn more about the product offerings, you can start by visiting the vendors' Web sites. Here's a list for starters.

ArborText	`http://www.arbortext.com`
Electronic Book Technologies	`http://www.ebt.com`
Frame Technology	`http://www.frame.com`
HaL Computer Systems	`http://www.hal.com`
Interleaf	`http://www.ileaf.com`
Microsoft	`http://www.microsoft.com`
SoftQuad	`http://www.sq.com`

What's interesting about some of these sites is that they are examples of their own products. The Electronic Book Technologies site is an example of their DynaWeb product. Other products are listed in "The Work Tools Shopping List" in Resources for the Web Chef.

Developing your own direction

You can use this model for another purpose as well. Instead of using it as a way to catalog tools, you can use it to clarify what you want to do.

For example, suppose you don't want to dive into SGML and information databases right away, but set them as long-term goals. You can use our model to plot a path to get there. That path will include short-term solutions, such as translators and using Web servers as information databases.

WHERE'S THIS HEADED?

Anyone who's decided to put up a Web site must wonder at least once along the way what the next big development is going to be. How primitive is this Web stuff going to look when the next big thing does arrive? Such thoughts tempt us to hold back a little on the Web investments of time and money, just so we don't stick our neck out too far. And so go the little dialogs in your head, bouncing back and forth between "Better safe than sorry" and "Nothing ventured, nothing gained."

Electronic publishing is changing faster than anyone can hope to keep on top of. But if you pull back a bit, the perspective makes it feel less like a white-water rafting trip without paddles.

Web itself is a clue

If we remember our own first experiences with the Web, a lot of the buzz came from two things that we experienced:

- Flying across the globe with the greatest of ease, not knowing that we did, and getting excited when we realized that we had.

- Creating a Web page and watching it displayed in a browser.

These are direct examples of some threads going on in information technology and computing in general, and we can thank the Web for bringing it home—literally.

At the simplest level, the big changes are about making information easier to share and making computers easier to use. One phrase for these trends is *location transparency*. That is, the users of the information don't have to know about all the ugly stuff going on underneath. It just happens. Part of the trend toward making computers easier to use is letting end users create their own systems. That is, instead of having to be a programmer, all you'll need are wordprocessing-level skills.

What are some of the names?

Let's have a look at some of the emerging trends and technologies that may lie in our future.

OLE and Publish and Subscribe

The beginnings of these trends—and some catchy and not-so-catchy naming—can be seen in the early part of the 1990s with Microsoft's OLE (Object Linking and Embedding) and Apple's Publish and Subscribe. There are differences between the two, but the general idea is to be able to have a piece of one document stuck in another document. It's better than copy-and-paste because the embedded or subscribed piece is connected to the original file. That way, you don't have to worry about someone using an out-of-date version of something that you created. Changes to the original are reflected in the copy.

They're similar to a Web hypertext link because the link, at least in the case of Publish and Subscribe, can go across a network. Here's a picture comparing the two.

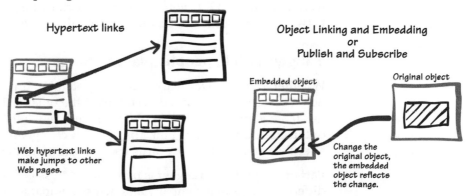

Hypertext links

Web hypertext links make jumps to other Web pages.

Object Linking and Embedding
or
Publish and Subscribe

Embedded object

Original object

Change the original object, the embedded object reflects the change.

You must admit, the idea of OLE and Publish and Subscribe is better than hypertext links. Instead of a jump to another location, you could actually construct a *virtual* view of a document made up of pieces from one or more other documents. The pieces don't have to be just text; they can be graphics and pieces of spreadsheets. Ah, to be able to do something like this across the Internet.

OpenDoc

The competition for OLE is OpenDoc, which is supported by a consortium that includes Apple, IBM, Novell, Adobe, Oracle, Sun, and Xerox. OpenDoc and OLE both represent a trend toward *document-centered* ways of working. That is, instead of thinking about what programs to use, you concentrate on the document you are creating.

The method of working in OpenDoc, for example, is to start with a container and drag and drop pieces into that container. For example, you could start with a wordprocessing document and drag other documents or pieces of other documents into it. But it doesn't have to stop there. You can also drag graphic, video, or sound elements into it. To edit a piece, you just double-click the piece. You don't have to track down the program that created it.

The other thing that you don't have to think about with OpenDoc is where those pieces live on the network. Just work with them as if they were on your own disk drive.

You can learn more about OpenDoc by visiting the following sites.

Component Integration Laboratories, Inc.	`http://www.cilabs.org`
OpenDoc Home Page	`http://www.info.apple.com/opendoc`

Interestingly enough—at least at the time this book is being written— to learn more about OLE, you'll have more luck looking at comparisons between OpenDoc and OLE than visiting the Microsoft Web site.

Taligent: Pink, people, places, things

Whether Taligent ever reaches its full potential, it needs to be included here because it's a natural descendant of the other technologies covered so far. It's a joint venture of Apple, IBM, and Hewlett-Packard that started out inside Apple as the "Pink" project, which legend has it was named after the color of the index cards used at one point in the project's history.

Part of the problem Taligent is trying to address is the sheer number of different things in a company and across companies that makes it really tough to share information and work together in general. This frustration arises from different types of computers, different operating systems, different computer interfaces, different file formats, and different applications.

Where OLE and OpenDoc promise *document-centered* ways of working, Taligent offers *task-centered* computing. Their metaphor for working on a task is *people, places, and things.*

They're ambitious as heck. For example, they want their stuff to run transparently on different hardware and operating systems. They also want to create a layer of *frameworks* for programmers to use as building blocks so they don't have to sweat things like file conversions and communications.

It doesn't stop there. Taligent also continues the trend of breaking applications up into smaller functional parts, similar to OpenDoc. So, instead of bloating a word processor with drawing-and-charting tools, spellchecker, thesaurus, communications program, and pizza cutter, all the pieces remain separate application parts. Use 'em if you need 'em; dump 'em and save disk and memory if you don't.

As we said, it might not all come to pass, but such ideas make you think about how good things might be. If they pull this off, we'll all be sitting around bragging about how we used to actually write HTML code in the old days.

You can get some information at their Web site:

```
http://www.taligent.com
```

Have a look at their glossary of terms to get a feel for their way of thinking.

Beyond the desktop metaphor: VRML and MBone

Okay, we've looked at *document-centered* with OLE and OpenDoc, and *task-centered* with Taligent. They both represent ways of trying to make working with computers like working in the real world. Even the original desktop metaphor of folders, files, documents, and trash cans was an attempt to do real-world modeling. Where can things go from here? Well, what about even more real-world modeling?

Two Internet technologies give us previews of what may lie in this direction. They are VRML and MBone.

VRML

VRML (Virtual Reality Modeling Language) started out in late 1993 as a three-dimensional interface to the Web, created by Mark Pesci and Tony Parisi. Out of the First International Conference on the World Wide Web came an initiative, headed by Mark Pesci and Brian Behlendorf, to develop a specification for a "common language to specify 3-D scene description and WWW hyperlinks."

The aim was to provide the basis for the next generation of Web browsers, which would be able to interpret VRML and run over a bandwidth as slow as a 14.4 modem.

Out of the specification work came an agreement to use Open Inventor ASCII File Format from Silicon Graphics, Inc. One peek at examples of that format will tell you that you probably won't be coding in VRML the way you coded in HTML. More likely, you'll use a graphical tool that will write out to this format.

You can learn more about VRML by reading Marc Pesci's own account of it at the following location:

`http://www.sgi.com/Products/WebFORCE/WebSpace/VRMLBackgrounder.html`

There're also good jumping-off points at the Virtual Reality Modeling Language (VRML) Forum and the San Diego Supercomputer Center VRML Repository at the following sites:

`http://vrml.wired.com`

`http://www.sdsc.edu/vrm`

To get an idea of what this type of computer interface might look like, visit the visions at the following site:

`http://vrml.wired.com/concepts/visions.html`

There, Mark Pesci describes five ways in which virtual worlds can be applied:

- The United States Holocaust Museum: A space that can be visited by everyone, with modeling that would be far more "evocative" than text and pictures alone.

- The United States Library of Congress: A virtual place that is "*intrinsically* navigable," which looks like a library in the real world.

- Earth: Take all that data that we have about the earth and represent them virtually. Also, an interface for "planetary management," being able to simulate and monitor global activity and the effects of our actions on the earth.

- The WorldWide Marketplace: A virtual physical marketplace that is not advertising, but representations of the places themselves. The sense would be less of a big department store, and more like Marrakesh.

- The Agora and the Senate: Augment self-governance through a system of virtual "town meetings."

In changing ways of interacting with computers, creating virtual worlds brings things closer to the physical world. However, the town meeting example needs one more ingredient: interactivity. That is, it's nice to be able to go and look, but it'd be even better to have a dialog. This is where the capabilities of MBone come in.

MBone

MBone (Multicast Backbone) provides the plumbing to multicast audio and video. You can do this as one person to a bunch of others (one-to-many delivery) and a bunch of people to each other (many-to-many delivery).

Named by Steve Casner of the University of Southern California and using an addressing standard developed by Steve Deering of Xerox Palo Alto Research Center, MBone has been around since 1992. It's a *virtual network*, sharing the general plumbing of Internet. Internet works by breaking up your information into little packets that find their own way to the destination where it is put back together ("Beam me up, Scotty"). Mbone uses *tunneling*, a scheme in which multicast packets are encapsulated inside regular Internet packets.

The applications of MBone, besides simple video and audio, include shared whiteboards and virtual meetings.

A good jumping-off point to learn more is the following Yahoo location:

```
http://www.yahoo.com/Computers/Multimedia/MBONE
```

You can find technical information at the MBone Information Web, maintained by Vinay Kumar at Enterprise Integration Technology (EIT), who has also done application development work:

```
http://www.eit.com/techinfo/mbone/mbone.html
```

This is one of those technologies that makes you wonder why more isn't happening with it.

Environments that can dance: CGI scripts to Hot Java

One of the pieces you need to get interactivity to work is a little gizmo to go off and do things based on something that you've done. On the Web, CGI (Common Gateway Interface) scripts are the way to do this. For example, when you use one of those fill-in-the-blanks forms and click the Submit button, what goes running around behind the scenes is a CGI script. When you visit a Web page, and it displays your domain name, the type of Web browser you're using, and lets you know that you're visitor 3,832, that's a CGI script.

All this happens on the Web server side of things. There's also the possibility of having the dancing happen on your machine at the browser end of things. That's the idea behind Sun Microsystem's Hot Java.

With a Hot Java browser, a little program transparently (there's that word again) slithers across the network to your browser. Instead of the software *install* processes that we're all accustomed to, the program automatically ends up on your machine and runs. This is scary and intriguing at the same time.

You can learn more about why this might not be as dangerous as it sounds by visiting the Web site:

```
http://java.sun.com
```

The white paper at the following site has more details:

```
http://java.sun.com/1.0alpha3/doc/overview/hotjava
```

Whoa. And we thought the Web was hot. As we can see from all the stuff hanging out in the future, we got a way to go still.

WHAT'S MY ROLE?

How big is this Web thing? And where will it take us? Telepathic transmission of holographic images? Who knows? Perhaps the best we can do is to try to put the Web in a bit of perspective, lest we drown in hype and speculation.

A lot of people liken the effect of the Web to that of printing with movable type. Gutenberg made printing and distributing information a thousand times less expensive than before. As a result, ordinary folks could afford books. Knowledge that had been the sacred preserve of princes and priests became available to all.

Today the Web is producing a similar revolution. Information once hermetically sealed in remote university libraries, accessible only to those with gobs of leisure time or an academic stipend, are now accessible to all. Citizens are actually reading drafts of laws while they are still in Congress and perusing the transcripts of famous trials. If, at two in the morning, you need to know the technical specifications of a product, you can find out in just a few minutes.

Sounds pretty grand for something that requires authors to revert to hand coding documents the way they did in 1979. To understand the gap between the reality and potential of the Web, we need to shift metaphorical gears.

Instead of thinking of the Web as a printing press, perhaps we should think of it as the Model T automobile. The Model T revolutionized transportation. It was not the first automobile. It was not the fanciest. It was not even the best. But it was cheap enough that ordinary people could afford it and simple enough that they could operate it. The Model T succeeded because it did not try to be all things to all people. You could get it in any color so long as it was black.

The Model T changed the world. Farmers could deliver their produce before it spoiled. Factory workers no longer needed to live in the grimy shadow of the plant. Families could vacation where and when they wanted to, unfettered by the timetables of the railroads. The Model T made where you lived less important than what you did.

The Web is providing similar benefits, especially to individuals and small businesses. Your home page can be just as impressive as that of the largest corporation. You can communicate your message, not just to people in your town, but to people around the globe. Your Web pages can answer questions, promote your product, or explain your policy—24 hours a day, 7 days a week, throughout the planet. With the Web at your command, you are not limited by who you are or where you are. On the Web, what matters is what you have to say.

RESOURCES FOR THE WEB CHEF

THE WORK TOOLS SHOPPING LIST

On the CD-ROM ...

resourcs
    resourcs.htm

Instant meals: A banquet sans bandwidth

Some of the programs mentioned in the shopping lists are included on the enclosed CD-ROM for your convenience. You can copy any program marked with an XXX icon to a temporary directory (or folder) on your hard drive, uncompress them, and install them—no muss, no fuss, no connect time required.

By the way, the tables themselves are also on the CD-ROM, stored in the *resourcs* directory in HTML format--with live links for all the URL, FTP, and e-mail references contained therein. So, if you already have a browser installed, open the home page for this chapter (/*resourcs* /*resourcs.htm*) as a local file, and link directly to the tool sources from there.

The tables on the following pages list some of the more common tools you'll need in your Web kitchen to create your pages and resources, browse around the Web itself, and sample the efforts of others. It's a fairly thorough list, but we make no claims that it's complete; if we've left off your favorite freeware browser—or worse, neglected to mention the shareware converter that you slaved nights and weekends over—we extend our humble apologies.

The Web world moves too fast for hard copy publishing to keep up with, anyway; by the time you read this, there will be new versions, new functions and capabilities, and new products out there. Consider these tables as a baseline or starting point; keep an eye on the industry periodicals and discussion groups identified in "References for the Insatiable" (page 605) for updates to tools and products.

Caveat Webster

These URLs and e-mail addresses were tested prior to publication, but the Internet is a very fluid place; you may find the occasional *Error 404* in spite of our best efforts. Don't despair: If the Webmaster of the site didn't leave you any cookie-crumb links to lead you to its new home, use one of the search mechanisms to find your way.

Keep in mind, too, that simply by listing a resource here, or by providing a copy of a program on the CD-ROM, the authors and the publisher are not endorsing any particular platform, product, process, reference, resource, or lifestyle.

Apple Macintosh

TCP/IP Applications: Macintosh		
Name	**Developer or Source**	**Available from/by:**
MacTCP	Apple Corporation *http://www.apple.com* MacTCP is included in System 7.5. Various commercial developers incorporate MacTCP into their SLIP/PPP product suites.	Commercial product. Contact: (800) 769-2775 *http://www.info.apple.com/support/askapl.html*
TCP/Connect II	InterCon Systems Corporation *http://www.intercon.com* TCP/IP stack is included in full Internet/SLIP tools suite (see below).	Commercial product. Contact *info@intercon.com* (703) 709-5500

Internet Tools Suites: Macintosh		
Name	**Developer or Source**	**Available from/by:**
Internet Valet	Software Ventures *http://www.svcdudes.com*	Commercial product. Contact: *valet-info@svcdudes.com*
OpenDoor	OpenDoor *http://www.opendoor.com/webdoor* Includes the WebDoor authoring product.	Commercial product available only to users of OpenDoor's Macintosh-based Internet services. Contact: *info@opendoor.com*
TCP/Connect II	InterCon Systems Corporation *http://www.intercon.com* Full suite of TCP/IP products.	Commercial product. Contact *info@intercon.com* (703) 709-5500 30-day demo version available via WWW from: *http://www.intercon.com/download.html*
VersaTerm, Versatilities	Synergy Software Full suite of TCP/IP products.	Commercial product. Contact: *maxwell@sales.synergy.com* (610) 779-0522

Web Browsers: Macintosh		
Name	**Developer or Source**	**Available from/by:**
Emacs w3-mode	William M. Perry A WWW browser for emacs.	Freeware/shareware available via anonymous FTP from: *ftp.cs.indiana.edu/pub/elisp/w3*
Enhanced NCSA Mosaic	Spyglass, Inc. *http://www.spyglass.com* Spyglass is the commercial developer and primary licensee of Mosaic from NCSA.	Spyglass does not sell or distribute individual Mosaic licenses; rather, it sublicenses rights to other (at last count, nearly 30) vendors. Contact: *info@spyglass.com* (800) 500-4411 (613) 729-7974 *http://www.spyglass.com/five/oems_licensees.html* Displays a list of licensed vendors (with links to those vendors where available).
MacWeb	TradeWave Corporation (Formerly Enterprise Integration Network, Inc., aka EINet.) *http://www.EINet.net/EINet/EINet.html*	Commercial product. Contact: *info@einet.net* (800) 844-4638 (512) 433-5300 Evaluation copy available via WWW from: *http://www.EINet.net/EINet/MacWeb/MacWebHome.html*
Mosaic for Macintosh	National Center for Supercomputing Applications (NCSA) *http://www.ncsa.uiuc.edu* The granddaddy of 'em all.	Freeware/shareware available via anonymous FTP from: *ftp.ncsa.uiuc.edu/Mac/Mosaic*
Netscape Navigator	Netscape Communications Corp. *http://home.netscape.com*	Commercial product. Contact *info@netscape.com* (415) 254-1900 Single-user evaluation (and beta) copies available via WWW from: *http://www.netscape.com* or via anonymous FTP from: *ftp.mcom.com/netscape*
Pipeline	The Pipeline *http://www.pipeline.com* Proprietary browser for Pipeline accounts only.	Commercial product bundled with Pipeline account subscription. Contact: (212) 267-3636

Web Browsers: Macintosh		
Name	Developer or Source	Available from/by:
SAMBA	R Cailliau, N Pellow CERN PTG	Shareware/freeware available via anonymous FTP from: *info.cern.ch/ftp/pub/www/bin/mac*
WebShark	InterCon Systems, Inc. *http://www.intercon.com*	Commercial product, integrated into TCP/Connect II suite. Contact: *sales@intercon.con*

Helper Applications: Macintosh		
Name	Developer or Source	Available from/by:
Acrobat Reader	Adobe Corporation *http://www.adobe.com* Mini-viewer for Adobe PDF files.	Freeware via WWW from: *http://www.adobe.com/Software.html#acrordr*
AVI-Quick	AVI to QuickTime converter	Freeware/shareware available via anonymous FTP from: *ftp.hyperarchive.lcs.mit.edu/HyperArchive/Archive/grf/util* *ftp.sumex-aim.stanford.edu/info-mac/grf/util* and various mirror sites.
Co-motion for Internet	Bittco Solutions *info@bittco.com* *http://www.bittco.com* Real-time collaboration or interaction via the WWW.	Commercial product. Contact: *info@bittco.com* (800) 265-2726 Demo versions for participating in Bittco-sponsored sessions are available via WWW from: *http://www.bittco.com/BittcoSphere2/LiveWire/livewire.html*
Common Ground Viewer	Common Ground Software *http://www.commonground.com* Mini-viewer for Common Ground digital paper files.	Commercial product. Contact: (415) 802-5800 Freeware/evaluation copy of mini-viewer is available via WWW from: *http://www.commonground.com*

Helper Applications: Macintosh		
Name	**Developer or Source**	**Available from/by:**
GIFConverter	Kevin Mitchell *74017.2573@compuserve.com* Image viewer for multiple formats.	Freeware/shareware available via anonymous FTP from: *ftp.mac.archive.umich.edu* *ftp.sumex-aim.stanford.edu/info-mac/grf/util* and various mirror sites.
Giffer	Viewer for graphics in GIF format.	Freeware/shareware available via anonymous FTP from: *oak.oakland.edu* *mac.archive.umich.edu* and various mirror sites.
Global Chat	Prospero Systems Research *http://www.prospero.com/aboutprospero.html* Real-time collaboration or interaction via the WWW.	Commercial product. Contact: *jcarey@prospero.com* (415) 731-8114 Demo version for personal or educational use is available via WWW at: *http://www.prospero.com/globalchat*
HotJava Viewer	Sun Microsystems *http://www.sun.com* 3-D viewer for Java worlds and objects.	Viewer will be available via WWW from: *http://java.sun.com/* (Not released at time of publication.)
JPEGView	Aaron Giles GIF and JPEG image viewer.	Freeware/shareware available via anonymous FTP from: *ftp.clemson.edu/pub/Mosaic/Mosaic_for_Macs/Helpers* *ftp.sumex-aim.stanford.edu/info-mac/grf/util* and various mirror sites.
NetPhone	Electric Magic *http://www.emagic.com* Full-duplex voice connectivity via the Internet.	Commercial product. Contact: (415) 759-4100

Helper Applications: Macintosh		
Name	Developer or Source	Available from/by:
QuickTime VR viewer	Apple Corporation *http://www.apple.com*	Freeware runtime viewer for VRML worlds and objects available via WWW from: *http://quicktime.apple.com* *http://qtvr.quicktime.apple.com*
Real Audio	Progressive Networks *http://www.realaudio.com* Real-time audio player.	Beta version available via WWW from: *http://www.realaudio.com*
SoundMachine	AU sound file player.	Anonymous FTP from: *ftp.clemson.edu/pub/Mosaic/Mosaic_for_Macs/Helpers* *ftp.sumex-aim.stanford.edu/info-mac/grf/util* and various mirror sites.
Sparkle	MPEG player and converter	Freeware/shareware available via anonymous FTP from: *ftp.clemson.edu/pub/Mosaic/Mosaic_for_Macs/Helpers* *ftp.sumex-aim.stanford.edu/info-mac/grf/util* and various mirror sites.
WorldView	Intervista, Inc. *http://www.hyperio.com/intervista* 3-D viewer of VRML files	Freeware runtime viewer for VRML worlds and objects available via WWW from: *http://www.hyperio.com/intervista*

HTML Authoring Tools: Macintosh		
Name	Developer or Source	Available from/by:
Alpha	Peter Keleher	Freeware/shareware available via WWW from: *http://www.cs.umd.edu/~keleher/alpha.html*
Arachnid	Robert McBurney University of Iowa *robert-mcburney@uiowa.edu*	Shareware/freeware available via WWW from: *http://sec-look.uiowa.edu/about/projects/arachnid-page.html*

HTML Authoring Tools: Macintosh		
Name	**Developer or Source**	**Available from/by:**
BBEdit / BBEdit Lite	Bare Bones Software *bbsw@netcom.com* *http://www.tiac.net/biz/ bbsw/*	Commercial product. Contact: *bbsw@netcom.com* (508) 651-3561 Lite version available at: *ftp.std.com/pub/bbedit/freeware/ bbedit-lite-30.hqx* Full demo version available at: *ftp.netcom.com/pub/bb/bbsw/bbedit-31-demo.hqx*
BBEdit HTML Extensions	Lindsay Davies *Lindsay.Davies@sheffield.ac.uk*	Shareware/freeware available via WWW from: *http://www.york.ac.uk/~ld11/ BBEditTools.html*
Ceneca PageMill	Ceneca Communications, Inc. *http://www.ceneca.com* Web authoring platform.	Commercial product. *Contact: info@ceneca.com* Phone (415) 842-6810 *http://www.ceneca.com/Products/PageMill.html*
Common Ground Internet Publisher	Common Ground Software *http://www.commonground.com* Digital paper publishing application; not released at publication.	Commercial product. Contact: (415) 802-5800
FrameMaker 5.0	Frame Technology Corp. *comments@frame.com* *http://www.frame.com* New version has built-in export to HTML format.	Commercial product. Contact: *comments@frame.com* (800) U4-FRAME *http://www.frame.com/PRODUCTS/ fm5.html#firstpage*
High Tea	Dr. R. (Stan) Stanier *ras7@bton.ac.uk*	Shareware/freeware available via WWW from: *http://www.w3.org/hypertext/WWW/Tools/ High-Tea.html*
HTML Editor	Rick Giles	Shareware/freeware available via WWW from: *http://dragon.acadiau.ca/~giles/HTML_Editor/ Documentation.html*

HTML Authoring Tools: Macintosh		
Name	**Developer or Source**	**Available from/by:**
HTML Web Weaver	Robert Best III *http://www.potsdam.edu/web.weaver*	Shareware predecessor to World Wide Web Weaver; available via anonymous FTP from: *ftp.potsdam.edu/pub/HTML_Web_Weaver/* *World_Wide_Web_Weaver1.0*
Simple HTML Editor (SHE)	Eric Lease Morgan NCSU Libraries *eric_morgan@ncsu.edu*	Shareware/freeware via anonymous FTP from: *ftp.lib.ncsu.edu/pub/software/mac/* *simple-html-editor.hqx*
WebDoor	OpenDoor *http://www.opendoor.com/WebDoor/* *WebDoor.html*	Commercial product available only to users of OpenDoor Internet services.
WordPerfect 3.5 with Internet Publisher	Novell Applications Group *http://www.novell.com/ busaptoc.htm*	Commercial product, with Internet Publisher applet included in recent product upgrade. Contact: (801) 429-7900
World Wide Web Weaver (prerelease)	Best Enterprises Robert Best III *Robert.Best@potsdam.edu* *http://www.student.potsdam.edu/Web.* *Weaver/About.html*	Commercial product. Contact: *Best@Northnet.org* (315)265-0930 Prerelease version available via anonymous FTP from: *ftp.potsdam.edu/pub/ HTML_Web_Weaver/* *WebWeaver2.5.2.sit.hqx*

Source-to-HTML Converters: Macintosh		
Name	**Developer or Source**	**Available from/by:**
BeyondPress	Astrobyte *http://www.astrobyte.com* Quark to HTML converter.	Commercial product. Contact: *Support@astrobyte.com* *http://www.astrobyte.com/Astrobyte/* *BeyondPressInfo.html*
Dave	Jeff Boulter The Bucknellian *http://www.bucknell.edu/bucknellian* PageMaker to HTML converter.	Shareware/freeware available via WWW from: *http://www.bucknell.edu/bucknellian/dave/*
HTML Markdown	Scott J. Kleper Converts HTML files into regular text files.	Shareware/freeware via anonymous FTP from: *http://htc.rit.edu/markdown.html*

Source-to-HTML Converters: Macintosh		
Name	**Developer or Source**	**Available from/by:**
HTML Translator (ClarisWorks upgrade)	Claris Corporation *http://www.claris.com*	Commercial product, included in recent product upgrade.
QT2WWW	Jeremy Hylton Converts text file containing Quark tags to HTML file.	Shareware/freeware available via WWW from: *http://the-tech.mit.edu/~jeremy/qt2www.html*
WebMaker (2.0)	The Harlequin Group Limited *http://webserver.harlequin.com* FrameMaker to HTML converter.	Commercial product. Contact: *web@harlequin.com* *http://webserver.harlequin.com/webmaker/2.0/*
XLTOHTML	R. Trenthem Rhodes College Computer Center Converts Excel 4.0 and 5.0 to HTML.	Shareware/freeware via anonymous FTP from: *http://www.rhodes.edu/software/readme.html*

See also:	Yahoo's List of HTML Converters at:
	    http://www.yahoo.com/Computers_and_Internet/Internet/World_Wide_Web/ HTML_Converters/
	W3O's List of Filters and Conversion Tools at:
	    http://www.w3.org/hypertext/WWW/Tools/Word_proc_filters.html	

Web Crafting Utilities: Macintosh		
Name	**Developer or Source**	**Available from/by:**
WebMap	City Net Express *http://www.city.net/* Image map creation software.	Commercial product. Contact: *http://www.city.net/* Prerelease version available via WWW at: *http://www.city.net/cnx/software/ webmap.html*

IBM OS/2 Warp

TCP/IP applications

OS/2 Warp comes equipped with TCP/IP connectivity included in its Internet Connection suite.

Internet Tool Suites

Although the Internet Connection built into OS/2 Warp is a fully functional Internet tool suite, computers using OS/2 Warp can also run products designed for Microsoft Windows 3.1 or Windows for Workgroups 3.11 environments.

Internet Tools Suites: OS/2 Warp		
Name	**Developer or Source**	**Available from/by:**
Chameleon TCP/IP	NetManage, Inc. *http://www.netmanage.com*	Commercial product. Contact: *sales@netmanage.com* (408) 973-7171
Emissary	Wollongong Group *http://www.twg.com*	Commercial product. Contact: *sales@twg.com*
Explore OnNet for Windows	FTP Software, Inc. *http://www.ftp.com/mkt_info/explore.html*	Commercial product. Contact: *sales@ftp.com* (800) 282-4387 (508) 685-3300
Internet Anywhere	Mortice Kern Systems, Inc. *http:/www.mks.com/internet*	Commercial product available with Portal account subscription. Contact: *iasales@mks.com* (519) 883-3242
Internet In A Box	Spry, Inc. *http://www.spry.com/intabox.html*	Commercial product. Contact: *iboxinfo24@spry.com* (800) 557-9614, extension 24
Internet Office	Spry Inc. *http://www.spry.com* LAN/WAN suite of Internet applications.	Commercial product. Contact: *iboxinfo24@spry.com* (800) 557-9614, extension 24 *http://www.spry.com/sp_prod/air/as_home.html*
InternetWorks	BookLink Technologies, Inc. *http://www.booklink.com/*	Commercial product. Contact: *info@booklink.com* (800) 453-7873
Mariner	Network Computing Devices *http://www.ncd.com*	Commercial product. Contact: *mariner@ncd.com* (415) 694-0650
NaviPress	Navisoft *http://www.navisoft.com/ index.htm* Includes browser in suite.	Commercial product. Contact: *info@navisoft.* Prerelease version may be available via WWW from: *http://www.navisoft.com*

Internet Tools Suites: OS/2 Warp		
Name	**Developer or Source**	**Available from/by:**
Quarterdeck Internet Suite	Quarterdeck Corporation *http://www.qdeck.com*	Commercial product. Contact: *info@qdeck.com* (310) 314-4263
WinTapestry/ SuperHighway Access for Windows	Frontier Technologies Corporation *http://www.frontiertech.com*	Commercial product. Contact: *superhighway@frontiertech.com* (414) 241-4555

Web Browsers: OS/2 Warp		
Name	**Developer or Source**	**Available from/by:**
Cello	Thomas Bruce Cornell University Legal Information Institute *http://ftp.law.cornell.edu/*	Shareware/freeware available via anonymous FTP from: *ftp.law.cornell.edu/pub/LII/cello* and various mirror sites.
Emacs w3-mode	William M. Perry A WWW browser for emacs environments.	Shareware/freeware available via anonymous FTP from: *ftp.cs.indiana.edu/pub/elisp/w3* and various mirror sites.
Enhanced NCSA Mosaic	Spyglass, Inc. *http://www.spyglass.com* Spyglass is the commercial developer and primary licensee of Mosaic from NCSA.	Spyglass does not sell or distribute individual Mosaic licenses; rather, it sublicenses rights to other (at last count, nearly 30) vendors. Contact: *info@spyglass.com* (800) 500-4411 (613) 729-7974 *http://www.spyglass.com/five/oems_licensees.html* Displays a list of licensed vendors (with links to those vendors where available).
I-COMM	Talent Communications, Inc. *http://www.best.com/~icomm/icomm.htm* *icomm@talentcom.com* I-COMM operates without a true TCP/IP connection. It requires a UNIX shell account.	Shareware/freeware available via anonymous FTP from: *ftp.best.com/pub/icomm* *ftp.oak.oakland.edu/pub3/simtel-win3/internet* and various mirror sites.

Web Browsers: OS/2 Warp		
Name	**Developer or Source**	**Available from/by:**
Internav	Phoenix Software Delphi Internet *http://www.ptltd.com* *http://www.delphi.com* Proprietary browser for Delphi accounts only.	Commercial product bundled with Delphi account subscription. Contact: (800) 452-0120
InternetWorks	BookLink Technologies, Inc. *http://www.booklink.com/*	Commercial product, bundled with MegaWeb (codename) Internet service subscription. Contact: (800) 453-7873 Beta version available via WWW from: *http://www.booklink.com/service/factshet.html#h*
Lynx	University of Kansas *http://www.cc.ukans.edu* Text-only browser for VT-100 terminal session.	Shareware/freeware available via anonymous FTP from: *ftp2.cc.ukans.edu/pub/WWW/lynx*
Mosaic for Windows	National Center for Supercomputing Applications (NCSA) *http:/www.ncsa.uiuc.edu* The granddaddy of 'em all.	Shareware/freeware available via anonymous FTP from: *ftp.ncsa.uiuc.edu/PC/Windows/Mosaic*
Netcruiser	Netcom, Inc. *http://www.netcom.com* Proprietary browser for Netcom accounts only.	Commercial product bundled with Netcom account subscription. Contact: *info@netcom.com* (800) 353-6600
Netscape Navigator	Netscape Communications Corp. *http://home.netscape.com*	Commercial product. Contact: *info@netscape.com* (415) 254-1900 Single-user evaluation (and beta) copies available via anonymous FTP from: *ftp.mcom.com/netscape*
Pipeline	The Pipeline *http:www.pipeline.com* Proprietary browser for Pipeline accounts only.	Commercial product bundled with Pipeline account subscription. Contact: (212) 267-3636

Web Browsers: OS/2 Warp		
Name	**Developer or Source**	**Available from/by:**
Quarterdeck Mosaic	Quarterdeck Corporation *http://www.qdeck.com*	Commercial product. Contact: *info@qdeck.com* (310) 314-4263 Evaluation/beta test version available via anonymous FTP from: *ftp://www.qdeck.com/beta*
SlipKnot	Macromind *http://www.interport.net/slipknot/slipknot.html* or e-mail: *slipknot@micromind.com* SlipKnot operates without SLIP or PPP through your regular UNIXshell account.	Shareware/freeware available via anonymous FTP from: *oak.oakland.edu/SimTel/win3/internet*
WebExplorer	IBM Corporation *http://www.ibm.com*	Commercial product; comes bundled with OS2/Warp. Contact: (800) 342-6672 (US) (800) 426-2255 (Canada) *http://www.raleigh.ibm.com/icw/icwprod.html*
WebSurfer	Netmanage, Inc. *http://www.netmanage.com*	Commercial product. Contact: *sales@netmanage.com* (408) 973-7171
WebSpace viewer	Template Graphics Software, Inc. *http://www.cts.com/~template* Viewer for SGI WebSpace 3-D worlds. (Not released at time of print.)	Commercial product. Contact: (619) 457-5359 Pre-release versions may be available for download via WWW from: *http://www.sd.tgs.com/~template/WebSpace*
WinWeb	TradeWave Corporation (Formerly Enterprise Integration Network, Inc., aka EINet.) *http://www.EINet.net/EINet/EINet.html*	Commercial product. Contact: *info@einet.net* (800) 844-4638 (512) 433-5300 Evaluation copy available via WWW from: *http://www.EINet.net/EINet/WinWeb/WinWebHome.html*

Helper Applications: OS/2 Warp		
Name	**Developer or Source**	**Available from/by:**
AAPLAY	DOS viewer for FLI files.	Shareware/freeware available via anonymous FTP from: *ftp.cica.indiana.edu* *oak.oakland.edu/pub* and various mirror sites.
Acrobat Reader	Adobe Corporation *http://www.adobe.com* Miniviewer for Adobe PDF files.	Shareware/freeware available via WWW from: *http://www.adobe.com/Software.html#acrordr*
Co-motion for Internet	Bittco Solutions *bittco@ccinet.ab.ca* *http://www.bittco.com* Real-time collaboration or interaction via the WWW.	Commercial product. Contact: *bittco@ccinet.ab.ca* (800) 265-2726 Demo versions for participating in Bittco-sponsored sessions are available via WWW from: *http://www.bittco.com/BittcoSphere2/LiveWire/livewire.html*
Common Ground Viewer	Common Ground Software *http://www.commonground.com* Mini-viewer for Common Ground digital paper files.	Commercial product. Contact: (415) 802-5800 Freeware/evaluation copy of mini-viewer is available via WWW from: *http://www.commonground.com*
CompuShow	DOS viewer for graphics in GIF, JPEG, TIFF, and Macpaint formats.	Shareware/freeware available via anonymous FTP from: *wuarchive.wustl.edu* *oak.oakland.edu/pub* and various mirror sites.
DigiPhone	Third Planet Publishing Full-duplex voice connectivity via the Internet.	Commercial product. Contact: (214) 713-2607
Director	David Walker Viewer for video files in Director format.	Shareware/freeware available via anonymous FTP from: *http:www.portal.com/~dwalker/dirhome.html*

Helper Applications: OS/2 Warp		
Name	**Developer or Source**	**Available from/by:**
DVPEG	DOS viewer for JPEG files.	Shareware/freeware available via anonymous FTP from: *ftp.cica.indiana.edu* *wuarchive.wustl.edu* and various mirror sites.
Global Chat	Prospero Systems Research *http://www.prospero.com/ aboutprospero.html* Real-time collaboration or interaction via the WWW.	Commercial product. Contact: *jcarey@prospero.com* (415) 731-8114 Demo version for personal or educational use is available via WWW at: *http://www.prospero.com/globalchat*
Graphic Workshop	Viewer for wide range of graphics formats.	Shareware/freeware available via anonymous FTP from: *ftp.cica.indiana.edu* *wuarchive.wustl.edu* and various mirror sites.
Kaleida Media Player	Kaleida Labs *http://www.kaleida.com* Player for ScriptX objects.	Commercial product. Contact: *kaleida.direct@kaleida.com* (800) 6-KALEIDA
Lview	Leonardo Haddad Loureiro *mmedia@world.std.com* Viewer for wide range of graphics formats.	Shareware/freeware available via anonymous FTP from: *ftp.cica.indiana.edu* *wuarchive.wustl.edu* and various mirror sites.
MPEG	MPEG viewer.	Shareware/freeware available via anonymous FTP from: *ftp.gatekeeper.dec.com/pub/micro/msdos/ win3/desktop* and various mirror sites.

Helper Applications: OS/2 Warp		
Name	**Developer or Source**	**Available from/by:**
Paint Shop Pro	Viewer for wide range of graphics formats.	Shareware/freeware available via anonymous FTP from: *ftp.cica.indiana.edu* *oak.oakland.edu/pub* and various mirror sites.
QuickTime Viewer	Apple Corporation *http://quicktime.apple.com* QuickTime movie player.	Commercial product. Contact: *info@apple.com* (800) 769-2775
Real Audio	Progressive Networks *http://www.realaudio.com* Real-time audio player	Commercial product. Beta version available via WWW from: *http://www.realaudio.com*
VFWRun	AVI viewer.	Shareware/freeware available via anonymous FTP from: *ftp.cica.indiana.edu* *oak.oakland.edu/pub* and various mirror sites.
WebSpace viewer	Template Graphics Software, Inc. *http://www.cts.com/~template* Viewer for SGI WebSpace 3-D worlds. (Not released at time of publication.)	Commercial product. Contact: (619) 457-5359 Prerelease versions may be available for download via WWW from: *http://www.sd.tgs.com/~template/WebSpace*
WorldView	Intervista, Inc. *http://www.hyperiom.com/intervista* 3-D viewer of VRML files.	Commercial product. Contact: *dagobert@netcom.com* Demo version available via WWW from: *http://www.hyperion.com/intervista*
WPLANY	Player for sound files in VOC, AU, and SND formats.	Shareware/freeware available via anonymous FTP from: *ftp.cdrom.com/.22/* and various mirror sites.

Helper Applications: OS/2 Warp		
Name	**Developer or Source**	**Available from/by:**
Xing MPEG	MPEG viewer.	Shareware/freeware available via anonymous FTP from: *wuarchive.wustl.edu* *oak.oakland.edu/pub* and various mirror sites.

Web Authoring Tools: OS/2 Warp		
Name	**Developer or Source**	**Available from/by:**
Build/2	IBM Corporation *http://www.ibm.com*	Commercial product. Contact: (800) 342-6672 (US) (800) 426-2255 (Canada)
Common Ground Internet Publisher	Common Ground Software *http://www.commonground.com* (Not released at time of publication.)	Commercial product. Contact: (415) 802-5800
CU_HTML.DOT	Anton S. Y. Lam Kenneth Y.P. Wong Chinese University of Hong Kong Word for Windows (2.0 and 6.0) template.	Shareware available via WWW from: *http://www.cuhk.hk/csc/cu_html/cu_html.htm*
FrameMaker 5.0	Frame Technology Corp. *http://www.frame.com* Integrated export to HTML format.	Commercial product. Contact: *comments@frame.com* (800) U4-FRAME *http://www.frame.com/PRODUCTS/ fm5.html#firstpage*
GT_HTML.DOT	Jeffrey L. Grover, John H. Davis III, Bob Johnston Georgia Tech Research Institute *gt_html@gatech.edu* Word for Windows (2.0 and 6.0) template.	Shareware available via WWW at: *http://www.gatech.edu/word_html/release.htm*
HotDog	Sausage Software *http://www.sausage.com*	Commercial product. Contact: *sales@sausage.com* 61-3-9434-7267 (Australia) Evaluation copy available via WWW from: *http://www.sausage.com*

Web Authoring Tools: OS/2 Warp		
Name	**Developer or Source**	**Available from/by:**
HotMetaL Pro	SoftQuad, Inc. *http://www.sq.com*	Commercial product. Contact: *hotmetal@sq.com* (800) 387-2777 Limited demo version available via anonymous FTP at: *ftp.gatekeep.dec.com/pub/net/infosys/ncsa/web/html/hotmetal*
HTML Assistant Pro	Brooklyn North Software Works *http://fox.nstn.ca/~harawitz/ index.html*	Commercial product. Contact: *harawitz@fox.nstn.ns.ca* (902) 493-6080 Limited introductory version at *ftp://ftp.cs.dal.ca/*
HTML HyperEdit	Steve Hancock Curtin University Perth, Australia	Freeware available via WWW from: *http://www.curtin.edu.au/curtin/dept/cc/packages/htmledit/home.html* Or by anonymous FTP from: *info.curtin.edu.au:/pub/internet/windows/hyperedit/htmledit.zip*
HTML Writer	Kris Nosack	Shareware available via anonymous FTP from: *lal.cs.byu.edu/pub/www/tools*
HTMLed	Peter Crenshaw	Precommercial "light" version available as shareware via WWW from: *http://www.ist.ca/htmled/*
HTMLed Pro	Internet Software Technologies *http://www.ist.ca*	Commercial product. Contact: *sales@ist.ca* A time-limited demo may be available via WWW from: *http://www.ist.ca/*
InContext Spider	InContext Systems *http://www.incontext.ca*	Commercial product. Contact: (301) 571-9464 (800) 263-0127
Internet Assistant	Microsoft Corp. *http://www.microsoft.com* Word extensions.	Commercial product extension. Contact: (800) 360-7561 Available as freeware via WWW from: *http://www.microsoft.com/MSOffice/Word/ia/chcklist.htm*

Web Authoring Tools: OS/2 Warp		
Name	**Developer or Source**	**Available from/by:**
InterNotes Web Publisher	Lotus Development Corp. *http://www.lotus.com*	Commercial product. Contact: (800) 346-1305 *http://www.lotus.com/inotes*
Live Markup Pro	MediaTech, Inc. *http://www.mediatec.com/mediatech*	Commercial product. Contact: *webmaster@mediatec.com* 30-day demo available via WWW from: *http://www.digimark.net/mediatech*
NaviPress	Navisoft *http://www.navisoft.com/ index.htm* Includes browser in suite.	Commercial product. Contact: *info@navisoft.* Prerelease version may be available at corporate Web address: *http://www.navisoft.com*
Web Wizard	David Geller	Shareware/freeware available via WWW at: *http://www.halcyon.com/webwizard* Also available via anonymous FTP from: *ftp.halcyon.com:/local/webwizard*
WebAuthor	Quarterdeck Corporation *http://www.qdeck.com/ Webauthor/fact.html* Extensions for Word for Windows 6.0; also available as part of an Internet suite.	Commercial product. Contact: *info@qdeck.com* (310) 392-9851
WebEdit	KnowledgeWorks *http://wwwnt.the.group.net/webedit/ webedit.htm*	Shareware/freeware available via WWW from: *http://wwwnt.the.group.net/webedit/webedit.htm*
WebWorks Publisher	Quadralay Corporation *http://www.quadralay.com* Uses FrameMaker as engine for Web publishing environment.	Commercial product. Contact: *info@quadralay.com* (512) 305-0240
WordPerfect Internet Publisher	Novell Applications Group *http://www.novell.com*	Extension to commercial product. Contact: (801) 429-7900 Available free via WWW from: *http://www.novell.com/busaptoc.htm*

Source-to-HTML Converters: OS/2 Warp		
Name	**Developer or Source**	**Available from/by:**
HTML Translator (ClarisWorks upgrade)	Claris Corporation *http://www.claris.com*	Commercial product, included in recent product upgrade. Contact: (408) 727-8227
HTMLCon	DOS program that converts HTML files to ASCII text.	Freeware/shareware via anonymous FTP from: *ftp.crl.com/ftp/users/ro/mikekell/ftp/htmlcon.exe*
Panorama **Panorama PRO**	SoftQuad, Inc. *http://www.sq.com* SGML to HTML converter.	Commercial product (Pro) Contact: *panorama-order@sq.com* (800) 387-2777 Limited demo version available via WWW from: *http://www.oclc.org:5046/oclc/research/panorama/panorama.html*
PM2HTML	Alessandro Agostini Stefano Cerreti Florence Research Area CNR PageMaker to HTML converter.	Shareware/freeware available via anonymous FTP from: *ftp.area.fi.cnr.it*
QT2WWW	Jeremy Hylton Converts text file containing Quark tags to HTML.	Shareware/freeware available via WWW from: *http://the-tech.mit.edu/~jeremy/qt2www.html*
Web Publisher	Skisoft, Inc. *http://www.skisoft.com/skisoft* Converts RTF files to HTML; supports tables.	Commercial product. Contact: *info@skisoft.com* Phone:(617) 863-1876 30-day free trial version available via WWW from: *http://www.skisoft.com/skisoft*
WebMaker (2.0)	The Harlequin Group Limited *http://webserver.harlequin.com* FrameMaker to HTML converter.	Commercial product. Contact: *web@harlequin.com* *http://webserver.harlequin.com/webmaker/2.0/*
XL2HTML	Jordan Evans Swales & Associates, Inc. NASA Systems Engineering Excel spreadsheet to HTML converter.	Freeware via anonymous FTP from: *http://www710.gsfc.nasa.gov/704/dgd/xl1html.html*

Source-to-HTML Converters: OS/2 Warp		
Name	**Developer or Source**	**Available from/by:**
See also:	Yahoo's List of HTML Converters at: *http://www.yahoo.com/Computers_and_Internet/Internet/World_Wide_Web/ HTML_Converters/* W3O's List of Filters and Conversion Tools at: *http://www.w3.org/hypertext/WWW/Tools/Word_proc_filters.html*	

Web Crafter Utilities: OS/2 Warp		
Name	**Developer or Source**	**Available from/by:**
AnchorPage	Iconovex Corp. *http://iconovex.com* Web page index generator; comes with RTFact, an RTF-to-HTML utility.	Commercial product. Contact: *74064.440@compuserve* (800) 943-0292
Background Assistant	Brooklyn North Software Works *http://fox.nstn.ca/~harawitz/ index.html*	Full-featured version is included in HTML Assistant Pro. Contact: *sales@brooknorth.bedford.ns.ca* Demo version available via WWW from: *http://fox.nstn.ca/~harawitz/abtbgast.html* Or via anonymous FTP from: *ftp.cs.dal.ca/htmlass*
Thumbs Plus	Creates thumbnails, useful for designing Web clusters.	Shareware/freeware available via anonymous FTP from: *ftp://ftp.cdarchive.com/FTP_server/pub/ dos-windows/thmpls.exe*
WebForms v1.0	Q&D Software Interactive forms-building tool.	Shareware/freeware available via WWW from: *http://www.intac.com/~dversch/*

Microsoft Windows (Versions 3.1 or Windows for Workgroups 3.11)

What about Windows '95 and Microsoft Network?

(We *knew* you'd ask that!) The short answer is that as this book was going to press, there were significant intangibles and, shall we say, uncertainties about Windows '95 and its Internet-related offerings. Rather than contend with restraining orders and rollout schedules and the like, we opted for the simplest route: Let's wait and see.

(Besides, we might want to write a sequel!)

If you want to know specifics about Windows 95's Internet capabilities, keep an eye on the Internet periodicals and general computing publications—they'll be sure to be full of info. (The most common publications are listed in "Raiding the icebox: periodicals worth fishing out of the stack" on page 615.)

TCP/IP Applications: Windows		
Name	**Developer or Source**	**Available from/by:**
Chameleon Sampler	NetManage, Inc. Sampler is a (free) demo version of commercial product; it provides only TCP/IP and SLIP support.	Demo version available by anonymous FTP from: *ftp.netmanage.com/pub/demos/chameleon/* The demo version is also included in several Internet and WWW books currently on the market.
Trumpet WinSock	Peter Tattam Trumpet Software International *info@trumpet.com.au*	Usually available from your ISP; also by anonymous FTP from: *ftp.cdrom.com /.22/cica* and various mirror sites.

Internet Tool Suites: Windows		
Name	**Developer or Source**	**Available from/by:**
Chameleon TCP/IP	NetManage, Inc. *http://www.netmanage.com*	Commercial product. Contact: *sales@netmanage.com* (408) 973-7171
Emissary	Wollongong Group *http://www.twg.com*	Commercial product. Contact: *sales@twg.com*
Explore OnNet for Windows	FTP Software, Inc. *http://www.ftp.com/mkt_info/ explore.html*	Commercial product. Contact: *sales@ftp.com* (800) 282-4387 (508) 685-3300

Internet Tool Suites: Windows		
Name	**Developer or Source**	**Available from/by:**
InterAp	California Software *http://www.calsoft.com*	Commercial product. Contact: *sales@calsoft.com* (714) 675-9906 30-day evaluation version available via WWW from: *ftp://www.interap.com*
Internet Anywhere	Mortice Kern Systems, Inc. *http:/www.mks.com/internet*	Commercial product available with Portal account subscription. Contact: *iasales@mks.com* (519) 883-3242
Internet Connection for Windows	IBM Corporation *http://www.ibm.com*	Commercial product. Contact: (800) 342-6672 (US) (800) 426-2255 (Canada) Demo version available via WWW at: *http://www.raleigh.ibm.com/icw/icwdemo.html*
Internet In A Box	Spry, Inc. *http://www.spry.com/intabox.html*	Commercial product. Contact: *iboxinfo24@spry.com* (800) 557-9614, extension 24 *http://www.spry.com/sp_prod/air/as_home.html*
Internet Office	Spry Inc. *http://www.spry.com* LAN/WAN suite of Internet applications.	Commercial product. Contact: *iboxinfo24@spry.com* (800) 557-9614, extension 24 *http://www.spry.com/sp_prod/air/as_home.html*
InternetWorks	BookLink Technologies, Inc. *http://www.booklink.com/*	Commercial product. Contact: *info@booklink.com* (800) 453-7873
Mariner	Network Computing Devices *http://www.ncd.com*	Commercial product. Contact: *mariner@ncd.com* (415) 694-0650
NaviPress	Navisoft *http://www.navisoft.com/ index.htm* Includes browser in suite.	Commercial product. Contact: *info@navisoft.* Prerelease version may be available via WWW from: *http://www.navisoft.com*

Internet Tool Suites: Windows		
Name	**Developer or Source**	**Available from/by:**
Quarterdeck Internet Suite	Quarterdeck Corporation *http://www.qdeck.com*	Commercial product. Contact: *info@qdeck.com* (310) 314-4263
SuperHighway Access for Windows	Frontier Technologies Corporation *http://www.frontiertech.com*	Commercial product. Contact: *superhighway@frontiertech.com* (414) 241-4555

Web Browsers: Windows		
Name	**Developer or Source**	**Available from/by:**
Cello	Thomas Bruce Cornell University Legal Information Institute *http://ftp.law.cornell.edu/*	Shareware/freeware available via anonymous FTP from: *ftp.law.cornell.edu/pub/LII/cello* and various mirror sites.
Emacs w3-mode	William M. Perry A WWW browser for emacs environments.	Shareware/freeware available via anonymous FTP from: *ftp.cs.indiana.edu/pub/elisp/w3* and various mirror sites.
Enhanced NCSA Mosaic	Spyglass, Inc. *http://www.spyglass.com* Spyglass is the commercial developer and primary licensee of Mosaic from NCSA.	Spyglass does not sell or distribute individual Mosaic licenses; rather, it sublicenses rights to other (at last count, nearly 30) vendors. Contact: *info@spyglass.com* (800) 500-4411 (613) 729-7974 *http://www.spyglass.com/five/oems_licensees.html* Displays a list of licensed vendors (with links to those vendors where available).
I-COMM	Talent Communications, Inc. *http://www.best.com/~icomm/icomm.htm* *icomm@talentcom.com* I-COMM operates without a true TCP/IP connection. It requires a UNIX shell account.	Shareware/freeware available via anonymous FTP from: *ftp.best.com/pub/icomm* *ftp.oak.oakland.edu/pub3/simtel-win3/internet* and various mirror sites.

Web Browsers: Windows		
Name	**Developer or Source**	**Available from/by:**
Internav	Phoenix Software Delphi Internet *http://www.ptltd.com* *http://www.delphi.com* Proprietary browser for Delphi accounts only.	Commercial product bundled with Delphi account subscription. Contact: (800) 452-0120
InternetWorks	BookLink Technologies, Inc. *http://www.booklink.com/*	Commercial product, bundled with MegaWeb (codename) Internet service subscription. Contact: (800) 453-7873 Beta version available via WWW from: *http://www.booklink.com/service/factshet.html#h*
Lynx	University of Kansas *http://www.cc.ukans.edu* Text-only browser for VT-100 terminal session.	Anonymous FTP from: *ftp2.cc.ukans.edu/pub/WWW/lynx*
Mosaic for Windows	National Center for Supercomputing Applications (NCSA) *http:/www.ncsa.uiuc.edu* The granddaddy of 'em all.	Anonymous FTP from: *ftp.ncsa.uiuc.edu/PC/Windows/Mosaic*
Netcruiser	Netcom, Inc. *http://www.netcom.com* Proprietary browser for Netcom accounts only.	Commercial product bundled with Netcom account subscription. Contact: *info@netcom.com* (800) 353-6600
Netscape Navigator	Netscape Communications Corp. *http://home.netscape.com*	Commercial product. Contact: *info@netscape.com* (415) 254-1900 Single-user evaluation (and beta) copies available via anonymous FTP from: *ftp.mcom.com/netscape*
Pipeline	The Pipeline *http:www.pipeline.com* Proprietary browser for Pipeline accounts only.	Commercial product bundled with Pipeline account subscription. Contact: (212) 267-3636

Web Browsers: Windows		
Name	Developer or Source	Available from/by:
Quarterdeck Mosaic	Quarterdeck Corporation *http://www.qdeck.com*	Commercial product. Contact: *info@qdeck.com* (310) 314-4263 Beta test version available via anonymous FTP from: *ftp://www.qdeck.com/beta*
SlipKnot	Macromind *http://www.interport.net/slipknot/slipknot.html* or e-mail: *slipknot@micromind.com* SlipKnot operates without SLIP or PPP through your regular UNIX shell account.	Shareware/freeware available via anonymous FTP from: *oak.oakland.edu/SimTel/win3/internet*
WebExplorer	IBM Corporation *http://www.ibm.com* Comes bundled with OS2/Warp; also available as standalone browser for Windows.	Commercial product. Contact: (800) 342-6672 (US) (800) 426-2255 (Canada) *http://www.raleigh.ibm.com/icw/icwprod.html*
WebSurfer	Netmanage, Inc. *http://www.netmanage.com* Included with the Chameleon TCP/IP software package.	Commercial product. Contact: *sales@netmanage.com* (408) 973-7171
WinWeb	TradeWave Corporation (Formerly Enterprise Integration Network, Inc., aka EINet.) *http://www.EINet.net/EINet/EINet.html*	Commercial product. Contact: *info@einet.net* (800) 844-4638 (512) 433-5300 Evaluation copy available via WWW from: *http://www.EINet.net/EINet/WinWeb/WinWebHome.html*

Helper Applications: Windows		
Name	**Developer or Source**	**Available from/by:**
AAPLAY	DOS viewer for FLI files.	Shareware/freeware available via anonymous FTP from: *ftp.cica.indiana.edu* *oak.oakland.edu/pub* and various mirror sites.
Acrobat Reader	Adobe Corporation *http://www.adobe.com* Miniviewer for Adobe PDF files.	Freeware via WWW from: *http://www.adobe.com/ Software.html#acrordr*
Co-motion for Internet	Bittco Solutions *info@bittco.com* *http://www.bittco.com* Real-time collaboration or interaction via the WWW.	Commercial product. Contact: *info@bittco.com* (800) 265-2726 Demo versions for participating in Bittco-sponsored sessions are available via WWW from: *http://www.bittco.com/BittcoSphere2/LiveWire/ livewire.html*
Common Ground Viewer	Common Ground Software *http://www.commonground.com* Mini-viewer for Common Ground digital paper files.	Commercial product. Contact: (415) 802-5800 Freeware/evaluation copy of mini-viewer is available via WWW from: *http://www.commonground.com*
CompuShow	DOS viewer for graphics in GIF, JPEG, TIFF, and Macpaint formats.	Shareware/freeware available via anonymous FTP from: *wuarchive.wustl.edu* *oak.oakland.edu/pub* and various mirror sites.
DigiPhone	Third Planet Publishing Full-duplex voice connectivity via the Internet.	Commercial product. Contact: (214) 713-2607
Director	David Walker Viewer for video files in Director format.	Shareware/freeware available via anonymous FTP from: *http:www.portal.com/~dwalker/dirhome.html*

Helper Applications: Windows		
Name	**Developer or Source**	**Available from/by:**
DVPEG	DOS viewer for JPEG files.	Shareware/freeware available via anonymous FTP from: *ftp.cica.indiana.edu* *wuarchive.wustl.edu* and various mirror sites.
Global Chat	Prospero Systems Research *http://www.prospero.com/ aboutprospero.html* Real-time collaboration or interaction via the WWW.	Commercial product. Contact: *jcarey@prospero.com* (415) 731-8114 Demo version for personal or educational use is available via WWW at: *http://www.prospero.com/globalchat*
Graphic Workshop	Viewer for wide range of graphics formats.	Shareware/freeware available via anonymous FTP from: *ftp.cica.indiana.edu* *wuarchive.wustl.edu* and various mirror sites.
Kaleida Media Player	Kaleida Labs *http://www.kaleida.com* Player for ScriptX objects.	Commercial product. Contact: *kaleida.direct@kaleida.com* (800) 6-KALEIDA
Lview	Leonardo Haddad Loureiro *mmedia@world.std.com* Viewer for wide range of graphics formats.	Shareware/freeware available via anonymous FTP from: *ftp.cica.indiana.edu* *wuarchive.wustl.edu* and various mirror sites.
MPEG	MPEG viewer.	Shareware/freeware available via anonymous FTP from: *ftp.gatekeeper.dec.com/pub/micro/msdos/win3/ desktop* and various mirror sites.

Helper Applications: Windows		
Name	**Developer or Source**	**Available from/by:**
Paint Shop Pro	Viewer for wide range of graphics formats.	Shareware/freeware available via anonymous FTP from: *ftp.cica.indiana.edu* *oak.oakland.edu/pub* and various mirror sites.
QuickTime Viewer	Apple Corporation *http://quicktime.apple.com* QuickTime movie player.	Commercial product. Contact: *info@apple.com*
Real Audio	Progressive Networks *http://www.realaudio.com* Real-time audio player	Commercial product. Beta version available via WWW from: *http://www.realaudio.com*
VFWRun	AVI viewer.	Shareware/freeware available via anonymous FTP from: *ftp.cica.indiana.edu* *oak.oakland.edu/pub* and various mirror sites.
WebSpace Viewer	Template Graphics Software, Inc. *http://www.cts.com/~template* Viewer for SGI WebSpace 3-D worlds. (Not released at time of publication.)	Commercial product. Contact: (619) 457-5359 Prerelease versions may be available for download via WWW from: *http://www.sd.tgs.com/~template/WebSpace*
WorldView	Intervista, Inc. *http://www.hyperiom.com/intervista* 3-D viewer of VRML files.	Commercial product. Contact: *dagobert@netcom.com* Demo version available via WWW from: *http://www.hyperion.com/intervista*
WPLANY	Player for sound files in VOC, AU, and SND formats.	Shareware/freeware available via anonymous FTP from: *ftp.cdrom.com/.22/* and various mirror sites.

Helper Applications: Windows		
Name	**Developer or Source**	**Available from/by:**
Xing MPEG	MPEG viewer.	Shareware/freeware available via anonymous FTP from: *wuarchive.wustl.edu* *oak.oakland.edu/pub* and various mirror sites.

Web Authoring Tools: Windows		
Name	**Developer or Source**	**Available from/by:**
Common Ground Internet Publisher	Common Ground Software *http://www.commonground.com*	Commercial product. Contact: (415) 802-5800
CU_HTML.DOT	Anton S. Y. Lam Kenneth Y.P. Wong Chinese University of Hong Kong Word for Windows (2.0 and 6.0) template.	Shareware available via WWW from: *http://www.cuhk.hk/csc/cu_html/cu_html.htm*
FrameMaker 5.0	Frame Technology Corp. *http://www.frame.com* Built-in export to HTML format.	Commercial product. Contact: *comments@frame.com* (800) U4-FRAME *http://www.frame.com/PRODUCTS/ fm5.html#firstpage*
GT_HTML.DOT	Jeffrey L. Grover, John H. Davis III, Bob Johnston Georgia Tech Research Institute *gt_html@gatech.edu* Word for Windows (2.0 and 6.0) template.	Shareware available via WWW at: *http://www.gatech.edu/word_html/release.htm*
HotDog	Sausage Software *http://www.sausage.com*	Commercial product. Contact: *sales@sausage.com* 61-3-9434-7267 (Australia) Evaluation copy available via WWW from: *http://www.sausage.com*

Web Authoring Tools: Windows		
Name	**Developer or Source**	**Available from/by:**
HotMetaL Pro	SoftQuad, Inc. *http://www.sq.com*	Commercial product. Contact: *hotmetal@sq.com* (800) 387-2777 Limited demo version available via anonymous FTP at: *ftp.gatekeep.dec.com/pub/net/infosys/ncsa/web/ html/hotmetal*
HTML Assistant Pro	Brooklyn North Software Works *http://fox.nstn.ca/~harawitz/ index.html*	Commercial product. Contact: *harawitz@fox.nstn.ns.ca* (902) 493-6080 Limited introductory version at: *ftp://ftp.cs.dal.ca/*
HTML HyperEdit	Steve Hancock Curtin University Perth, Australia	Freeware available via WWW from: *http://www.curtin.edu.au/curtin/dept/cc/packages/ htmledit/home.html* Or by anonymous FTP from: *info.curtin.edu.au:/pub/internet/ windows/hyperedit/htmledit.zip*
HTML Writer	Kris Nosack	Shareware available via anonymous FTP from: *lal.cs.byu.edu/pub/www/tools*
HTMLed	Peter Crenshaw	Precommercial "light" version as shareware available via WWW from: *http://www.ist.ca/htmled/*
HTMLed Pro	Internet Software Technologies *http://www.ist.ca*	Commercial product. Contact: *sales@ist.ca* A time-limited demo may be available via WWW from: *http://www.ist.ca/*
InContext Spider	InContext Systems *http://www.incontext.ca*	Commercial product. Contact: (301) 571-9464 (800) 263-0127
Internet Assistant	Microsoft Corp. *http://www.microsoft.com* Word extensions.	Commercial product extension. Contact: (800) 360-7561 Available as freeware via WWW from: *http://www.microsoft.com/MSOffice/Word/ia/ chcklist.htm*

Web Authoring Tools: Windows		
Name	**Developer or Source**	**Available from/by:**
InterNotes Web Publisher	Lotus Development Corp. *http://www.lotus.com* **Note**: Windows NT only.	Commercial product. Contact: (800) 346-1305 *http://www.lotus.com/inotes*
Live Markup Pro	MediaTech, Inc. *http://www.mediatec.com/mediatech*	Commercial product. Contact: *webmaster@mediatec.com* 30-day demo available via WWW from: *http://www.digimark.net/mediatech*
NaviPress	Navisoft *http://www.navisoft.com/ index.htm* Includes browser in suite.	Commercial product. Contact: *info@navisoft.com* Prerelease version may be available via WWW from: *http://www.navisoft.com*
Web Wizard	David Geller	Freeware available via WWW at: *http://www.halcyon.com/webwizard* Also available via anonymous FTP from: *ftp.halcyon.com:/local/webwizard*
WebAuthor	Quarterdeck Corporation *http://www.qdeck.com/ Webauthor/fact.html* Extensions for Word for Windows 6.0.	Commercial product; also available as part of an Internet suite. Contact: *info@qdeck.com* (310) 392-9851
WebEdit	KnowledgeWorks *http://wwwnt.thegroup.net/webedit/web edit.htm*	Shareware. A 30-day evaluation copy is available via WWW from: *http://wwwnt.thegroup.net/webedit/webedit.htm*
WebWorks Publisher	Quadralay Corporation *http://www.quadralay.com* Uses FrameMaker as engine for Web publishing environment.	Commercial product. Contact: *info@quadralay.com* (512) 305-0240
WordPerfect Internet Publisher	Novell Applications Group *http://www.novell.com*	Extension to commercial product. Contact: (801) 429-7900 Available free via WWW from: *http://www.novell.com/busaptoc.htm*

Source-to-HTML Converters: Windows		
Name	**Developer or Source**	**Available from/by:**
HTML translator (ClarisWorks upgrade)	Claris Corporation *http://www.claris.com*	Commercial product extensions, included in product upgrade. Contact: *http://www.claris.com*
HTMLCon	DOS program that converts HTML files to ASCII text.	Freeware/shareware via anonymous FTP from: *ftp.crl.com/ftp/users/ro/mikekell/ftp/htmlcon.exe*
Panorama Panorama PRO	SoftQuad, Inc. *http://www.sq.com* SGML to HTML converter.	Commercial product (Pro). Contact: *panorama-order@sq.com* (800) 387-2777 Limited demo version available via WWW from: *http://www.oclc.org:5046/oclc/research/panorama/panorama.html*
PM2HTML	Alessandro Agostini Stefano Cerreti Florence Research Area CNR PageMaker to HTML converter.	Shareware/freeware available via anonymous FTP from: *ftp.area.fi.cnr.it*
QT2WWW	Jeremy Hylton Converts text file containing Quark tags to HTML.	Shareware/freeware available via WWW from: *http://the-tech.mit.edu/~jeremy/qt2www.html*
Web Publisher	Skisoft, Inc. *http://www.skisoft.com/skisoft* Converts RTF files to HTML; supports tables.	Commercial product. Contact: *info@skisoft.com* Phone:(617) 863-1876 30-day free trial version available via WWW from: *http://www.skisoft.com/skisoft*
WebMaker (2.0)	The Harlequin Group Limited *http://webserver.harlequin.com* FrameMaker to HTML converter.	Commercial product. Contact: *web@harlequin.com* *http://webserver.harlequin.com/webmaker/2.0/*
XL2HTML	Jordan Evans Swales & Associates, Inc. NASA Systems Engineering Excel to HTML converter.	Freeware via anonymous FTP from: *http://www710.gsfc.nasa.gov/704/dgd/xl1html.html*

Source-to-HTML Converters: Windows		
Name	**Developer or Source**	**Available from/by:**
See also:	Yahoo's List of HTML Converters at: *http://www.yahoo.com/Computers_and_Internet/Internet/World_Wide_Web/ HTML_Converters/* W3O's List of Filters and Conversion Tools at: *http://www.w3.org/hypertext/WWW/Tools/Word_proc_filters.html*	

Web Crafter Utilities: Windows		
Name	**Developer or Source**	**Available from/by:**
AnchorPage	Iconovex Corp. *http://iconovex.com* Web page index generator; comes with RTFact, an RTF-to-HTML utility.	Commercial product. Contact: *74064.440@compuserve* (800) 943-0292
Background Assistant	Brooklyn North Software Works *http://fox.nstn.ca/~harawitz/ index.html* Background editing and creation utility; a full-featured version is included in HTML Assistant Pro.	Commercial product. Contact: *sales@brooknorth.bedford.ns.ca* Demo version available via WWW from: *http://fox.nstn.ca/~harawitz/abtbgast.html*
Thumbs Plus	Creates thumbnails, useful for designing Web clusters.	Shareware/freeware available via anonymous FTP from: *ftp://ftp.cdarchive.com/FTP_server/pub/ dos-windows/thmpls.exe*
WebForms v1.0	Q&D Software Interactive forms-building tool.	Shareware/freeware available via WWW from: *http://www.intac.com/~dversch/*

UNIX

TCP/IP applications

TCP/IP is built into the UNIX operating system; as such, external or extra TCP/IP applications are not neccesary. As usual, UNIX did it right the first time.

Internet Tool Suites: UNIX		
Name	**Developer or Source**	**Available from/by:**
WebFORCE	Silicon Graphics, Inc. *http://www.sgi.com* Authoring, viewing, and server platform that supports SGI's 3-D VRML implementation.	Commercial product. Contact: *info@sgi.com* *http://www.sgi.com/Products/WebFORCE*
Java	Sun Microsystems *http://java.sun.com* Java is an object-oriented language for developing Internet applications, including 3-D objects.	Commercial product. Contact: *java@java.sun.com* (800) 820-9995 (415) 336-0018

Web Browsers: UNIX		
Name	**Developer or Source**	**Available from/by:**
Arena	The World Wide Web Consortium *http://www.w3.org/hypertext/WWW/Consortium/* Supports HTML 3.0 specifications.	Shareware/freeware available via WWW from: *http://www.w3.org/hypertext/WWW/Arena/*
Chimera	John Kilburg *john@isri.unlv.edu* Based on Athena widget set; Motif isn't required.	Shareware/freeware available via WWW from: *http://www.unlv.edu/chimera/*
Enhanced NCSA Mosaic	Spyglass, Inc. *http://www.spyglass.com* Spyglass is the commercial developer and primary licensee of Mosaic from NCSA.	Spyglass does not sell or distribute individual Mosaic licenses; rather, it sublicenses rights to other (at last count, nearly 30) vendors. Contact: *info@spyglass.com* (800) 500-4411 (613) 729-7974 *http://www.spyglass.com/five/oems_licensees.html* Displays a list of licensed vendors (with links to those vendors where available).
Hot Java	Sun Microsystems *http://java.sun.com* WWW browser that supports 3-D and other objects written in Java.	Commercial product (not yet released). Contact: *info@sun.com*

Web Browsers: UNIX		
Name	**Developer or Source**	**Available from/by:**
MidasWWW	Tony Johnson *http://www.w3.org/hypertext/WWW/ MidasWWW/Announce1.html*	Freeware available via anonymous FTP from: *freehep.scri.fsu.edu/networking_news_e-mail/ midaswww/midaswww_1.0.tar.Z*
Mosaic for X	National Center for Supercomputing Applications (NCSA) *http://www.ncsa.uiuc.edu*	Freeware/shareware available via anonymous FTP from: *ftp.ncsa.uiuc.edu/X/Mosaic*
Netscape Navigator	Netscape Communications Corp. *http://home.netscape.com*	Commercial product. Contact: *info@netscape.com* (415) 254-1900 Single-user evaluation (and beta) copies available via WWW from: *http://home.netscape.com*

Helper Applications: UNIX		
Name	**Developer or Source**	**Available from/by:**
AudioFile	Audio player handling a bunch of different formats; compiles on most UNIX boxes.	Shareware/freeware available via WWW from: *ftp://ftp.dec.com/pub/DEC/AF*
Ghostscript/ Ghostview (Aladdin)	Russell Lang Artifex Software, Inc. Aladdin version of the popular Postscript file viewer.	Freeware available via WWW from: *ftp://prep.ai.mit.edu/pub/gnu/* and various mirror sites.
Ghostscript/ Ghostview (GNU)	GNU version of the popular Postscript file viewer.	GNU General Public license, available via WWW from: *ftp://prep.ai.mit.edu/pub/gnu/* and various mirror sites.
MPEG-I	Multi-Stream System Layer encoder/decoder/player set.	Shareware/freeware available via WWW from: *ftp://flash.bu.edu/pub/code*
WebSpace	Silicon Graphics (developer) *http://www.sgi.com* VRML viewer for SGI platform.	Commercial product. Evaluation copy is available via WWW from: *http://www.sgi.com/Products/WebFORCE/ WebSpace*

Helper Applications: UNIX		
Name	**Developer or Source**	**Available from/by:**
X Play Gizmo	Alan Braverman Software Development Group NCSA *alanb@ncsa.uiuc.edu* Audio/movie control panel.	Shareware/freeware available via WWW from: *ftp://ftp.ncsa.uiuc.edu/Mosaic/Unix/viewers/ xplaygizmo/*
XAnim	Mark Podlipec 3 Federal St. Billerica, MA 01821 *podlipec@wellfleet.com* XAnim is a program for viewing a wide variety of animation formats under X11.	Shareware/freeware available via WWW from: *http://www.portal.com/~podlipec/home.html*
Xplay	A sound player for SunOS 4.1.x systems.	Shareware/freeware available via WWW from: *ftp://ftp.ai.mit.edu/pub/xplay/*

See also:	The healthy collection of MPEG players at:
	
	  ftp://ftp.crs4.it/mpeg/programs/
	
	X Consortium's FTP Server at:
	
	  ftp://ftp.x.org
	
	NCSA's Anonymous FTP Server at:
	
	  ftp://ftp.ncsa.uiuc.edu/Mosaic/Unix/viewers/	

Web Authoring Tools: UNIX		
Name	**Developer or Source**	**Available from/by:**
ASHE (A Simple HTML Editor)	John R. Punin *puninj@cs.rpi.edu*	Shareware/freeware available via WWW from: *ftp://ftp.cs.rpi.edu/pub/puninj/ASHE*
WYSIWYG HTML Editor	Nick Williams City University *http://web.cs.city.ac.uk* X-Windows HTML editor based on Andrew toolkit.	Shareware/freeware available via WWW from: *http://web.cs.city.ac.uk;80/homes/njw/htmltext/ htmltext.html*

Web Authoring Tools: UNIX		
Name	**Developer or Source**	**Available from/by:**
Common Ground Internet Publisher	Common Ground Software *http://www.commonground.com*	Commercial product. Contact: (415) 802-5800
Cyberleaf	Interleaf Corporation *http://www.ileaf.com*	Commercial product. Contact: *i-direct@ileaf.com* (800) 955-5323 *http://www.ileaf.com/ip.html*
FrameMaker 5.0	Frame Technology Corp. *http://www.frame.com* Built-in export to HTML format	Commercial product. Contact: *comments@frame.com* (800) U4-FRAME *http://www.frame.com/PRODUCTS/fm5.html#firstpage*
HotMetaL Pro	SoftQuad, Inc. *http://www.sq.com*	Commercial product. Contact: *hotmetal@sq.com* (800) 387-2777 Free limited version available via WWW from: *http://www.sq.com/products/hotmetal*
PHOENIX	Lee Newberg, Ph.D. University of Chicago *L-Newberg@UChicago.EDU* *http://http.bsd.uchicago.edu/~l-newberg/phoenix.html*	GNU General Public License, available via WWW from: *http://www.bsd.uchicago.edu/pub/phoenix/*
tkHTML	Liem Bahneman University of Washington HTML editor based on tk.	Shareware/freeware available via anonymous FTP from: *ftp.u.washington.edu:/public/roland/tkHTML*
WebForce	Silicon Graphics *http://www.sgi.com* VRML-based development suite.	Commercial product. Contact: *http://www.sgi.com/Products/WebFORCE*
WebPages	IT Solutions *http://www.pages.com*	Commercial product. Contact: *info@its.com* (312) 474-7700 (800) 394-4487 *http://www.pages.com/products/WebPages.htmld/index.html*

Web Authoring Tools: UNIX		
Name	**Developer or Source**	**Available from/by:**
WebWorks Publisher	Quadralay Corporation *http://www.quadralay.com* Uses FrameMaker as engine for Web publishing environment.	Commercial product. Contact: *info@quadralay.com* (512) 305-0240

Source-to-HTML Converters: UNIX		
Name	**Developer or Source**	**Available from/by:**
miftrans	Jim McBeath C code for MIF to HTML converter.	Freeware available via anonymous FTP from: *ftp://ftp.alumni.caltech.edu/pub/mcbeath/web/miftran/*
qt2www	Jeremy Hylton Converts text file containing Quark tags to HTML.	Shareware/freeware available via WWW from: *http://the-tech.mit.edu/~jeremy/qt2www.html*
WebMaker (2.0)	The Harlequin Group Limited *http://webserver.harlequin.com* FrameMaker to HTML converter.	Commercial product. Contact: *web@harlequin.com* *http://webserver.harlequin.com/webmaker/2.0/*
WebMaker (1.4)	CERN *http://www.cern.ch/WebMaker/WebMaker.html* Converts FrameMaker files to HTML.	Shareware/freeware available via WWW from: *http://www.cern.ch/WebMaker/distribution.html*
wp2x	Raymond Chen WordPerfect 5.1 to HTML (among others).	Freeware available via WWW from: *http://www.milkyway.com/People/Michael_Richardson/wp2x.html*
See also:	Yahoo's List of HTML Converters at: *http://www.yahoo.com/Computers_and_Internet/Internet/World_Wide_Web/HTML_Converters/* W3O's List of Filters and Conversion Tools at: *http://www.w3.org/hypertext/WWW/Tools/Word_proc_filters.html*	

Web Crafter Utilities: UNIX		
Name	**Developer or Source**	**Available from/by:**
ChURL (Check URL)	Computer-Aided Eng. Network University of Michigan *http://www.engin.umich.edu:80/college/* Link validation application.	Currently freeware available via WWW from: *http://www.engin.umich.edu/~yunke/ scripts/churl/*
net.Form	net.Genesis *http://www.netgen.com/products/ products.html* Server forms generator.	Commercial product. Contact: *netform-sales@netgen.com*
Ovation	Visual Engineering Inc. *http://www.cdrom.com/pub/viseng* Presentation software, exports to multiple file formats, new version to support HTML linking.	Commercial product Contact: *info@ve.com* (408) 452-0600 An evaluation copy is available via WWW from: *http://www.cdrom.com/pub/viseng/www/ HomeSeries/slide003.html*
Sesame Navigator	Ubique, Inc. *http://www.ubique.com/* "Virtual room" real-time interaction application.	Commercial product. Contact: *info@ubique.com* (415) 896-2434 Evaluation version available via WWW from: *http://www.ubique.com/*
XV	John Bradley *xv@devo.dccs.upenn.edu* *http://www.sun.com/sunsoft/catlink/ xv/xv.html* World-class graphics conversion and manipulation tool.	Shareware/freeware available via WWW from: *ftp://ftp.cis.upenn.edu/pub/xv*

REFERENCES FOR THE INSATIABLE

Last but not least, we've collected a fair number of references along the way: Web sites, publications, and even books (remember *those*?) that may be of some help to you as you hone your skills as a Web chef. We've included these references on the CD-ROM also, so that you can use the links (when provided) to access information directly — or, at the very least, cut-and-paste those book titles into that email to your purchasing department. Happy reading!

Online References: On the Web, about the Web

On the CD-ROM ...

resourcs
   webinfo.htm

Here's a detailed list of some of our favorite (or most recommended) sources for hints, tutorials, resources, support, and inspiration throughout the Web. For easy access, we've divided them into these catagories:

- Web resources (general)
- Design guides
- HTML guides
- HTML specifications
- Advanced features
- Media and multimedia
- VRML and things virtual
- Helper apps, viewers, and utilities
- Background textures and colors
- Business information sources on the Web
- Useful mailing lists
- Newsgroups of interest
- Other useful stuff

Remember, we've also provided a series of tables with live links to all of these resources on the CD-ROM.

Web Resources (General)	
Description / Source	**URL**
Home Page Construction Set	*http://nyx10.cs.du.edu:8001/~esasaki/hpcs/*
HTML Resources	*http://oneworld.wa.com/htmldev/devpage/ dev-page1.html#doc-a-1-3*
HTML Validation Service	*http://www.halsoft.com/html-val-svc/*
HTML/WWW Mentor Page	*http://www.mindspring.com/guild/index.html*
Mosaic User Authentication Tutorial	*http://wintermute.ncsa.uiuc.edu:8080/ auth-tutorial/tutorial.html*
NetLinks! Newbie Help Link	*http://www.interlog.com/~csteele/newbie.html*
Point Survey ratings system	*http://www.pointcom.com*
Quality, Guidelines & Standards for Internet Information Resources	*http://coombs.anu.edu.au/SpecialProj/QLTY/QltyHo me.html*
URL-Minder (Tracks designated pages and notifies you of changes.)	*http://www.netmind.com/URL-minder/ URL-minder.html*
WAIS Tutorial	*http://wintermute.ncsa.uiuc.edu:8080/ wais-tutorial/wais.html*
Web & HTML authoring pointers	*http://oneworld.wa.com/htmldev/devpage/ dev-page.html*
Web (everything you wanted to know and then some)	*http://www.yahoo.com/Computers/ World_Wide_Web/*
Web design tips and pointers to resources	*http://gagme.wwa.com/~boba/masters1.html*
Web Developers's Virtual Library	*http://WWW.Stars.com*
Jon Wiederspan's Mac WWW Development Guide	*http://www.uwtc.washington.edu/Computing/ WWW/mac/Directory.html*
WWW FAQ	*http://sunsite.unc.edu/boutell/faq/www_faq.html*

Design Guides	
Description / Source	**URL**
English language usage	*http://www.best.com/~dsiegel/tips/usage.html*
Graphic design tricks	*http://www.best.com/~dsiegel/tips/graphics.html*
HTML Style Sheet by the Learning Technologies Center at Cornell University	*http://frazier.cit.cornell.edu/style/style.html*
Netscape Corporation's Web Design Guide	*http://home.mcom.com/assist/net_sites/index.html*
Style Your Sheet	*http://www.links.net/webpub/style.html*
Sun Guide to Interface Design	*http://www.sun.com/sun-on-net/www.sun.com/ uidesign*
Typography and legibility tips	*http://www.best.com/~dsiegel/tips/typography.html*
Yale C/AIM WWW Style Manual	*http://info.med.yale.edu/caim/ StyleManual_Top.HTML*

HTML Guides	
Description / Source	**URL**
Bare Bones Guide to HTML	*http://www.access.digex.net/~werbach/ home.html*
Basic HTML (Pointers to guides)	*http://www.hypermall.com/tk/basic.html*
Beginner's Guide to HTML	*http://www.ncsa.uiuc.edu/demoweb /html-primer.html*
Beginner's Guide to URLs	*http://www.ncsa.uiuc.edu/demoweb/url-primer.html*
Composing Good HTML	*http://www.willamette.edu/ html-composition/strict-html.html*
Crash Course in Writing HTML	*http://www.ziff.com/~eamonn/crash_course.html*
Guide to URLs	*http://www.netspace.org/users/dwb/url-guide.html*
HTML Guides	*http://union.ncsa.uiuc.edu:80/HyperNews/ get/www/html/guides.html*

HTML Guides	
Description / Source	**URL**
HTML Information Center	*http://iconovex.com/HTMLPAGE.HTM*
HTML Quick Reference Guide	*http://kuhttp.cc.ukans.edu/lynx_help/ HTML_quick.html*
HTML Style Guide & Test Suite	*http://www.best.com/~dsiegel/vestibule/ set_netscape.html*
NCSA's classic HTML Primer	*http://www.ncsa.uiuc.edu/General/Internet/WWW/ HTMLPrimer.html*
Tim Berners-Lee's HTML Style Guide	*http://www.w3.org/hypertext/WWW/Provider/ Style/Overview.html*
URLs (list of sources)	*http://www.yahoo.com/Computers/ World_Wide_Web/Programming/ URLs___Universal_Resource_Identifiers/*

HTML Specifications	
Description / Source	**URL**
HTML 2.0 DTD	*http://www.halsoft.com/sgml/html-2.0 /DTD-HOME.html*
HTML 3.0 DTD	*http://www.halsoft.com:80/sgml/ html-3.0/DTD-HOME.html*
HTML Specification	*http://www.w3.org/hypertext/WWW/MarkUp/ MarkUp.html*
HTML Specifications, including the Internet Engineering Task Force draft for HTML 3.0	*http://www.w3.org/hypertext/WWW/MarkUp/ html3/CoverPage.html*

Advanced Features	
Description / Source	**URL**
CGI Beginner's Tutorial	*http://www.catt.ncsu.edu/~bex/tutor/ index.html*
CGI FAQ	*http://www.best.com/~hedlund/cgi-faq/ faq-general.html*

Advanced Features	
Description / Source	**URL**
CGI Programmer's Reference: Browser Survey	*http://www.halcyon.com/htbin/ browser-survey*
Common Gateway Interface Overview	*http://hoohoo.ncsa.uiuc.edu/cgi/ overview.html*
Dynamic documents (Netscape)	*http://home.netscape.com/assist/net_sites /dynamic_docs.html*
Forms (mostly tutorials)	*http://www.yahoo.com/Computers/ World_Wide_Web/Programming/Forms/*
Letting users search your Web pages	*http://www-rlg.stanford.edu/home/jpl/ websearch.html*
Perl and WWW support page from Reed University	*http://www.ee.pdx.edu/~rseymour/wwwperl/*
Tables, How-To (Netscape)	*http://home.netscape.com/assist/net_sites/tables.html*
University of Florida's Perl Programming Archive	*http://www.cis.ufl.edu/perl/*

Media and Multimedia	
Description / Source	**URL**
Audio formats guide	*http://cuiwww.unige.ch/OSG/AudioFormats/*
FAQ for Transparent GIFs	*http://dragon.jpl.nasa.gov/~adam/transparent.html*
Icons sources	*http://www.yahoo.com/Computers/ World_Wide_Web/Programming/Icons/*
Introduction to MIDI	*http://www.eeb.ele.tue.nl/midi/intro.html*
Kai's Power Tricks and Tips for Photoshop	*http://the-tech.mit.edu/KPT/*
MBONE overview	*http://www.research.att.com/mbone-faq.html*
MIDI Home page (also includes many sources of MIDI files	*http://www.eeb.ele.tue.nl/midi/index.html*
MIME media types	*ftp://ftp.isi.edu/in-notes/iana/ assignments/media-types/media-types*

Media and Multimedia	
Description / Source	URL
MIME type suffixes	http://www.w3.org/hypertext/WWW/Daemon/User/Config/Suffixes.html
Multimedia resources (Good selection of UNIX tools)	http://viswiz.gmd.de/MultimediaInfo/
Multimedia Tutorials	http://galen.med.virginia.edu/~smb4v/tutorial.html
Music Resources on the Internet	http://www.music.indiana.edu/misc/music_resources.html
Recommended file formats for WWW documents	http://sd-www.jsc.nasa.gov/web_formats.html
Stock footage (Global Village) Online database of over 1 million video clips and images.	http://nbn.nbn.com/footage/
Working with images	http://frazier.cit.cornell.edu/style/images.html

VRML and Things Virtual	
Description / Source	URL
Lawrence Livermore National Laboratory's VRML Test Page	http://dsed.llnl.gov/documents/WWWtest.html
San Diego Supercomputer Center's VRML Repository	http://www.sdsc.edu/vrml
Virtual Reality Modeling Language resources, links, and information	http://VRML.wired.com

Helper Apps, Viewers, and Utilities	
Description / Source	URL
Graphical Information Map Tutorial	http://wintermute.ncsa.uiuc.edu:8080/map-tutorial/image-maps.html
Helper Applications	http://home.mcom.com/MCOM/tricks_docs/helper_docs/index.html
HTML Checker script Weblint	http://www.khoros.unm.edu/staff/neilb/weblint.html

Helper Apps, Viewers, and Utilities	
Description / Source	**URL**
HTML Validation Service	*http://www.halsoft.com/html-val-svc/*
Imagemaps (mostly tools for creating)	*http://www.yahoo.com/Computers/ World_Wide_Web/Programming/Imagemaps/*
Index maker script	*http://cs.sau.edu/~mkruse/www/scripts/ indexer.html*
Link verifier (part of Webtest tool suite)	*http://wsk.eit.com/wsk/dist/doc/admin/ webtest/verify_links.html*
Link verifier lvrfy	*http://www.cs.dartmouth.edu/~crow/lvrfy.html*
QuickTime converters and utilities	*http://www.astro.nwu.edu/lentz/mac/qt/ home-qt.html*
Transparent GIFs	*http://www.yahoo.com/Computers/ World_Wide_Web/Programming/ Transparent_Image*

Background Textures and Colors	
Description / Source	**URL**
Background sources	*http://www.yahoo.com/Computers/ World_Wide_Web/Programming/Backgrounds/*
Backgrounds by Achille Hui	*http://drizzle.stanford.edu/~achille/ images/misc/backgrounds/*
Backgrounds from Netscape (public domain)	*http://home.netscape.com/home/bg/ backgrounds.html*
Backgrounds, How-To (Netscape)	*http://home.netscape.com/assist/net_sites/bg /index.html*
Color References jump page	*http://gagme.wwa.com/~boba/masters1.html*
Color RGBtoHex program	*http://www.lne.com/Web/Examples/rgb.html*
Color sampler	*http://www.interport.net/~giant/COLOR/ hype_color.html*
Color specifier and editor for backgrounds	*http://www.infocom.net/~bbs/cgi-bin/colorEditor.cgi*

Background Textures and Colors	
Description / Source	**URL**
Color wheel for picking colors (Requires Netscape 1.1 browser)	*http://www.biola.edu/cgi-bin/colorserve/ colorserve.html*
RGB Hex Color Chart	*http://phoenix.phoenix.net:80/~jacobson/ rgb.html*
RGB to Hex converter	*http://www.univox.com/rgb2hex.html*

Business Information Resources	
Description / Source	**URL**
American Stock Exchange	*http://www.amex.com*
Dun & Bradstreet business reports	*http://www.dbisna.com*
Global Trade Point Network	*http://www.unicc.org*
International Import Export Business Exchange	*http://www.imex.com*
International Trade Admin. (U.S. Dept. of Commerce)	*http://www.ita.doc.gov*
Internet Marketing Surveys & Information	*http://www.activmedia.com*
Links: 2000 — Marketing and Advertising on the Net	*http://www2000.ogsm.vanderbilt.edu/links.cgi*
MCI Small Business Center	*http://www.mci.com/SmallBiz/*
New York Stock Exchange	*http://www.nyse.com*
University of Michigan Economic Bulletin Board	*gopher://una.h.lib.umich.edu:70:70/11/ebb*

Mailing Lists and Newsgroups	
Description / Source	**URL**
Acrobat / PDF listserve	To subscribe: send *SUBSCRIBE PDF-L Your name your_ID@your_domain* in message body to: *Majordomo@binc.net*

Mailing Lists and Newsgroups	
Description / Source	**URL**
Copyright issues discussion group	To subscribe: send *subscribe cni-copyright your_real_name* in message body to: *LISTPROC@CNI.ORG*
HTML authoring discussion	To subscribe: send *subscribe html-list your_real_name* in message body to: *listserv@netcentral.net*
HTML/WWW Developers	To subscribe: send *subscribe wwwdev (your name)* in message body to: *LISTSERV@LISTSERV.UNB.CA*
SGML discussion	To subscribe: send *subscribe SGML-L (your name)* in message body to: *LISTSERV%DHDURZ1.BITNET@* *CUNYVM.CUNY.EDU*
SGML discussion	To subscribe: send *subscribe comp-std-sgml your_real_name* in message body to: *comp-std-sgml-request@naggum.no*
Usability issues discussion group	To subscribe: send *subscribe utest your_real_name* in message body to: *listproc@hubcap.clemson.edu*
Usenet Newsgroups of interest	*comp.infosystems.www* *comp.infosystems.www.advocacy* *comp.infosystems.www.browsers.mac* *comp.infosystems.www.browsers.misc* *comp.infosystems.www.browsers.ms-windows* *comp.infosystems.www.browsers.x* *comp.infosystems.www.servers.ms-windows* *comp.infosystems.www.servers.unix* *comp.infosystems.www.servers.mac* *comp.infosystems.www.servers.misc* *comp.infosystems.www.authoring.html* *comp.infosystems.www.authoring.cgi* *comp.infosystems.www.authoring.images* *comp.infosystems.www.authoring.misc*

Mailing Lists and Newsgroups	
Description / Source	**URL**
Web design discussion group	To subscribe: send *subscribe web-design you@your.domain (your name)* in message body to: *web-design-request@angel.net*

Other Useful Stuff	
Description / Source	**URL**
American Society of Indexers	*http://www.missouri.edu/~libnh/ASI/*
Announcement services	*http://www.yahoo.com/Computers/ World_Wide_Web/Announcement_Services/*
Apple's e-World Web City	*http://www.eworld.com/general*
Ask Dr. Internet	*http://promo.net/gut/*
Desktop publishing resources	*http://degaulle.hil.unb.ca/ UNB_G_Services/GSHomePage.html*
E-Mail Infobot -- send subject <help> to get a list of helpful information	*infobot@infomania.com*
Human-computer interaction topics (Bowling Green University)	*http://hydra.bgsu.edu/HCI/*
Internet Public Library (University of Michigan)	*http://ipl.sils.umich.edu/*
ISO 8859-1 table	*http://www.uni-passau.de/~ramsch/iso8859-1.html*
NewsPage	*http://www.newspage.com*
Online Computer Library Center	*http://www.oclc.org*
The Well-Connected Mac	*http://rever.nmsu.edu/~elharo/faq/Macintosh.html*
WebChat	*http://www.irsociety.com/webchat/webchat.html*
Windows Resources	*ftp://ftp.cdrom.com/.5/cica/winsock/*

Raiding the icebox: periodicals worth fishing out of the stack

On the CD-ROM ...
resourcs
webpubs.htm

Okay, okay, one can't be online all the time, can one? Here's our list of compelling periodicals that somehow get dog-eared before they head to the recycle bin. These are (almost) all Internet- or WWW-related; *Byte* is included as an antidote to the, um, enthusiasm of the rest. Of course, your favorite general-purpose computer magazines will also feature WWW information on occasion.

Byte   `http://www.byte.com/`

Interactive Age   `http://techweb.cmp.com/ia`

Interactive Week   `http://www.interactive-week.com`

Internet World   `http://www.mecklerweb.com/mags/iw/iwhome.htm`

NetGuide   `http://techweb.cmp.com/net/current/`

New Media   `http://www.macromedia.com/Brain/New.media/index.html`

WebWeek   `http://www.mecklerweb.com/mags/ww/wwhome.htm`

Wired   `http://www.hotwired.com/`

Publications

Last but by no means least, the actual bookshelf: trade and technical books that you may find useful, and that will certainly impress those in neighboring cubicles.

Ames, Andrea L., David R. Nadeau, John L. Moreland and Robert H. Russ. *The VRML Sourcebook*. New York: John Wiley & Sons, Inc., 1995. *http://www.wiley.com/CompBooks/CompBooks.html*

Armstrong, James. *HTML Pocket Reference Card*. Seattle: Specialized Systems Consultants, Inc., 1994. *http://www.ssc.com/ssc/new.html*.

Aronson, Larry. *HTML Manual of Style*. Emeryville, CA: Ziff-Davis Press, 1994.

Cronin, Mary J. *Doing More Business on the Internet*. New York: Van Nostrand Reinhold, 1995.

December, John and Neil Randall. *The World Wide Web Unleashed (Second Edition)*. Indianapolis: Sams Publishing 1995. *http://www.rpi.edu/~decemj/works/wwwu.html*.

Deep, John. *Developing CGI Applications with Perl*. New York: John Wiley & Sons, Inc., 1995. *http://www.wiley.com/CompBooks/CompBooks.html*

Dougherty, Dale, Paula Ferguson, and Richard Koman. *The Mosaic Handbook*. Sebastopol, CA: O'Reilly & Associates, 1994. *http://gnn.com/gnn/bus/ora/index.html*.

Ellsworth, Jill H. and Matthew V. *The Internet Business Book.* New York: John Wiley & Sons, Inc., 1994. *http://www.wiley.com/CompBooks/CompBooks.html*

————*Marketing on the Internet: Multimedia Strategies for the World Wide Web.* New York: John Wiley & Sons, Inc., 1995. *http://www.wiley.com/CompBooks/CompBooks.html.*

Flynn, Peter. *The World Wide Web Handbook.* Stanford, CT:: International Thomson Computer Press, 1995.

Ford, Andrew. *Spinning the Web: How to Provide Information on the Internet.* New York: Van Nostrand Reinhold, 1994.

Fry, Andrew and David Paul. *How to Publish on the Internet.* New York: Warner Books, 1995. *http://www.pathfinder.com/@@s8C9RmCmcgAAQEsY/twep/Features/How_Pub_Web/Welcome.html/.*

Gilster, Paul. *Finding It On The Internet.* New York: John Wiley & Sons, Inc., 1994. *http://www.wiley.com/CompBooks/CompBooks.html*

————*The Internet Navigator.* New York: John Wiley & Sons, Inc., 1994. *http://www.wiley.com/CompBooks/CompBooks.html.*

————*The Mosaic Navigator.* New York: John Wiley & Sons, Inc., 1995. *http://www.wiley.com/CompBooks/CompBooks.html.*

Graham, Ian S. *The HTML Sourcebook.* New York: John Wiley and Sons, Inc., 1995. *http://www.wiley.com/CompBooks/CompBooks.htm*

Hoft, Nancy L. *International Technical Communication: How to Export Information About High Technology.* New York: John Wiley & Sons, Inc., 1995.

Horton, William K. *Designing and Writing Online Documentation: Hypermedia for Self-supporting Products,* 2nd. Edition. New York: John Wiley & Sons, Inc., 1994.

————*Illustrating Computer Documentation: The Art of Presenting Information Graphically on Paper and Online.* New York: John Wiley & Sons, Inc., 1991.

————*The Icon Book: Visual Symbols for Computer Systems and Documentation.* New York: John Wiley & Sons, Inc., 1994.

Ivens, Kathy. *The Internet Warp Book.* Rocklin, CA: Prima Publishing, 1995. *http://www.webcom.com/~prima/The_Internet_Warp_Book.html*

Lemay, Laura. *Teach Yourself More Web Publishing with HTML in a Week.* Indianapolis: Sams.net, 1995. *http://slack.lne.com/lemay/theBook/index.html.*

————*Teach Yourself Web Publishing with HTML in a Week.* Indianapolis; Sams Publishing, 1995. *http://slack.lne.com/lemay/theBook/index.html.*

Liu, Cricket, Jerry Peek, Russ Jones, Bryan Buus and Adrian NyeRuss. *Managing Internet Information Services.* Sebastopol, CA: O'Reilly & Associates, 1994. *http://gnn.com/gnn/bus/ora/item/miis.html.*

Morris, Mary. *HTML Authoring for Fun & Profit.* Englewood Cliffs, NJ: Prentice Hall, 1995.

Murray, James D. and van Ryper, William. *Encyclopedia of Graphics File Formats.* Sebastopol, CA: O'Reilly & Associates, 1994. *http://gnn.com/gnn/bus/ora/index.html*

net.Genesis and Devra Hall. 1995. *Build A Web Site*. Rocklin, CA: Prima Publishing. ISBN 0-76150-064-2 *http://www.netgen.com/book/*.

Pfaffenberger, Bryan. *World Wide Web Bible*. New York: MIS Press, 1995.

Sterne, Jim. World Wide Web Marketing. New York: John Wiley & Sons, Inc., 1995. *http://www.wiley.com/CompBooks/CompBooks.html*

USING THE CD-ROM

Inside the back cover of this book, you'll find an object, shiny and round. It may look like a CD-ROM, but it is really a pantry for the Web chef. Our pantry contains all the recipics, fixings, and sample dishes shown throughout the book. But to get them from the pantry to your stove or table, you've got to do a little computer work.

First shoot a rabbit

An old recipe for rabbit stew began with the instructions, "First go out and shoot a rabbit." The first step in using the CD-ROM is to install a CD-ROM drive. Chances are you either already have a CD-ROM drive working. If you do, fine. If you don't, you should. We won't tell you how—that's another book—but we have it on good authority that mere mortals have done it. One of us authors even got one working in less than two months.

Mount the disk

No taxidermy implied. The next step is to add the CD-ROM to your file system. On Mac and Windows systems that means "Put it in." For UNIX systems, the procedure depends on which sect of UNIX runs your machine, whether you are using one of the graphical interfaces or whether you were high school typing champ, and what brand of CD-ROM you have. As a now-infamous Help message says, "contact your UNIX counsellor."

While you're at it, make sure you know how to copy files from the CD-ROM to your hard disk. You'll need that skill later.

The way the files appear (as names or icons) will depend on which operating system but the names of the files and the organization of directories and files is essentially the same. If you just can't wait to learn what's on the CD-ROM, turn to "What's on the CD-ROM" on page 621.

Just looking

For a preview of your tour, see "What's on the CD-ROM" on page 621.

If you like looking at the pictures in a cookbook before concocting any of the dishes, you're in luck. Just fire up a Web browser and point it at homepage.htm at the top level of the CD-ROM. If you like a straightforward guided tour, just park your cursor over the [Next] button and click, click, click. If you hate guided tours and want to tear off on your own, go ahead, there are lots of links there.

One caution: Many of the examples and templates are made up of placeholders and are self-contained. That means that their navigational buttons do not point back to the navigational pages that are part of your tour. Pages that are part of the tour contain our distinctive Cookbook emblem. You'll recognize it by the Chef's hat on the left edge. Here's one from an example:

You can always get back to the tour by using the Back command of your browser.

Rolling up your sleeves

Ready to start cooking? To use the templates and examples on the CD-ROM, you will need to copy them to your hard disk first. For the complex templates and examples, ones consisting of more than a single file, we strongly recommend that you copy the whole directory. That way you get all the icons, graphics, and related pages used by the recipe. You can throw out the ones you don't need—once you've crafted replacements for them.

Again, how you copy from the CD-ROM is a personal matter between you and your operating system of choice. It's really the same basic procedure as copying files from a floppy disk. In most cases, you can click and drag a folder or subdirectory icon from the CD-ROM window to your hard drive window, and your operating system will do the rest.

If you do not know how to copy files from your CD-ROM to your hard disk, dust off the manuals for your operating system—or ask a friend. Learn to do this and other basic tasks such as running programs, creating directories, and deleting files. Without these basic skills, you won't get far with the CD-ROM.

Unpacking the implements

Almost all of the tools provided on the CD-ROM are squished in some platform-specific manner to make them more manageable, and then given specific file name extensions to indicate their file type. Here's what those extensions mean:

Operating system	File extension	Decompression program
Macintosh	.sea	Self-extracting archive; copy it to its own subdirectory and double-click to make it expand.
	.hqx	Convert from BinHex4.0; you'll get either application files or a self-extracting archive that will, when expanded, create application files.
OS/2	.exe	Either a self-extracting archive or the actual program executable file; copy it to its own subdirectory and double-click to find out.
Unix	.gz	A file compressed with GNU's GZIP; use GZIP or compatible utility to uncompress.
	.tar	A tape archive file; use the UNIX **tar** utility to extract files from archive format.
	.Z	A file compressed with the UNIX **compress** command; use the UNIX **uncompress** command to expand.
	.tgz	A file that was "tar'd" (archived to a tape file) and then compressed with GZIP; use GZIP to uncompress, then use **tar** to extract files from tape archive format.
Windows	.exe	Either a self-extracting archive or the actual program executable file; copy it to its own subdirectory and double-click to find out.

Each tool has its own folder on the CD-ROM. In each folder is a compressed or BinHexed version of the tool; in most cases (except the UNIX tools), the compressed file is in a self-extracting format, which means that you run it, just like a program, in order to extract the files that it holds.

Most folders also contain a subdirectory called `exploded`. The `exploded` subdirectory (no ordinance implied) contains all the files extracted from the compressed file in the directory above.

We've provided this exploded subdirectory for your convenience. If the tool is fairly simple, these extracted files are probably all the program files you'll need, ready to run; copy 'em over to your hard disk and have at it. If it's a more sophisticated tool, these extracted files will be the installation files you need to formally install the program.

For example, the directory MOSAIC (in Windows Tools) contains:

- The self-extracting file MOS20FB.EXE

- The subdirectory exploded, which contains the installation files for the Mosaic browser.

To try out or use a tool like this, you'll need to follow this general procedure:

1. Create a new, empty subdirectory (or folder) on your hard disk to hold the tool.

2. Copy to its new home either the compressed file or the entire exploded subdirectory/folder.

Now you're ready to expand and install the program. Here's how:

1. If you copied the exploded subdirectory, go to Step 2.

    If you copied a self-extracting file (with an .exe or .sea extension), double-click on it. It will expand to either the full-blown application, or to a series of installation files (depending on how the program developer set up the installation routine).

    If you copied a compressed file for a UNIX tool, use an appropriate utility to uncompress it.

Some UNIX tools and resources are provided as binaries, which you'll have to compile for your particular platform. If you haven't contacted your UNIX counsellor by now, you may need to.

2. Next, look for a readme or similarly-named file; if you find one, open it in a basic editor (SimpleText, pico, Notepad, etc.) and peruse it for installation instructions. The readme file will probably spell out the shareware or registration policy of the program's creator, and may provide all the operating instructions you're going to get, so it's worth a look.

3. Look in your new directory/folder for an executable file called install or setup.

    - If you find it, double-click on it, and the program will begin its installation routine. Follow the prompts during the installation routine to get the program up and running.

    - If you can't find either one, that probably means that no further installation or extracting is necessary; look for the application itself and crank it up.

4. Try out the program.

5. If you like it, be sure to register your copy and pay whatever license fees the creator requests.

   If you don't like it, and you want to remove it from your system, look in the online help or the `readme` file for instructions on uninstalling the software. Uninstalling lets the program clean up after itself in system files and system folders—better to do this than to simply blow away the program and leave the remainders behind.

What's on the CD-ROM?

We've loaded the CD-ROM with tools, templates, graphics, examples, case studies, and other goodies to make authoring Web pages easy and fun. There are two ways you can get a sense of what's on the disk. You can read about it here, or you can read about it on the disk. To read on the disk, just point your browser at the CD-ROM's home page. It's `homepage.htm` at the top level of the CD-ROM. Once there, just repeatedly pound the Next button to wend your way through the disk, pausing to sample its delights. Have a nice tour.

Want to read about it here? OK, we'll walk you through the main directories on the disk and point out what you'll find.

Two nearly identical versions for the price of one

First, a little technotalk. Everything is on the disk twice. On the disk are two partitions. One is the standard ISO-9669 CD-ROM format and the other is a Macintosh Hierarchical File System (HFS) format. If you are on a Mac, you see the Mac partition. If you are on a DOS, Windows, or UNIX system, you see the ISO partition.

Heads up!

As long as you use this CD-ROM on a single system, you probably won't notice the differences between Mac and PC text files. But, if you move things around on a mixed-system network, watch out for it.

The names and arrangement of directories are the same, but there are a few slight differences.

Text is not text is not text

Text files are not quite the same on the Mac as text files on other systems. On the Mac, text files mark the end of each line with a new-line character. On the PC, text files mark the end of lines with a combination of a carriage-return and a new-line character. Most browsers ignore the differences and many word processors are smart enough to convert on the fly. However, many text editors and HTML-editors are not. If you open a Mac text file on a PC text editor, all the lines slew together and some black blobs litter the screen. If you open a PC text file on a Mac text editor, all lines begin with a fat square block. For that reason, the text files on the Mac partition are in Mac format and the ones on the ISO side are in PC format.

Windows version of John Wiley & Sons, Inc., catalog

The Windows version of John Wiley and Sons, Inc., online catalog is included only on the ISO partition. It consists of the file `catalog.exe` and the directory `catalog` at the top level of the CD-ROM. To install the catalog, from Windows run the file `catalog.exe` and follow the prompts.

Other differences

There are a few other differences. Since they concern specific directories only, they are included with the description of the individual directory.

First an overview

At the top level, the CD-ROM contains these directories:

Directory	What it contains
`about`	Web pages about this book and its authors
`catalog`	John Wiley & Sons, Inc., online catalog (for Windows only)
`examples`	Examples, case studies, alternative techniques shown in the text.
`ingrdnts`	Templates for ingredients you can add to your Web pages, as described in Chapter 5 and 7.
`meals`	Templates for complete clusters of Web pages, as described in Chapter 11.
`recipes`	Templates for whole Web pages, as described in Chapter 4.
`resourcs`	Icons, page banners, sound bites, and other resources.
`tools`	Browsers, HTML editors, file-format converters, and other utility programs.

Let's take a look at them one at a time.

The about **directory**

The about directory houses Web pages about this book and its authors. As an incentive to reading our biographies, we'd point out that they took little time to prepare, since we used our own Biography template (found in the recipes directory.)

The catalog **directory**

The catalog directory, which appears only on the ISO partition, contains the contents of the John Wiley & Sons, Inc., online catalog. If you want to shop for some other fine books, get into Windows and run the file catalog.exe, which is on the top level of the CD-ROM. It will install the catalog on your Windows system.

The examples **directory**

For a complete list of the examples on the CD-ROM and links that let you jump to them, point your browser at:

examples
    examples.htm

The examples directory houses the many examples you find throughout the book. Want to borrow one? Help yourself. Want to see what something shown in a picture really looks like on the screen? Go ahead, it's probably here in this directory.

By *examples* we mean pages or parts of pages with actual content in them. Examples are different from templates, which have placeholders for content. Of course, nothing stops you from using one of these examples as a template.

The example directory is organized by chapter:

```
example
    chap3
    chap4
    chap6
    chap8
    chap9
```

You probably noticed that some of the chapters, such as 7 and 11 are missing. This is usually because they discuss templates which are in separate top-level directories.

Within each of the chapter folders, you may find subfolders for groups of examples or case studies. For instance, within the folder for Chapter 6, which deals with media and multimedia, you find these folders:

```
chap6
    icons
    movies
    pictures
    sounds
    text
```

You may want to follow along through the examples as you read the book.

The `ingrdnts` directory

The `ingrdnts` directory contains the bits and pieces of great Web-pages-to-be. They are the templates for headings, lists, tables, forms, and other components of Web pages. These are discussed in Chapters 5 and 7.

The templates are in two forms: as text files and as Rich Text Format (RTF) files. Each form is in a separate subdirectory within `ingrdnts`:

```
ingrdnts
    as_rtf
    as_text
```

Within these directories the ingredients are stored as individual files and all together in a single file, called `allinone.rtf` or `allinone.txt`. Some people like to open the all-in-one file and cut and paste from it. Others like to pinpoint where they want a particular element and then use the Insert or Import command to suck in the file for a particular element.

The `meals` directory

For an overview, with links that let you jump into each cluster, browse to:

```
meals
    meals.htm
```

The `meals` directory contains the templates for complete clusters of pages, as discussed in Chapter 11. Each cluster is in its own folder:

```
meals
    catalog
    grid
    hierarch
    howto
    newsmag
    onref
    sequence
    training
```

The `recipes` **directory**

For an overview, with links that let you jump into each page template, browse to:

recipes
    recipes.htm

A complete example of each of these page-types is included in:

examples
    chap4

The `recipes` directory contains templates for the most common kinds of Web pages you will want to create. These are discussed in Chapter 4. Each template is in a separate directory along with all the icons it uses and placeholders for any graphics it contains. The directories are:

```
recipes
    biograph
    book
    catalog
    contents
    course
    download
    generic
    glossary
    homepage
    howto
    index
    mmedia
    news
    organiz
    register
    research
    survey
    trouble
```

The `resourcs` **directory**

The `resourcs` directory contains resources. Resources are things that help you quickly put together Web pages and test them. Within `resourcs` are several directories of goodies:

Directory	What it contains
`banners`	GIF images used as page banners in templates and examples.
`genicons`	General-purpose icons.
`mediaicn`	Media-icons. GIF images used to trigger sound, music, video, and so forth.
`navicons`	Navigational icons. GIF images for Next, Previous, Up, Home buttons and more.
`pictures`	Images for placeholders and testing your ability to display various formats.
`rulers`	GIF images for measuring distances in pixels on the screen.
`sounds`	Sound bites for testing your ability to playback various sound file formats.

Directory	What it contains
swashes	Colorful bars and lines for dividing Web pages.
video	Video clips in various file formats to test your ability to play moving pictures.

The tools **directory**

In the tools directory you will find browsers, HTML editors, file-format converters, and other utility programs to simplify your task of creating Web pages. These are organized by operating system:

```
tools
    mac
    os2
    unix
    windows
```

Take a look at what's available for your system. We can't be too specific here because we're still negotiating and acquiring the best goodies we can.

Here you may notice some differences between the Macintosh and ISO partitions. The Macintosh tools in the mac directory on the ISO partition are in BinHex4.0 format (.hqx). On the Mac partition they exist as compressed self-extracting archives (.sea) and as uncompressed folders as well.

One thing we should point out is that much of the included software is shareware. This does not mean it is free. It does not mean you bought it with the book. It means that its creator has generously agreed to share a copy with you. If you use it, you are honor bound to pay the creator the requested fee. (For some it may be only a postcard.) You'll find the terms by which you may use the software in its read-me file, splash screen, or About panel.

Other tools are special limited-editions (limited in capabilities, not quantities) or self-expiring models. Please read and comply with the manufacturer's conditions for their use. If you like any of them, go ahead and buy a copy or two.

Within each of the operating-system folders is a Web-page version of the Shopping List shown earlier in this chapter. The one for the Macintosh, for example, is called shopmac.htm. These pages contain links to vendors of even more products for each operating system.

INDEX

3-D browsers (3-D players), 51–52

A

C

H

I

P

T

CATCH THE
Technology Wave
WITH WILEY COMPUTER BOOKS

Internet Business Kit

JILL H. ELLSWORTH AND
MATTHEW V. ELLSWORTH

This is an affordable, all-in-one *Internet Business Kit* that lets you get your business up on the Internet without hassles or steep learning curves! *The Internet Business Kit* is a complete package that includes the software and five easy steps to quickly get your business up on the Internet and develop a winning business plan. The package helps you open up an Internet account, set up a Web page storefront, use e-mail, access information, take orders, and conduct market research and much, much more.

ISBN# 0-471-13327-2
Price $69.95 US/$84.95 CAN
2 book/CD-ROM set
1995

Designing Interactive Documents with Adobe Acrobat Pro

JOHN DEEP

This book/CD-ROM set provides all the background necessary and a graphical tutorial to show how to use Adobe Acrobat Pro to professional interactive documents combining graphics and hypertext links. Real life examples demonstrate how you can create everything from interactive advertising to dynamic electronic books that can be browsed by the World Wide Web.

ISBN# 0-471-12789-2
Price $34.95 US/$48.95 CAN
Book/CD-ROM
416 pp. 1995

World Wide Web Marketing

JIM STERNE

If you're a marketing pro eager to tap into the commercial potential of the Internet but you are drowning in techno-babble, this book is for you. Written by the expert on Internet marketing, this non-technical guide to Web marketing strategy offers tested tips on everything from managing your company's image to finding customers and selling products to monitoring your success online.

ISBN# 0-471-12843-0
Price $24.95 US/$32.50 CAN
paper 336 pp. 1995

Online Resources for Business

ALFRED GLOSSBRENNER &
JOHN ROSENBERG

Whether you're doing market research or sizing up the competition, you won't want to venture online without this resource. This guide helps you find the information your company needs to stay competitive.

Online experts Glossbrenner and Rosenberg give you the bottom line on the business services - DIALOG, Lexis/Nexis, Dow Jones, and NewsNet; the consumer services - Compuserve, America Online, and Prodigy; and the Internet. They tell you what type of information is available from each service, how much it costs and discuss sophisticated search strategies, tools and techniques.

ISBN# 0-471-11354-9
Price $24.95 US/$34.95 CAN
paper 384 pp. 1995